Christian Moderns

THE ANTHROPOLOGY OF CHRISTIANITY

Edited by Joel Robbins

Christian Moderns

Freedom and Fetish in the Mission Encounter

WEBB KEANE

University of California Press

BERKELEY   LOS ANGELES   LONDON

University of California Press, one of the most distinguished university presses in the United States, enriches lives around the world by advancing scholarship in the humanities, social sciences, and natural sciences. Its activities are supported by the UC Press Foundation and by philanthropic contributions from individuals and institutions. For more information, visit www.ucpress.edu.

Parts of this book were previously published in different form: chapter 5 as "Religious Change and Historical Reflection in Anakalang, West Sumba, Indonesia," *Journal of Southeast Asian Studies* 26 (2), 1995: 289–306; chapter 6 as "Sincerity, 'Modernity,' and the Protestants," *Cultural Anthropology* 17 (1), 2002: 65–92; chapter 7 as "From Fetishism to Sincerity: Agency, the Speaking Subject, and Their Historicity in the Context of Religious Conversion," *Comparative Studies in Society and History* 39 (4), 1997: 674–93, reprinted with the permission of Cambridge University Press; chapter 8 as "Materialism, Missionaries, and Modern Subjects in Colonial Indonesia," in *Conversion to Modernities: The Globalization of Christianity,* ed. Peter van der Veer (New York: Routledge, 1996), 137–70, copyright © 1996 by Peter van der Veer, reproduced by permission of Routledge/Taylor & Francis Group, LLC; chapter 9 as "The Spoken House: Text, Act, and Object in Eastern Indonesia," *American Ethnologist* 22 (1), 1995: 102–24, copyright © by the American Anthropological Association; and chapter 10 as "Money Is No Object: Materiality, Desire, and Modernity in an Indonesian Society," in *The Empire of Things: Regimes of Value and Material Culture,* ed. Fred R. Myers (Santa Fe, NM: School of American Research Press, 2001), reprinted by permission, copyright © 2001 by the School of American Research, Santa Fe.

University of California Press
Berkeley and Los Angeles, California

University of California Press, Ltd.
London, England

Library of Congress Cataloging-in-Publication Data
Keane, Webb, 1955–
     Christian moderns : freedom and fetish in the mission encounter / Webb Keane.
         p.   cm. — (Anthropology of Christianity ; 1)
     Includes bibliographical references and index.
     ISBN-13: 978-0-520-24651-5 (cloth : alk. paper)
     ISBN-10: 0-520-24651-9 (cloth : alk. paper)
     ISBN-13: 978-0-520-24652-2 (pbk. : alk. paper)
     ISBN-10: 0-520-24652-7 (pbk. : alk. paper)
         1. Missions—Indonesia—History. 2. Missions, Dutch—History. 3. Calvinism—
Comparative studies. 4. Religion and culture. 5. Conversion—Christianity.
6. Netherlands—Religion. 7. Indonesia—Religion. I. Title.
     BV3340.K38 2007
     306.6′66425986—dc22   2006019220

Manufactured in the United States of America
16   15   14   13   12   11   10   09   08   07
10   9   8   7   6   5   4   3   2   1
This book is printed on New Leaf EcoBook 50, a 100% recycled fiber of which 50% is de-inked post-consumer waste, processed chlorine-free. EcoBook 50 is acid-free and meets the minimum requirements of ANSI/ASTM D5634–01 *(Permanence of Paper).*♾

For A & C

Contents

Illustrations

Acknowledgments

Some fifteen years ago, Peter van der Veer asked the opening question in my first campus job interview. Looking at me across the table, he said dryly, "When I was a little boy in the Netherlands, each Sunday in church we gave our guilders for the mission in Sumba. Now I want to know what happened with my money." My dissertation had been on quite a different topic, and history does not record my answer. But they hired me. Thus Peter and I began a conversation about religion and colonialism that has extended on and off over the years. So many years, so many conversations, so many debts. At the risk of inadvertently leaving some out, I must mention Arjun Appadurai, the late Bernard S. Cohn, E. Valentine Daniel, Nicholas Dirks, Nancy Farriss, Susan Gal, Marilyn Ivy, John Lucy, Daniel Miller, Nancy Munn, Fred Myers, John Pemberton, William Pietz, Christopher Pinney, Elizabeth Povinelli, Vicente Rafael, Marshall Sahlins, Rafael Sánchez, Bambi Schieffelin, Robert Sharf, James T. Siegel, Peter Stallybrass, George Steinmetz, Ann Stoler, Greg Urban, Michael Warner, and, collectively, the members of the Ethnohistory Seminar (University of Pennsylvania), the Committee for the Study of Social Transformation (University of Michigan), and the Michicagoan Faculty Workshop in linguistic anthropology (Universities of Chicago and Michigan).

Numerous early versions of this project benefited from the responses and challenges of many teachers, colleagues, and students, including Julia P. Adams, Danna Agmon, Richard Bauman, Lauren Berlant, Maurice Bloch, Susan Blum, Charles Briggs, Fenella Cannell, Emily Carter, William Christian, Simon Coleman, Jean Comaroff, J. Joseph Errington, Courtney Handman, Nina Kammerer, Rita Kipp, Gábor Klaniczay, Vassilios Lambropoulos, Alaina Lemon, Bruce Mannheim, Hirokazu Miyazaki, Erik Mueggler, Sherry Ortner, Gretchen Pfeil, Annelise Riles, Susan Rodgers, William Sax,

Lee Schlesinger, Michael Silverstein, and David Thomas. Peter van Rooden has been an unfailingly prompt, precise, and humorous advisor on Dutch religion. Don Herzog has been asking some of the most astute and difficult questions anyone could hope for; if I have been able to respond adequately to even half of them, I will be proud. Jacqueline Vel provided me with valuable, hard-to-find writings about the church and mission. Janet Hoskins and Joel Kuipers have been steadfast companions in Sumba and beyond. Philip Yampolsky's knack for finding the most obscure resources has been of great help more than once. And I've been able to count on Patsy Spyer's generous support everywhere, from Chicago to Jakarta to Leiden.

For their comments on full drafts of book chapters, sometimes on short notice, my special thanks to Talal Asad, Dipesh Chakrabarty, Vincent Crapanzano, Gillian Feeley-Harnik, William Hanks, Charles Hirschkind, Judith T. Irvine, Jennifer Johnson-Hanks, Sonja Luehrmann, Phyllis Mack, Saba Mahmood, Raphael Sanchez, Patricia Spyer, and Peter van Rooden. And above all, for the enormous task of commenting on the entire manuscript, my especially deep gratitude to Don Brenneis, Don Herzog, Adela Pinch, Joel Robbins, and Danilyn Rutherford. Bonita Hurd has been an unusually astute copyeditor. Frank Cody prepared the index.

During the years this book has been brewing, I have benefited from considerable institutional generosity, starting with the backing of my academic departments, first at the University of Pennsylvania, then at Michigan. Fieldwork in Indonesia and archival research in the Netherlands was supported by grants from the Southeast Asia Council of the Association for Asian Studies with funds from the Luce Foundation, Wenner-Gren Foundation for Anthropological Research, Social Science Research Council, and American Council of Learned Societies, and by a U.S. Department of Education Fulbright-Hays Fellowship. I was also sponsored by the Lembaga Ilmu Pengetahuan Indonesia and Universitas Nusa Cendana. I had time for writing this book thanks to support from the Center for Advanced Study in the Behavioral Sciences (Stanford) funded by the Andrew W. Mellon Foundation, Institute for the Humanities (Ann Arbor), Institute for Advanced Study (Princeton), National Endowment for the Humanities, and the John Simon Guggenheim Foundation.

I presented early versions of several parts of this book at annual meetings of the American Anthropological Association, American Ethnological Society, Association for Asian Studies, and Association of Social Anthropologists of the United Kingdom and Commonwealth, and at workshops or lectures at the Center for Advanced Study in the Behavioral Sciences; Center for the Critical Analysis of Contemporary Culture (Rutgers University); City University of New York; Columbia University; Cornell University; Harvard University; Heidelberg University; Institute for Advanced Study; Institute for Global Studies in Culture, Power, and History (Johns Hopkins University); London School of Economics; National University of Singapore; New York University; Research Center for Religion and Society (University of Amsterdam); School of American Research; University College London; University of California, Berkeley; University of California, San Diego; University of California, Santa Cruz; University of Chicago; University of Pennsylvania; Princeton University; Stanford University; and Yale University. At the University of Michigan, I presented parts of this project to the Anthro-History Workshop, the Committee for the Study of Social Transformation, the Institute for the Humanities, and the Linguistic Anthropology Lab. I am grateful to the participants for so many thoughtful discussions.

Having said that this book is a response to a question put to me during an academic interview, I should also make clear that it grew out of long conversations and sometimes very pointed questions during my residence in Sumba from 1985 to 1987 and in 1993. The people I knew best tended not to be the sort to let one off the hook easily. They probed my thoughts, beliefs, habits, and in some cases, the state of my soul at least as far as I could ever have probed theirs. It is difficult to single out individuals from two years of constant encounters, some of the most casual of which were among the most revealing. But I must acknowledge the deep hospitality of Bapak Augustinas U. Sabarua and Ibu Mariana R. Kahi Kawurung, who, with their extended family in several locations, gave me a home and much more. I also recognize the invaluable assistance of Bapak U. S. Kababa, Umbu Dewa Damaràka, Umbu Pàda Buli Yora, Ubu Kàna Dapa Namung, Umbu Siwa Djurumanu, Umbu Kuala Ngara Ata, Pendeta S. Kadiwangu, Ibu Firas, Ratu Ngongu, and the family of Leng Kep. Although all whom I asked for permission agreed to let me use their names in my writing, in the end I have decided to use pseudonyms except for matters of clear public record. All translations from Anakalangese, Indonesian, and Dutch are my own unless otherwise noted. Quotations from conversations are from my own field notes when no citation is given. In transcriptions from Anakalangese, subscripts indicate implosive consonants; for further details on Anakalangese, see Keane 1997c: xxvii–xxix.

Adela Pinch's intellectual contribution marks every page of this book, which is amazing, considering her ongoing conspiracy with Clara Keane to remind me of what really matters.

Introduction

In 1649, in the midst of one of the most violent periods in modern English history, a time of civil war and regicide, John Milton wrote a polemic against royal tyranny. Called *Eikonoklastes*, it was a response on behalf of the Parliamentarians to *Eikon Basilike*, supposedly a posthumous publication by King Charles I, who had been executed a few months previously. The latter work, a royalist bid for sympathy, had portrayed the king as a pious man much given to prayer. In the course of his reply, Milton attacked the use of fixed, published prayers. Writing of verbal formulae, such as those that had been established a century earlier in the *Book of Common Prayer*, he said, "[T]o imprison and confine by force, into a Pinfold of sett words, those two most unimprisonable things, our Prayer [and] that Divine Spirit of utterance that moves them, is a tyranny that would have longer hands than those Giants who threatn'd bondage to Heav'n" (1962: 505).

Milton's reference to tyranny is no mere rhetorical flourish. The context was a struggle between Parliament and royal rule, as well as between kinds of Protestantism, and for Milton the question of human freedom was as much at stake in how one speaks as it was in how one is governed. His disagreement was not with the words of the published prayers in themselves: "But suppose them savoury words and unmix'd, suppose them *Manna* it self, yet if they shall be hoarded up and enjoynd us, while God every morning raines down new expressions into our hearts, in stead of being fit to use, they will be found like reserv'd *Manna*, rather *to breed wormes and stink*" (1962: 505, emphasis in the original). The problem, rather, lies in the abridgment of one's freedom to speak. To follow a published text when praying is to submit one's inner spirit to the "outward dictates of men" (1962: 506). Milton's argument aligns a set of mutually reinforcing oppositions between self and social others, movement and stasis, expenditure of the new and hoarding of the old, inner and outward, immaterial spirit and material text, and, ultimately, freedom and bondage. He expresses what I call a semiotic ideology, which links political power and the spiritual disciplines of the self.[1]

Seventeenth-century England lies far from the nineteenth- and twentieth-century missionaries and converts with whom this book is concerned and the colonial and postcolonial worlds they inhabited. But in important respects, Milton's remarks foreshadow my central themes. We can hear an echo of Milton in the common complaint Calvinists were directing against their Catholic neighbors on the Indonesian island of Sumba in the 1990s. Good Protestants pray with their eyes shut. Catholics, by contrast, do so with open eyes. Why? So they can read the words of their prayer books instead of speaking from within. This, I was often told, shows they are no better—and hardly more modern—than Sumba's unconverted ancestral ritualists, who (Calvinists claimed) worship stones and pieces of gold and thus surrender their agency to that of demons, imagined or real. Failing to recognize their own agency, the Calvinist might muse, it is no wonder pagans are excluded from modern citizenship by the Indonesian state, which requires its people to belong to a monotheistic religion. And like pagans, the Calvinist would sometimes add, Catholics even worship statues of the Virgin Mary as if they were alive. In short, by preserving dangerously misguided practices from the past, Catholics and pagans have been left behind by the times. In this slide from texts to fetishes, we may again recall Milton, for whom, according to one insightful commentator, to follow written prayers is "to commit the act of idolatry" (Targoff 2001: 37). Submitting to fixed discursive forms is not only a theological error or an affront to God; it threatens to undermine the agency proper to humans.[2]

1. Similar oppositions run through another important debate of the period: how and, particularly, through what ways of speaking might ministers legitimately *represent* their parishioners before God (Targoff 2001: 25, 38–52)? Here too, even for Protestants opposed to Milton's Puritanism, liturgical form is inseparable from the political theory of governance.

2. The reader may ask, What of the agency of God, who is the ultimate source of the words Milton is talking about? As will become apparent in the chapters that follow, there are two answers. First, in practice, the actual struggles that follow from these questions are perforce carried out among humans. Second, theologically, even the famously predestinarian Calvinists with whom I am most concerned eventually ruled questions about God's agency more or less out of court. It is not for humans to speculate about the purposes of a transcendent being. In addition, for God's will to be fulfilled, humans must make use of the agency that is properly theirs. In Milton's case, God may rain down words, but it is humans who must decide to use them. For these reasons, among others, ideas that have religious sources could enter into more secular discourses.

AGENCY, WORDS, THINGS

But what does "agency" mean if it can be undermined by printed texts or statues? And why should agency have anything to do with historical progress? What kind of human subject does such a concept of agency presume? In what kinds of actions ought that subject to engage? What kinds should it avoid? In order to answer these questions, I explore the dilemmas raised when Dutch Calvinist missionaries and their converts encounter ancestral ritual on an island in Southeast Asia. I suggest that their dilemmas can shed light on those faced by other people in quite different contexts, with quite different purposes, even secular activists or scholars trying to understand social change. For many of the questions with which Calvinists and other Protestants have wrestled in religious terms also arise, within different frames of reference, for others. When, for example, the feminist philosopher Judith Butler describes how power forms the subject, she writes, "Subjection consists precisely in this fundamental dependency on a discourse we never chose but that, paradoxically, initiates and sustains our agency" (1997: 2). It is surely no criticism of her overall thesis to observe that this seems paradoxical only given certain assumptions about agency and discourse, that is, a certain semiotic ideology. But on reflection, this semiotic ideology should not, in its basic form, seem unfamiliar to most of my readers. We can find variations on these themes across a wide range of discursive fields at the beginning of the twenty-first century.

Agency has been a ubiquitous topic in historical and anthropological writing for at least a generation. It has long been a critical element in the analysis of social structure and history. But the moral value of agency goes beyond theoretical questions. As Talal Asad remarks, "The doctrine of action has become essential to our recognition of other people's humanity" (1996: 272). It is precisely because agency is so closely tied to certain ideas about humanity that the search for its traces has become an ethical imperative for much contemporary writing about feminism, the politics of recognition, democracy, rights, and postcolonialism, among other things. For anthropologists and historians, the quest for local agency is often portrayed as an antidote to earlier assumptions about tradition-bound natives and timeless structures or to triumphalist narratives of empire and modernity. To seek out historical agency has therefore become an essential part of taking account of "all the players in the game" (Comaroff and Comaroff 1991: 9).

Here, however, we encounter a central dilemma. The quest for agency often seems tacitly to be informed by the humanist assumption that self-transformation is not only a central fact of history but also a good that exceeds local systems of value. This view of self-transformation has sources, sometimes only half acknowledged, in European intellectual, moral, and even theological history. But however much the social theorist, ethnographer, historian, or political activist may want to take seriously other people's self-consciousness, we cannot assume in advance that this self-consciousness will coincide with what we would take to be a convincing account of their actions and the consequences that follow from them. The problem is not just a matter of having failed to take into account "the native point of view" but also follows from the inseparability of people's self-understanding from the historical specificity of the concrete practices and semiotic forms in which their self-understanding is embedded. A number of critics (e.g., Anderson 2000; Chakrabarty 2000; Mahmood 2005; Povinelli 2002) have pointed out that the resulting ethical, political, and legal dilemmas raise serious questions about the concepts of agency that have been presupposed by certain predominant ideas about humanity in the Euro-American West. More than this, however, by exploring the struggles over questions of agency in the mission encounter between Calvinists and ancestral ritualists, I show that "our" dilemmas do not simply arise from the encounter with "others." Some of those paradoxes are implicit in the prevailing concepts of agency from the start.

The encounter of Dutch Calvinists and their Sumbanese interlocutors provides a sharp enough contrast, at great enough distance, that it will help us discern more clearly both a number of assumptions that might otherwise pass unremarked and the paradoxes they produce. If there is any shared ground between Protestant and more secular traditions, it should be most apparent when both stand in a situation of maximum difference from something else. The colonial encounter offers such a situation. My analysis centers on the interactions among Calvinist missionaries in the colonial Dutch East Indies and then independent Indonesia, their converts from a system of ancestral ritual, and those who resisted conversion. Their collective story starts as an encounter between two sides, but its postcolonial consequences produce a tangle of relations and possible positions that is far more complex.

Although much of this book is about language and material things, it is when Milton finds language and things to be pertinent to the moral problems of freedom that he comes closest to expressing the key link between semiotic ideology and what we could call a moral narrative of modernity. In the chapters that follow, I argue that the sorting out of proper relations among, and boundaries between, words, things, and subjects is often driven by the question "What beings have agency?" Therefore this sorting out is fraught with moral implications. In Bruno Latour's terms, it involves the work of purification. One way these moral implications are manifested is in a widespread set of intuitions about historical progress. These intuitions center on the idea that modernity is, or ought to be, a story of human liberation from a host of false beliefs and fetishisms that undermine freedom. There are some obvious empirical difficulties that any such effort to reduce history to a single narrative runs into and, of course, many alternative ideas about modernity. But this association of modernity with the emancipated subject has been powerful across a range of contexts. Versions of it underlie everything from venerable depictions of religion as an opiate, to liberal ideas about self-fulfillment, to Western denunciations of Islam.

This book is not, on the whole, meant to provide explanations *of* history. Rather, my interest is in sorting out how people use and make sense of words and things and their bearing on agency. I am especially concerned with the moral quandaries that, given certain background assumptions about the human subject, words and things can seem to pose for those who use them. In their material and formal properties, and in the ways people have responded to those properties, words and things have an incorrigibly historical dimension. They are in constant motion. Moreover, in some circumstances, people's ideas about words, things, and people include assumptions *about* history—for example, that history can be understood as a narrative of moral liberation. I argue that the assumptions about words and things that some Protestant and secular traditions share contribute to commonsense notions about the agency and freedom that often are supposed to define persons within those same traditions. Some recurrent paradoxes arise amid the resulting efforts to distinguish persons from the materiality of both words and things.

The specific circumstances involving Calvinism, the colonial encounter, and their postcolonial consequences on which I focus are thus situated within an encompassing story about Protestant efforts to escape some of the apparent implications of the ways human subjects are embedded in social and material worlds. This effort often focuses on semiotic form. (I will explain what I mean by *semiotic* shortly. I should mention here, however, that it does *not* refer to approaches that treat social phenomena as if they were texts to be read or messages to be decoded. Indeed, such treatments of social things as texts or codes are themselves historically specific manifestations of the work of purification.) Semiotic form can include such things as the sounds of words, the constraints of speech genres, the perishability of books, the replicable shapes of money, the meatiness of animals, the feel of cloth, the shape of houses, musical tones, the fleshiness of human bodies, and the habits of physical gestures. Many of these things come under scrutiny by religious evangelists and other reformers.

Moral questions about semiotic form recur in a variety of ways throughout the long history of Christian reform and revitalization movements. In widely different institutional settings, theological vocabularies, and political circumstances, religious reformers have grappled with the relations between what they understand to be oppositions, such as immanence and transcendence, materiality and spirit, determinism and freedom. Today, in an intellectual world that often prides itself on having surpassed modernity, to say nothing of the Enlightenment or religious belief, these oppositions may seem archaic, and the problems they pose vanishingly distant. But the long religious background is crucial for any critical understanding of the terms by which we try to understand words, things, and agency. How these terms are understood has also played a role in how Euro-Americans have understood themselves to be modern and construed modernity's others. The missionary encounter and the attendant problems of radical conversion provide one context in which this background and its links to the idea of modernity can be rendered especially visible.

PROTESTANTS AND MODERNS

This conceptual background underpins my basic historical argument, which situates the colonial encounter within a Protestant strand that runs through or in parallel to certain ways of understanding modernity, what might be called the moral narrative of modernity. This narrative, which I discuss in more detail in the next chapter, takes many forms, of which those associated with liberal thought have been among the most influential. Briefly, in this narrative, progress is not only a matter of improvements in technology, economic well-being, or health but is also, and perhaps above all, about human emancipation and self-mastery. If in the past, humans were in thrall to illegitimate rulers, rigid traditions, and unreal fetishes, as they become modern they realize the true character of human agency. Conversely, those who seem to persist in displacing their own agency onto such rulers, traditions, or fetishes are out of step with the times, anachronistic premoderns or antimoderns.

What makes this a specifically Protestant strand is that the narrative tends, often only by implication, to link moral progress to practices of detachment from and reevaluation of materiality. One of the core problems with which the Protestant Reformation wrestled was the role of material mediations in spiritual life. To be sure, the problem was hardly confined to Protestantism or even Christianity.[3] But the Reformation instigated a long series of efforts to change the role and moral value of semiotic forms in relation to ways of speaking, liturgical objects, the conscience, the body, written texts, material culture, ecclesiastical offices, money, and God. Their specific outcomes are especially pertinent both in today's Euro-American West and in much of its former colonial territories, and have shaped many familiar theoretical efforts to understand them. Certain aspects of the familiar narratives of modernity cannot be discerned unless we understand the persistence of this religious attack on semiotic form in the Western world. The religious attack on semiotic form converges with other familiar ideas, such as the Kantian claim that human freedom depends on moral autonomy, which became central to later secular liberal institutions.

In some important strands of this tradition, the materiality of signifying practices comes to be identified with external constraints on the autonomy of human agents. Thus, this materiality can, in some respects, seem to pose a threat to freedom that demands a serious response. Freedom, in this light, seems to depend on the dematerialization of what is most definitive of humans, whether that be understood as the soul, thoughts, belief, or, say, the meanings of words. The religious background to ideas of modern freedom helps make sense of the impetus behind what Latour (1993) has called purification. Latour defines purification as the drive to draw a clear line between humans and nonhumans, between the world of agency and that of natural determinism. He claims that so-called modernity is characterized by the work of purification. The reader may feel that Latour's portrait makes use of too broad a brush yet still draw from it some useful questions. And even if we were to accept Latour's portrayal of modernity, we should nonetheless be puzzled by the impetus to purify that he identifies with it. For there is no *necessary* reason to think that semiotic form or, indeed, any apparently external objects should be a threat to humans requiring that clear lines be drawn between them. The difference between things and humans, nature and culture, or object and subject does become a problem, however, given a particular semiotic ideology and a particular set of assumptions about the human subject and its agency. One clear and historically influential expression of this ideology was developed within Calvinism.

3. The general problem of semiotic form is a recurring theme in many religious movements. For more on linguistic form as a problem for religions generally, see Keane 1997b, 2004.

THE MISSION ENCOUNTER

These assumptions can be hard to see. In this book, I make them more visible by exploring their manifestations in a religious borderland (though one that is neither geographical, nor, in all cases, sociological) in the encounter between people who start from sharply contrasting assumptions. This is the encounter that took place over the course of the twentieth century between the Calvinist missionaries and their converts and the ancestral ritualists on Sumba in the colonial Dutch East Indies and post-colonial Indonesia. Like all such encounters, this one is complex, and the people involved could take quite different positions toward one another depending on circumstances. But in order to clarify their largely tacit assumptions about words and things, humans and agency, I focus on the contrastive moments in which Calvinists and ancestral ritualists are posed as two clear sides to an encounter. In this respect, I am also working along the lines by which they themselves tended to simplify their own perceptions of the encounter.

The encounter was not, for the most part, a violent one, and from their arrival in 1904 until after the church was taken over by Sumbanese in the 1940s, and still well into the 1970s, the Calvinists were not notably successful. That religious missions played a complex and sometimes contradictory role within the workings of colonial domination is by now well known, even if the exact nature of that role is still debated (see, for example, Beidelman 1982; Comaroff and Comaroff 1991, 1997; Peel 1995; Pels 1999; Rafael 1993; Ranger and Weller 1975; Schneider and Lindenbaum 1987; van der Veer and Lehmann 1999). Colonial power was, of course, a necessary condition for the missionary project here, but it remains somewhat tangential to the main story I want to tell. This is for three reasons. First, where postcolonial societies have made Christianity their own, we miss something crucial if we see in their claims only the effects of colonialism. Second, the mission encounter helps make more visible some critical themes that run through the more domestic history of Christianity well before, and after, colonialism (see chapter 1).

The third reason relates to the particular historical conditions under which the mission operated. During the colonial period, the Dutch missionaries in Sumba had little support from the distant centers of government and were rarely in a position of much direct coercive power. Moreover, as strict Calvinists, they were worried about the depth and sincerity of conversions, and so ruled out many possible strategies that they saw as reliant on external pressure or bribery. In attempting to convert the Sumbanese, they were forced to talk, to explain themselves, to attempt to understand those whom they were addressing, who were forced to explain themselves in turn. Although the conversations were always between unequals, at no time was either side in full command of the terms of discourse.[4] For generations, some of the most contentious points around which this talk circled were the proper places of words and things in the moral and spiritual life of the person and their implications for human agency. This was as much the case in debates about family, wealth, and death as in debates about ritual. Now the foreign missionaries have mostly left; Sumbanese are converting other Sumbanese, and money and commodities are part of the scene, along with an Indonesian nation-state and new forms of cultural and religious politics. Over the century, the debates touched on everything from prayer to houses, from meat to money and marriage. But the conversations continue, provoked in new ways by the same fundamental problems.

I find my point of greatest leverage in the colonial encounter and its postcolonial wake, as missionaries, converts, and the recalcitrant grapple with the apparent contradictions between the materiality of semiotic form and the nature and value of human beings. But before I discuss the specifics of this missionary encounter, in part 2 of this book, the background I have sketched out here must be filled in further. This introduction lays out some of the general conceptual issues. In the next chapter I turn to the global spread of Christianity in general, and Protestantism in particular, in order to bring out the moral themes in certain narratives of modernity. In chapter 2, I consider some aspects of Protestant semiotic ideology and creedal practice, with special focus on their implications for the idea of agency. The three subsequent chapters address the categories of religion, culture, and history.

OBJECTIFICATION, OBJECTS, AND THE SUBJECT

Western social thought has long been shaped by two master historical narratives that seem complementary, or opposed, yet which also reinforce each other in certain respects. Karl Marx (1967a, 1967b, 1978a, 1978b) and Martin Heidegger (1962, 1977), exemplifying these two narratives, each tells a story about the estrangement that defines the condition of modernity. It is

4. Nor were these missionaries unusual in their lack of direct power or their insistence on sincerity; compare the African situation discussed by, for instance, J. D. Y. Peel (1995).

a definition that sets "us"—those who accept their place in these stories—apart from our predecessors and also, at least by implication, from some of our contemporaries: those who are not yet modern. To see what the two narratives share, given their great complexity and vast political and conceptual divergences, requires some drastic simplification. So let us say, for purposes of establishing the context of what follows, that for Marx this estrangement involves abstraction of that which was concrete, decontextualization of that which lives within a context of social relations, and alienation of persons from the results of their activity. For Heidegger, it includes a denial of temporality, and the taking of the world as so many objects from which we stand apart. Despite their profound differences, these two stories share this denouement, that modernity is distinguished by what I call objectification, and that objectification has serious consequences for human subjects.

Objectification, at least in the more common negative uses of the word, is more often invoked than defined; those who use the term often assume we should by now know what it is and what is wrong with it. It connotes a lack of agency and even motion, a distancing from the world, a lack of self-recognition, an abuse of others. It can stand for a complex family of concepts that includes reification (Lukács 1971), the synoptic illusion (Bourdieu 1977), disembedding (Polanyi 1944), abstraction and fetishism (Marx again), and many others. Certainly we can tease these concepts apart analytically (see Nussbaum 1995), but what interests me here is their affinities and the ease with which one can slip among them as they come to be consolidated within the narratives of modernity. One of the central themes of this book is the way epistemological claims are taken to have moral implications, the way one's assumptions about language, for instance, come to be intertwined with how one understands the human subject. To see the moral implications of epistemological claims requires the suspension of some of the more familiar uses of such concepts as objectification or fetishism. I discuss the concept of fetishism in chapter 2. Here, a brief word about objectification. One reason why it is difficult to look critically at a concept like objectification is that it so often is treated as something already understood, as obvious. Objectification is commonly both taken to be an effect of power and, in turn, believed to contribute to its reproduction, and so the discussion quickly skips over it in order to get to power itself.

One purpose of this book is to provide an alternative to the assumptions about objectification that are implicit in many of the classic and more recent criticisms of modernity. A good example of what I mean by these criticisms is Timothy Mitchell's important portrayal of incipient modernity in Egypt

(1988). It is certainly one of the most sophisticated recent accounts of the links among power, modernity, and objectification, and I find much of what he says to be persuasive.[5] Drawing on Heidegger's "The Age of the World Picture" (1977), as read in light of the work of Jacques Derrida and Michel Foucault, Mitchell describes colonialism's most profound effects on its subjects as being products of what he calls representation. By representation, he means both a relation of standing-for and the ontology that relation is supposed to produce. Representations, in this account, involve a distinction between model and reality, such as a panorama and an actual landscape, or a map and a city. Representations offer a privileged location to a viewer, such that both viewer and model clearly stand apart from the reality being represented, rendering that reality as an object (1988: 7–10). This, Mitchell tells us, is distinctively modern and Western. The modern West is a world in which representation produces the effect of there being a world of objects that exist external to it, and of subjects that stand outside that world, which is made available for them by means of these representations. Those subjects assume an ontological distinction between material things and their abstract structures, linked by universal semiosis, "a world of signs" (1988: 14).[6] Mitchell sees this effect as producing the distinction between material bodies and immaterial souls, and as complicit in the creation of colonial order, both political and, as the producer of truth-effects, conceptual.

Mitchell is attempting to trace links between alienation as it has been understood in political economy and the forms of estrangement described in the phenomenology of experience, the perspectives I have identified with Marx and Heidegger, respectively. As I have suggested, although the two perspectives show the world from vastly different positions, in certain respects they both express, and further contribute to, an underlying narrative about modernity and its costs, the effects of life disembedded from previous unities, and the consequences of estrangement. With this general critical story I have no quarrel. Moreover, I am deeply sympathetic with the effort to work at the intersection of political economy and phenomenology. Rather, the problem I address concerns how these two perspectives have come to project modernity's others and, thus, unwittingly help consolidate

---

5. Mitchell refers to "objectness" and "objective," concepts that, in his writing, are encompassed within the overarching rubric of "representation."

6. Typical of those working in the tradition of continental philosophy, Mitchell uses the word *semiosis* to refer to what is, in effect, a Saussurean model of signifiers and signifieds, in which meaning is established by differences, under the doctrine of the arbitrariness of the sign. I criticize the Saussurean model below. What I mean by *semiotics* in this book works with a very different tradition and set of assumptions.

a moral narrative of modernity. For, on the one hand, the distancing effects that Mitchell describes have long been associated with liberation. One version of the moral narrative of modernity says that it is precisely in their ability to stand apart from the world and see it clearly that moderns have come to master it. It is this desire for mastery that Mitchell attacks. On the other hand, by seeing representations as exterior to humans, and for that reason a source of oppression for them, he also reproduces the very dichotomies that bolster the moral narrative he wants to expose.

The story Mitchell tells depends in part on a depiction of the non-Western, nonmodern world in terms derived, by means of inversion, from an understanding of representation that is thoroughly entangled with some common views of modernity. In short, Mitchell's analysis is most compelling—and most generalizable—when it asks about the consequences of representational practices for subjects and the colonial orders that produce them. And yet in certain respects it remains too simple, insofar as it depends on too restricted an account of representation, such that no one but the "moderns" could ever stand apart from their own experience. Lurking behind this account remains, as the invocation of Heidegger should suggest, a certain notion of modern disenchantment and alienation—and thus, by back-projection, of nonmodern enchantment and unities, of which we must be wary.

This book responds in two ways. One is to draw out some themes in the genealogy of the moral (and, by implication, political) critique of objectification. The other is to bring into view some alternatives by showing *multiple* modalities of object creation, decontextualization, and distantiation, and showing that these are not confined to particular historical contexts or social arrangements. Such a view may help us get away from a romantic, perhaps even condescending, view of others as a back-projection from who we *think* we are. Thus it may be a first step toward a response to the complaint, somewhere, by the Indian psychologist and social critic Ashis Nandy that "it is not India's job to be the opposite of the West." The point is not to abolish difference in the name of universals, but to thwart the inclination to turn all differences into versions of just one big opposition, that is, into inversions of ourselves. This effort may also help us appreciate the real difficulties posed by some of the more familiar ways of thinking about and giving value to agency.

In this book, I do not follow the more common anthropological strategy of challenging the assumptions of the West or its vision of modernity by posing against it, through ethnographic portrayal, a wholly alternative cultural world. I do not reject the value of this anthropological strategy out of hand, despite its evident flaws, and its influence on my previous book is certainly apparent (Keane 1997c). My approach here, however, is different. First, in the more ethnographic parts of this book, I focus on an encounter at what the Dutch missionaries saw as a religious frontier. At many junctures in this book, in order to clarify the picture, I treat this encounter as if it had just two sides, the Calvinists and *marapu* followers, that is, the adherents of Sumbanese ancestral ritual. But this is a strategic oversimplification, and in the course of the twentieth century any clear sociological division into two sides makes less and less sense. In some circumstances, for example, Sumbanese Christians stand alongside the Dutch and face marapu followers; in others, all marapu followers and Christians, both Dutch and Sumbanese, stand together and face the rest of Indonesia and, beyond that, the world of Islam. The clash in question here is less one between peoples, or even cultures, than it is between semiotic ideologies. Second, in discussing the more general historical background, I suggest—and can do no more than suggest—that the mission encounter replays themes of encounter and reflexivity that run through the long history of religious form *within* the West that began well before the colonial and postcolonial era.

LANGUAGE AS A MORAL PROBLEM

In the critical tradition that produced the dominant ideas of objectification I have sketched here, the idea of the *object* perforce appears against the background of ideas about the *subject*. It is this background that retains elements of religious and humanist genealogies that much contemporary social thought seems to have left far behind it. These are the valorization of agency, and a certain model of the freedom of a human subject. Within the mainstream philosophical tradition, this model of freedom emerged out of the Enlightenment when it grounded morality in autonomy (Schneewind 1998). I do not rehearse here the familiar postmodernist criticisms of this tradition. But to set the stage for what follows, there are two points about this story that I must note here and elaborate on in the next chapter. First, this story about modernity as the emergence of a relatively more free subject is a story not only about the difference between present and past but also about the West's difference from the non-West (Mahmood 2005; van der Veer 1996, 2001). Second, although the conceptual side of the story is usually framed within the history of philosophy, and its consequences often discussed in the secular terms of most political thought, its broader social impact and deeper effects on subjective life—what Foucault might have called its capillary effects—depend at least as much on religious teachings and practices. One point at which these two aspects of the moral narrative of modernity meet is in the missionary encounter with those who are not Christian, not Western, and not "modern."

Why should words or things pose moral problems for humans? Let me start with the observation that signifying practices can be experienced in contrasting ways. On the one hand, as vehicles of meaning and inhabitable dispositions, signifying practices form an intimate component of subjective experience and its cognizability. On the other hand, as concrete, publicly accessible forms, they can present themselves to subjects as external objects of experience. Now, the way I have formulated this opposition may seem to offer the very subject-object, immaterial-material, distinctions that I subject to critical scrutiny in this book. I insist on the distinction here, however, because it is analytically important to keep in mind the ways in which things and words are *not* wholly products of human intentions, mastered by human actions, and that they are not saturated with meanings. They are potentially objects in both the conceptual and material meanings of the word. The challenge that words and things can pose to persons is therefore not just a problem for the observer and the theoretician but is often a recurrent instigation *within* action itself. In their modality as objective semiotic forms, signifying practices *can,* in some circumstances, offer themselves up to reflection. Given the right background assumptions about the world, the objective character of signifying practices can even become a source of moral or political anxiety, demanding active intervention. At that point, the very materiality of semiotic forms can become, in effect, an agent provocateur of historical change.

Within the analysis of objectification, language plays a special role. For one thing, the reflexive capacities of language itself give it an important mediating and regulating function relative to other semiotic domains (see Lucy 1993; Lee 1997). But in addition, language is itself subject to special modes of objectification. Central to the objectification of language is the process of entextualization. Linguistic anthropologists developed this term to describe how chunks of discourse come to be extractable from particular contexts and thereby made portable (see especially Bauman and Briggs 1990; Kuipers 1990; Silverstein and Urban 1996). The process commonly involves elimination of linguistic features that anchor any stretch of discourse in some immediate context, such as pronouns, temporal and spatial indexes, references that depend on shared knowledge between interlocutors, and so forth (Hanks 1992, 1996). These chunks of discourse, or "texts," can thereby circulate and be recontextualized, inserted into new contexts. This movement of language through decontextualized and recontextualized modalities forms one condition for the possibility of cultural circulation, including that of religion, by means of scriptures, sermons, prayers, creeds, hymns, didactic literature, and so forth.

But in some times and circumstances, people may find this propensity for language to move among contexts to be problematic, even morally troubling. For example, the decontextualization of language can reinforce authority by offering it an apparently transcendental position from which to speak. Conversely, decontextualization can put the sources, intentions, or sincerity of a stretch of discourse in doubt, undermining those who would use it. Derrida (1982) points out, when he discusses the so-called iterability inherent to the very structure of language, that this propensity invites "nonserious" uses of language, such as mimicry, sarcasm, and insincerity, as well as uses unintended by the author, such as magic, divination, or, say, the devil's ways of quoting scripture. For those who think verbal meaning depends on clear intentions, or who seek truly sincere forms of self-expression, the possibility of nonserious language can be troubling. And as Richard Bauman and Charles Briggs (2003) have argued, efforts to regulate language in the face of that worry can have disturbing and sometimes counterintuitive political consequences.

In part 2 of this book I discuss some of the ways in which the objectification of language can seem to be a moral problem for the speaking subject in the light cast by the encounter between Calvinists and Sumbanese ancestral ritualists. These problems include the misuse of scripture as a tool for divination, the expectation that prayers will bring about material results, and reliance on formulaic or rhetorical turns of phrase. One response, by the Calvinists, is to insist that words are merely the external expression of inner thoughts. The dangers posed by entextualized language should, in effect, be constrained by the norm of sincerity. Words should be contextualized relative to the speaker's intent to convey ideas. The norm of sincerity and its moral ramifications depend on the idea that language could be transparent, that it could be a clear and direct vehicle for the communication of thoughts from one person to another. Words should be subject to the agency of a speaker who stands apart from the words he or she masters (see chapter 7).

The important point is that these are not just ideas about language. They are about people. According to Richard Bauman and Charles Briggs (2003), for example, in seventeenth-century and eighteenth-century western

Europe the speaker of sincere, transparent language came to be seen as normatively superior to those who engaged in insincere or rhetorical speech, which for some English thinkers was a necessary foundation for both the polity and good science. Such a person's word could be trusted. Writing about the same historical period, Steven Shapin (1994) has argued that trust in another's word was critical to the acceptance of experimental methods in early modern science. Since the general public could not witness experiments, it was the reliability of the report that mediated between the scientist's experiences and the general production of knowledge. Politically, from the eighteenth century onward, a speaker of transparent, sincere words came to be identified with the responsible and disinterested participant in the public sphere, as one who, in Michael Warner's portrayal (2002), is free of the interests and determinations of any particular social location. Similar expectations came to be common in more ordinary day-to-day interactions as well. I am not concerned here with evaluating the historical status of these specific claims. Rather, my interest is in the way they exemplify the articulation among language ideology, speaking (and reading and writing) practices, moral values, political institutions, and concepts of the person. What one believes about language, in this case, has implications for what one expects of other persons, including oneself, and what those others themselves expect.

SEMIOTIC IDEOLOGY

Linguistic anthropologists call what one believes about language a language ideology. In Judith Irvine's formulation, language ideology is "a cultural system of ideas about social and linguistic relationships, together with their loading of moral and political interests" (1989: 255). These ideas respond to people's experience of language itself. As Michael Silverstein puts it, in one of the earliest definitions, such ideologies (note the plural) are "sets of beliefs about language articulated by users as a rationalization or justification of perceived language structure and use" (1979: 193). Language ideologies, however, do not just reflect on language as it is given: people act on the basis of those reflections. They try to change or preserve certain ways of speaking and criticize or emulate other speakers. These efforts can be as subtle as the intuition that people from certain backgrounds are not quite trustworthy, or a hesitance to express certain values in one's mother tongue; they can be as violent as the state suppression of minority languages. Language ideologies therefore play a crucial role in the social and political dynamics of language structure and use (Hill 1985; Kroskrity 2000; Schieffelin, Woolard, and Kroskrity 1998; Woolard and Schieffelin 1994).

Three aspects of the concept of linguistic ideology are worth stressing here. First, to the extent that language ideology responds to the speaker's awareness of language, it is predicated on some capacity to take language as an object within experience. That is, it involves at least some incipient form of objectification. Given the range of observed language ideologies across and within societies, the objectification of language in some sense of the term is apparently ubiquitous and hardly restricted to special social or historical circumstances. Second, this awareness is necessarily partial. This is due, in part, simply to the inaccessibility of linguistic structure to full awareness, the reason Franz Boas (1911) doubted speakers' analyses of their own language (see Irvine 2001).

But more to the point, partial awareness is a result of the ways in which awareness emerges from the speakers' locations within fields of social difference.[7] Language ideologies do not just express social difference, they play a crucial role in producing—in objectifying and making inhabitable—the categories by which social difference is understood and evaluated. Moreover, since the power effects of language (and of semiotic form more generally) are not fully determinate—the "same" forms can, for example, have quite different implications in different contexts—ideological mediation is a necessary component of any political consequences that might follow from form. At the same time, *ideology* here does *not* mean false consciousness or systematic deception. By using the word *ideology*, most linguistic anthropologists are stressing the productive effects of reflexive awareness. Third, language ideology plays a causal role within the historical transformation of language itself. It is a source of linguistic play, of judgments about variations in speech styles and linguistic repertoires and thus about the people associated with them, it gives rise to language reform and purification movements, and so forth. All of these have consequences for language structure, practices, and their larger sociopolitical effects.

With the idea of semiotic ideology, I am expanding on certain implications of these observations.[8] Theorists of language ideology make clear that, to the extent that objectification is a precondition for reflective awareness, it is not necessarily the *end* of dynamic processes, but rather a particular

---

7. The degree to which speakers can be fully aware of their language ideologies is subject to considerable debate (see Kroskrity 2004 for a useful summary).

8. For a use of *semiotic ideology* that develops similar observations in a somewhat different direction, see Parmentier 1994.

moment within them.[9] Language ideology thus seems to be one special instance of a more general principle of reflexivity within the ongoing creation and transformation of social phenomena. Indeed, most accounts of language ideology describe consequences that extend far beyond language in any strict sense of the term. Judith Irvine (1989), for example, has demonstrated a wide range of ways in which language articulates with political economy. Moreover, the reflexivity peculiar to language seems to play an especially important role in regulating other semiotic domains.

Why then extend the idea of linguistic ideology as "semiotic ideology"? For two reasons. First, the very distinction between what counts as language and what does not is itself constructed ideologically, and it differs across historical and social contexts. Second, there are places in this book in which my primary focus is on material objects, in contexts where the role of language is not necessarily definitive. As Christopher Pinney (2005) has argued, we must consider the ways in which material things work independently of, or in contradiction to, their discursive surround. Otherwise we risk treating humans as if their capacity to endow the world with meaning had no limits, and, I would add, as if the world could hold no further surprises for them. Since consequences and corollaries can include the full range of signifying practices and their various kinds of materiality, the more encompassing concept of semiotic ideology seems to be called for. In this book, language ideology plays a central role, but this role links it to other semiotic domains. It is a matter of semiotic ideology whether speakers even consider words to be radically distinct from things in the first place.

This emphasis on materiality means more than just insisting on the materiality of the world within which signifying practices take place. It means that ideas and the practices they involve have not only logical but also causal effects on one another across a potentially wide range of apparently distinct social fields. They are parts of what we could call a *representational economy*. That is, practices and associated ideologies exist in dynamic relations with one another such that changes in one domain can have consequences for others. It is such a representational economy that Mary Poovey (1998) portrays when, for example, she argues that early methods of bookkeeping in England had moral connotations and should be understood in relation to elite knowledge projects such as rhetoric or natural philosophy. Indeed, the parallels that Timothy Mitchell draws among colonial exhibitions, pedagogy, images of the body, city plans, and print

---

9. Here I am extending an argument that I began to lay out, in a preliminary form, in Keane 1997c; see also Keane 2003b; Silverstein and Urban 1996.

technology can also be seen as effects of a representational economy. The idea of representational economy is meant to situate words, things, and persons (along with other agentive beings such as spirits) dynamically within the same world with one another. It is meant to show how secular intellectuals, nationalist politicians, market traders, and religious missionaries might be acting in the same field of ideas and values, and what, say, money, prayer, and promises might have to do with one another. But the idea of representational economy is not intended to take the place of culture, episteme, or historical formation. The idea is not meant to be totalizing but rather to allow for the multiple possibilities immanent in any given moment, sometimes even across different contexts within individual lives.

Representational economies are doubly heterogeneous. First, within a given representational economy, its different elements are subject to different kinds of processes (changes in speech registers are not produced by the same causes and do not have the same consequences as those in theological doctrine, institutional arrangements, or economic value). Second, in any given social context, multiple representational economies are likely to be in play; the United States at the beginning of the twenty-first century is hardly unique in its ability to contain both biblical literalists and rational choice economists. As Dipesh Chakrabarty (2000) has argued, it is an error of historicism to treat as anachronistic those who seem not to fit into a particular narrative (a point I develop in chapter 4).

But although the elements within a representational economy interact with one another, that interaction is not in itself sufficient to make them mutually reinforcing. As I show below, similar semiotic forms such as a spoken text (chapter 9) or money in an offering dish (chapter 10) can enter into very different kinds of moral actions, depending on the semiotic ideologies of those who use them.[10] Within a representational economy, therefore, semiotic ideology plays a crucial mediating role. My attention to encounters in a religious borderland is meant to make this visible.

The different elements of a representational economy (for instance, norms for handling money, liturgical conventions, and domestic arrangements) are subject to different causal logics and temporalities. Norms for handling money are directly affected by financial institutions that may be

---

10. Recent insightful work in other Christian contexts exemplifies the point. Birgit Meyer (2003, 2004), for instance, shows that secular film producers in Ghana make use of Pentecostalism because its temptations, demons, and exorcisms provide great possibilities for melodrama. The producers do not thereby become Pentecostal, although they may inadvertently reinforce the doctrinal message.

responding to influences and goals very different from the theologies that shape liturgical conventions. That elements within a representational economy cohere at any given moment, or seem to, is always something that requires explanation. In some circumstances, it is one of the tasks of church doctrines and disciplines, for instance, to achieve this effect of coherence. But coherence is not always achieved in so purposeful a way. More generally, different kinds of practices and institutions affect one another within a representational economy, but it is the logic of a semiotic ideology that helps bring the effects into alignment.

Thus, in a debate about correct ways of praying, for example, the concept of sincerity ties ways of speaking to the model of words as conventional expressions of inner thoughts, to the norm that semiotic forms should be subordinate to immaterial meanings, and to moral evaluations of persons as responsible agents (see chapter 6). To that extent, the moral value of sincerity is an aspect of language ideology (see chapter 7). But the norm of sincerity functions within a larger representational economy that includes the constituting of social relations by means of material goods. Sincerity in this context means that material objects should be taken to stand apart from the people who own and transact them. When used, for instance, in marriage exchange or ceremonies, objects ought only to express immaterial meanings and not serve as tokens of economic value or media of magical power (see chapter 8). The separation of words from things is reinforced by a nascent ideology of referential speech that encourages the treatment of verbal performances as texts (see chapter 9). The ideal of abstraction exemplified by the treatment of valuables as expressions of immaterial meanings reaches its most developed form in ideas surrounding money (see chapter 10).

The idea of semiotic ideology is meant to capture these practices involving words and things within the same frame. By viewing words and things together within one frame, we can see how they interact within a single representational economy such that changes in some domains can have consequences in others. For example, changing theological views can alter the nature of moral claims, ideas about agency and responsibility, and the ways in which they draw lines between animate subjects and inanimate objects. Changes in legal responsibility or the technological manipulation of life may, in turn, induce changes in theological arguments. It is for reasons like this that battles over apparently minor matters such as the use of a prayer book can be taken so seriously by the combatants. They involve basic assumptions about what kinds of beings inhabit the world, what counts as a possible agent, and thus what are the preconditions for and consequences of moral action.

MATERIALITY

In the context of a study of religious conversion and the moral narrative of modernity, the idea of semiotic ideology is meant to do two things. It aims to show why moral arguments may focus on semiotic forms. It is also intended to open up approaches to the question of objectification that do not derive from the teleological destination of modernity. To make this second point, I draw attention to the materiality of semiotic form. This must be taken into account even in understanding language. Because of its duplex character, the experience of speech is complex (Jakobson 1957; Silverstein 1976). One the one hand, it plays a special role in the experience of subjectivity, as inner speech. On the other, it is in the experience of language as structured sounds or textual forms—for example, encountered in instances of actual language use—that "we recognize the external discourse [of other speakers] as external by virtue of its sensible character" (Urban 1996: 23). Language ideology responds to the phenomenal forms that make language available as a potential object of apperception, intuitions, and reflexive thought. But these potentially work in tension with the experience of inner speech.

Like language ideology, then, semiotic ideology is a reflection upon, and an attempt to organize, people's experiences of the materiality of semiotic form. Not only language but also music, visual imagery, food, architecture, gesture, and anything else that enters into actual semiotic practice functions within perceptible experience by virtue of its material properties (see Keane 2003c). These things have repeatable forms that are a minimal condition of their recognizability across instances, of their circulation across social space, and of their capacity for temporal extension. But people's ability to recognize those forms as "the same" depends on certain ways of framing them, since their very materiality means they are always open to other unrealized possibilities. The hard metallic offerings of certain Sumbanese rituals could, by assimilation to coins, become a metonym of monetary value; the wooden ancestor tablets of a Chinese village could become Maoist firewood; an early Florentine altar could become Fine Art. Semiotic forms exist as much within a representational economy of causes and effects as within a realm of logics and meanings. This materiality is a precondition for their social existence. It is also the condition for their historical mutability, their openness to an unspecifiable range of future possibilities.

I stress this materiality, and its articulations with mute causality, against the effects of certain assumptions built into the model of the sign developed by Ferdinand de Saussure (1983) that stubbornly persist in much post-structuralist thought. These assumptions derive from his methodological distinction between speech and linguistic system. The most important are these: the radical distinction between signs and the world; and the doctrine of arbitrariness, which held that there are in principle no relations between signs and the world signified except for those established by the conventions of the system itself, commonly understood as a code shared among its users. As a result, what Saussure called *semiology* concerned only virtual types, never concrete tokens. Although language, for Saussure, did have form, which is the basis of the system of differences, it did not have materiality in any consequential respect. As a synchronic system, it functioned within a logic in which causality had no place.[11] Saussurean analysis has produced enduring insights into the character of language as a virtual system of denotations, but efforts to bring it to bear on language practices or other, nonlinguistic, semiotic domains have fared far less well.

When I use the word *semiotic* in this book, however, it is within a tradition that has set itself strongly against this Saussurean abstraction of the sign. Some of the foci of this countertradition—which draws on Charles S. Peirce's model of the sign, as well as on aspects of phenomenology, sociolinguistics, and the writings of Bakhtin (1981, 1986), Goffman (1981), and Vološinov (1973)—have been indexicality, poetic form, and speech genre (see Lee 1997). Indexicality refers to those modes of signification that function by means of real connections between whatever is taken to be a sign and some actually existing object of signification. The connections might be juxtaposition (pointing finger and thing being pointed at) or cause and effect (smoke emanating from fire). Poetics, following Roman Jakobson, looks at the effects of patterned linguistic form (e.g., rhythm, rhyme, or other parallelisms) on language users' intuitions of significance and coherence. Speech genre, like other sociolinguistic phenomena, such as register, similarly concerns the formal constraints to which people intuitively respond in using language, and the ways these are embedded within material activities as well as social interaction. This is not the place to review the substantial

---

11. Note that Saussure's historical analysis did not have the influence outside linguistics that his synchronic analysis had.

literature on these topics; I simply point out some of the ways an understanding of semiotic form demands attention to materiality. Although the examples I mention have been linguistic, there are important implications for the wider field of semiotic modalities, such as exchange valuables, money, the meat distributed at feasts, and architectural form, which I explore in the chapters that follow.

THE WORK OF PURIFICATION

One reason the wider appeal of Saussure's abstraction of signs from social and material worlds has been so persistent is, perhaps, that it participates in the larger historical process that Bruno Latour calls the work of purification. The work of purification, according to Latour, is an overarching project of making separations—of humans from nonhumans, nature from society, objects as sources of determination from objects that we make use of, and the Kantian things-in-themselves from the transcendental subject (1993: 10–11, 33, 53, 56). When the work of purification turns to what Latour calls the separation of "signs and things[,] . . . material causality from human fantasy" (1993: 35), it seems to me he is talking about precisely the division between the dematerialized linguistic sign postulated by Saussure and the material reality assumed by his critics.

One of Latour's main goals, as I understand him, is to resituate the place of science within the Euro-American West's understanding of itself and its modernity. Although this project is different from the one that engages me here, two aspects of Latour's account are pertinent to the story I am telling. One is the assertion that purification is never entirely successful. The other is the moral subtext that seems to run through Latour's historical narrative, that purification is driven by the sense that there is something scandalous or threatening about the mixing of humans and things, culture and nature. I suggest that the social role of semiotic form helps explain the first, and the religious dimension of the concept of modernity provides part of the second. Consider first the failure of purification. Even while moderns are trying to separate things, Latour asserts, hybrids are proliferating. These include things that mix nature and culture, things and humans, like psychotropic drugs, hybrid corn, and frozen embryos (1993: 49). But he tells us little about why this is happening. Latour's background is in science studies, and the hybrids with which he is most concerned involve technological manipulation. But both the ubiquity of so-called hybrids, and the sense of scandal they can generate, have sources beyond the history of science and technology. The materiality of semiotic form is inescapable; to the extent that it mediates even inner subjectivity, it renders full purification impossible.

The other point important to my argument concerns the historical narrative of modernity. Latour asserts that purification is part of the way in which the modern has come to be defined as "a new regime, an acceleration, a rupture, a revolution in time" (1993: 10). But modernity is not just a certain historical period, one among many. The story involves winners and losers. More than that, it has a value-laden subtext: "The obscurity of the olden days, which illegitimately blended together social needs and natural reality, meanings and mechanisms, signs and things, gave way to a luminous dawn that cleanly separated material causality from human fantasy" (1993: 35). To put it in terms that might be more recognizable to the people about whom I write in this book, modernity is often told as the outcome of a story of moral redemption.

As far as I know, Latour does not really explain what drives purification, gives it direction, or endows it moral force. I think one reason is that he sees this as largely a story about science and its separation from politics, the two sides exemplified by his central protagonists, Robert Boyle and Thomas Hobbes. Religion appears briefly in the narrative only as one more thing affected by purification: God is eliminated from the public scene and exiled to the individual's heart (Latour 1993: 33). But if we place the work of purification within the context of the Reformation attack on certain aspects of semiotic form, we may recognize one source of its moral impetus. To invoke Latour once more, he captures the anthropological perspective when he writes: "The ethnologist of our world must take up her position at the common locus where roles, actions and abilities are distributed—those that make it possible to define one entity as animal or material and another as a free agent; one as endowed with consciousness, another as mechanical, and still another as unconscious and incompetent. Our ethnologist must even compare the always different ways of defining—or not defining—matter, law, consciousness and animals' souls, without using modern metaphysics as a vantage point" (1993: 15). But as I argue over the next several chapters, this is not the ethnologist's task alone. It is also, in a quite distinct key, to be sure, the task of the reformer. When religious reformers and their most hardworking heirs, the missionaries at what they took to be the religious frontier, set to work, it was often precisely on making these distinctions. In this respect, they make some of the core assumptions of their Euro-American world visible and reveal some of the moral imperatives and anxieties these entail—as we can see with the help of the ones they are trying to save. When they grapple, say, with the proper place of objects in the lives of subjects or with the possibilities and limits of human agency, or when they attempt to sort out what is ethically acceptable, or even simply believable, across cultural difference, they take on problems that should look familiar. However estranged the ethnographer may be from either set of protagonists—for both the missionaries and their interlocutors can seem to live in distant moral and conceptual worlds—they must in these respects be understood as his or her coevals. When I argue, in the later chapters of this book, that the imputation of fetishism is prone to redound onto the accuser, I am not simply describing a problem peculiar to missionaries. I am pointing to paradoxes we may face ourselves.

SYNOPSIS AND OVERVIEW

The book is divided into three parts. Part 1 explains my approach to Protestantism and its relationship to the moral narrative of modernity, part 2 looks closely at certain aspects of the encounter between Calvinism and ancestral ritual on the island of Sumba, and part 3 turns to some contemporary ramifications of this encounter beyond the specifically religious.

The four chapters in part 1 differ in character from those that make up the rest of the book. They sketch the most pertinent dimensions of the larger context within which I situate the mission, colonialism, and conversion on Sumba. Whereas parts 2 and 3 analyze specific ethnographic and historical materials from the mission encounter and afterward, these first four chapters work at a very different level of generality. They touch on a number of topics, such as the concept of modernity, the globalization of Christianity, the category of religion, and postcolonial historical consciousness, each of which properly demands its own monograph, if not a whole field of study. My treatment of them here is not meant to be a thorough or definitive demonstration. The purpose, rather, is to make explicit the larger framework that informs my approach in subsequent chapters. Part 1 thus attempts to work against some of the occasional, unintended consequences of one of anthropology's great virtues, a particularism so scrupulous it can sometimes obscure our view of large contexts and deny us the insights we might gain from comparing cases. This effort is particularly important when the very people with whom we are most immediately concerned insist that an important part of their lives involves something both global and transcendental. In chapter 1, I begin by sketching some general aspects of Christianity in the contemporary world, stressing its global reach and the challenge it poses for those who would say that to become modern is, perforce, to become secular. I define *modernity* as an idea that has become a ubiquitous part of historical consciousness, and argue that certain aspects of the more liberatory narratives of modernity draw on concepts and values that were also expressed by, and perhaps in part derive from, the Protestant Reformation (though no doubt the influences run both ways). In chapter 2, I discuss Calvinism as a semiotic ideology. I analyze the ways that textual forms such as the creed facilitate the global circulation not just of a doctrine and but also of a model for how one might take active command over one's inner thoughts. It is a model that enters into certain ideas about human freedom. In chapter 3, I turn to the genealogy of the concepts of religion and culture. Here I look especially at nineteenth-century efforts to distinguish between the two so that reformers and missionaries could change one but not the other. These efforts encountered practical and conceptual dilemmas that persist today. In chapter 4, I consider some of the problems for people's sense of history that arise in the context of radical religious conversion. People have grappled with questions like How do we know the past has been put behind us? In what forms does the past persist? Is the apparent persistence of the past a threat or a source of value for us? I draw attention to some of the practices that help produce the experience of rupture or continuity. These questions return again in chapter 5, which opens the second part of the book.

With part 2, I take a closer look at the encounter between Dutch Calvinism and ancestral ritual. The setting is Sumba, an island of eastern Indonesia, which was missionized by the neo-orthodox Reformed Churches in the Netherlands (Gereformeerde Kerken in Nederland) from the first years of the twentieth century. The mission was replaced by the self-governing Christian Church of Sumba (Gereja Kristen Sumba) in the 1940s. By the last quarter of the twentieth century, when I carried out my fieldwork there, a Christian majority (mostly members of the Gereja Kristen Sumba, and a smaller number of Catholics and evangelicals) was emerging on the island.[12] The argument of part 2 centers on the concept of fetishism as a precipitate of the encounter between semiotic ideologies. In contrast to

---

12. I discuss aspects of this history in chapters 3, 4, and 5. Translating denominational titles can be confusing, since all Dutch Calvinists called themselves "reformed." The English word translates two Dutch words, *hervormde* and the older linguistic form *gereformeerde*. The mainstream Reformed Church (Hervormde Kerk) was the nineteenth-century heir to the official church of the Dutch Republic after the disestablishment of 1795. The name Gereformeerde Kerken refers to neo-orthodox Calvinists who seceded from the Hervormde Kerk in the nineteenth cen-

many in the Marxist or Freudian traditions, I use *fetishism* not to assert my own correct view of agency, but rather in an attempt to gain insight into the stakes when people differ over the locus of agency. I use the word to denote the imputation to others of a false understanding of the divisions between human and nonhuman, subject and object, an error that threatens human agency. That is, the idea that others are fetishists is part of the work of purification. The four chapters of part 2 look at arguments about people, words, and things, mostly in the context of religious practice, where the issues are brought into sharpest focus.

Chapter 5 centers on the oratory in an event that took place in 1986, when one Sumbanese elder attempted to explain his conversion to Christianity, make his peace with the past, and claim a crucial historical role for himself. To do this, however, he appropriated a speech genre whose pragmatic underpinnings work at double cross purposes to his assertions: the past persists where there was supposed to be change, and is changed where it is supposed to have been preserved. Semiotic form offers a degree of resistance to the intentions of those who would use it and retains some independence of the changing semiotic ideologies that mediate its uses. Chapter 6 concerns the duplex character of words, their forms and meanings, as they arise in different approaches to prayer. I follow arguments between Calvinists and marapu ritualists about what words can and cannot do. This chapter brings into focus many of the core problems for human agency and for the religious goal of transcendence that are posed by the materiality of language. Chapter 7 also focuses on language but concentrates on its speakers. I look at sincerity as a moral ideal for the human subject, as it applies both to words and to the use of material goods in marriage exchange. This juxtaposition shows how ideas elaborated with respect to words can have implications for things as well, as Christians argue that certain exchange valuables should be understood only as symbolic expressions of ideas, not as economic goods. The discussion of material things is developed further in chapter 8, which follows a series of debates among Dutch missionaries themselves, and between them and the unconverted Sumbanese. The debates center on how

---

tury (to further confuse matters, at the end of the twentieth century, the two churches began a process of merging once more). The Gereformeerde Kerken's insistence on local autonomy is marked by the use of the plural *churches (kerken)*. I refer to the mainstream Hervormde Kerk as the Reformed Church. Depending on the context, I refer to the successionists as the neo-orthodox or Reformed Churches, or sometimes just Calvinists. When the context makes clear whom I mean, I sometimes refer to them as Protestants or Christians. Note that in Indonesian the word *Kristen* (Christian) often refers to Protestants, in contrast to *Katolik*.

Christians should cope with the sacrificial offerings distributed in feasts, which are a central part of Sumbanese social life. As these debates make evident, Christians' efforts to maintain discrete boundaries between materiality and meaning lead to serious conundrums.

Part 3 examines semiotic ideology, which I introduce through Calvinism, as it appears in less explicitly religious contexts. In chapter 9, I look at what happens to objectified bits of language—ritual texts—as their function shifts from the uncertain effort to bridge an ontological gap between humans and spirits to a stabilized display of cultural knowledge. Here we have an exemplary instance of the kind of objectifying representation Mitchell sees as defining modernity. I show that the emergent semiotic ideology within which the display of culture works is indeed new, but it draws on older modes of entextualization. In chapter 10, I briefly discuss the emergence of money and the commodity form in Sumbanese life. These are the forms about which the strongest claims about modernity's abstractions have traditionally been made. I look at them in the context of an encounter between two semiotic ideologies.

THE PROBLEM OF WRITING ABOUT CHRISTIANITY

Some final remarks. First, sometimes it still surprises me to discover I have written a book in which Christianity plays so large a role. In the end, I find that the topic has allowed me to address a wide range of theoretical problems that have long provoked me. Moreover, it has allowed me to do so in conversation with religious believers who are hardly likely to grant me special ethnographic authority, and who speak from within a tradition that has helped shape the vocabulary of social thought in which I work. But the realization that I could think about words, things, and agency through Christianity was a long time coming. When I began writing what became the earliest parts of this book, it did not seem likely that Christianity in itself was going to have a significant part in the outcome. The instigation certainly did not come from my own background, in which I was exposed to a highly political strain of Quakerism mixed with a mild Episcopalianism, behind which were the dimmest genealogical ghosts of Irish Catholics, Danish Lutherans, and, across a vast distance, what one could imagine as scary Hawthornian Puritans. Anyway, I came from a city about which Lenny Bruce once quipped, "All New Yorkers are Jewish." And as I grew up downtown in the sixties and seventies, there were Santeria botanicas down the street, and around every corner there might be Hare Krishna chanters,

Black Muslim preachers, or Zen beats. But for all that, it was easy enough in this context to appreciate Donne and Emerson, Giotto and Rothko, while leaving the theology out. One could read even the Bible as a student of art and literature, as the words of one well-known title invited us to do. Aside, perhaps, from my reading of Weber's *Protestant Ethic* and Augustine's *Confessions*, it was the man whom I call Umbu Neka who first provoked me to think about Christianity at length (see chapter 5). Much of my field-work, and many of my closest relationships, were with the non-Christians I call marapu followers. But Umbu Neka, along with the members of my own Sumbanese household, and several other friends, colleagues, and acquaintances in Sumba, forced me to take their religion seriously and to grapple with the fact that they assumed this was also the religion of *tau jiawa kaka* (white foreigners) like me. In one respect, this book is an effort to pick up parts of conversations I had let drop and—belatedly and in a foreign register—enter into them again.

As a first principle, in this book I treat Christianity as what Marcel Mauss (1990) would have called a "social fact." By social fact, I mean simply this: Christianity, its ideas, institutions, social formations, political identities, hopes, desires, fears, norms, and practices, both everyday and extraordinary, *exist* for an remarkably large and varied number of people. Christianity may be part of a taken-for-granted background or a fervent frontline concern, the tone of people's engagement may be indifferent or passionate, but for them it is there. But this raises a well-known conundrum. The study of religion, even more than other anthropological topics (Keane 2003b), has provoked vehement debates over the observer's position. Susan Harding summarizes one view when she writes, "Social scientists and professed unbelievers in general do not let themselves get close enough to 'belief' to understand it" (2000: 36). We may take her point yet still recognize that, as a blanket statement, this assertion depends on a specific idea of understanding, as well as a particular assumption about the place of belief in religion. The privilege it accords to subjective experience is something we should not accept uncritically (see Scott 1991 for a major statement of the problem; see Sharf 2000 for discussions of religious experience in particular). As Talal Asad (1993) and others have argued, the special role given to inner belief in many contemporary views of religion has specific historical sources and political entailments. It is perhaps worth noting, then, that Harding's own remark comes in the context of her brilliant demonstration of the role that texts and ways of speaking that originate from other people play in constituting the inner experience of belief (which is perhaps why she puts that word in scare quotes). The point is not to dismiss experience, but to recognize how it is situated and by what forms of mediation, and, when it *is* privileged, to ask why and to investigate the implications.

Much of anthropology's comparative imagination, whether it is brought to bear on colonial encounters, on the present-day forces of globalization, or, at another plane, on the problem of other minds, still commonly depends on certain largely unexamined notions about the West. In much anthropological writing, focused as it is on developing the complexity and nuance of its ethnographic portrayals, the author's contrastive background notions about the West are often unexamined, crude, and even ill-informed. Moreover, anthropologists are only slowly coming to grips with the centrality of Christianity to so much of what we consider to be "the West": its discourses, values, and practices (see Cannell 2005, 2006; Masuzawa 2005; Robbins 2004a). But Christianity is no longer just a story about the West: it has become central to understanding the world after colonialism.

This book, with its focus on Calvinists, differs somewhat from many contemporary ethnographies of Christianity in at least one respect. I cannot say, as did F. E. Williams about his own pioneering work on Melanesian Christians, that, "[i]n eighteen years of anthropologizing, I have never been so bored" (quoted in Douglas 2001: 617). But members of the Reformed Churches, whether Dutch or Indonesian, are among the least puzzling or flamboyant of Christians. They are not millenarian or even revivalist. The state does not view them as dangerous subversives, like the Branch Davidians (Faubion 2001), nor can one make any strong claim that they are a wellspring of political resistance, like South African Zionists (Comaroff 1985). They have not elaborated an alternative cosmology or created new rituals, and do not commonly undergo demonic possession or take part in exorcisms or even, usually, listen to fire-and-brimstone preaching. The hymns of the Reformed Churches sound like those one might hear in a mainstream Protestant service in the United States. Despite the theological importance of original sin and the possibility of damnation, these do not normally figure prominently in their sensibilities. Even the doctrines of election and predestination have, in practice, become muted. Most of the time, their politics are not extraordinarily "repugnant," in contrast to the people about whom Susan Harding (1991) has written. And so far, at least, they have been lucky enough to escape the horrific interreligious violence that has engulfed some of their coreligionists elsewhere in Indonesia. For this lack of drama and color, I claim these virtues: first, the seeming ordinariness of the Reformed Churches may help us see that quality of everydayness in which religion can have some of its most important consequences. For whether we take our cue from the sexual chatter of Foucault's Victorians, from the dinner table of Bourdieu's workers, from Weber's bookkeepers, or from the humble purchase of cloth in Marx, surely some of the most momentous historical processes take place at the level of everyday life. Second, if the flamboyance of some denominations makes them intriguing, it can also keep them exotic. If my intuition is right, and certain assumptions within secular thought do parallel, and in some cases draw from, religious sources, we are more likely to notice the affinity where the religion seems less Other.

In spite of my specific ethnographic focus on Calvinism, at several points in this book I speak of Christianity or Protestantism. These terms encompass an immense and constantly changing variety of sects, styles, and worldviews. Protestantism alone ranges from the privatistic individualism of modern liberal Quakerism to the highly public expressiveness of some evangelical churches (Harding 2000), from the asceticisms of early Puritans to the gospel of prosperity's celebration of wealth (Coleman 2000), from the restraint of low church Anglicanism to the exuberance of Pentecostalism (Austin-Broos 1997; Meyer 2004; Robbins 2004b), from biblical literalists (Crapanzano 2000) to those who treasure the materiality of the Bible (Rutherford 2003) or refuse to read the scriptural texts at all (Engelke 2004b). In the pages that follow, I address internal differences in detail when they are important. But it should also be said at the start that insisting on these differences too much runs against the claims of many Christian churches to be part of a single, universal phenomenon, and thus may cause us to lose sight of the actual consequences of those claims. Much of what I have written here concerns Protestantism; given its history, with too great an emphasis on distinctions we also risk missing something of the effects of the contrast, self-defined or otherwise, between Protestantism and its rivals. In this contrastive context, the Christian emphasis on proselytization and conversion, at least in the Protestant forms with which I am most concerned here, entails *some* broad shared underlying vision of the subject to be converted and the historical trajectories involved.

My emphasis in this book is on the practices, and their animating ideas, by which Christianity becomes inhabitable and practicable. These ideas and practices are presupposed by, and thus crucial to understanding, the institutions, political goals, and social identities that have been the more usual topics of much recent ethnographic and historical writing about the religion. I also suggest that aspects of Christianity form part of the background of some of the key concepts, anxieties, modes of acting, and morality of many self-consciously secular projects.

To that end, this book takes doctrines seriously. There are simply too many things that we cannot understand if we do not also listen to what religious believers have to say about their cosmos and its implications for how they set about acting in, and on, the world. The historian Phyllis Mack got it right when she made the following observation in the midst of her social and political study of the Reformation in the mid-sixteenth-century Lowlands. First she quotes Claude Lévi-Strauss in *Tristes Tropiques,* describing Nicolas Durand de Villegaignon's Calvinist community in Brazil in 1566: "Where they should have been working to keep themselves alive, they spent week after week in insane discussions. How should one interpret the Last Supper? . . . [T]hey went so far as to send an emissary to Europe to ask Calvin to adjudicate on certain knotty points." Mack then remarks, "One might safely assume, I think, that these Calvinists were not insane, and that if they had not considered the Last Supper to be of ultimate importance they would not have traveled to Brazil in the first place" (1978: 108; typo corrected). Doctrinal problems are not only *about* the world: they function, often in practical and concrete terms, *within* that world. If this is true in general, it is especially important to bear in mind when trying to understand such doctrinally driven forces as reform movements and missionization.

This book centers on an encounter over the course of which the different sides took on different identities. It is not about "the West and the rest" insofar as Sumbanese Christians can, in certain circumstances, stand with the Dutch as they face their unconverted neighbors—or more threatening, if more distant, Islam. The crucial difference is between semiotic ideologies and practices, which are not isomorphic with the sociological entities involved. Sociological identity is further complicated by the question of ethnographic specificity. I begin the book with a discussion of Christianity and Protestantism as global, historical phenomena. I then turn to European missionaries. The Sumbanese themselves do not really enter the story until part 2, beginning with chapter 5. Because of the focus on the encounter, much of this book follows the tendency of the earlier missionaries and present-day Sumbanese Christian Church (Gereja Kristen Sumba) and speaks of "Sumba" as a whole. Often the missionary writings do not specify localities with any greater precision than that, and I am forced to follow my sources in their generality. When I draw on my own fieldwork, I refer to Anakalang, a borderland district between east and west Sumba. But depending on the questions one asks and the things one wants to accomplish, Sumba is divisible into indefinitely greater degrees of ethnographic specificity. Present-day Sumba contains a number of districts whose inhabitants speak one or more languages from a set of closely related languages that are most divergent at either end of the island. The districts are also marked by numerous social structural and ritual distinctions. Anthropological convention has therefore treated the island as home to some half dozen distinct societies.[13] My own fieldwork followed this convention, and indeed, given the difficulty of learning even one Sumbanese language, that was plenty. But the convention is also something of a fiction. Internally, the districts are divided by loyalties to village and clan that may override any sense of greater unity. At the same time, in many respects, Sumbanese recognize a degree of kinship with one another and similarities in cultural principles. The similarities become more relevant under some circumstances than others, and within the framework of the Indonesian nation-state, familiar processes of ethnicization are at work (Hoskins 1993; Keane 1997a; Kuipers 1998). One of the most visible institutions of a unified Sumbanese identity is the Sumbanese Christian Church.

Finally, a brief remark on what this book is and is not. I do not pretend to give a full history or ethnography of either the Dutch mission or Sumbanese Protestantism, and I make only passing reference to Sumbanese Catholicism. I am aware of how much is left out. But the task I have set myself is neither that of setting the record straight nor that of portraying a totalizable world so that everything has been accounted for. First, my purpose in this book is to convey insights drawn from an encounter. It is an encounter in which each side extends away from the meeting place in numerous other directions. As I have noted above, in certain respects it makes no sense to speak in terms of "two sides." We can see this when the Sumbanese become Christian or the Dutch grow nostalgic for pre-Christian Sumba, and they find themselves allied with one another against the non-Christians around them in both Indonesia and the Netherlands. This leads me to the second point: if we see missionization as part of the work of purification, we should consider the possibility that purification works to sort out semiotic potentials that the missionary may, in some ways, *share* with the unconverted—the tempting vitality of the fetish, the tangibility and resistance of words, the possibility of hidden thoughts, the question of responsibility, the desire for the unattainable, and the experience of suffering. At this point, perhaps, readers may even discover, as Johannes Fabian (1983) long ago urged them to, that Dutch missionaries, Sumbanese Christians, and

---

13. For contemporary ethnographies of Sumba in this vein, see Forth 1981; Geirnaert-Martin 1992; Hoskins 1993; Keane 1997c; Kuipers 1990. Forshee 2001 provides a useful perspective by following textile producers and marketers in their travels and commercial ties beyond particular localities.

ancestral ritualists are their coevals. Finally, because I am trying to think about assumptions that can be hard to stand apart from, I have found it most useful to work closely with some key topoi—debates about prayer or meat, for instance. There is a cost to being selective, but I hope the result is worth it. Rather than attempting to light up everything, at risk of flattening out all detail and depth, I hope the reader will benefit from the relief cast against shadows.

PART I

Locating Protestantism

Waingapu, East Sumba, 1986. Photo by Webb Keane.

1   Religion's Reach

They trespass, Authors to themselves in all,
Both what they judge and what they choose; for so
I form'd them free, and free they must remain,
Till they enthrall themselves.

JOHN MILTON, *Paradise Lost*, book 3, lines 122–25

You have no eyes for something that took two millennia to
prevail? . . . There is nothing strange about this: all long
developments are difficult to see in the round.

FRIEDRICH NIETZSCHE, *Genealogy of Morals*, first essay, no. VIII

Beginning in the last decades of the twentieth century, militant Christianity's dramatic emergence into public view, alongside politicized Islam, has had at least the virtue of upturning much conventional wisdom. It appears now that religion is no more likely to wither away than (contrary to Engel's famous prediction) is the state. Nor is the march of history necessarily a triumph of technocratic rationality or cool utilitarian calculation. The resulting intellectual unsettlement is certainly useful, although a glance through the newspaper suggests it will rapidly give rise to yet more, newly revised, sorts of conventional wisdom. But the high visibility of the more flamboyant kinds of evangelical or charismatic religion may lead us to lose sight of other, perhaps more lastingly pervasive, aspects of Christianity. This book focuses on Dutch Calvinists to explore some long-running themes that run through Protestant Christianity in the forms that were, for much of its Euro-American history, mainstream. After all, well into the twentieth century, Protestantism was a thoroughly familiar part of the moral, political, and conceptual world in much of the Euro-American West, even for the most unreligious—or non-Christian—individuals; increasingly, this is true across much of the globe. Certain of the themes I explore within Protes-

---

Epigraphs: John Milton, *Paradise Lost: Complete Poems and Major Prose*, ed. Merritt Y. Hughes (1674; Indianapolis: Bobbs-Merrill, 1957), 261; Friedrich Nietzsche, *The Birth of Tragedy and the Genealogy of Morals*, trans. Francis Golfing (1887; Garden City, NY: Doubleday, 1956), 168.

tantism, especially Calvinism, are also found in habits, practices, and ways of thinking not usually seen as religious.[1] In fact, if the new role of so-called fundamentalist religion in the contemporary public world shocks some observers, this may be due in part to the ways it challenges their basic understandings about human freedom and its realization in history that, in certain respects, are found in other more or less self-consciously religious and secular discourses.[2]

At the center of this book is the promulgation of Dutch Calvinism on a Southeast Asian island. The book is therefore necessarily also about colonialism and its postcolonial wake. And it speaks as well about the idea of becoming modern, with all the promises, threats, and paradoxes this involves. Immediately the reader may seek some assurance: I do not propose that we return to that well-trod narrative trail so brilliantly blazed by Max Weber (1946, 1958). In order to explain why, I begin by situating Calvinism and the mission movement within a larger frame. Often over the course of this book I treat Calvinism as expressing a general cluster of ideas, practices, and social forces. This treatment of what is, after all, not even the largest of Protestant, much less Christian, denominations today requires justification. For some time now, a host of evangelical and charismatic movements, including Pentecostalism, the prosperity gospel, and various sorts of televangelism, have been the fastest-growing and most visible kinds of Protestantism across much of the globe. These movements are hardly made up of austere followers of Calvinism; in many ways they may be seen as reactions against that austerity.

One classic justification for paying special attention to Calvinism lies in its peculiar position within the history of Euro-American capitalism or political thought. The former is most famously identified with Weber; the latter is exemplified by Michael Walzer's remark, directed especially, I imag-

---

1. I use the categories "religious" and "secular" here as common terms of self-description within the contexts being discussed. For a more critical discussion of the category "religion," see chapter 3.

2. Saba Mahmood (2005) asserts that liberal thinkers and activists tend to portray freedom as the exertion of agency against the confines of tradition and other obstacles, which they conceive as being wholly external to the individual. The extent to which religion is itself considered to be one of those obstacles (and not playing a more constitutive role) is a constant problem within this view of freedom. Even those liberals who argue for religious tolerance can have difficulty dealing with religious demands that seem, from the perspective of liberalism, to restrict the individual's autonomy. For a parallel critique of the "crypto-normative" claims of feminism, see Anderson 2000. As I suggest below, these very notions of freedom and its value have sources, or at least strong parallels, in certain aspects of the Protestant tradition.

ine, to secular intellectuals, that "Calvinist saintliness, after all, has scarred us all" (1974: vii). Along with these authors, I do accept the basic thesis that Calvinism played a critical historical role in the Euro-American world, especially in the period before the pietistic and evangelical revivals, if not necessarily in the specific ways they have claimed. But this is not my main concern here. Although this book is about historical phenomena, it is not, except at moments, intended as a work of historical explanation as such.

In this chapter I take an approach to the importance of Calvinism somewhat distinct from those associated with Weber and Walzer. Through a look at Calvinism, I aim to clarify certain themes that recur in various ways in a number of different Protestant contexts. These themes concern the concept of agency and approaches to its exercise, the disciplining of interior belief, the work of purification, and the semiotic ideologies these presuppose. The themes are manifested especially in recurrent practical and theological questions about language, materiality, and their implications for humans. They are certainly not the only themes to be found in Christianity, Protestantism, or even Dutch Calvinism, nor do they rule out all sorts of contrary ones. But the moral and ontological problems I examine here do come into especially sharp focus in the missionary encounters that were characteristic of many colonial contexts. For one thing, these were often situations that seemed to call for radical conversion. By this I mean conversion between religions seen as vastly different—above all, the conversion of people who seemed to lack not just scriptures and monotheistic creeds but even a proper sense of the distinction between humans and inanimate things. Encounters such as these cast into deep relief some features of Protestant Christianity that might be found in more secular practices and discourses as well.

I am interested in these religious questions in particular for the ways they illuminate some widespread ideas about modernity, especially its moral dimensions, and for its associations with certain notions of freedom. Some of these themes are doctrinal: others are more tacitly embedded within practices. At some points in the discussion that follows, I speak of Calvinism as an exemplary case that helps us see certain things more clearly. Less frequently, I also suggest that Calvinism has directly helped to produce and circulate the ideas and practices by which these themes have become ubiquitous. The actual historical effects of Calvinism and other Protestant groups on realms beyond religion are, perhaps, most evident in the colonial missions. But I do not want to make strong causal claims about the historical role of Calvinism. To say that Calvinism helps us see some familiar aspects of the idea of agency more clearly is not to say that it is necessarily the *source* of this idea. Sometimes it is just an especially clear *vehicle* for it.

For very good reasons, anthropologists and historians have developed a scrupulously keen wariness about the perils of overgeneralization. What could invite those perils more than the effort to speak of something as vast and complex as "Protestantism" or "Christianity"? Given the tendentious and sometimes pernicious ends that such generalities can serve, the responsible procedure may be to confine oneself to the most carefully located and circumscribed claims. Yet this strategy too has its drawbacks. One is simply empirical: the circulation of church members, funds, institutional arrangements, scriptures, hymns, sermons, and practices means virtually no Christian community is purely local in nature. Another is doctrinal: most Christians surely claim at least some kind of commonality with other Christians, even if only far enough to assert that others have got it wrong and should know better. Behind this sense of potential commonality lies a long history of texts, doctrines, institutions, and practices in which as much is shared, circulated, or reinvented as is distinguished and differentiated. To focus entirely on the local case may lead us to miss some crucial aspects of the religion. These include the sense church members have of being part of something larger. They also include the fundamental, long-running conceptual and moral arguments, as well as the sociopolitical movements, out of which any specific church emerged. To speak only in local terms is to risk making it appear as if Christianity were created from scratch each time, or that each church exists in splendid isolation.

Before turning to the Dutch Calvinists of Sumba, then, I propose a series of contexts. I will tease out some of the themes that Calvinism shares with other kinds of Christianity, other modes of proselytization. This chapter begins by portraying Christianity as a global religion; from there I turn to Protestantism and then Calvinism. Of course this approach, directed as it is toward Calvinism, means that certain aspects of Protestantism and Christianity come to the fore while others remain in the background. Even something as widely shared as the Apostles' Creed, which I discuss in the next chapter, can produce consequences quite different in, say, colonial Spanish America than in twentieth-century northern Europe, and such pre-scripted, as opposed to spontaneous, forms are eschewed altogether by some evangelical groups.

The perspective on Christian globalization that I take in this chapter is determined by my interest in semiotic forms and the ideologies by which they are taken to have moral implications. This provides some of the background for my turn in the next chapter to the creed form, the idea of having mastery over one's thoughts, and the impetus to purify, which Bruno Latour (1993) claims is characteristic of modernity. I argue that the drive to purify the world of so-called hybrids, as he puts it, is best understood against the background of the religious themes I have been drawing out here.

Latour also says that purification never succeeds. Indeed, religious histories show that attempts at purification produce results that seem to be inherently unstable. In attempting to make sense of this failure, I introduce one of the central themes of this book. One source of the failure of purification is the inescapable materiality that semiotic form introduces into even the most transcendentalizing projects. With this point, in fact, my argument opens up again to find a place for those evangelical groups that eschew creeds, or faiths that favor communities and priestly authority over solitary introspection. It is not my purpose here to engage in a large-scale examination of history. But one might speculate that one factor that has entered into the production of Christianity's sheer complexity is precisely the recurrent conflict between purifying projects of transcendence and countermovements toward materialization, each provoking the other (see Klaniczay 1990).

THE CHRISTIANITY OF GLOBALIZATION

When one of the first anthropologists to focus on globalization, Ulf Hannerz, wanted to designate the interconnectedness of today's world, he turned to Alfred Kroeber's appropriation of the classical Greek word *ecumene*, in its original sense of "the entire inhabited world" (Hannerz 1996: 6–7). But we may hear echoes of something else in this word, something at once more common and more specific. The *Oxford English Dictionary* defines *ecumenical* this way: "(1; *Eccl.*) Belonging to or representing the whole (Christian) world, or the universal church; general, universal, catholic; specifically, applied to the general councils of the early church, and (in modern use) of the Roman Catholic Church (and hence occasionally to a general assembly of some other ecclesiastical body); also assumed as a title by the Patriarch of Constantinople; formerly sometimes applied to the Pope of Rome" (1989: 64). This is followed by attestations dating from the mid–sixteenth century—precisely that moment when the presumed universality of the Roman Catholic Church was being thrown violently into doubt—and this, from the *Daily Telegraph* in 1970: "The cause of ecumenism has received no setback. It might indeed be enhanced, if the Archbishop [of Canterbury] were to receive and accept an invitation to be present in Rome at the canonisation ceremony."

As these definitions suggest, *ecumene* does not refer simply to a positive fact, an objective matter of scale. Rather, the word suggests that, when it came to naming the global as a unity, until recently a capacity to imagine totality was often inseparable from the expansive community, and perhaps the embracing ontology, of a given universalizing religion.

Of course globalization as a matter of circulating bodies and goods, economic forces, and cultural incitements does not depend on anyone's *concept* of the global. Yet, as Arjun Appadurai (1996) has argued, globalization is realized in the movement of persons, their ideas, and their desires in ways that cannot be reduced to either political economy or diaspora. Indeed, demography alone (even combined with economics) is surely insufficient to account for the power of globalization, without the ideas and images people bring with them. If globalization means more than the objective circulation of people and money, it is not merely a matter of imagination. Ideas, like everything else, circulate insofar as they have some medium. They are materialized in specific semiotic forms. Speech styles, financial instruments, televised performances, magazines, fashions in clothing or food, and institutional forms (from revolutionary cells to the most ordinary bureaucracies): each has its own temporality and its own distinct local and causal modality. It is by virtue of possessing semiotic form that ideas enter into the world of causes and consequences and thus can be set into motion.

To the extent that religious proselytizing is a globalizing force, the semiotic forms that religions produce are crucial to understanding that force. The globalization of Protestant Christianity was facilitated by the development of certain semiotic forms and ideologies. Some of these have become inseparable from even the purportedly secular narratives of modernity.[3] In the next chapter I look closely at one set of semiotic ideologies and one particular practical form, the creed. But first, in this one, I sketch out the larger context of the global spread of Christianity and its relationship to the moral narrative of modernity.

Evangelizing religions have been crucial forces in the translocal circulation of people, practices, and ideas since Buddhism spread out of South Asia

---

3. Clearly not *all* the forms that proselytization has taken enter those narratives. Thus, for instance, the emphasis on formal institutions, sacred sites, and collectivities characteristic of the missions of early Iberian Catholicism in the colonial Americas do not play the same role as do the more recent Protestant practices that are my central concern in this book.

in the first century B.C.E. But full-fledged Christian globalization took form within colonialism.[4] And conversely, colonialism was shaped by Christianity. Missionaries usually aspired to both a more far-reaching and a deeper transformation of colonized peoples than did either administrators or business interests (Beidelman 1982; Comaroff and Comaroff 1991; Huber and Lutkehaus 1999; Cooper and Stoler 1997). Given missionaries' greater commitments of time and attention to daily life, their effectiveness too was often much greater. The particular forms taken by colonialism's long-term influence in many parts of the postcolonial world are surely marked, in some way, by missionaries' moral impetus to improve the world.[5]

That moral impetus is embodied in everyday *practices*—the stuff of Michel Foucault's "capillary power" (1980: 39). Potentially unlimited, these can include learning a creed and catechism, setting out on pilgrimages, reading and discussing scripture, praying, singing hymns, listening to sermons, attending regular church services, undergoing confession, even diary-keeping and the introspective probing of one's thoughts, desires, and motives. These practices are well suited for evangelism, since many of them can be so readily detached from particular social contexts and made available for universal circulation.

As a result, it should be no surprise that, at the beginning of the twenty-first century, one-third of the world's population is Christian, and that one-third of those Christians live in former colonies. The largest number of non-German missionary sisters in the sister order of the Society of the Divine Word is Indonesian—this organization is especially active in Brazil, Botswana, Ghana, and Europe (Huber and Lutkehaus 1999: 21–22). The

4. After the early colonial missions of Iberian Catholicism, in Western Christianity the next great wave of global missionization did not arise until the promptings of the pietistic and evangelical revivals in northern Europe and America at the end of the eighteenth century (van Rooden 1996; Stanley 2001). Eastern Christianity saw a parallel movement accompanying Russia's imperial expansion.

5. That missionaries themselves often had deeply ambivalent relations not only to the colonial systems in which they were embedded but also to modernity is well known; see, for example, Clifford 1982 for a discussion of Maurice Leenhardt in Melanesia and Comaroff and Comaroff 1991 on British nonconformists in South Africa. This ambivalence could be reinforced by the relative autonomy of the mission societies that developed from the end of the eighteenth century on. A historian of Dutch religion has pointed out that the mission society itself was an institutional form—the voluntary organization—that presupposed a distinction between public and private spheres (van Rooden 1996). These societies drew their support from the private sphere at home and tended to see their potential mission field as so many individual souls that, ideally, could be approached without reference to existing national boundaries. This could put them at odds with colonial orders.

looming schism within the Anglican Church over the appointment of a gay bishop in the United States is to a large degree being driven by African bishops. The largest Christian missionary movement in the world today comes out of Korea (Walls 2001: 25). Even where Christians are a minority, it was often Christian schools, or those modeled on them, that educated the first generations of nationalist elites in the early and mid–twentieth century (Comaroff 1985: 129; Keyes 1996: 284). In Indonesia, for instance, where Christians are about 9 percent of an otherwise largely Muslim population, the most powerful general of the last generation and the most influential newspaper editors were Christian.[6]

Here I want to point out two aspects of religious globalization. One concerns the concept of the global, the other certain empirical characteristics of global religion. The conceptual aspect, as I have suggested, is implicit in the religious background to the now secularized word *ecumene*. Although evangelists have not always aspired to global reach, the universalizing implications of a transcendental faith are surely there for those willing to take the point. By the nineteenth century, supported by the other expansive visions that accompanied colonialism, as well as by totalizing cosmologies, evangelizing efforts often presupposed a global whole of potential converts. For example, the fundamentalist Protestant group called the Summer Institute of Linguistics draws from the Book of Revelations a claim that the millennium will not arrive until the Bible has been translated into every language on earth, no matter how obscure.[7] The doctrine provides a perspective from which the world can be seen as composed of a singular collection of like entities (languages and their speakers), the set of which can be brought to completion. The Summer Institute of Linguistics is only carrying to an extreme a logic whose potential might be found in *any* religious creed that claims to be true for all humans.[8]

Certain empirical consequences of this global spread are worth bearing in mind for any anthropological approach to Christianity. The more recent

6. For the claims that Christians played a special role in twentieth-century Indonesian history precisely because of the rupture with tradition produced by their minority status, see van Klinken 2003.

7. I draw here on conversations with Courtney Handman about her preliminary fieldwork on the Summer Institute of Linguistics in Papua New Guinea.

8. It has been argued that nineteenth-century Protestant missions' ideas about the unity of humankind were strongly influenced by the eighteenth-century Enlightenment (Stanley 2001: 10). But in many cases, the very possibility of evangelization seems to depend on some sort of assumption about human unity, a point recognized at least as early as Thomas Aquinas's *Summa Contra Gentiles* (Stanley 2001; also MacCormack 1991: 45), if not the epistles of Saint Paul.

forms of colonial proselytization and conversion may have been instigated by the Euro-American West, but in the postcolonial world their dynamic extends well beyond their sources. Christianity has become "our" religion for a large part of the non-Western world and is not seen as foreign. For instance, Wesleyan Methodism is considered to be a core component of Fijian ethnic identity, a definitive point of contrast to Indo-Fijians and other Polynesians. Similar instances can be found across the Pacific and Southeast Asia. One result is that a significant part of proselytization today originates from non-Western sources or takes place within communities, for instance, in revivalist movements *among* Christians.[9] It is simply not sufficient to think of Christianity as a question of contact or influence, or as the responsibility of a limited number of actors. As an ethnographer of South American Catholicism puts it, missions are "an ensemble production that is well past its first act" (Orta 2002: 712; compare Barker 1990; Robbins 2004a, 2004b).

Since churches are often linked to other churches across the globe, they are significant facilitators of global flows in their own right. As members of the Swedish Faith Movement study evangelical videotapes, they may even take up American body language and speaking styles as part of their expression of a global faith (Coleman 2000). So it is not enough for anthropologists to take note of Christianity only insofar as it forms an expression of purportedly *local* identity. Although many churches are marked by ethnonyms or toponyms (the United Church of Zambia, the Church of Lanka, the Protestant Christian Batak Church) and play crucial roles in the consolidation of local identities and factional political strife, this is hardly the only story. For example, members of the Christian Church of Sumba (Gereja Kristen Sumba) do not, in the first instance, see their Christianity as distinctively "Sumbanese" but insist they are part of a church with *global* reach. They receive money and advice from the Netherlands, send students to theological schools on Java, and teach the Heidelberg Catechism. In some respects Christianity has no locality, either sociologically (institutions and people circulate), culturally (ideas and practices circulate), or ontologically (its truth-claims are universal).[10] Local religious practice is rarely entirely free from ties to spatially dispersed structures or from circulating ideas and

9. Even a century ago, the Ambonese were carrying the faith to other parts of Indonesia, and Fijians to New Guinea (Errington and Gewertz 1995: 92; see also Whiteman 1983).

10. The church historian Peter van Rooden (2002) writes, "All world religions derive their strength, it is almost a matter of definition, from their supralocal organisations, not from their rootedness in local communities." To this spatial

persons. Correlatively, concrete practices are rarely entirely separable from some foundations in more abstract theological doctrines. Thus, the act of proselytizing a religion may end up confounding the oppositions both between the global and the local, and between the elite and the popular. Indeed, the very *lack* of locality can be a crucial part of that religion's appeal.

Despite this vigor, Christianity has, at least until recently, remained somewhat offstage for anthropologists of globalization.[11] For instance, the index to Ulf Hannerz's book *Transnational Connections* has no entries for *Christianity, missionary,* or even *religion*. Hannerz is in very good company, with, for instance, Eric Wolf and his *Europe and the People without History* (1982). And if globalization is a story about modernity, one can hardly blame them, of course. After all, it has been a commonplace since Max Weber—if not since August Comte—that secularism is one of the hallmarks of modernity. It has long been conventional to identify modernity with a mechanistic worldview, the scientific method, the rise of capitalism, industrialization, urbanization, an elaborate division of labor, nation-states, the growth of the bureaucratic organizations, mass media, and, in association with them all, inexorable secularization. Definitions of secularization vary from an emphasis on the separation of public from private spheres, with the relegation of religion to the latter, to statistical declines in participation in religious institutions (Bruce 1992). The historical trajectory remains more or less the same, however. Even Max Weber (1958) portrayed the Protestant Ethic as eventuating in an iron cage of distinctly nonsectarian construction.[12]

---

extensiveness we should add a temporal dimension, for in many parts of the formerly colonized world, young people are growing up in communities that have been Christian for as long as anyone can remember, even as far back as the beginning of local recorded history (in Fiji for more than 150 years; in Indonesia's Maluku and parts of the Philippines, for more than 300; to say nothing of Mexico, Brazil, and the Andes). Van Klinken (2003) argues that self-consciously local, mission-derived Christian communities in Indonesia were sociologically and culturally conservative. The individuals whose conversion set them *apart* from their communities and led them into cosmopolitan affiliations with the European bourgeoisie were the ones most likely to become significant political actors.

11. Anthropologists of Christianity abound (see Cannell 2005, 2005), but those of globalization are not always in conversation with them. This relative oversight may be due in part to certain disciplinary commitments peculiar to anthropology. The role of Christianity in globalization has certainly drawn the attention of others, ranging from Jacques Derrida in his discussion of "globalatinization" (Derrida and Vattimo 1998) to sociologists such as Peter Beyer (1994).

12. For examples of the classic argument that Protestantism was a crucial element in the development of modernity, see Troeltsch 1958 and Weber 1958. For

But the daily newspaper should make it obvious that religion has not retreated to the private sphere (see Casanova 1994). If news from the Middle East, Northern Ireland, or Sri Lanka, or, for that matter, Amsterdam and Copenhagen, does not demonstrate religion's persistence in public events, a glance at American presidential politics should confirm it. And for further confirmation we could look to the seven foreign ministers who held up the signing of a constitution for the European Union by demanding it acknowledge Europe's Christian heritage (*New York Times*, May 26, 2004, p. A12). There are those who respond that such appearances of religion in public are mere historic relics, or that they are desperate reactions against incipient modernity; when Salman Rushdie said the problem with Islam was it had never gone through the Enlightenment, he was merely honing the dull edge of conventional wisdom. Conventional wisdom, in this case, may not only be wrong, it may be dangerous too. At the very least, it requires reexamination.

THE MORAL NARRATIVE OF "MODERNITY"

One way Christian imaginaries have had an effect across the postcolonial world emerges from their coupling with certain concepts of modernity, and vice versa. The coupling is twofold. Empirically, as a result of colonial and para-colonial circulation, many people first experienced what they understood to be modernity as having a Christian face. Conceptually, there are aspects of the very idea of modernity that seem to have been shaped in a dialectical relationship to a moral understanding of progress and agency. This moral narrative has affinities with aspects of Protestantism, especially as it developed in the era of evangelical and Enlightenment challenges.

Modernity is certainly a word in danger of meaning everything and nothing. Taken as the outcome of a teleological narrative, any particular characterization of modernity faces a complex and unpredictable world brimming with counterexamples. What makes us think history should even *have* a single narrative? Yet to pluralize "modernities" invites self-contradiction (see, for example, Gaonkar 1999). Given modernity's genealogy as a totalizing category, how could such a plurality of other modernities or alternative modernities be rendered coherent? At best, modernity is a concept we should treat with cautious circumspection.

---

recent anthropological arguments against the identification of modernity with secularization, see Asad 2003 and van der Veer 1996.

But there is one indisputable empirical claim we *can* make about "modernity." As an *idea*, it has a pervasive and powerful role in the popular imagination wherever we look, from the Nahuatl *moderno* in Mexico (Hill 1985) to the Anakalangese *moderen* in Indonesia. Across the ethnographic spectrum, the idea of the modern is crucial to people's historical self-understanding. It is part of both elite and popular discourses, imaginings, and desires. And it is hardly a neutral matter. Questions on the subject can be terribly fraught: What does it take to be modern? What are its promises and its threats? Who is included or excluded? Are we there yet? How can we get out of it? Whatever we may think of modernity as a category of empirical analysis, this at least is true: the idea of the modern has become a ubiquitous social fact.

Even if we see modernity only as a widespread form of historical imagination, it has a daunting degree of heterogeneity. For many people, it seems to mean simply unimaginable wealth (see, for example, Knauft 2002: 6; Meyer 2003: 212). For others, it promises life without labor, where pushing a button gets you everything, or life without illness. To yet others it is about better food; there are people in Sumba who insist that "modern" food is surely much softer than their own maize, tubers, and rice. And these are just the more positive visions—modernity without Auschwitz, Hiroshima, or the Gulag.

But in its more optimistic versions, the idea of modernity commonly seems to include two distinctive features: rupture from a traditional past, and progress into a better future. Thus, when Jean and John Comaroff define modernity, in the context of the colonization of southern Africa, they call it "an ideological formation in terms of which societies valorize their own practices by contrast to the specter of barbarism and other marks of negation" (1997: 32). This is surely too narrow in some respects—for one thing, modernity is as much a story people tell about *their own past* as about *others*—but it captures something important: the narrative often has a normative, even moralistic, thrust to it. For much of the twentieth century, Indonesians were admonished, from higher authorities both left and right, that they *must* become modern—that to resist would be to harm the nation itself. Wherever the world has been called "developing," similar stories could be told. The moral subtext to such imperatives may underlie people's responses to economic collapse in Zambia, where, James Ferguson writes, "what had been lost . . . was not simply the material comforts and satisfactions . . . but the sense of legitimate expectation that had come with them—a certain ethos of hopefulness, self-respect, and optimism" (1999: 12). Material deprivation may be an objective fact—but abjection is the stuff of morality. History, in this narrative, involves an implicit vision of the good (see Taylor 1999: 157).

Linked to moral underpinnings, this narrative often is made up of another component too, a call for humans to *act* upon their history. Foucault, voicing Baudelaire, asserts that modernity involves an "ironic heroization of the present" and demands that one produce oneself (1992: 312). With or without the Parisian irony, the heroic sense is widespread. One important narrative about modernity relates that human agency had been misrecognized in the form of fetishes, despots, and demons onto whom it had been projected. In this story, the true character of human agency is eventually revealed and thus recaptured. Since Marx and Feuerbach, if not Voltaire, the call to self-recognition, traced across historical time, often involves realizing that agency falsely imputed to deities is in fact human. Commonly this story of error disabused is taken to lead inexorably to the secular vision of modernity, replacing gods with humans at the center of the action. J. B. Schneewind's 1998 history of modern moral philosophy bears the title *The Invention of Autonomy*. It is a history in which self-recognition is one precondition for a new sense of independence.

But the moral character of the narrative predates Voltaire and Marx. One theme within the Protestant Reformation, for instance, was the idea of restoring agency to its proper subjects. To reveal more directly the ultimate divine agent meant liberating individuals from the domination of illegitimate clerics and their rituals, and restoring to people their own principled agency, including freedom to read (if not necessarily to interpret) scripture and form congregations.[13] And even if the early reformers did not necessarily see themselves as radicals, they can be seen as responding to one set of possibilities (though, no doubt, only one of a number) that can be found within the very idea of proselytization, for proselytization emphasizes change, positively viewed and, usually, actively sought. As the church historian Jaroslav Pelikan puts it, "Every Christian church wants to define

---

13. See Troeltsch's early claim that the "thought of freedom, of personality, of the autonomous self" derives ultimately from certain strains of Protestantism, rather than, say, the Renaissance, and had an important influence on modern ideas of political freedom and the separation of church and state later associated with secularism (1958: 36, 117; see also Troeltsch 1931: 688–89). To be sure, Troeltsch was hardly a neutral observer: as Tomoko Masuzawa (2005) argues, despite his role as a scholar of world religion, he remained a theologian who was committed to demonstrating the universality of Christianity. Nonetheless, his argument is important. Although early Protestantism was dominated by its own forms of clerical authority, it did sow the seeds for later, more radical religious movements with antiauthoritarian dimensions.

itself as *catholic* [in the inclusive rather than denominational sense], *evangelical,* and *reformed,* at least in some sense" (2003: xiii, emphasis in the original), a claim that conjoins universal scope and purposeful change.

The pattern of recurrent reform movements can take what Judith Irvine and Susan Gal have called fractal recursivity, "the projection of an opposition, salient at some level of relationship, onto some other level" (2000: 38). Each reformer is capable of projecting onto the older institution vices similar to those against which the earlier dispensation had earlier defined itself. If Calvinists could portray Catholics in terms similar to those by which Catholics portrayed Jews, Muslims, and pagans, so too could rebels against Calvinist authority in their turn. The restlessness of Protestant Christianity, which today is producing new factions and denominations at an extraordinary pace, is driven by this sense of revival, restoration, and reform; however routinized the religion becomes, transformation remains a lurking possibility. This transformation is not necessarily a conversion, much less the radical conversion from non-Christianity (or even nonreligion) to Christianity. But when some evangelical groups conflate the two and portray even revivals within the church as conversion, they are perhaps picking up on a logic already immanent in the reforming character to which Pelikan refers.[14] As many evangelical groups maintain, one is never converted once and for all. This strong model of conversion places transformation at the very center of authority.

Thus it should be no surprise that, according to Michael Walzer, writing of the Euro-American world in the light of early Calvinism, "progress was first imagined in terms of a Christian history and an imminent millennium" (1974: 12). The extraordinary ongoing dynamic of Christian revivalism in the late twentieth and early twenty-first centuries means that even settled communities of Christians can be subjected to conversion all over again. In Latin America at the beginning of the twenty-first century, the centuries-old rapprochement between local deities and Spanish Catholicism is under vigorous attack by Pentecostal evangelists. Similar internal missionization is taking place in formerly Anglican parts of Melanesia and Calvinist enclaves in Indonesia. What this means is that conversion remains an issue long after the initial missionization. Therefore, in any given instance, there

---

14. The Pentecostal distinction between the initial stage of justification, at baptism, and a later stage of sanctification, marked by glossolalia, is one example of the extension of the logic of conversion within a single church (see Austin-Broos 1997: 18).

is likely to be an unpredictable struggle between the taken-for-granted of established churches and the sharpened self-consciousness of zealous reformers.

One result is that the possibility of conversion can seem to promise an Archimedean point by which the very foundations of society itself can be examined and criticized. In nineteenth-century India, according to Gauri Viswanathan (1998), Christianity seemed to its converts to promise social liberation (see also Prakash 2003). Papua New Guinean evangelicals in recent decades have assaulted the perpetuation of old local traditions by Anglican fellow villagers and defended their acts in the name of the universal human right to religious expression (Errington and Gewertz 1995: 115). And writing of a historically Catholic Nicaragua in the mid–twentieth century, Roger Lancaster called its revolution a "religious revitalization movement," and observed that even Marxists took "atheism" to mean political despair—a denial of the moral thrust of history and the special role that human agency plays in it (1988: 20). If the idea of modernity includes a moral narrative about human liberation, it is a story that often draws on religious subtexts about the possibilities for, and the value of, self-consciousness.

SUBJECT AND SELF-CONSCIOUSNESS

Viewed in the context of the moral narrative of modernity, the radical conversion from false to true religion, from no religion to religion, or even from religion to no religion dramatically expresses the general possibilities and virtues of self-transformation. As a ubiquitous source of globally circulating ideas, people, and mundane practices, religious proselytization offers conceptual and practical paradigms by which transformation can become an inhabitable, practicable possibility and a moral imperative. This transformation is both historical and social in its sweep, but also subjective and capillary in its embodiments. One the one hand, there is the reconfiguring of entire societies, altering the very course of history itself: Constantine converts Rome. Social reconfiguration, for example, was an important goal of Iberian Catholicism in the Americas. But, on the other hand, this transformation is effected by the saving of individuals: Saul struck on the road to Damascus. When asked, "Hast thou a Wife and Children?" the protagonist of Bunyan's *Pilgrims' Progress* replies, "Yes, but I am so laden with this burden, that I cannot take that pleasure in them as formerly: methinks, I am as if I had none" (1960: 17), having left them behind as he seeks his personal salvation. Such has been the potentially antisocial demand made by many Protestant missions.

Proselytization may foster the imagining of global communities and transcendental realities, but it makes these real through concrete practices, some of which have their effect in intimate and subjective domains. The quotidian practices of the universal religions, like mass media, nationalism, and other translocal mediations, invite a host of vernacular cosmopolitanisms. What Benedict Anderson (1983) said of the everyday experiences that underwrite national "imagined communities" is surely at least as germane to religious communities, if not more so: when people gather in church each Sunday, they are invited to imagine that other Christians are doing so simultaneously around the world (see Robbins 2004a: 175). But historical agency, in the context of the predominant post-eighteenth-century forms of proselytization, often centers on the individual subject. Even when Christianity is a source of social critique, it is a critique that commonly hinges on individual capacities for action. One of the stronger expressions of this point is Kenelm Burridge's claim that the modern individual produced by Christian conversion is defined by "the capacity to deliberately step outside custom, tradition, and given social roles, rights, and obligations, scrutinize them, formulate a moral critique, and . . . envisage a new social order governed by new moralities" (1978: 13–14). This is only one, rather celebratory and selective, formulation, but it expresses clearly how agency, morality, and objectification (the capacity to step outside and scrutinize) can function together.

Let me be clear, the point here is *not* that Protestantism introduces agency, or even individualism, into a world that formerly had lacked them.[15] First, such a claim presumes an untenable view of the world before missionaries. Second, any real effects Protestant missions have had on the world may be impossible to fully disentangle from the host of other historical forces that have been their contemporaries. But Protestantism has offered influential expressions of the high moral value of agency. In many cases, such as those I discuss in this book, it ties that moral value to the preliminary task of getting people to see what beings in the world are actually agents (God and humans, not spirits or fetishes) and what kinds of agency properly belong to them. Protestantism has been an important source of practices that foster particular kinds of self-consciousness about agency

15. Nor am I saying that what is apparently secular is actually, in some definitive and essential sense, "religious" (for this debate, see Blumenberg 1983; Löwith 1949).

and the possibilities for action—for instance, what may or may not be accomplished by human agents, what by divine ones. That sense of agency works in conjunction with distinctive forms of self-understanding about the internal constitution and dispositions of human subjects. Moreover, those kinds of Protestant Christianity with which I am most concerned here have produced semiotic ideologies that take the properties of words and things as potential threats to the true understanding of agency, with serious moral consequences. In this chapter, I discuss the concept of agency, especially within Calvinism, then, in the next chapter, I turn to Calvinist semiotic ideology and an exemplary practice, the saying of creeds.

Philosophers as different as Charles S. Peirce (1934, para. 421), Charles Taylor (1985), and Donald Davidson (1980) all give special weight to actors' self-awareness in their various analyses of intentional action. For example, in many accounts, it is the actor's reflexive capacity to give a description to an action that makes an act coherent over time. This reflexive capacity seems implicit as well in the concept of a meaningful event that lies at the heart of Weberian sociology. That is, the object of a properly sociological or historical description in this tradition is brought about by purposeful people who think they know what they are doing—joining political parties, not suffering earthquakes. By these accounts, having a particular concept *of* agency should have consequences for how one acts.

Psychoanalysts, cognitive psychologists, and critics of ideology will immediately point out that such models of action which depend on high degrees of self-consciousness at best are marred by what they leave out. But the concept of agency that runs through the moral narrative of modernity is largely one in which self-awareness is a condition for freedom. Here I briefly propose some terms by which one can understand the relationship between action and metalevel concepts of action, which take on more ethnographic specificity in the second part of this book.

To the extent that people's actions are guided by self-awareness, they are shaped by available concepts of the kind of act being undertaken; that is, metapragmatic categories (see Silverstein 1976, 1993). Such a reflexive understanding of agency has consequences for the actions it frames. These metapragmatic concepts derive from cultural, that is, publicly circulating, categories for kinds of actions and actors. Being cultural, these reflexive categories are necessarily historical in character: they both persist and change over time. The metapragmatic category of agency helps organize relations among kinds of acts, of media, and of actors. It concerns such things as whether agency itself is a good or something to be subordinated to a higher good, such as tradition, the law, the good, or divine mandate.

The concept of agency can therefore enter into the work of purification, guiding people as they try to sort out which kinds of beings do or do not have agency. For societies differ as to whether agency tends to be understood as, say, amoral willfulness or moral liberation, whether spirits, statues, stones, songs, or texts, classes, masses, nations, or only individuals, can be agents or not. As I argue in subsequent chapters, an important part of the work of purification that links Protestantism to the idea of modernity is concerned with agency. One of the chief aims of the work of purification, as undertaken by Protestant missionaries, is to establish the proper locus of agency in the world by sorting out correct from mistaken imputations of agency. God, Christ, and humans, for instance, have agency in their respective ways— priestly words, pagan sacrifices, and ancestral spirits do not. For strict Calvinists, prayer should express thanks to or even petition God, but it should not undertake to cause direct consequences in the world (see chapter 6).[16] So too the slaughtering of animals and distribution of meat must be no more than the sharing of food or, at most, the outward expression of what is actually an immaterial meaning (see chapter 8). The false imputation of agency is not mere error: it can have grave moral consequences. It is this sense of the moral danger of mislocated agency that is conveyed by the derogatory accusation of fetishism. The Calvinists' efforts to sort out proper forms of agency, allocate them to proper agents, and eliminate false agents and immoral actions constitute the central topic of part 2 of this book.

In locating certain kinds of agency in persons, and in according agency a special value, Protestantism converges with the subjective dimension of the idea of modernity as moral progress. Taken as a narrative of liberation, the idea of modernity commonly includes the emergence of some version of the human subject that is distinguished by its heightened knowledge of, and efforts to realize itself through, its capacities as a self-aware agent. By

16. The continued pertinence of the question was made evident in an essay that appeared on the editorial page of the *New York Times* as I was copyediting this book (see Raymond J. Lawrence, "Faith-Based Medicine," April 11, 2006, p. A21). The author, an Episcopal minister, applauded a scientific report stating that prayer has no healing powers. He wrote that if prayer were known to have such effects, religion "would be degraded to a kind of commercial enterprise, like Burger King, where one expects to get what one pays for." Prayers "of praise, thanksgiving and repentance" are rightly held in higher esteem than the "magical wing of religion." His words, expressing the long-standing mainstream Protestant position, closely echo those of the missionaries I quote in chapter 6. But the appearance of his essay in so prominent a position in the newspaper of record surely testifies to the vitality of that "magical wing of religion" that he opposes.

subject here, I mean historically and culturally specific, and semiotically mediated, constructions of the nature of the human and its capacities (Cascardi 1992). In contrast to more psychologically oriented perspectives, this concept, perhaps most familiar as portrayed by Foucault (e.g., 1979, 1983), focuses on forms of self-understanding immanent in public discourses, political formations, practical disciplines, and associated modes of activity.

To be sure, there are competing romantic and authoritarian views of modernity that develop quite different narratives—of modernity as alienation or as a fall from older communal harmonies, for instance. But the core features of the idea that most concern me here are those summarized by Marshall Berman (1982) and Charles Taylor (1989; see also Habermas 1987). This idea includes a special privilege accorded to the individual's agency, inwardness, and freedom and a vastly expanded vision of the possibilities for individual self-creation. We can, in fact, find versions of these ideas in other times and places. But, as Charles Taylor has argued, one thing that marks the distinctiveness of their modern version is that these possibilities are supposed to pertain to everyone, not just social elites or religious virtuosi.

At the heart of this version of the modern subject is the conjunction of personal and historical self-transformation with a vision of a self that must be abstracted from material and social entanglements. This abstraction seems critical to the idea of moral autonomy. Some version of this autonomy is a precondition for the existence of the rights-bearing, morally accountable citizen (Comaroff and Comaroff 1997: 32, 61). It also underwrites the political authority of the abstract, disinterested participant in the public sphere (Warner 2002). Autonomy characterizes the view of human nature that is presupposed by liberal critics of Islam, who assume that "all human beings have an innate desire for freedom, that we all somehow seek to assert autonomy when allowed to do so, that human agency primarily consists of acts that challenge social norms" (Mahmood 2005: 5). Even less optimistic narratives about less liberal regimes may draw on the self-governing subject in significant ways. When, for example, Foucault took Jeremy Bentham's panopticon to exemplify a modern disciplinary order (Foucault 1979), the moral agency of the prisoner played a crucial role. For, once the prisoner has internalized the warden's invisible gaze, he has in effect made it his own and does the work himself. The panopticon certainly does not require a Protestant or even, say, Counter-Reformation subject, but Protestant ideas that link agency to introspection and interiority provide this subject with an important way of understanding itself.

PROTESTANT AGENCY

To say that Protestant Christianity historically has been a crucial model for taking one's destiny in hand may seem paradoxical. After all, theologically it is God who is the ultimate agent. Protestant doctrines of grace also stress the role of divine agency in the individual's conversion. But however much the believer may hold God as the ultimate agent, the action occurs within the context of human practices. These vary widely, of course: verbal practice alone can range from the quiet of Quaker introspection to the passionate volume of Baptist testimony and Pentecostal speaking in tongues; bodily disciplines from fast to feast, from immobility to ecstatic dance. But almost no model of conversion relies on divine intervention alone without a significant element of human agency. Take the example of American fundamentalist Bible-believers—people who form intimate and closely monitored personal relations with the kind of Jesus who might tell them, for instance, to slow down when they are driving near a police speed trap. As the psychological anthropologist Tanya Luhrmann (2004) shows, even they engage in purposeful activities of Bible reading, study groups, prayer, and internal disciplines of visualization that are meant to invite divine visitations. These believers are not just passively sitting back and waiting for something to happen.[17] So too, as Michael Walzer argues, the ultimate predestinarians, the early Calvinists, were among the most strenuous in their own modes of *self*-discipline and most activist in changing the mundane world around them. And some people, like the Urapmin of highland Papua New Guinea, did not wait for the missionaries to arrive but set out to get religion on their own, and they have ended up with the sort of Pentecostal millenarianism many casual observers might consider antithetical to the assertion of human agency (Robbins 2004a).

The main protagonist in several of the influential early interpretations of modernity is Calvinism. Calvinism is associated with a strong version of the doctrine of predestination that would seem to rule out any serious role for human agency.[18] But, as Weber (1958) points out, the Calvinist doctri-

17. In effect, this is the other side of the point developed by James Faubion (2001) concerning Christians, and by Charles Hirschkind (2001) and Saba Mahmood (2005) concerning Muslims, that discipline forms an important alternative to liberal models of agency, since it involves intentionally orienting oneself toward an external agent. The discussions in these three books should also be compared to the insightful discussion of Fijian Christian "abeyance" of agency in Miyazaki 2000.

18. A pessimistic view of the power of the will goes back to Saint Augustine. Calvinism came to emphasize predestination partly as an attack on the agency asserted by the Catholic Church, which claimed for itself the power to grant merit

nal emphasis on predestination hardly resulted in passive acceptance of divine will.[19] Indeed, at first neither outsiders nor the faithful took predestination to be a defining tenet of Calvinism, and the 1566 creed that was adopted across the Netherlands did not even mention it (Mack 1978: 122).[20] For, while maintaining that God determined everything that happens, Calvin also asserted that, since God was fundamentally beyond human comprehension, it would be presumptuous at best to make any effort to understand these mysteries (Benedict 2002: 86; Schneewind 1998: 32–35).

In practical terms, as Weber recognized, Calvin's doctrine ultimately threw humans back on their own resources. One result was that Calvinists eventually came to see themselves as being located between two extremes within Protestantism. On the one hand, the Anabaptists sought to preserve their purity in a kingdom of God kept wholly separate from this world. On the other hand, Lutherans were seen as overly conciliatory, keeping the world as they found it, seeking to change only hearts. Within this field, Calvinists saw their distinctiveness as lying in worldly actions, the reformation of religion entailing the reformation of society as well (van Til 2001: 20). This is why, according to one historian of Calvinism, "[o]ne reason the faith proved so compelling to so many was that it inspired dreams of a dramatic transformation of manners, morals, and the social order" (Benedict 2002: xvi). The dynamism this entailed was expressed by a slogan coined in the Netherlands in the sixteenth century, which has been taken as a motto by many Reformed churches today: *Ecclesia reformata, quia semper reformanda* (The Reformed Church because always reforming; see Benedict

---

that could counteract a lifetime of sin right up to the very moment of death. But Calvinist doctrine distinguishes between predestination, which determines ultimate salvation, and providence, which governs daily life. Weber's thesis applies more to the former than to the latter.

19. What Weber took to be typically Calvinist was in fact only one subspecies, English experimental predestinarianism (Benedict 2002). It was associated with the effort to restrict church membership to visible saints. Holding that signs of grace could be discerned in one's experience, this doctrine produced the highly developed self-discipline and anxious introspection made famous by the early New Englanders, and it took its most prominent institutional form in Congregationalism.

20. It was not until the early seventeenth century, in response to internal schisms and Catholic apologetics, that the doctrine attained sharper clarity. The core assertions of Calvinism were codified by the synod of Dort (1618–1619), summarized in the famous rubric TULIP: total depravity (original sin affects all aspects of the person's being), unconditional election (salvation derives from God's will alone; no human deeds can alter that), limited atonement (Christ died only for those who are saved), irresistible grace, and the perseverance of the saints (nothing can cause one to lose one's salvation).

2002: xvi). The predestinarian emphasis peaked in the early seventeenth century; by the nineteenth century, mainstream Calvinism had in practice become voluntaristic (Benedict 2002: 328; Kipp 1990: 19). In the mid–twentieth century, a historian writing from within the faith expressed a positive self-image of the Calvinist as "a reformer and a dangerous character to encounter on moral and political issues. He is a man with a mission to bring to realization the will of God in human society" (McNeill 1954: 436). Despite its well-earned reputation for social authoritarianism, Calvinism implicitly linked social change to self-transformation, and this in turn to self-consciousness. John Milton expressed the first link between self-transformation and social transformation in his eulogy of Oliver Cromwell: "A commander first over himself; the conqueror of himself, it was over himself he had learnt most to triumph. Hence he went to encounter with an external enemy as a veteran accomplished in all military duties" (quoted in Walzer 1974: 315). To understand the particular forms that this general dynamic took, and its role in the work of purification, requires a look at Calvinists' worries about materiality and mediation—that is, their semiotic ideology and the practices with which it is involved.

2 Beliefs, Words, and Selves

Hard Texts *are* Nuts (*I will not call them* Cheaters)
Whose Shells *do keep their* Kirnels *from the* Eaters.
Ope then the Shells, and you shall have the Meat,
They here are brought, for you to crack and eat.

JOHN BUNYAN, *The Pilgrim's Progress,* part 2

Concepts such as agency are rarely made explicit, but rather are presupposed by the ways people act and evaluate the actions of others. These presuppositions are not just a matter of private thought but are embedded in the public forms that actions take. This is one reason why reformers and other purifiers, when they try to sort out what is or is not an agent, often focus on semiotic forms. When they do so, they draw on the sets of assumptions I call semiotic ideology. By forging links among different ideas and values, semiotic ideology serves as a guide to what words and things can or cannot do, and to how they facilitate or impinge on the capacities of human and divine agents. When the early Protestant reformers directed their energies toward such things as material sacralia or liturgical modes of action, they did so because they saw them as having a bearing on priestly agency, the individual conscience, and the transcendent character of God. Sacralia and liturgies, priesthoods and the idea of conscience, were part of a representational economy in which each had practical and conceptual consequences for the others. These and related issues continued to provoke the purifying endeavors of twentieth-century missionaries. In the second half of the book, I show that we cannot fully understand the particular issues that provoked the Dutch missionaries and their Sumbanese interlocutors, or the passion with which the issues were fought, without a grasp of the semiotic ideologies involved on both sides. Here I sketch some of the earlier doctrinal back-

---

Epigraph: John Bunyan, *The Pilgrim's Progress from This World to That Which Is to Come,* ed. James Blanton Wharey (1678–1684; Oxford: Oxford University Press, 1960), 263.

ground to those ideologies, then turn to some dimensions of the larger question of how beliefs are made inhabitable in practices.

The two most popular, dramatic, and visible actions taken by the early Protestant reformers were the vernacularization of scripture (which produced the Reformation's first English martyrs) and the destruction of material images in the churches. One major stake in both cases was the locus of agency. To translate scripture was to wrest the capacity of interpretation from Roman Catholic clerics, who had interposed themselves between God and the reader. Iconoclasm, especially when coupled with attacks on Catholic interpretations of the Eucharist, could be a flamboyant denial of the power of material things to mediate divine actions. Protestantism has provided some of the terms by which the purification process has become generalized to the non-Protestant and even non-Christian world.[1]

After the destruction of religious images in the churches, one of the core, defining features of the early Reformation was its attack on Catholic ritual, especially the Eucharist. This attack centered on questions of action, such as "Do the sacraments, under certain ritual conditions, actually undergo transubstantiation?" "Can priestly actions effect transformations of that order?" and, in the face of such claims, "What manner of agent, and thus what kind of being, is a priest supposed to be?" According to Calvin, Catholic Eucharistic practices were "veritable inventions of the devil" and "most wicked infamy and unbearable blasphemy" (quoted in Benedict 2002: 85). Although the argument against Catholic sacramental practice depended on the claim that it lacked any scriptural basis, the argument was animated by political and ontological questions of agency, of *who* can do *what*. If Holy Communion has the substantial effects that Catholicism claims for it, and only a priest can conduct the rite, then, in the Calvinist view, the priest is virtually a kind of magician (Mack 1978: 109). Calvin insisted that the Eucharist was only symbolic (1949: see especially bk. 4, chap. 14, paras. 17–18). It is a form of expression whose basis is fully distinct from its material embodiment. To understand the distinction, we must understand a semiotic ideology that mediates between an ontology of persons and agencies, on the one hand, and the concreteness of semiotic practices and possible actions, on the other.

1. For instance, Talal Asad points out that, when orientalists claim Muslims lack modern agency, one example they give is Muslims' supposed passive submission to the coercion of the Qur'anic text (2003: 10–11).

CALVINISM'S SEMIOTIC IDEOLOGY

One way the early Protestant reformers defined themselves against Roman Catholicism was by their insistence that ritual has no efficacy in and of itself. Rather, those who partake in such things as the communion meal must *already* possess faith, and this faith must be the basis for their fellowship with one another. It is in this context that we should understand the special prominence of Calvinist questions of doctrine, for they had a direct bearing on the very possibility of forming congregations.

The distinctiveness of Calvinist doctrine was anticipated by Ulrich Zwingli's initial break with Lutherans over the Eucharist (precisely that doctrinal problem which Lévi-Strauss considered insane, in his remark about the missionaries in Brazil that I quoted in the introduction). Although Lutheran doctrine departed from Roman Catholic orthodoxy, it nonetheless retained some concept of transubstantiation. Luther held that, for the believer, in the context of the rite itself, Christ was really present in the wafer and wine. By contrast, Calvin maintained that the Eucharist was "symbolic," and described Luther's view as "a carnal and crass conception of God" (quoted in Benedict 2002: 86; also see Niesel 1956).[2] The Calvinist position involved two claims, that transubstantiation has no scriptural basis, and that it fostered unwarranted clerical privileges—a claim about the textual mediation of divine will, on the one hand, and about the human usurpation of divine agency, on the other.

Calvin asserted that the material embodiment of the Eucharist, like all divine expressions, exists only because of the incapacities of humans: "As men are made known by countenance and speech, so God utters His voice to us by the voice of the prophets, and in the sacraments takes, as it were, a visible form, from which He may be known by us according to our feeble capacity" (Commentary on John 5:37, quoted in Wallace 1953: 22).[3] Ulti-

2. The older view goes back to Thomas Aquinas, who adapted the Aristotelian distinction between accident and substance to explain why the Eucharist could be *both* bread and wine (accident, which is the stuff of experience) *and* Christ (substance, which is in principle unobservable) (MacCormack 1991: 28; Pelikan 1989: 501). The split represented in these Reformation debates manifests the breakdown of that accident/substance distinction. Among other things, Calvin's position shows how hard it had become by this historical moment to imagine that the different substances could have the same accidents (an observation I owe to Don Herzog).

3. Compare this to the Orthodox tradition, which sees iconoclasm as a heretical denial of the second person of the Trinity, since it applies the unrepresentability of God the Father to the incarnation of Christ. As Saint Theophanes wrote in the ninth

mately the efficacy of the rite derives from divine agency. But Calvin concludes that this efficacy is mediated not by any material practice in itself but by the faith of the communicants, in conjunction with God's actions.

From this strenuous denial of material mediations follow certain other semiotic implications. For one thing, if communion is only a sign of grace already achieved, attention shifts from the rite itself to the signs of grace *as signs*, subordinated to that which they signify. Second, the minister's authority comes from moral leadership not material practice. The minister, then, is emphatically an ordinary human, albeit one marked by a legitimate call to office. His primary function is to teach. Above all, this means preaching. Stripped of their imagery by waves of iconoclasm (Eire 1986; Mack 1978; Wandel 1995), the edifices of the Reformed Churches looked like lecture halls, the altar replaced as a focus of attention by the pulpit. In many cases, the churches were decorated only with placards bearing the Ten Commandments and other scriptural passages (Benedict 2002: 497), an apt materialization of the highly textual orientation of the movement. The emphasis on texts and speaking led to an elaboration and explication of linguistic ideology. These centered on the scriptural word and the human voice.

For Calvinists, neither sound nor linguistic form have any power in themselves. As one early reformer put it: "There is no power and efficacy inherent in the physical voice, unless God has penetrated into the [ministers'] souls by the authority of His Spirit and . . . has inwardly taught the minds of the men, and has breathed on them with His unseen breath, by which the mist of the blind mind having been driven away, their souls may be able to direct their gaze towards the blazing beams of the heavenly light" (Pierre Viret, quoted in Mack 1978: 110). The invocation of invisible divine influence is, among other things, one way of accounting for the pragmatic effects of language. It also forms a point of intersection between semiotic ideology and moral values, in a more subtle but perhaps more pervasive way than the more dramatic forms of iconoclasm. And of course it compels the inward search even in the effort to utter outward words. A sense of the scandalous, or perhaps merely ludicrous, nature of this relationship to language was expressed in a French Catholic satire directed at the reformers in 1556, which said of one that "he makes up a prayer from his imagination" (quoted in Benedict 2002: 492). The dematerialization of

---

century, "No one could describe the Word of the Father; But when He took flesh from you, O Theotokos [the Virgin Mary], He consented to be described" (quoted in Ouspensky 1992: 151).

meaning and pragmatic effect that seemed to the believer to be the marks of sincerity could, in the eyes of the skeptic, just as easily seem to be mere insubstantiality. If one does not accept that the individual speaker can obtain divine inspiration, one hears merely idiosyncratic invention and, it would seem, the empty sounds produced by a willful self. Because the human heart is wicked, Calvinist suspicion could produce its own hyper-hermeneutic, a probing of signs for what might lie behind them.

The Protestant Reformation promoted a revived interest in the scriptural text, Calvinism most of all: "Reformed worship was characterized by a par-ticularly single-minded focus on the sacred text of the Bible as preached, read, and sung, and by a zeal to eliminate all unscriptural elements from the liturgy" (Benedict 2002: 490). Similarly, Calvinism placed special emphasis on making Bible reading the center of family worship and recasting indi-viduals' thoughts in the scriptural mode. This did not necessarily require that the Bible be taken literally, and could encourage kinds of figurative reading (Frei 1974). One version of figurative reading could be to take bib-lical words as more or less explicit commands, to treat the text as an instruc-tion manual (Crapanzano 2000: 146). Luther, Zwingli, and Calvin did not claim that every word of the Bible was divinely inspired, only that the essen-tial message was assured and accurately conveyed to the scribes. Stricter bib-lical literalisms emerged later, beginning with seventeenth-century responses to Catholic apologetics (Benedict 2002: 301). In the nineteenth century, Calvinist literalism drew further encouragement from Scottish Common Sense philosophy. Thomas Reid's assurance that external reality was just as it appeared to be seemed to reinforce the perspicuity of scripture (Harris 1998: 14). If anything, the literalist position was hardened in the nineteenth-century reaction against critical scholarship (see Crapanzano 2000; Harding 2000). Literalism could become one way of controlling bibli-cal interpretation in the absence of other institutional controls.

But even scriptural literalists had to have some way of coping with com-peting interpretations of scriptural passages.[4] For the nineteenth-century

---

4. The Web site for a group advocating the abolition of creeds, since they com-pete with the authority of the Bible, says even Luther and Calvin were unfaithful to the doctrine *sola scriptura* (by scripture alone), since they produced creeds (www.bible.ca/sola-scriptura-start.htm, accessed September 25, 2005). But the Web site authors' own view of the Bible depends, among other things, on their assump-tion that if you give "every verse in the Bible on a single topic to 100 people . . . they will all agree." That this has notoriously not turned out to be the case is, of course, one motive for the production of creeds, as a means of regulating interpretation.

neo-orthodox Calvinists, the explanation was formulated by Abraham Kuyper.[5] One of Kuyper's problems was to respond to nineteenth-century science without denying its success. In opposition to those who sought to put religion on a more scientific footing, Kuyper asserted that the regenerate soul does not need discursive demonstration but only the immediacy of faith; there is nothing in the text of the Bible per se that will make us accept its authority. This helps explain why different readers of the same passages could come to different conclusions. In making this argument, Kuyper not only is reproducing a familiar distinction between ideal and material but also is denying conceptual efficacy to semiotic form, even in scriptural texts.

This seems to be part of a general devaluation of materiality, because, along the same lines, Kuyper argued against *all* forms of empirical demonstration of religious truth. In reply to Cartesian skepticism and Baconian empiricism, Kuyper argued that it is only by virtue of faith that our ego believes even our own senses (Harris 1998: 215–16). I take this to imply that what I have described as suspicion of semiosis, and dematerialization of the sign's essence, do not only go together but, for a Calvinist, also can be distinguishing features of the state of salvation. The unsaved seek reasons for belief in words and other sensible forms of evidence; not so the saved. Kuyper held that the Logos of God, as expressed in scripture, is different from his spoken words and "indicates merely the psyche of thought independent of its somatic clothing in language and sound" (1898: 477).[6] This reasoning, turning as it does on the general character of language, links religious dematerialization to a more general suspicion of semiosis.

Here we see the full-fledged view that signifying form is a superficial garb laid upon more fundamental, if immaterial, meanings. It is a view hardly restricted to religious doctrine. Indeed, it is widespread and enters into some of the moral narratives of modernity. A version of the distinction between signifying form and immaterial meanings appears, for example, in another way in Ferdinand de Saussure's model of the so-called arbitrary signifier and its purely conceptual signified (see Keane 2003c).[7] But if the Saussurean model is driven by a modernist effort to produce a rigorous and

5. Kuyper, to whom I return in chapter 3, was a founder of the Reformed Churches, the denomination that sponsored the mission to Sumba.

6. In this respect he is not far from the orthodox position established by Saint Augustine and Thomas Aquinas, in which Logos, as God's word, was compared in human experience to one's inner thoughts, contrasted to spoken words.

7. As I noted at the beginning of this chapter, I do not intend to make strong causal claims for Calvinism's historical role, but it might be worth noting here that

autonomous science of language, in Kuyper we see more clearly the moral implications of the dematerialization of signs. For Kuyper, there was nothing either in the linguistic form or the auditory materiality that helps the word achieve its effects. This view of signs was not simply due to a spiritualization of the world, though surely it is that, but followed from the problem of accounting for different responses to the experience of an otherwise shared, objective world.

Writing in the late nineteenth century, Kuyper was reacting to developments in philology and science, on the one hand, and to pietistic revivals, on the other. But he was also hearkening back directly to Calvin. For Calvin, the theological foundation for this dematerialization lay in the vastness of the gap between God and humans. This is one reason why Calvin finds less radical semiotics, such as that of Luther, to be so offensive, as they lessen the transcendence of divinity. Any communication of God with humans results from a humanization of form, which is therefore also a veiling of something that otherwise would overwhelm us. In the case of the New Testament, God reveals himself in Christ, which amounts to an act of self-humiliation. The attitude toward the material is clearly expressed in Calvin's discussion of the phrase "Word as made flesh," which appears in John:

> The word *flesh* expresses the meaning of the evangelist more forcibly
> than if he said that *He was made man.* He intended to show to what a
> mean and despicable condition *(vilem et abiectam conditionem)* the
> Son of God on our account descended from the height of His heavenly
> glory. When Scripture speaks of man contemptuously, it calls him *flesh.*
> Now though there be so wide a distance between the spiritual glory of
> the *Speech* of God and the abominable filth of our flesh *(putidas carnis
> nostrae sordes),* yet the Son of God stooped so low as to take upon
> Himself that *flesh* subject to so many miseries. (Commentary on John
> 1:14, quoted in Wallace 1953: 11–12, italics in the original)[8]

Thus the word is identified with the body in a derogatory sense. And to fix one's attention upon the word or other sign in itself, rather than the meaning, is tantamount to the vice of pride. To counteract this temptation,

---

Saussure himself came from Geneva, which had been Calvin's great stronghold. One may speculate that, even despite the intervening centuries, the basic teachings and unspoken assumptions of Calvinism were part of the taken-for-granted world within which he was raised.

8. Wallace's translations are based on the standard edition, Baum et al. 1863–1900. For Calvinists who did not denigrate the fleshly body, see Mack 1992; compare Bynum's 1995 discussion of how body could be seen as a problem in the context of pre-Reformation ideas about resurrection.

God's signs point beyond themselves to a more transcendental realm. "There were, no doubt, various appearances under which God made himself known to the holy fathers in ancient times; but in all cases he refrained from using signs which might induce them to make for themselves idols" (Commentary on Matthew 17:5, quoted in Wallace 1953: 80). For instance, according to Deuteronomy 4:11, "The Holy Spirit appeared under the form of a dove, but as it instantly vanished, who does not see that in this symbol of a moment, the faithful were admonished to regard the Spirit as invisible, to be contented with His power and grace, and not call for any external figure" (Calvin 1949: bk. 1, chap. 2, para. 3). Only by means of such mysterious and transcendent signs can humans be cured of pride and the curiosity it produces. Notice the implication that idolatry can fix upon words as much as upon material objects. To attend too much to the form of the sign is not simply an error, it is an expression of human arrogance. Semiotic ideology can have strong moral implications.

If words are bodily forms for meanings, they are nonetheless superior to other nonlinguistic matter. "Whenever God offered any sign to the holy Patriarchs, it was inseparably attached to doctrine without which our senses would gaze bewildered upon an unmeaning object" (Calvin 1949: bk. 4, chap. 14, para. 4). And "true acquaintance with God is made more by the ears than by the eyes. . . . God will proclaim His name so that Moses may know Him more by His voice than by His face, for speechless visions would be cold and altogether evanescent did they not borrow efficacy from words" (Commentary on Exodus 33:19, quoted in Wallace 1953: 72). The first quotation makes clear that an object lacks meaning in itself. It cannot provide its own metalanguage but requires completion by verbal explanation in the form of doctrine. Not only does Calvin presuppose a clear distinction between ideas and matter, but he also indicates, as the second passage seems to suggest, that it is language's capacity for conveying immaterial meanings that renders it the most suitable medium between merely material things and that which is fully divine. To be sure, representations of divine words—that is, their semiotic forms—are subordinate to Logos, as human words are subordinate to thought. But their special relationship to the latter member of each pair grants words a privileged mediating role. That role, however, depends on a correct understanding of the nature of words and their distinction both from concepts and from things. These are matters of semiotic ideology. The proper treatment of language called for purification.

The theological purification of language coexisted with similar purification movements in the name of scientific objectivity. The Royal Society in seventeenth-century England, for instance, sought to cleanse language of the rhetorical excesses that would interfere with a proper, transparent relationship to the objects of denotation (Bauman and Briggs 2003), a goal that appears to persist in, for example, the logical positivism of the early twentieth century. Language and the world of objects must, in this ideology, be understood to stand clearly and distinctly in separate domains, the former attached to the latter by the terms of proper reference. And it may take considerable disciplinary effort to achieve this separation. Some Protestant language reforms contributed to the same emerging semiotic ideology demanded by science; to that extent, at least, they were operating within the same representational economy. The purification of language for science could take on moral undertones, just as the purification of language for religion could reinforce the separation of material objects from the world of meanings and of agents.

TEXT, BELIEF, AND THE CREED PARADIGM

Calvinism's semiotic ideology sharpened the distinction between material expression and immaterial meaning and put them in a hierarchical relation to one another, endowing this distinction with grave moral consequences. It privileged belief, associated with immaterial meaning, over practices that threatened to subordinate belief to material form. The work of purification was an exertion of agency in its own right, but agency and belief are linked in more specific ways. To see this requires stepping back from the particulars of Calvinism and returning to a characteristic practice of Christianity more generally, the saying of creeds.

Calvinist semiotic ideology is one instance of a larger historical process that has led, within the narrative of modernity, to the defining of religion. I discuss the definition of religion in more detail in chapter 3. Here I am concerned with a Western view of religion that had become powerful by the nineteenth century, which identified it "as a set of propositions to which believers gave assent" (Asad 1993: 41). This made religion a matter not of material disciplines or of ritual practices, for example, but of subjective beliefs. The focus on propositions is part of a larger semiotic ideology, the belief that language functions primarily (and properly) to refer to or denote objects in a world that lies apart from it, in order to communicate ideas that lie within one person to another listener or reader. But for that ideology to take on historical and social consequence, it must be embedded within pervasive practical disciplines. Religion is not just the propositions but *the giving of assent to* those propositions. One important template for the relationship between these terms, *proposition* and *assent,* is the creed.

In the previous chapter, I showed some of the ways Christianity has become global in scope. Certainly one proximate condition that made this dissemination possible was Western colonization. But the effect of Christianity on subjectivities, and the religion's continued mobility, depends on the portability and intimacy of specific practices as well. I suggest that some of these religious practices also play a key role in fostering the moral narrative of modernity. For one thing, the pervasive presence of Christian discourses, not just in churches but in schools, the press, mass entertainment, and so forth, has probably influenced all sorts and manners of people in ways that more elite forms of philosophy, political thought, and science have not. But neither religion nor the moral narrative of modernity is confined to the imagination. They offer ways of inhabiting that which they make imaginable. In the most direct terms, Christianity circulates by means of concrete practices such as confession, catechism, creeds, sermons, prayers, hymns, scripture reading, and introspective disciplines. These practices articulate public doctrine and subjective experiences. They bring together elites—the theologians and other teachers, the state authorities, the priests—and everyone else. Christianity, like the other major proselytizing religions, has been extremely successful in creating semiotic forms that can circulate across an indefinitely wide range of contexts, and that make doctrine believable, impressive, morally commanding, and above all, part of an inhabitable world. These forms include bodily habits such as kneeling or crossing oneself, institutions such as seminaries, and obligations such as tithing. And, as observed at least since Weber, they can be inseparable from less explicitly religious things such as accounting practices, domestic arrangements, and architecture (Comaroff and Comaroff 1991). But the force of doctrine has been supported especially by texts.[9]

Protestant liturgies and their practical extensions into daily life often underwrite a certain entextualization of the world. As I discussed in the introduction, this mode of objectification brings out the aspects of language that are not anchored in or dependent on a particular context. It allows language to be extracted from one context and inserted into others. The entex-

---

9. Of course textual, bodily, and other semiotic forms often work together. See, for example, William Hanks's incisive account (2000) of the broader effects induced by the dialogue form and associated disciplines by which the Roman Catholic catechism was taught in Spanish colonial America.

tualizing practices that have facilitated the circulation of Christianity include the sermon (which itself usually centers on the recontextualizing of a bit of scriptural text), prayer, catechism, aspects of the confession or testimony, and private reading and interpretation of scripture.[10] Here I want to look at one example of this textualization, what I call the creed paradigm. This involves looking at the creed and its implications more generally for the relations among semiotic form, semiotic ideology, and the subject.

The creed, an explicit statement of religious tenets and the norms for its verbal performance, is unique to the evangelizing, scripture-based religions.[11] Like scripture, hymns, and prayers, the creed contributes to the global circulation of evangelical religion. Moreover, the creed gives doctrine an explicit form; it tends to place the primary locus of religion in the believer, not institutions; it dwells on differences among religions; and by taking textual form, it makes religion highly portable across contexts. The circulation of modular forms such as creeds works against the localizing forces on which anthropologists of global religions have tended to focus. Danilyn Rutherford (2003) has argued that in Biak (western New Guinea) an important part of the value of scripture and liturgy is precisely their distant origins and capacity for unlimited circulation. Confronted with the enormous ethnolinguistic diversity of Papua New Guinea, people say, "[N]o matter where you go . . . there is only one Bible" (Errington and Gewertz 1995: 95). And surely similar intuitions are common elsewhere. This lack of location can, in some contexts, become part of the practical power of Christian semiotic forms.

As a practice, the creed can form a paradigm for subjective agency. By this I do not mean that creeds teach certain beliefs, or that these beliefs must be ultimate values or meanings. Of course they may be, but their power does not depend on the matter. After all, most people are probably not ardent believers, and no doubt many are indifferent toward or even skeptical of the prevailing religion. All the evidence suggests this indifference and skepticism are ubiquitous and not peculiar to supposedly secular

10. To say the Lord's Prayer is to recontextualize the words originally given in the scripture (Matthew 6:9–13). Harding (2000) gives a detailed account of the ways more generally in which American fundamentalists work to "stand in the gaps" between scripture and everyday life and make scriptural language their own. For sermons, see Besnier 1995; Peacock and Tyson 1989; Schieffelin 2000.

11. According to Pelikan and Hotchkiss, behind the Christian creeds stands the Jewish Shema, "Hear, O Israel: The Lord our God is one Lord" (2003a: 7). But note that this is the repetition of a commandment rather than an explicit, first-person declaration of faith. The first creed to be officially adopted as binding on the universal church came out of Constantine's council at Nicaea in 325 C.E. (Pelikan 2003: 9).

modernity. Furthermore, even shared creeds can be used in different ways, with different intended effects across denominations. Although semiotic forms are consequential, any particular effects depend on their conjunction with social, political, and other forces (see Irvine 1982; Keane 2004). Semiotic form may be powerful, but in itself it is not *automatically* efficacious in any particular way.

The impact of the creed as a paradigm lies, in part, in the more ordinary domain of semiotic practices and the semiotic ideologies of everyday life. A creed, in the most commonly circulating forms today, looks like a series of propositions about the world. But these propositions are peculiar in certain respects. First, usually they are formulaic and are carefully worked to condense complex arguments about doctrine into a readily learned and reproduced form.[12]

Consider, for example, the Apostles' Creed:

> I believe in God, the Father Almighty, Creator of heaven and earth. And in Jesus Christ, his only Son, our Lord, who was conceived of the Holy Spirit, born of the Virgin Mary, suffered under Pontius Pilate, was crucified, died, and was buried; he descended into hell. On the third day he rose from the dead; he ascended into heaven, sits at the right hand of God the Father Almighty. Then he shall come to judge the living and the dead. I believe in the Holy Spirit, the holy catholic church, the communion of saints, the forgiveness of sins, the resurrection of the body, and the life everlasting. Amen. (Pelikan and Hotchkiss 2003a: 669)[13]

A single sentence summarizes core doctrine about the first person of the Trinity, the next three sentences that of the second person (Jesus Christ), and the final sentence that of the third, the Holy Spirit. The entire English text amounts to a mere twelve phrases, plus *Amen*.

But these sentences are a particular kind of statement: they are attached to a performative of assent. The first word of the Latin text is *Credo*, I believe.[14] The Apostles' Creed states an objective claim (it is the case that

---

12. Not all creeds are so short that they can be easily memorized and recited, but even the longer ones are designed to provide some economical means of mastering a more complex whole.

13. The present text dates to the early eighth century and seems to be an expansion of a second-century baptismal formula. According to Pelikan, it was admired by Luther and Calvin for its simplicity and, currently, is the most common baptismal formula in Western Christianity (Pelikan and Hotchkiss 2003a: 667).

14. In some circumstances, such as baptisms, they can be performative in the strict sense defined by J. L. Austin (1955), since the very saying of a creed can be a constitutive part of the act of becoming Christian. Conversion to Islam can make use of similar performative means.

"Jesus . . . was conceived of the Holy Spirit"). As such it appears to be merely a proposition. But it begins with the explicit reflexive first-person assertion "I believe." It asserts the speaker's alignment with the claims (the speaker says: the statement "Jesus was conceived of the Holy Spirit" is true about the world and I hold that it is true). Moreover, it publicly reports this alignment (saying in effect that "Jesus was conceived of the Holy Spirit" is true about the world and I hold that it is true, and I hereby state so before a listener [divine and, often, human as well]).

The creed paradigm takes the publicly circulating form of an assertion (and as such could, for example, be performed as an act of solidarity with a congregation or in defiance of a mob). The paradigm—in accord with Saint Paul's dictum "For man believes with his heart and so is justified, and he confesses with his lips and so is saved" (*Epistle to the Romans* 10:10)— treats interior belief as not sufficient. It publicly represents the speaker as taking responsibility for his or her own thoughts. To be sure, the schoolboy may memorize a creed as mere rote, and certainly many ritualized public recitations of the creed do not seem to demand much personal responsibility. But the persistent recurrence of religious reform movements suggests that the semiotic form of the creed entails a normative tilt toward taking responsibility for those words, making them one's own.

There is an apparent paradox here, since the creed takes the *form* of a proposition, and thus seems to put the speaker in an exterior third-person relationship to her own beliefs, as that of a subject to an object world. As Wittgenstein remarks, belief statements are peculiar since they seem to invite the notion of having more than one voice: " 'Judging from what I say, *this* is what I believe.' . . . One would have to fill out the picture with behavior indicating that two people were speaking through my mouth" (1953: 192). The sense of paradox, however, depends on a prior normative linguistic ideology that one speaker should have only one voice (Bakhtin 1981; see Keane 2001). The creed, as an implicitly public performance, places the speaker's belief within the context of a public world of words. Moreover, these are words over which the speaker has no control other than utterance and acceptance. Despite the first-person form, the speaker of the creed may not deviate from the exact words of the text as established within the authority of a specific tradition.[15] In this way, semiotic form

15. I cannot pursue here the intriguing question of the pronoun, except to note that the Nicene Creed of 381 C.E. replaced the first-person plural of earlier creeds with the singular. It stood this way until Vatican II restored the plural, over a millennium and a half later (Pelikan 2003: 50).

facilitates a disciplinary practice that tends toward bringing inner thoughts into line with public doctrine.[16] It seems to put the speaker on record as *starting* with the text and *then* taking responsibility for the match between her words, her thoughts, and ultimately, the world itself. However private the inner world of thoughts may be supposed to be, this taking of responsibility is itself a public act before human and divine witnesses.

AGENCY TOWARD THE SELF'S THOUGHTS

Since the words of the spoken creed seemingly make transparent the speaker's inner thoughts, this stance toward one's own words is a model for both sincerity and responsibility. The creed exemplifies (and teaches) a norm of taking responsibility for one's thoughts and, thus, a distinction between the immateriality of thought and the materiality of its expressions, mediated by the norm of sincerity. It leaves open a variety of stances toward the materiality of expression. Radicals like the early Quakers, for instance, took material—that is, textual—forms to represent the illegitimate intrusion of social others (Bauman 1983). But even when Roman Catholic apologists defended words, along with other liturgical forms, against such attacks words remained subordinate to belief. Blaise Pascal writes, "The external must be joined to the internal to obtain anything from God, that is to say, we must kneel to pray with the lips, etc., in order that proud man, who would not submit himself to God, may now be subject to the creature. . . . [To] refuse to join [the external] to the internal is pride" (1958: 250). In saying this, he seems to be insisting on the inferiority of the speaking body. This is why subjection to the body humbles the proud.

The creed form encourages a view of religion within which verbalized beliefs hold a privileged position. The first-person statement of a text is belief's prototypical semiotic form. It thereby offers a paradigm for being agentive toward one's own thoughts, as a subject toward a world of objects. However much one may insist that faith is ultimately due to grace, Calvinism, like many other denominations, still requires some response on the part of the believer. Given this sense of responsibility, agency toward one's beliefs or thoughts can become a crucial precondition for sincere conversion, at least in its most demanding forms.

16. The Third Synod of Toledo (589 C.E.), for instance, resolved that the creed be chanted by congregations "to strengthen the vacillating minds of men" (Pelikan 2003: 180). But both Augustine and Aquinas held that the creed ultimately is only making explicit what people already believe (Pelikan 2003: 341).

For all practical purposes, the more one insists on the transcendence of a God who should not be expected to intervene in everyday affairs, the more the human agent is likely to come to the foreground. In many respects, then, the model of the agency of the believer who can articulate and take responsibility for his or her faith may come to resemble less religious versions of internal agency. Conversely, given the importance of the ideal of sincere conversion for much of Western history, it should not be surprising that this ideal in turn influenced ideas about inner agency more generally. Again, I am not attempting to give a historical account of influences, but rather am trying to make certain background assumptions easier to see. For example, a glance at some versions of inner agency that have been developed in moral and political philosophy shows how they can be linked to the idea of freedom. In his own version of the moral narrative of modernity, Charles Taylor (1989) takes John Locke's view of the mind (1975) as paradigmatic. Taylor considers Locke's emphasis on one's ability to stand back from, evaluate, and reform one's very desires (comparable, perhaps, to what Daniel Dennett calls "second order desires" [1976]), and the general expectation that one ought to do so, to be crucial to the development of the modern self. A parallel version of this highly cognized and agentive ideal of self-reform appears in quite a different historical narrative, Foucault's portrayal of disciplinary self-inspection. Foucault describes this discipline as a crucial component of the forms of power that he claims originate more generally in Christianity's invention of the "pastoral power" derived from knowing what is inside people's minds (1983: 214).[17]

Such ways of formulating agency are more than psychological speculations: they are meant to have a bearing on moral and political questions. Thus the philosopher Stuart Hampshire's description of inner agency, an ability to stand back and evaluate one's inner thoughts, is part of his account of individual freedom. He writes, "[B]eliefs are those thoughts which I endorse as true. I do not merely find them occurring or lingering: I decide in their favour. . . . A belief is a thought from which a man cannot dissociate himself" (1975: 97–98). This is a stipulative definition, specifying what, for Hampshire, counts as "belief." It more closely resembles the kinds of explicit beliefs that are stated in creeds than, for example, in the taken-for-granted background of ordinary activity like "my coat is in the closet." And we may

17. One might then surmise that, for the more pietistic Protestants, "pastoral power" becomes internalized. Crucial to the ideology of conversion I am describing here, at least in its more austere versions, is the idea that conversion is supposed not to be mediated by social others, such as priests or other authorities (see, for example, Soeffner's 1997 account of Lutheranism).

be skeptical of its focus on the bright light of self-possessed reason. But Hampshire's definition does exemplify a certain vision of the healthy, virtuous—and, perhaps, fully "modern"—person that is built into some of the background assumptions and everyday disciplines of democratic society. Locke held that political liberty depended on the mind's ability to stand back from desires in order to evaluate them and remake itself (a function of what Taylor calls objectification). This vision of self-consciousness directs us to take, as one commentator remarks, "responsibility for oneself (including one's thoughts)" and involves a special sense of agency and authority distinct from outwardly directed actions (Moran 2001: 114).

Again, we can gain a sense of the generality of this concept of agency by the appearance of a parallel version in Michel Foucault's darker account of modernity, in which the subject is "tied to his own identity by a conscience or self-knowledge" (1983: 212). Self-knowledge, according to Judith Butler's reading of Foucault, involves self-objectification (1997: 22). That is, semiotic forms such as texts or verbal formulae ("I believe") and categories ("homosexual") play a crucial part in developing the kinds of self-awareness that Foucault and Butler take to be distinctive of modernity. As I argue in part 2 of this book, in circumstances in which the creed is taken as a paradigm for the more general norm of sincerity, this norm is likely to obscure the crucial role played by the external, textual dimensions of the performance. The production of sincerity and the self-consciousness it involves depend on objectification. Yet the norm of sincerity and self-consciousness also tend to presuppose an abstract view of the subject such that objectification can be troubling.

The early Protestant reformers treated the creed as a speech act that takes place between speaker and God (Pelikan 2003: 56). Yet even for the Protestants, creeds are not normally supposed to be spoken in solitude or in silent inner speech, but rather collectively and aloud. If creeds perform a paradigm of the expression of an inward act (thought and assent), they enact it within and for a public. In certain respects, they are constitutive of a public. Like any text, of course, creeds are inherently repeatable "out of context" (just as I can quote them here) and are therefore available for use in an unlimited number of possible circumstances and for an indefinite number of functions. They are, however, central in two key practices. One is baptism, a performance of transition between states. The boundary of the religion is marked by the verbal assertion of beliefs. The other key practice is the recitation of the creed by an assembled congregation. Apparently the early Christian creeds derived from catechisms and baptismal pedagogy: they are remnants of dialogues, the answers to questions that begin "Do you believe that" (Pelikan 2003: 50). "So we preach and so you believed" (1 Corinthians 15:3–11). Preaching and confession are, in effect, interdependent moments of entextualization and recontextualization, as the congregation affirms its assent to doctrines that are also expounded in sermons and scriptural readings. And whether or not there is ultimately a divine addressee, the congregation and, potentially, outsiders such as hostile regimes, competing sects, and unbelievers are often what, in Erving Goffman's words, could be called ratified overhearers (1981). In many cases, such overhearers are an evangelical and political target of the performance.

In the pre-Reformation era, collective recitation of a creed was often linked to the penitential system that the reformers rejected. The reformers instead stressed the sincerity and privacy of the creed (Pelikan 2003: 55–56). Religious materializations such as rituals, offerings, priesthoods, sacred sites, relics, communities, holy books, and bodily disciplines persisted but usually in a position subordinate to that of statements of belief. Yet even were one to insist that belief is the very heart of religion, that insistence still depends on, and circulates by means of, semiotic forms. And the tension between these—the purported immateriality of ideas or transcendence of the souls that pertain to them, and the materiality of their embodiments—has been a persistent problem in many salvationist religions. This may be one reason why reformers at times, as during the early Reformation, devoted so much of their energy to scriptural translation and the destruction of material images.

We might look on the creed paradigm in Bruno Latour's terms as part of the work of purification. Certainly, at the level of propositional content, creeds were created in order to establish correct doctrine and expunge deviations. They tend to emerge when one must distinguish one's beliefs from those of others; thus, for instance, the Indonesian Batak Creed starts with a denial of twelve heresies before it gets to any positive claims (Pelikan and Hotchkiss 2003b: 543–55). And creeds offer the speaking subject a discursive position from which to state that difference and claim responsibility for it.

But the work of purification goes well beyond the *content* of doctrines. Creeds make beliefs available in the foreground. Their status is much like that of beliefs as described by Hampshire: they are objects for one's full consciousness and, therefore, things in relation to which one stands as an agent, being able to chose to commit oneself to them. Within this semiotic ideology, it is by virtue of that very objectification that verbalized beliefs enter into the exercise of freedom. In the context of the Calvinist mission, this is why real conversion requires that a speaker's words be sincere expressions of ideas that are truly understood, a point to which I return in chapter 7. At stake is not just the transmission of correct doctrine but also the production of human subjects who are (relatively) free because they fully grasp the agency that is rightly theirs.

It should not be surprising, then, to find that the semiotic form exemplified by the creed is not confined to religion. Such distinctively modern forms of political self-assertion as the Declaration of Independence, the preamble to the United States Constitution ("We the people"), the United Nations Universal Declaration of Human Rights, and perhaps even the Boy Scout's oath, may take some of their force from a history of creeds.[18] The Pledge of Allegiance, recited every morning in American schools, seems to mold citizenship in a similar mode of subjectivization. Such small, repeated, habitual semiotic practices are some of the ways in which the capillary effects of historical forces can be felt well beyond the category of religion as conventionally understood, and work toward shaping persons at an intimate level. They also, we should note, help render illegitimate *other* materializations of thought and personhood (see Bauman and Briggs 2003). Yet other materializations continue to reemerge—rhetorics, imageries, gestures, fetishisms—and so the instigation to purify is continually renewed.

FETISHISM AND PURIFICATION'S FAILURES

In discussing the modern subject, I described it as normatively abstracted from material and social entanglements in the name of greater freedom. This abstraction is the outcome of the work of purification that draws on models of redemption and even religious paradigms for taking an agentive stance toward one's inner thoughts. The goal of abstraction is one aspect of Protestant conversion that has provided both new concepts and new practices by which those concepts become inhabitable in ordinary lives. These concepts and practices have given content and direction to the processes Latour has called "purification." The work of purification aims to create "entirely distinct ontological zones: that of human beings on the one hand;

18. Of the Declaration of Human Rights, Pelikan writes, "In its definition of itself as a code and a 'common standard' that is intent on achieving 'a common understanding,' which is to be kept 'constantly in mind,' it aspires to function as a shared 'rule of faith' and of conduct, much as creeds do" (2003: 304–5). For the constitutive effects of the textual character of the Declaration of Independence, see Lee 1997; Warner 1990.

that of nonhumans on the other" (1993: 10–11). When Latour describes actual examples of purification, they tend to be the work of elite practitioners of science (Boyle) or political philosophy (Hobbes). But Latour does not give a strong explanation of what drives the purification or of what organizes the various different domains of action such that they fall into an overarching tendency with a single direction and lend it the sense of moral progress. One source of a moral impetus to purification may, however, be found in religious reform. Viewed in this light, Michael Walzer's assertion that "Protestantism tended to push visibility and invisibility, morality and salvation, further and further apart" can be seen as an account of the urge to purify (1974: 25). To that extent, Protestantism has been a guide for and expression of purification. It has provided some crucial means by which purification might enter into ordinary lives well beyond the elite spheres of science, theology, or philosophy.

Purification requires an opponent, that which is to be purified. One of the many categories by which the opponents of purification were named was "fetishism." Put briefly, the idea of fetishism concerns the sorting out of potential agents and modes of action in the world. Developing a suggestion of William Pietz's (1985), I define fetishism as an imputation directed at others who have purportedly confounded the proper boundaries between agentive subjects and mere objects. The accusation sorts the universe into things (bodies, rocks) that are material and subject to natural law, and other things (souls, thoughts) that are immaterial and subject to other forces—human agency, say, or divine intervention.

In the context of religious conversion, to misunderstand these distinctions could be a source of moral peril. In more secular contexts, the correct sorting out could be a precondition for moral, political, and scientific progress. An example of this sorting out can be seen in the philosopher Susan Nieman's version of the moral narrative of modernity: "Radically separating what earlier ages called natural from moral evils was thus part of the meaning of modernity. Modern conceptions of evil were developed in the attempt to stop blaming God for the state of the world, and to take responsibility for it on our own" (2002: 3). The distinction among agents and other causes shapes what one can expect, what one can hope for. Thus the fetishist is not only mistaken, she denies her own agency. To surrender one's agency to stones, statues, or even written texts is to diminish one's responsibility. For those who argue that one's freedom depends on the sense of responsibility that comes of understanding one's own agency, fetishism or its analogues can be a source of political self-betrayal.

This purification process, undertaken in the name of religious reform and of modernity, became a paradigm well beyond Western or Christian societies. For example, according the historian Gyan Prakash, the prestige of science in colonial India was associated with a project to "constitute religion by stripping it of what appeared unscientific and irrational" (2003: 41). This was to be accomplished by dividing indigenous culture into religion and magic. Thus the Hindu reformist movement Arya Samaj, founded in 1875, denounced ancestor rituals, priesthood, the caste system, and idol worship as superstitious corruption. Once these material accretions were stripped away, Hinduism would be revealed to possess a dematerialized spirituality and thus a universality equal to that of Protestant Christianity.[19]

Similar reform movements elsewhere sought to purify Roman Catholicism, Buddhism, Islam, and Judaism.[20] Over the last century or so, in their elite forms, the reformist parts of these religions have converged with one another in important ways. First, in many cases, religious reform worked in tandem with the promotion of science in the name of modernity. Science and religion are both hoped-for outcomes of purification processes. Second, in many cases the paradigm seems to be the antiritualism of the Protestant Reformation. The reformers typically aim to replace ritual with beliefs at the center of religion. Third, the result should be to restore human and divine agency to their respective proper locations relative to each other and to natural law. To the extent these reforms have become generalized across religious reform movements, they tend to be identified with modernity itself.

And yet, a long view of the history of Christianity suggests that purification does not fully succeed. One scholar of medieval European religion states in summarizing the conceptual terms of this history: "A significant part of Christian doctrine completely rejects the constraints of life on earth, makes every attempt to overcome them, and opposes them with superior, universal norms, in the name of transcendency. Yet, at the opposite pole, we can find—for the *self-same* constraints—approval, religious sanctification and deduction from divine command" (Klaniczay 1990: 31, italics in the

19. The dematerialization of religion and the dematerialization of the person understood in more secular terms seem to go hand in hand. According to Taylor, the main current of philosophical and literary visions of the modern self centers on modes of self-consciousness that depend on the assumption that consciousness can be fully disembodied and the self not placed in the world along with other natural things (1989: 170–76).

20. See, for instance, Eickelman 2000; Gombrich and Obeyesekere 1988; Orta 2002; Sharf 1995.

original). If Luther and Calvin undertook to purify the church of Roman Catholic trappings, their austerities and institutional forms were challenged in turn by new textual forms and institutions, new rites and spiritual enthusiasms, and even the eudemonic bodily practices of today's hugely successful Pentecostalism (Austin-Broos 1997; Robbins 2004b). Doctrinal struggles such as these are, of course, the outcomes of complex political, social, and theological histories. But if we attend to the clashes in semiotic ideologies they involve, they might help illuminate conflicts that have taken place in quite different historical contexts.

The value accorded to transcendence in traditions like Calvinism encourages efforts at abstraction, to play down the materiality of semiotic form in order to arrive at a disembodied spirit, a pure idea, or an unsullied faith. This goal, however, cannot reproduce itself without generating new semiotic forms.[21] Latour says that the work of purification inadvertently produces new hybrids. But why should that be? One approach to the production of hybrids is this: Once semiotic forms are introduced into a social world, they become available as materials for experience on which further work is carried out. They can become objects of reflection, sources of disciplinary practice, points of contention, or sources of anxiety. For example, some of the major actions taken by the Protestant reformers were responses to the sheer materiality of the liturgical forms and material objects that existed in the world of late medieval Europe, which reformers saw as an affront to the divine transcendence. But the reformers could not help but produce new forms—creeds, sermons, hymns, houses of worship, even (over the protests of some reformers) clerical garb. These forms could never be fully confined to their original contexts or definitively subordinated to their "true," immaterial meanings. They risked being fetishized, producing new hybrids. That risk is inseparable from their efficacy, the capacity that semiotic forms have of being recontextualized. Although the risk of semiotic form is inherent, it is only troubling, and liable to provoke reactions, when viewed within the values and ideas of certain semiotic ideologies.

A Russian Orthodox theologian writes, "There is, in different forms, a permanency to iconoclasm. Suffice it to think of the Albigensians in medieval France, the Judaizers in fifteenth-century Russia, and finally, of the Protestant Reformation" (Ouspensky 1992: 119). One need not adopt his no doubt highly interested perspective to suspect that some core aspects of

---

21. Another complicating factor, of course, is the doctrine of incarnation. My concern here, however, is more with the pragmatic difficulty posed by any medium, rather than the more specific and conceptual domain of doctrine.

the basic semiotic problem of materialization recur in quite different historical contexts. But the semiotic problem is necessarily both historical in its outcome and productive of history in its dynamics. High ideals, doctrines, and ideologies cannot exist socially or be transmitted without some semiotic embodiment, which necessarily imposes certain conditions on them (such as iterability, contingencies of form, and the hazards inherent in the processes of decontextualization and recontextualization) that may contradict the purposes of those who create them.

Latour says that, although modernity is a project of purification, purification never entirely succeeds. There are surely many reasons for this. What I mean to stress here is that this inability to achieve complete purification is *inherent* in the very materiality of semiotic form. This is apparent, for example, in the perpetually recurring efforts at religious purification that run through the histories of scriptural religions. In their modernist versions, reformers' efforts to strip away superstition, instrumental reason, idolatry, and fetishism are undertaken in the name of greater spirituality on the part of the human, and greater transcendence on the part of the divine. Even the most austere forms of mystical unknowing ultimately involve some semiotic medium; even the denial of words begins as a response to words and, in most cases, includes some way of displaying that denial (see Keane 1997b, 2004). Semiotic form requires material instantiation. The purification process can never fully separate the material from the nonmaterial and stabilize the difference. We can see this in the creed paradigm. For a creed to function, it must take a stable linguistic form independent of the speaker and be capable of circulating among other possible speakers. It cannot work without some material expression. In Latour's terms, it is a hybrid, a mixture of those domains that purification tries to keep separate, such as material and nonmaterial, natural and cultural. This is why the imputation of fetishism is so persistent in clashes between different ontologies.

On the other hand, if purification does not fully succeed, nonetheless purification efforts continue to appear. The work of purification and the imputation of fetishism are not restricted to matters of high doctrine. Since the fetish concept comes into play in the effort to establish the real locus of agency in the world, it has implications for all sorts of human activities. This is one reason for the persistence of the urge to effect purification in the face of the material dimensions of semiotic form. For instance, the distribution of possible agents affects jurisprudence, delimiting the range of possible responsible actors and thus the scope of blame and punishment. In much humbler domains, it can affect the very problem of suffering. To suffer is to be the patient of an agent. As a concept that informs the work of purification, fetishism guides the effort to determine what will count as possible agents, and thus how one can and must—or must not—deal with suffering, whether one prays in order to heal or merely to express empathy. The appeal of new understandings of agency is especially apparent where, over and over again, conversions are instigated by immediate and mundane causes of suffering: sickness, the death of children, impoverishment, social domination or marginality, fear of the dead. One of the central things conversion does is change the relations of agent and patient, and of subject and object. The idea of fetishism attends to the border between actor and patient. It opens up new potential agents and modes of action. In this context, we can see how the imputation of fetishism, and the effort to free people from it, can lead to the work of purification in a way that has real consequences for ordinary people as they seek out solace, cures, and culprits.[22]

The themes I have highlighted within Protestant Christianity by looking at Calvinism, and the aspect of the idea of modernity to which I have tried to link them, tend to abstract the human subject from its material entanglements in the name of freedom and authenticity. In this understanding of freedom, we can see one suppressed link between modernist rationality and proselytizing religion: the value of freedom and abstraction lies, at least in part, in their offer of transcendence. The constitution of the human subject in contrast to objects is a persistent and disturbing problem for many ideologies of modernity. It worries both high theory and everyday practices. Even in its most abstract and transcendent, the human subject cannot free itself from objectification. It retains a body, depends on objects, and speaks by means of publicly known, material forms of speech. People cannot free themselves from the practices by which they are embedded in the world of other persons. And the semiotic forms of those practices can bring into sharp focus the presence of other persons, a certain immediacy even of the distant and the dead. Calvinism is an especially rich ethnographic domain for exploring this irresolvable tension between abstraction and material (and thus social) mediations. The tension is thrown into sharp relief in the colonial encounter not just with other religions but also with religion's Others. In the colonial world, freedom links the moral narrative of modernity to a Western sense of self. As Peter van der Veer remarks, "[I]t

---

22. The reconceptualization and redistribution of agency has consequences independent of immediate efficacy. For example, as Peter Pels observes of colonial east Africa, "[i]f the missionaries were unsuccessful in solving the problems created from day to day by secret evil agencies, their increasing monopoly of the spiritual realm forced Walguru to rely more and more on the secular healing" of medicines (1999: 296–97).

is in the opposition of freedom and unfreedom that the Christian West distinguishes itself from its Others" (1996: 3). The contrast hinges in part on concepts such as custom, tradition, and culture, which function as that to which the native is in thrall, and whose difference from the freedom promised by religion poses such troubling difficulties.

3   Religion, Culture, and the Colonies

I suggested in the previous chapter that some of the roots of the drive to purification inherent in certain moral narratives of modernity reach into the history of religious reform. Religious arguments that demand the spiritualization of humans, and that insist souls are distinct from their physical embodiments, can also encourage less specifically religious worries about the materiality of objects and the human agency of subjects. In many cases, the efforts of religious reformers and evangelists propel these demands and worries into the smallest capillaries of everyday life and commonplace habits. One of my major purposes in the second part of this book is to demonstrate these claims in greater detail. But first I want to continue developing, in terms doubtlessly both too broad and too limited, some aspects of the global context within which the mission encounter can be situated. I proceed through the use of a key few examples meant to bring out some of the relevant aspects of that context. This chapter concerns the category "religion" and proposes that some of the dominant ways in which it is usually understood within Western narratives of secular modernity are themselves affiliated with the work of purification. The heart of the chapter is my discussion of the distinctly Protestant treatment of religion by the Victorian anthropologist E. B. Tylor and the echoes of that formulation in early Dutch ethnography and missiology.

Purification can work by sharpening distinctions among categories and domains of social life. One of the most conventional characterizations of modern society in Western social thought, exemplified in the foundational works of Marx, Weber, and Durkheim, is that it separates such domains as religion, economy, family, and politics. Compartmentalization forms the defining contrast to societies in which these elements are thoroughly bound together into what Marcel Mauss (1990) called a "total social fact."

The conceptual compartmentalization of religion accompanied the well-known political and institutional processes in the eighteenth and nineteenth centuries that produced the formal separation of church and state in the United States and parts of Europe. Religion, in these narratives of modernity, does not necessarily disappear, but it finds its proper place, confined to the private sphere of interior belief, individuals, and the congregations they voluntarily form. For religion to maintain its proper place requires a vigilant policing of conceptual and, often, juridical boundaries. This policing, in turn, contributes to the configuring of religion as a knowable entity, an object in the world, both for those who are religious and those who are not.

The global spread of Christianity, therefore, was not just the inculcation of a new religious doctrine but also, in many cases, the introduction of a new category of religion altogether. This category of religion often worked in tandem with a semiotic ideology that assumed a sharp distinction between signs and the world they signified. This distinction commonly contributed to the contemporaneous effort to define the specific domain of the cultural. To be sure, neither Christianity nor any particular semiotic ideology is the only element in what is certainly a complex history. But my aim here is to focus on the contribution of Protestantism, especially the major semiotic elements, to the production of the categories of religion and culture that played, and continue to play, a crucial role in the moral narrative of modernity.

RELIGION AS A CATEGORY

If religion is a knowable object, what manner of object is it? To the extent that religion is defined in terms of practices, habits, moral imperatives, values, institutions, and beliefs that persist over time and circulate within communities that are identified with a particular religion, it can seem to be cultural. But there has long been a tendency to identify the cultural with localities.[1] By contrast, as I argued in the previous chapters, religious pros-

---

1. The attack on the identification of culture with place is exemplified by Appadurai 1986b. Although there are important thinkers in anthropology who do not treat culture as a bounded entity (Franz Boas, for one; see Keane 2003b), and there is growing interest in the unbounded circulation of cultural phenomena (see, for example, Appadurai 1996; Hannerz 1996; Urban 2001), the idea of culture often still centers on human differences among communities. This idea tends to be spatialized, in contrast to the universalizing claims of natural science and scriptural religion and to the less spatialized principles of difference, such as class or gender.

elytization is often distinguished by a refusal to be confined to localities. Evangelizing and salvationist religions may make claims to what is, in principle, an potentially unbounded spatial and temporal range.[2] And in practice these spatial and temporal assertions can force people to confront the problem of culture. When, for instance, early Christians needed to deal with the habits, stories, or even the temples and statues they had inherited from their own past in classical pagan antiquity, or when nineteenth-century Europeans encountered vastly different habits, stories, and objects in their various colonial worlds, they were compelled to make decisions about which should be altered or abandoned, which could be kept. As the historian Sabine MacCormack observes of one of the earliest colonial missions to confront alien spirits, "If there is a European analogy to the Andes around 1660, it is not medieval Europe, where Christianity could be taken for granted. Rather it is the late antique Mediterranean, where even Christians were deeply divided as to how much of their pagan past could permissibly be salvaged and how much of it simply had to be salvaged if meaningful existence was to continue" (1991: 11). By the end of the nineteenth century, the decision of what to salvage in colonial societies commonly hinged on whether the practice or idea in question could be defined as culture, and therefore more or less harmless, or as false religion. In much of the colonial world, where the institutional distinctions among religious, juridical, and political domains familiar to Europeans did not exist, this decision required the active creation of conceptual categories.

If religion is *not* cultural, then what is it? And if religions are cultural phenomena, but manifestly not cultures, what is the proper context for their analysis? What is culture if even a global religion, ranging across all kinds of social, linguistic, or political contexts, is cultural? These are not merely academic questions. They trouble missionaries and converts, as well as government officials, jurists, educators, development workers, and even the tourism industry. The difficulties arise within a family of problems faced by everyone from social theorists and ethnographers to political activists, as well as by religious believers across the spectrum.

The difficulties are compounded by the problem of genealogy. The categories "religion" and "culture" are, among other things, part of everyday Western folk sociology. Few anthropologists today can, without at least

2. Admittedly, this spatial expansiveness developed fully only after the advent of voluntary mission societies at the end of the eighteenth century. For only then did evangelization become a private enterprise independent of established churches and state institutions, and thus they could be seen as unfettered by national boundaries (van Rooden 1996).

some epistemological circumspection, assume that such categories simply describe things in the world.[3] In the Weberian tradition of social science, one might take them on as useful analytic constructs. More recent critiques have made it harder to accept the constructing of ideal types as a neutral procedure. For many critics, categories like religion and culture are not only historically recent and parochial in character, they are also politically dubious, and, it would follow, their applicability across cases is problematic at best. A common response to this critique is to jettison general categories in favor of more appropriate, that is, local, categories.[4] This turn has resulted in a number of by now familiar difficulties that would take me too far afield to lay out here (but see Keane 2003b). One point, however, must be stressed. The "local," as a privileged basis for knowledge, has itself become problematic.

As I mentioned above, critics of the culture concept have attacked the assumption that people are rooted in bounded places. But more directly relevant here is this: conceptual categories like religion and culture have been let out of the bag, and we are hardly in a position to scoop them back up again. Like "the modern," they are part of both elite and everyday discourses and mediate self-awareness just about everywhere; the categories have themselves become social facts. Moreover, in the case of those scripture-based, universalizing faiths most commonly called religions today, there *is* no obvious locality to which they can be tied. This is true sociologically (institutions and people circulate), culturally (ideas and practices circulate), and epistemologically (the dominant world religions make universal claims). Indeed, as I suggested in the previous chapters, part of the appeal of global religions may lie in their very lack of location.

This suggests that we adopt the categories for whatever purchase they might offer. But to accept existing categories demands, at least, considerable self-awareness. It asks us to reflect on what Foucault would call their genealogy and explore its implications. The problem is not, after all, simply a matter of finding conceptual clarification or better empirical evidence. The concepts of cultural analysis are too entangled with histories of domination and

---

3. My discussion here touches only on some limited aspects of the larger problem of defining religion. For further discussions of the implications of the attempt at definition, see especially Asad 1993, 2003; Masuzawa 1993, 2005; Saler 1993; Smith 1982.

4. In an early moment in this skeptical turn, Benedict Anderson remarked (in a footnote to his essay on the Javanese concept of power) that one could just as well have written of the Western concept of *sakti* (1972). But the observation did not prevent him from undertaking a thoroughly Weberian analysis in the body of the article.

exclusion for us to rest content with that. We need not accept the careless assertion that such entanglement—or even mere proximity—is tantamount to collusion with forces of domination or exclusion to recognize the serious need for ethical and epistemological circumspection.

Talal Asad traces contemporary definitions of religion as a universal and transhistorical entity back to the seventeenth century. Writing of Lord Herbert's attempt to define Natural Religion as the common denominator for all faiths, he says, "This emphasis on belief meant that henceforth religion could be conceived as a set of propositions to which believers gave assent, and which could therefore be judged and compared as between different religions and as against natural science" (1993: 40–41). This emphasis on belief is not just a matter of theoretical construction, however. It is also one of the ways religious reformers actively define themselves against the unreformed. This impels the dematerialization—the stripping away of bodily disciplines, rituals, icons, even texts—by which religious purification converges with the moral narrative of modernity. Dematerialized religion has consequences for agency. For example, Calvinist prayer is supposed to be the expression of a thought. Calvinists oppose their own uses of language to what they see as the materialist and instrumental efforts to influence the deities by pagans and Catholics (see chapter 6). This way of imputing to others a false understanding of agency is what I have dubbed "fetishism." One lasting result of the nineteenth-century definitions of religion and culture I discuss in this chapter is that the reformer tends to understand these differences within a historical narrative. This narrative involves a critical shift in semiotic ideology, by which humans are supposed to possess newly recognized forms of agency, but only to the extent that they come to realize that words and things do *not* have certain kinds of efficacy.

The distinction between religion and culture still, even in the early twenty-first century, bears the marks of its role in a fraught nineteenth-century endeavor. This distinction is a problem not only for social research but also for all sorts of other endeavors. Some of these are products of the formal separation of church and state. In many contemporary nation-states, for instance, whether an act, institution, or idea is categorized as religious has serious consequences for conscientious objectors to military service; for those who refuse to take oaths, receive inoculations, use internal combustion engines, work on the Sabbath, or allow their children to enter public schools; for refugees or those who wear distinctive clothing; and for the tax status of real estate. There is a less well-developed but growing cluster of similar juridical and political consequences for things that are categorized as cultural—practices that might otherwise be repugnant, for instance, may be tolerated and legally protected if they are cultural; songs and artistic motifs may be claimed as cultural property; claims that are unbelievable to the jurist nonetheless may be accepted as valid testimony in courts; and so forth (Kirsch 2001; Myers 2002; Povinelli 2002).

In this chapter I address the problem of religion insofar as it was an ethnographic question in the same context within which the anthropological concept of culture was being formulated. First I show some of the ways that the relations between the two raise problems in present-day religious and political spheres. I suggest that the shape these questions take today reflects the way in which the concepts were formulated in the nineteenth century. In order to get a better sense of the relations between these concepts, I then turn to three exemplary nineteenth-century figures: the English anthropologist Edward Burnett Tylor (1832–1917), the Dutch ethnographer-missionary Albert C. Kruyt (1869–1946), and the Dutch Calvinist theologian Abraham Kuyper (1837–1920). The work of these men, along with that of some of their associates, illustrates different dimensions of the theoretical and practical problems of defining the relations between religion and culture, and some of the consequences for the purification of semiotic form. In chapter 4, I turn to the encounter of the religious and the cultural from another angle, to ask what problems the apparent persistence of past cultural forms poses for a religious historical imagination whose future is at stake. The struggle of nineteenth-century and twentieth-century scholars, missionaries, and converts can shed light on some of the conceptual and ethical problems the categories of religion and culture still raise today. These problems help shape present-day understandings of objectification and abstraction.

LOCATING RELIGION

The problem of localizing Christianity goes back to Saint Paul's preaching to the Gentiles, and the subsequent missions to northern Europe in the centuries that followed. But not until the colonial and postcolonial context did the problem come to hinge explicitly on the emergent—and, often, mutually defining—concepts of culture and religion. In the last decades of the twentieth century, as the Dutch were wrestling with their past role as colonial masters, the question of religion and culture took on new and forceful shape. For the heirs of the mission movement, this question was inflected by practical happenstance. For example, in 1972, economic pressures forced the Dutch organizations that had been supporting the Christian Church of

Sumba (Gereja Kristen Sumba) to make drastic budget cutbacks and sharply reduce the number of workers sent overseas. This circumstance brought to the fore what had all along been a lingering set of conceptual and political questions.

To address these questions, a Dutch volume of reflections on relations between the Dutch and Sumbanese Reformed Churches began by asking "whether there is coming into existence something that should be called Sumbanese Christendom" (van Halsema et al. 1995: x) and ended with the assertion that "[o]ne of the new questions [arising from Sumbanese Christianity] is the sense-giving framework of a context stamped by another religion" (Holtrop and Vel 1995: 240). These simple sentences condense a host of problems: What is it to be "Sumbanese"?[5] What is "Christianity" when it is inflected or qualified by a locality—either that of the missionaries who conveyed it, or those who converted? And since that inflection is usually understood in cultural terms, what is culture to religion, or religion to culture? These are simultaneously political, social, and conceptual questions, but they are mediated semiotically—their mode of existence and their causal consequences depend on their embodiment and circulation in material forms.

At roughly the same time, in 1978, the Roman Catholic parish of Waingapu, East Sumba, celebrated its twenty-fifth anniversary. The Catholic mission had been more aggressive in making use of Sumbanese cultural forms, such as in adapting local songs as hymns, and had a local reputation for being an easier religion for marapu followers to enter. But, despite their doctrinal and institutional differences, the Catholic minority on Sumba faced some of the same problems as the Calvinists.

By the time of this celebration, many of the key players were Indonesians, mostly from Sumba and the neighboring islands. The keynote of the event was a newly written, culturally specific mass. In the booklet accom-

---

5. In the 1950s, the missionary linguist Louis Onvlee (1973g) pointed out that the concept of a "Sumbanese people," as opposed to more localized identities based on territories, clans, or linguistic distinctions, did not make sense. The idea of a *people* (Indonesian, *bangsa*) was fundamentally nationalist in character. In effect, a Sumbanese people does not become imaginable until *after* people come to think of themselves as Indonesians—"Sumbanese" is not the aggregation of all the clan and village identities but rather a historical precipitate of this larger category. In the 1980s and 1990s, this broad category was still of only limited relevance (see Keane 1997a). At that time, one of the chief ways in which the category was beginning to gain purchase was through the institutions of the Sumbanese Christian Church (see Steedly 1996 for a comparable situation in western Indonesia).

panying the mass, the author of the mass, a man from the nearby island of Flores, explained his motives:

> Culture is a manifestation of the human answer to our questions about ourselves and the world around us. This shows that Culture covers all aspects of human life, including religion. . . . The replacement, adaptation, and creation [of values] must be done in a cultural way too. . . . Religious truth takes shape, grows, is filled and communicated outward in the framework of the culture of its adherents. Without that, religious truth will not become an integral part that is able to function, becoming a source of inspiration, creation, and motivation for its adherents. For that reason, we face various tasks—to comprehend and reevaluate the Christianity that we have inherited in order to differentiate more sharply the Evangelical basis which is authentic and the basis in foreign culture (read: West) which has been closely tied with it in the history of the Christianizing journey to Indonesia. (Beding 1978: 92)

Texts like this can easily seem platitudinous. I think, however, we must take seriously what their authors are trying to accomplish, and recognize the complexity and contradictions of the concepts they presuppose. We must do so on two grounds: first, because these are real problems for them, and second, because these are problems we (as outsiders, at least in the moment of the analytic or observational stance) share *with* them—the problems are part of what makes them coeval with us, as it were. One of the most sophisticated recent ethnographers of Christianity insists, for instance, that the analyst "must attend to the cultural aspects of Christianity" (Robbins 2004a: 326), a task whose goal is both seemingly obvious and difficult to achieve. Nor are the questions confined to scholars and religious activists. In 2004, the writers of a constitution for the European Union found themselves, according to the *New York Times*, "bedeviled" by them (May 26, 2004, A12). Saying, "Of course, we have a Judeo-Christian past, but the constitution is inspired by a heritage that is cultural, religious and humanist all at once," the French foreign minister made it clear that a cultural past was acceptable in ways a purely religious one might not be. In a somewhat different formulation, the Polish foreign minister held that religion was acceptable, as long as it was understood as primarily a question of traditions: "We are not talking about a reference to Christian values, but to Christian traditions—hence to a historical fact that no one can change." In the next chapter I turn to the concept of history in light of religious proselytization and its temporality. In this one, I consider religion and culture. Since they are categories that have been created under specific circumstances, a better understanding of their genealogy is crucial both to understanding their currency as social facts in the world and to reconstructing their analytical and theoretical usefulness today.

The views of culture and religion expressed in the passages above reflect certain tensions in those concepts as they emerged within the colonial context, as well as the effect of postcolonial and transnational politics. Efforts to grapple with the concepts and their politics, in the context of global Christianity, have centered on the ideas of localization and inculturation. *Localization* reflects the anthropological interest in local particularity and the ability of societies to resist and transform "external" forces (see Robbins 2004b). *Inculturation* reflects missionary concerns. It was defined by the father general of the Jesuits as the "incarnation of the Christian life and of the Christian message in a particular cultural context, in such a way that this experience not only finds expression through elements proper to the culture in question, but becomes a principle that animates, directs, and unifies the culture, transforming and remaking it so as to bring about a 'new creation'" (Pedro Arrupe, *Selected Letters and Addresses* [1978], quoted in Pelikan 2003: 311). Such statements depend on a long and often troubled history of attempting to distinguish between religion and culture.[6] Part of the difficulty in doing so results from the work of purification, which posits a realm of beliefs, parceled out between religion and culture.

OBJECTS OF THE DISTANT GAZE

The distinction between religion and culture was formulated in the context of the separation of church and state. But in its nineteenth- and twentieth-century forms, it also emerged as part of a more general, and disturbing, problem of knowledge: how to distinguish and relate religion and science as two distinct, perhaps complementary, or even opposed, possibilities for the knowing and acting subject. In an era shaken by such things as Darwinism and new forms of biblical scholarship, the categories of religion, culture, and

---

6. The concept of inculturation in the postcolonial context has in some cases led to a shift in the terms of discussion. For example, some Catholics in Flores, north of Sumba, have argued that inculturation requires dialogue between *religions*. Even if the end result is Christianization, in order to initiate dialogue the local religions must be put on the same footing as Christianity. This means they must be provided with a theology (Barnes 1992: 171–72; for the idea of a specifically Toraja Christianity in central Sulawesi, compare Sinaga et al. 2004). But this view of the task still depends conceptually on the older problem of distinguishing between culture and religion.

science raised fraught questions, such as which domains were proper to each, how their respective institutional forms should treat one another, and whether one was about to supplant the other. The conflict between religious and self-consciously secularizing conceptual strategies may have been internal to nineteenth-century Europe, but it also has had enormous bearing on the contemporary postcolonial world. If the paradigm of modernity has been taken to be a secular Europe, then those for whom the gods are still agents in or beyond this world are relegated not simply to difference but, in historical terms, to anachronism (see chapter 4). These questions suggest what was at stake when the Victorians attempted to establish religion and culture as *objects* for scientific scrutiny.

E. B. Tylor was raised a member of the Society of Friends, or Quakers, who practiced an austere Protestantism marked by its strong opposition to ritual and other liturgical forms. The intellectual historian J. W. Burrow remarks that "the non-conformist background of Spencer and Tylor was perhaps as important as their rationalism in determining their attitude to primitive religion. It was an irony of that time that the men who had sufficient scientific detachment to treat religion as an element in social life essentially no different, from a sociological point of view, from any other, were, *ipso facto*, least likely to be able to appreciate what religion, particularly public, organized, ritualistic religion, meant to the worshipers themselves" (1966: 245). *Irony* may not be quite the right word in this case. That the scholarly perspective might be a *product* of the distant gaze is itself hardly surprising. Distance is, after all, usually considered to be a precondition for objectification. Yet the particulars of that distance remain worth attending to, for two reasons. First, as we would expect, the point of view of a Tylor or a Spencer fostered assumptions that continue to live within subsequent studies of religion even when carried out by different sorts of scholars under different circumstances. Second, it is a particular irony of the colonial situation with which I am most immediately concerned that some of the most influential missionaries worked within paradigms created by agnostics, skeptics, or people otherwise theologically unsympathetic.[7] And, conversely: comparisons with the colonized were, for the European

---

7. We might recall here that William Robertson Smith's early work in biblical scholarship, often considered a founding document in the anthropology of religion, was carried out while he was a professor at the Free Church College, a Calvinist institution in Aberdeen (McNeill 1954: 402). This research put him in serious jeopardy, as he became subject to heresy accusations. In something of an ironic reversal, Tomoko Masuzawa (2005) argues that the purportedly secular study of comparative religions today often harbors a Christian subtext.

powers, "crucial elements in defining one's modernity" (van der Veer 2001: 5; see likewise Chakrabarty 2000; Comaroff and Comaroff 1997; Dirks 1992; Stoler 2002; Thomas 1994).[8] Yet those who provided the crucial evidence for this difference, and helped shape the categories by which that evidence was interpreted, were often missionaries who had at best a profoundly ambivalent relationship to that very modernity.

There is also what Ian Hacking (1995) calls a "looping effect" present here. Objects of scholarly knowledge such as "animism," "fetishism," and, in their light, "religion" (as construed and reinterpreted in the context of the colonial encounter) were, at least in the early generations, constructed out of materials gathered to a large extent by missionaries. The labors of missionaries both as proselytizers and as ethnographers were, in turn, guided by these scholarly categories. And those who were studied and converted often took on those categories, which then transfigured their own self-understanding (see, for instance, Prakash 2003).

E. B. Tylor's formulations of the concepts of culture and animism can stand for certain broader currents that shaped the purifying efforts of both scholars and missionaries. He has a totemic role as the holder of the first academic position in anthropology in Great Britain (reader at Oxford in 1884, chair in 1896) and provider of classic definitions of religion ("the belief in Spiritual Beings" [1864: vol. 1, p. 424]) and culture ("Culture or Civilization, . . . is that complex whole which includes knowledge, belief, art, morals, law, custom, and any other capabilities and habits acquired by man as a member of society" [1864: vol. 1, p. 1]). More specifically, he had a direct influence on the Dutch missionaries and ethnographers who worked in the Dutch East Indies.

Burrow defines the central task of Victorian anthropology as an attempt to understand "non-rational modes of thought and conduct," by which he means the "reverential, ceremonial, status-ordered, as distinct from practical, calculating, 'useful.' . . . [The latter is that] which does not *per se* invite sociological explanation, for example, selling at the highest price and buying at the lowest" (1966: 2). Note three things about this characterization. First, the rational is posed in terms of market rationality on the British model of the self-organizing society, rather than, say, posed as religion produced by natural reason. Second, the social and cultural are essentially

8. A parallel self-definition was occurring at home. As Peter Pels remarks, debates about Victorian occultism such as that between E. B. Tylor and Alfred Russel Wallace were "sites of political contest about the proper constitution of the modern" (2003: 243). For the role played by the image of the *missionary* in the self-definition of the modern, see Priest 2001.

defined by negation, as the residue left when ends-means rationality has been eliminated. This distinction still underwrote many approaches to culture in the second half of the twentieth century. Finally, the nonrational here includes not only things a European might see as religious (the reverential and ceremonial) but also things seen as traditional, even in a presumably legal domain (status-ordered). The question of the relative rationality or irrationality of religion and culture continued to haunt ethnography in the Indies, and beyond, for a century.

The question of rationality is evident in trajectories of the principal scholars of comparative religion in the next generation after Tylor. R. R. Marett, James Frazer, and Andrew Lang all started out in the study of classical myth, whose irrationality in a world considered by the Victorians to be foundational to modern reason would be especially troubling (see Asad 2003; Veyne 1988). Tylor's interests did not have the same starting point, but his work helped facilitate theirs. He was instrumental in shifting the emphasis in evolutionary social theory away from law and social organization toward religion. In contrast to Henry Sumner Maine, John F. McLennan, and others, Tylor was uninterested in institutional or sociological forms. Not only did he direct his attention away from social organization, but when turning to religion, he treated it as, above all, a domain of the individual mind.[9]

Tylor's concept of culture was driven by two explicit projects. One was an argument against polygenics and for the shared origin of all humans (Stocking 1968). The other was his treatment of all human phenomena as subject to explanation in terms of natural law. The former led to both his concept of animism and his method of thought-experiments. The latter derives from the premise that, since humans share a single origin, we can assume a single human nature. When confronted with any cultural phenomenon, we should assume it to derive from intelligible motives, that is, reasons that we ourselves ought to be able to supply. Animism, therefore, must be the product of rational thought. Its error lies not in the reasoning powers of the animist but in the empirical premises, the animist having only limited knowledge to start with. The monogenist project also motivates the doctrine of "survivals," the idea that some aspects of social life are only remnants of earlier states of society and have lost their original

9. The heavy emphasis on belief became central to the definition of both religion and culture in what Skorupski (1976) calls the "intellectualist" lineage in anthropology, which centered on such problems as the rationality of so-called traditional religions (see, for example, Horton and Finnegan 1973; Wilson 1970) and, more recently, is converging with evolutionary psychology.

rationale. This doctrine provided a way of saving the hypothesis by providing an out when something cannot be explained by contemporary common sense. Notice that the logic of the survival can work to reinforce a Protestant semiotic ideology by providing an explanation for the distinction between ritual (empty forms that have survived) and the meanings they have lost.

The second project, the incorporation of humans under natural law, helps motivate the distinctive character of Tylor's magnum opus, *Primitive Culture* (1864), fully half of which is devoted to religion. In contrast, Lewis Henry Morgan's *Ancient Society* (1877) is concerned almost entirely with government, family, and property (although similarly motivated by the effort to adjudicate the relations between religion and science; see Feeley-Harnik 2001). As George Stocking points out, by focusing on religion, Tylor privileges that one aspect of culture in which explanations that make reference to nonnatural causes, such as divine mandate, might have seemed most likely to many of his readers (1968: 79). This would be the most effective way to demonstrate that even morality is part of nature. For Tylor, the locating of morality within nature underwrites an argument against the degenerationists. Since human culture in general, and morality in particular, are subject to natural laws, which are laws of evolution (*evolution* meant as a general notion of orderly development or progress rather than a specifically Darwinian mechanism of natural selection), then all human states are more or less the products of ongoing progress. Indeed, Stocking argues that Tylor's concept of culture does not lend itself to the more pluralistic treatment of culture that entered anthropology from the German tradition by way of Herder and Boas. Rather, Tylor tends to portray culture as pan-human, the important distinctions lying not among different cultures but rather among different stages reached in a single civilizing progress.

As the insistence on progress hints, there is another subtext to Tylor's treatment of religion. It is most famously expressed in the concluding statement of *Primitive Culture:* "It is a harsher, and at times even painful, office of ethnography to expose the remains of crude old culture which have passed into harmful superstition, and to mark these out for destruction. Yet this work, if less genial, is not less urgently needful for the good of mankind. Thus, active at once in aiding progress and in removing hindrance, the science of culture is essentially a reformer's science" (1864: vol. 2, p. 453). Tylor is not speaking here of political or social reform. Early in *Primitive Culture,* he announces, "It is with a sense of attempting an investigation which bears very closely upon the current theology of our own day that I have set myself to examine systematically, among the lower races, the development of animism" (1864: vol. 1, p. 21). He is a purifier, heir both to an Enlightenment contempt for superstition, tradition, and ceremony and to radical Protestantism's hostility to Catholicism.

An essentially Protestant position (and the semiotic ideology it involves) determines what will count as culture and thus, under Tylor's definition, religion. The definition implicitly sets culture in contrast to anything that might fall under instrumental or practical rationality. Tylor understands religious *practices* to be, above all, outward expressions of inner *beliefs.* Thus beliefs may vanish, leaving practices behind as survivals. In theory, those beliefs might derive from divine inspiration or the universal insights of natural religion. But his explanation of animism takes an empirical turn and places *humans* at the foundations of religion. By rendering religion a component of the more encompassing domain of culture, Tylor makes religion a matter of the mind, constrained by the "habits acquired by man as a member of society," and thereby subject to rational critique in the name of progress. And his anti-Catholicism was surely not indifferent to the slightly scandalous effects of conjoining "primitive" religion with those varieties closer to home.

Tylor thus provides the missionary with a paradoxical tool. On the one hand, by the end of the nineteenth century, most Protestant missions probably shared some ground with Tylor. Their preaching, teaching, and disciplinary endeavors could hope to succeed only to the extent that they were addressed to at least minimally reasonable humans subject to persuasion and learning. Tylor's concept of animism imputes to "primitives" a capacity for drawing conclusions from an objective world that they *share* with the missionaries. Moreover, this doctrine locates primitive religions not on the other side of a radical divide but within the same ontological terrain as the religion being promulgated by the missionaries. After all, it might have seemed more reasonable to determine that there were some human groups so low as to have *no* real religion at all. But Tylor ruled this out by fiat in establishing his "minimum definition": "By requiring in [the definition of religion] the belief in a supreme deity or of judgement after death, the adoration of idols or the practice of sacrifice, or other partially-diffused doctrines or rites, no doubt many tribes may be excluded from the category of religious. But such narrow definition has the fault of identifying religion rather with particular developments than with the deeper motive which underlies them" (1864: vol. 1, p. 424).

This invited the intellectually sympathetic missionary to seek out and develop the hidden commonalities among what would be understood as different species of the same genus, "religion." The invitation was reinforced by the doctrine of survivals, since the latter meant that "primitive" cultures could be improved by selective processes of elimination and, at least implicitly, that they could be brought up to the level of other civilizations. Yet, of course, the naturalism of this account of religion, and its subsumption under the overarching category of "culture," could potentially also threaten the theological foundations of the entire missionary project. If missionaries did not usually carry the logic so far, the categories with which they worked still produced their share of conundrums.

CULTURE AND THE MISSIONARY

In the Dutch East Indies, Tylor's account of animism directly influenced both missionary practice and the nascent, missionary-dominated field of colonial ethnography. Albert C. Kruyt was born in Java to a family that provided the Netherlands Mission Society (Nederlandsch Zendeling Genootschap) with several evangelists (Brouwer 1951).[10] Repatriated to the Netherlands at the age of eight, he graduated from the society's missionary training program.[11] Kruyt and his collaborator, Niclaus Adriani (a highly trained theologian and linguist with close family ties to missionary circles), seem to have devoted at least as much effort to ethnography as to conversion. They saw the latter task as requiring a movement on both sides of the religious divide. As Kruyt remarks in the preface to his great monograph on animism: "I myself, being active as a missionary in the Celebes, have more and more entered into the thoughts of the Toradja, whereby I have been able to bring . . . the Gospel to the people in a form that gives hope that they will accept something of the preaching in itself. Insofar as I would give as objective as possible a picture of animism in the following pages, I have set aside my standpoint as a Christian and missionary regarding these primitives' world and spirit views" (1906: vii).

10. The Netherlands Mission Society was founded in 1797 on the model of the London Missionary Society, by members of the Hervormde Kerk who had been influenced by the Pietist movement. A voluntaristic organization in the Enlightenment mode, the society was formed only two years after the disestablishment of the church in the Netherlands. As van Rooden observes, such independent missionary societies "define the originality of modern Western Christianity" (2002: 73).

11. The program was directed by the brother-in-law of G. A. Wilken, another Indies-born missionary-ethnographer. Wilken, in his own influential monograph on animism in the Indies (1884–1885), followed Tylor in taking animism to be the earliest stage of religious evolution.

This quotation nicely, if apparently unwittingly, expresses one of the core paradoxes of missionary ethnography, the tension between the relativizing perspective and the vocation to change the native. Kruyt and Adriani eventually produced four long ethnographies of the peoples of Sulawesi, theoretical studies of animism, two dictionaries and a grammar of indigenous languages, and solid ethnographic reports on other islands, including Sumba. Even the missionaries of the neo-orthodox Reformed Churches on Sumba, who disagreed with some of the Netherlands Mission Society's theological and missiological doctrines (Reenders 1995: 21), drew on the conceptual categories Kruyt and Adriani developed.

Kruyt's approach was based on that idea that, if conversion were not to produce superficial or syncretistic results, it should take place gradually and within an entire community. Therefore his mission work focused on culture, with the aim of producing a *volkskerk,* a people's church that would be the embodiment of a society. Conversion had to be a gradual process. As Kruyt writes, "[I]t always remains a riddle for me, who has come to know a primitive people in their life and work, how one might introduce Christianity as a development from these nature-god rites" (1906: ix). In order to decide what in the indigenous religion might be antecedent to, or suitable for developing into, Christianity required finer distinctions to be made among kinds of religion (animism, spiritism, fetishism, and so forth). Out of the effort to make such decisions, he collected and classified a wide range of data from his own and others' ethnographic research, compiled in *Animism in the Indies Archipelago* (1906). This work became one of the main guides for the research and thinking of the next generations of missionaries and ethnographers. Although the missionaries had the task of defining Christianity for the natives, and regulating it, the natives were supposed to decide for themselves which parts of their previous culture were compatible with that Christianity (Schrauwers 2000: 54). Of course in practice, the natives were hardly left to sort through their culture themselves. Nor is the question a simple matter of colonial transformations and local resistance: in Sumba, for instance, the Dutch were often frustrated in their efforts to preserve what they took to be local cultural forms by Sumbanese converts who saw them as too redolent of paganism.

The massive gathering of ethnographic data by people like Adriani and Kruyt was justified, in part, by the missionaries' need to take a hand in the task. That ethnographic project did not require theological or missiological unanimity. For instance, in contrast to Kruyt, the Reformed Churches' missiology held that local religions were entirely false and, unlike ancient Greek and Jewish beliefs, could not prepare their followers for a higher religion (Wellem 2004: 116). Nonetheless, its missionaries to Sumba were required to undergo formal training in the religion and culture of their respective mission fields; some of them eventually produced extensive, serious ethnographic writing. They had to know the false religion in order to combat it effectively, and the culture in order to convert people in accordance with, and thus with the support of, their particular way of living.

One of Kruyt's main revisions of the prevailing theories of primitive religion was the distinction between "animism," as a belief in a rather generalized soul substance (Dutch, *zielstof*), and "spiritism," a belief in and worship of a specific, identifiable, and enduring soul. Animism was produced under conditions of an original "communistic" society, in which the individual was subsumed under the collective: "[A]mong those people who still live an entirely communistic life, with whom the individual is entirely wrapped up in the community, the soul substance still entirely preserves the peculiar character of an all-animating life-force. . . . [T]he primitive man is thus not aware of 'his individuality' [Dutch, *niet van zijn 'ik-zijn' bewust is*] and the soul substance has little personality . . . [so] they have only a very vague representation of the life to come" (1906: 2–3). "Spiritism" represented an evolutionary advance, being associated with societies in which some individuality was appearing, at least in the person of the chief. Thus, for example, in the case of the To Pamona people of central Sulawesi, practices that could be identified with animism (and with an impersonal life force) should be suppressed as superstition. By contrast, practices identified with spiritism (and with a category of souls of the dead that retain some individuality) could be adapted to Christianity, since they were associated with a native awareness of life after death, on which Christian ideas of resurrection could be developed. In general, the insightful missionary-ethnographer should be able to look beneath *practices* and find a more abstract plane of *concepts*. Even missionaries of the Reformed Churches, which in principle denied any redeeming value in Sumbanese religion, tended in practice to work with similar logic. At this more abstract plane, translation into Christianity could be effected, a practical consequence of Calvinist semiotic ideology.

RELIGION AND THE OBJECT WORLD

I have suggested that culture, for those influenced by Tylor, is defined in contrast with instrumental rationality. The ground on which native rationality was to be adjudicated remained the background assumption that all humans share an objective world, since it was only against objective conditions that rationality could be determined. The ironies of the use of an objectivist ontology are strikingly evident in its role within the teachings of the theologian Abraham Kuyper. Kuyper, whose semiotic ideology I discussed in the previous chapter, was perhaps the most prominent exponent of anti-Enlightenment neo-orthodox Dutch Calvinism at the end of the nineteenth century (Harris 1998; McNeill 1954; Wintle 1987). Theologically hearkening back to Calvin, he also aimed at a radical restructuring of Dutch society and had no qualms about using distinctively modern institutions to that end. He was one of the leaders of the schism that produced the Reformed Churches (Gereformeerde Kerken), and he founded the Free University in Amsterdam (1880) in part to provide a home for scientists whose religious belief, he thought, had kept them out of more secular scientific institutions.[12] As head of the Netherlands' first political party, the Anti-Revolutionary Party, he served as a prime minister of the Netherlands (1901–1905). His work represents one way to reconcile the competing claims of science and religion by allocating each to a distinct domain—a process that can be seen as part of the larger process of what Latour calls purification. Kuyper's thought also exemplifies the extent to which the theologically conservative accepted, and even helped contribute to, the background assumptions of objectivist ontology.

Kuyper brought to full fruition the Dutch reaction against Enlightenment attacks on religion and against nineteenth-century Pietistic evangelicalism, and he was instrumental in exporting neo-orthodoxy, especially to America and Scotland. His reaction arose in the context of nineteenth-century struggles not just between Darwinians and antievolutionists but also, within Christianity, between modernism and biblical criticism, scripturalism, and evangelical revivalism. Two aspects of his movement are worth stressing here. First, Kuyper stood against the use of philological scholarship and rational apologetics to defend religion; he denied that faith could be proven or successfully conveyed by means of appeal to evidence (Benedict 2002: 338–39; Harris 1998: 208; McNeill 1954: 396). In the face of these movements, the Reformed Churches had become increasingly committed to the literal inerrancy of the Bible. As Vincent Crapanzano has

---

12. It was the Reformed Churches that sponsored the mission to Sumba (see chapter 4). The Free University was one of the two institutions at which their missionaries were allowed to undergo their obligatory training (Wellem 2004: 115). Louis Onvlee, Bible translator and ethnographer of Sumba, who will reappear in the chapters that follow, served as a professor at the Free University in his later years.

observed, one of the distinctive features of literalism is that it "focuses on the referential or semantic dimensions of language—more specifically on the word [by which Crapanzano means discrete lexical items rather than larger stretches of discourse]—rather than on its rhetorical or pragmatic (that is, its context-relating) dimensions" (2000: 2). This is a matter of the literalists' language ideology (and thus of semiotic ideology) and not necessarily an accurate reflection of their actual practices. For one thing, even literalists cannot take scripture completely at face value in every respect (Malley 2004). Moreover, as Susan Harding (2000) has shown very strikingly, people who claim to take scriptural language at its word can be masterful rhetoricians. The ideological emphasis on literalism can become one component of purification applied to language in, for example, efforts to strip away contextual features of meaning or the pragmatics of interaction, matters to which I return in the second and third parts of this book.

A second important aspect of Kuyper's movement is its relationship to science. Despite his rejection of rational proofs for religion, Kuyper (1899) argued that Calvinism does encourage and protect scientific inquiry into nature, because a proper understanding of God as creator requires us to take God's creation as lawlike and ordered. Faith that does not lead to science, he maintained, is in fact superstition. Kuyper assumes here a measure of reason based in shared access to the object world of scientific knowledge that may help us understand the distinction that people like Kruyt were making between acceptable and unacceptable components of "animistic" traditions. But the Calvinist also accepts a domain of miracles and redemption. They simply exist apart from the "normal" realm of natural law. In effect Kuyper used the doctrine of justification by faith alone to argue that meaning is underdetermined by experience. It is perhaps this underdetermination that led him to support the inculturation of liturgy in the colonies, a position that was an inescapable part of the historical moment— even as its actual fulfillment was subject to indefinite deferral.

ETHICS AND *ADAT*

The problem of culture for the missionaries was shaped by the theoretical concerns of the anthropologists they read, but it was also powerfully stimulated by the changing situation in the colonies. Although parts of the Indies had been under Dutch control since early in the seventeenth century, and certain regions converted to Christianity early on, serious efforts at missionization across the archipelago began only late in the nineteenth century. Until the Napoleonic wars bankrupted the enterprise, the Indies had been governed by the Dutch East India Company, a private commercial undertaking. Neither the Company nor the state rule that succeeded it encouraged the conversion of indigenous peoples, which they saw as politically destabilizing. A crucial transformation occurred at the end of the nineteenth century, when reformers in the Netherlands promulgated the idea that the Dutch owed a debt of honor to the Indies, from which they had profited so well. This found support from business interests that saw in the Indies potential markets and industrial labor forces, which required, however, a higher standard of living (Ricklefs 1981: 143). Under the resulting "Ethical Policy," colonial rule after 1901 was, for a period, supposed to be guided by concern for the welfare of the natives. Whereas the state had earlier discouraged proselytization, and had forbade it in Muslim areas, the Ethical Policy was open to demands by mission groups for religious freedom and education, though it still restricted mission groups' access to Muslims. At the same time, between 1904 and 1910, partly for geopolitical reasons, the colonial state completed the expansion of its control over the archipelago. This opened up more non-Muslim areas and made them relatively secure for missionary activity.

In contrast to missions to China, India, and elsewhere, those to the non-Muslim Indies were faced with ritual and discursive practices whose very status as religion was subject to debate. As Adriani wrote in 1919 of the people he encountered in central Sulawesi (due north of Sumba), "There is no word for religion in the Toraja language. . . . [I]t has no tenets, no developed doctrines about gods or man; it doesn't propagate itself, and belongs totally to the social circumstances within which the Toraja people have found themselves for some time" (quoted in Schrauwers 2000: 32). In intellectual terms, these circumstances would seem to have invited some rethinking of definitions of religion and its subspecies.

But circumstances made this more than a theoretical matter. The idea of the debt of honor, combined with the mid-nineteenth-century wave of Pietistic revivalism (the *réveil*), had inspired "Ethical Theology." In contrast to earlier missionaries, who tended to rely on Dutch or the trade-language Malay, with the aim of producing converts on the model of Dutchmen, proponents of the Ethical Theology were deeply concerned about the danger of inculcating superficial faith. In search of a deeper conversion, they emphasized the use of local languages and respect for indigenous cultures. Even someone as theologically conservative as Kuyper asserted, "Our western forms of confession and liturgy may not be laid on the converts from other peoples. God has not shaped all people alike. Therefore, eastern forms of hymn, prayer, and confession must arise out of their own bosom from the converted Javanese from their past experience" (Reenders 1995: 7). Of course underlying this position is a Calvinist anti-ritualism that would encourage at least a certain skepticism toward received liturgy of any sort.

Proponents of Ethical Theology sought to create a "people's church" *(volkskerk)* by the "appropriation" or inculturation *(toeeigenning)* of Christianity in such a way that the community would be converted without losing its distinctive ethos. The importance of inculturation as it was conceived by the Pietists was that it would support the development of a personal emotional bond between believer and God by situating the new religion within existing social networks and value systems. In practice, as we have seen in the case of Albert Kruyt, this goal forced the missions to decide what in the indigenous culture was and was not compatible with Christianity. It also demanded some decisions be made about what was or was not essential or dispensable in Christianity. Although Kuyper and his Reformed Churches were opposed to the Pietists, aspects of inculturation appear in the work of their own missionaries.[13]

In this context, one crucial term was *adat*. Adat (a word whose localizing implications are already implicit in its foreign derivation, having entered Malay from Arabic) has held a wide and changing set of denotations. It can refer to the unstated norms of personal deportment and social interaction, custom in general, explicit rules, or customary law, and it can refer to a more diffuse understanding of culture. It is a concept whose scholarly formulations have come to play a crucial practical and ideological role in Indonesian society quite broadly since the nineteenth century. Of particular importance for the present discussion is that adat has been defined in contrast to, and in coordination with, religion *(agama)*.[14]

In accordance with the nineteenth-century Dutch colonial model of the plural society, the population of the Indies was divided into broad categories

13. One example of how these groups could be interlinked is found in P. D. Chantepie de la Saussaye. Holder of the first Dutch doctorate in comparative religion, he was one of the principal figures in Ethical Theology, influenced by Pietism, and an opponent of Kuyper, although, like him, opposed as well to Enlightenment and liberalism. But he was also the chairman of the Netherlands Bible Society (see Swellengrebel 1974), which trained Louis Onvlee for his work on behalf of the Reformed Churches' mission to Sumba. Another example is that of Albert Kruyt himself, who visited and reported on Sumba (1921) with the cooperation of the missionaries, despite their apparent theological and missiological differences.

14. *Adat* also enters into contrastive relations with another Arabic loan word, *hukum* (law), in ways that do not directly concern us here (see Bowen 2003).

(Europeans, natives, and nonnative Orientals, such as Chinese), each of which would be governed by its own laws. Originally it was thought that natives would be governed by Islamic law. But Islam was also increasingly seen by the Dutch as a political threat. Adat seemed to offer a useful—and legitimately indigenous—alternative to the claims of Islam, especially to the political authority of its clerics. Although adat was not implemented within the system of colonial law until the twentieth century, the conceptual foundations were already being developed in the mid–nineteenth century by ethnologist missionaries such as G. A. Wilken, Kruyt, and Adriani.

An important contributor to the formulation of adat, who drew on the conceptual domain of Islam, was the Orientalist Christiaan Snouck Hurgronje (1857–1936), celebrated for having successfully entered Mecca in the 1880s disguised as a pilgrim. At the end of the century, he turned his attention to the strongly Islamic society of Aceh, in northern Sumatra. There the Dutch were facing the most prolonged and violent resistance to colonial rule they had ever encountered. The most militant leadership in the rebellion apparently consisted of Muslim clerics. On the basis of his expertise in Islam, Snouck Hurgronje was commissioned to undertake a study and make policy recommendations; one result was a now classic ethnographic monograph (Snouck Hurgronje 1906). What is most important for our purposes is his claim that the clerics were fundamentally external to village society, and they could thus be eliminated or neutralized with no serious consequences for the Acehnese overall. Here we see a sociological version of the logic by which Christian missionaries elsewhere attempted to define what is cultural and what is religious, to distinguish them from one another, in order to operate upon one without disturbing the other. In the Acehnese case, Snouck Hurgronje proposed that Islam itself remain intact; indeed, it would even be purified. This is because Islam was properly a religion of piety. Only where it attempted to function as a juridical system did it become a foreign, rigidly doctrinaire, and ultimately illegitimate imposition on the local world. That is, religion should get out of the business of politics and law and return to its proper domain, spirituality.

What is the deeper and more legitimate source of law? Where there is no tradition of a centralized state, law must be something that expresses the genius of the place, something distinctively local. Thus the Dutch conceptually set adat against the legal rulings of religious scholars as self-governance is set against rule imposed by social outsiders. But if adat is local, Islam, by contrast, at least in certain respects, was not, and its political authority in local societies could potentially be put into question. This was useful for the purpose of delegitimating the claims of Islam in one political context; but of course it might destabilize the work of Christian missionaries in another.

If the category of adat came to affect the meaning of religion, it also affected the idea of culture. Because adat was local, one could not assume it possessed the same principles across the archipelago. Rather, it required detailed empirical investigation in a series of localized case studies. One result was a tendency to identify behavioral norms with bounded localities and to assimilate persons to those places—to place the Batak in Batakland, the Balinese in Bali, as it were.[15] As I observed above (see footnote 1), this localization of the "native" is implicit in some, if not all, strands in the anthropological concept of culture. The postindependence Indonesian state inherited most of these assumptions from the colonial state, even when the New Order regime (1966–1998) attempted to reduce the content of adat to "traditional" clothing, marriage ceremonies, architecture, and the like. By the late twentieth century, adat sometimes took on new forcefulness as a source of authority opposed to the state (Bowen 2003: 59), but it retained that territorial logic: thus to oppose the state could often seem to lead to localism.

Whereas the Tylorian model of culture did not logically imply the existence of geographically and sociologically bounded cultures, Dutch conceptualizations of adat did. The school of adat and adat law studies focused on delineating adat-regions or -territories. Perhaps one reason for the difference was the territorialization of the respective institutions most interested in these topics. The colonial legal apparatus of the Indies attempted to distinguish among populations in order to codify and apply the appropriate laws (see Lev 1972). In a somewhat parallel move, when faced with the prospect of competition among the missionaries of different religious sects, the colonial state established a policy of one mission per people.[16] As a result, the missions were confronted not with an entire archipelago that they would have to render into manageable units, but with predetermined, highly circumscribed, domains. Catholics in western Flores had no immediate interest in fixing the precise relationship of the Manggarai to the Orthodox Calvinist mission's Sumbanese people, even though the two

---

15. Approaches to adat could stress either cultural or legal dimensions of the term, and the study of adat became an important part of both ethnographic and jurisprudential scholarship in the Netherlands during the twentieth century. The scholars who founded adat studies as a legal discipline, C. van Vollenhoven and F. D. E. van Ossenbruggen, both emphasized its local character.

16. Colonial policy here echoed cooperation and noncompetition policies worked out in world missionary conferences in 1854 and 1885 (McNeill 1954: 385).

islands were so close as to be visible from one another on a clear day. A missiological concern for inculturation could, in these circumstances, work in tandem with ethnographic particularism.

CULTURE AS THE OBJECT OF REFORM

Kruyt criticized government efforts to freeze adat in place by codification. After all, his whole evangelizing project, especially as it treated religion— at least non-Christian religion—as cultural, depended on the malleability of cultural forms. In this light, Kruyt justified missionary goals by asserting that adat was *not* an unchanging tradition, because "[w]henever the relations, the conditions of life, the mentality of the members of the society change, adat itself alters. . . . Adat is thus living; it alters itself whenever the men who observe it change" (1936: 42).

If a missionary is committed to the transformation of societies, then change must be possible or the whole effort would be futile. But what is subject to change and what is not? On the one hand, clearly *something* in the practices and ideas of the people being missionized must change. On the other, in at least some respect, the truth of Christianity itself is never supposed to change. By the twentieth century, it became conventional for Dutch missionaries to advocate the preservation of local cultures. What had to be changed was only local *religions*. Conversely, if Christian practices were to be adapted to local conditions—something that even Kuyper supported in principle—then only those elements that were not part of the essential core of the religion could be changed. They had to be cultural, which for Dutch missionaries typically meant things like hymns, costumes, and verbal metaphors. At any rate, in terms of Calvinist semiotic ideology, such superficial things could hardly be deemed essential.

But the missionary had to be wary, since the elements of practice taken up by this adaptation had to be, themselves, part of local culture, and not the pre-Christian religion. As a result, those who advocated the localization of Christianity had a reason to seek out differences between religion and culture. But in doing so, they risked participating in the purification processes that had contributed to secularization in the West, by confining religion to a distinct sphere apart from other domains of social life—a risk of which many were aware (Kipp 1990: 10). Those who saw religion and culture as inextricably bound together—as anthropologists in the tradition of Durkheim and Mauss did—tended to reject compromise and demand radical transformation. The question of what counted as religion and what as culture was, in practical terms, usually inescapable. Across the Indonesian mission fields there were fraught discussions as to the proper categorization of such things as burial sites, marriage exchanges, cross-cousin marriage, divorce, tooth filing, polygyny, and even naming practices.[17]

Kruyt and Adriani (along with their predecessor Wilken) dominated the missionary ethnology of the Indies in the late nineteenth and early twentieth centuries, but their reception by the more conservative missionaries of the Reformed Churches on Sumba was mixed. Two opposed visions of divine history were involved. Kruyt and Adriani treated indigenous practices as phases in the progressive development of the knowledge of God, and therefore the sensitive missionary could seek out elements of the local religion to use as a means of bringing the people to a higher level. But those who followed Kuyper saw these practices as apostasy from the original revelation, as "idol and devil worship" (Dutch, *afgoden- of duivelsdienst*) (Reenders 1995: 21–22). Yet Kuyper's insistence on congregational autonomy also led them to ponder how they could adapt the church to local societies.

In the Sumbanese mission, at one end of the spectrum, P. J. Lambooy proposed to use the Sumbanese word for ancestral spirits, *marapu*, to translate *God* (Lambooy 1930, 1937). This proposal goes beyond simply making a distinction between religion and culture. It seems to assume that, for the very speakers of the language themselves, the lexical form is so arbitrarily connected to its meaning that the two can be detached, and the form be attached to a new significance. Although this proposal was never taken up, most of the Protestant missionaries to Sumba did assume that adat and religion could be distinguished and an accommodation with adat should be reached (Reenders 1995: 30–31; Onvlee 1973h).

At the other end of the spectrum, L. P. Krijger (1932) argued that adat and marapu worship were indistinguishable, and therefore adat in its entirety

---

17. Regular synods of the Gereja Kristen Sumba since the 1950s have grappled with a number of these practices. For example, keening and the playing of mortuary gongs were for many years prohibited for being too closely associated with the marapu, and gifts can be brought to a funeral only as provisions for the guests, not as offerings. Until recently, the use of stone tombs in the central plaza of the village was also forbidden in some areas. Otherwise, the church allows most traditional internment practices as long as people understand that whether or not the internment is carried out correctly will in itself have no effect on the deceased's ability to enter heaven (Wellem 2004: 339–47). Some practices have proved especially contentious. At the end of the 1990s, for instance, despite several rulings on the subject, there remained considerable disagreement and ambiguity about the standing of polygynous marriages among church members and how to deal with them (Wellem 2004: 334–38). I discuss some of the other debates in detail in part 2.

must be opposed, since it was inextricable from Satan worship. S. J. P. Goossens, the missionary who most strongly insisted that religion and culture were inseparable, eventually went so far as to set up a separatist compound for his converts. In Goossens's compound, Christians could live apart from other Sumbanese, the better to eschew such things as tobacco and betel nut, whose sharing remains an essential medium of everyday Sumbanese sociability up to the present day. This was against the explicit mission policy of fostering good relations between converts and the rest of Sumbanese society. Goossens's extreme measures provoked the greatest crisis in the mission's history. He was eventually expelled from the mission society, and he set up his own Free Church (van den End 1987; Yewangoe 1995: 122).

Yet, for all the ferocity of his intolerance, Goossens recognized something that others like Lambooy did not. As Onvlee (1973c) himself pointed out in his well informed and sympathetic ethnographic writing about Sumba, even the ordinary etiquette of betel nut chewing was profoundly implicated in concepts of soul, reciprocity, and identity that pointed toward the spirit world. In the first generations, the general opinion held by Sumbanese converts themselves was closer to that of Goossens than of Lambooy. For instance, they rejected efforts by Dutch missionaries to introduce gong music into church services, on the grounds that the sound of the gongs would evoke memories of the marapu, if not actually attract the marapu themselves (Goossens 1987: 407; Onvlee 1987).[18] Even at the end of the twentieth century, proponents of inculturation complained of stubborn resistance by local congregations to the introduction of Sumbanese tunes, gongs, or dances in church (Wellem 2004: 272–74, 346–49). Similarly, Sumbanese rejected much of the effort to replace the Indonesian or Dutch languages with Sumbanese religious vocabulary. By the end of the twentieth century, the most common words for Christian concepts in Sumba tended to be taken from Indonesian, many of them having Arabic sources (such as *Allah*), or from more neutral semantic domains in Sumbanese languages

---

18. Dutch observers have suggested that this situation may have begun to change in the last decades of the twentieth century. They said that Sumbanese had begun "to ask themselves how far is it necessary to separate yourself from your own society and above all from your family if you are a Christian. . . . [Since] the number of Christians was increasing and they no longer held a minority position," Sumbanese Christians were beginning to feel they could return to certain practices, such as in-village burial, that they had rejected earlier (Holtrop and Vel 1995: 230–31). But the Sumbanese-born theologian F. D. Wellem (2004) portrays local congregations at the turn of the twenty-first century as still being theologically, liturgically, and culturally much more conservative than the Dutch or more cosmopolitan Indonesians.

(such as *Mori,* meaning "Lord").[19] There are many possible reasons why the more forceful efforts at indigenization did not readily take hold. But it seems that one may have been the poor fit between the local circumstances and a semiotic ideology that took words and material forms to be merely arbitrary expressions of abstract meanings, a problem to which I turn in chapter 4.

HISTORY, EVOLUTION, AND SEMIOTIC FORM

According to the mainstream of Calvinist semiotic ideology, language and liturgical practices should point to the immaterial ideas they express. We can see this in missionary ethnographies. For instance, Albert Kruyt's analysis of the religion of the To Pamona people of Sulawesi treated the associated rituals as expressions of beliefs that could be represented independently of the rituals themselves. In the context of Calvinism, Kruyt viewed ritual as a *leervorm,* a lesson of instruction in God's will (Schrauwers 2000: 187). The biblical word was a more direct expression of this will than ritual. This follows the Calvinist doctrine which states that, although all humans have knowledge of the basic moral law, "man is so shrouded in the darkness of errors" that this knowledge is obscured (Calvin 1949: bk. 2, chap. 8, para. 1). This is why we require the *written* law of scripture. The scriptural text works, however, because the reader is already possessed of "a readiness to obey" (Calvin 1949: bk. 2, chap. 7, para. 3–12). Ritual is less explicit than text, but text in turn is subordinate to innate knowledge. The explicit nature of the text is needed only because of the debilitating effects of Adam's Fall on that innate knowledge.

This theological position is congruent with elements in one important linguistic ideology common in post-Reformation Europe. In this view, of which the biblical literalism mentioned above is only one variant, the principal functions of language are referential and predicational (see Silverstein 1979; Bauman and Briggs 2003). This means the principal function of language is to denote meanings and refer to entities that exist in a world external to language. But in the context of animistic and, especially, fetishistic practices, this referential understanding of language could be understood to

19. In the 1990s, Sumbanese evangelists commonly taught that the couplets of Sumbanese ritual speech really refer to God, but that Satan had tricked people into applying them to ancestral spirits (Wellem 2004: 296). Despite this, Sumbanese Protestants seemed to prefer shifting vocabulary and even language away from the older poetic forms, rather than refunctionalizing those existing speech genres for Christian purposes (but see chapters 5 and 9 for another side of the story).

be the outcome of an evolutionary process, over the course of which the magical and ritualistic functions of language had gradually been eliminated. This evolutionary view presumably helps explain why Kruyt accepted animistic interpretations of Christian rites such as baptism (the view, for instance, that baptismal water has magical effects on the convert) as evidence that Christianity was becoming a meaningful part of the lives of former pagans. This acceptance would otherwise be curious, in view of the emphasis on interiority over external forms and strenuous rejection of any hint of magical interpretation of rites.

Kruyt's position resembles the Tylorian doctrine of survivals in postulating a distinction between form and belief, such that the former could persist while the latter disappears. But it also suggests a view of material disciplines, according to which faith in the discipline would eventually produce a more appropriate, and evolutionarily more advanced, mode of discipline centered on the production of assent to propositions. That is, progress has a semiotic component: people advance from faith in the signifier to having the capacity to pass beyond it to the signified. And indeed, Kruyt's mission, like many others, increasingly stressed verbal over other ritual forms. This may help explain why, besides the sermon, it is the singing of hymns, as an intermediate form between nonverbal ritual and purely verbal propositions, that so dominates contemporary churches in the region.

By the end of the twentieth century, the Dutch church-based aid workers and other supporters of the Sumbanese church had gained considerable sophistication, and they criticized their forebears (and present-day Gereja Kristen Sumba leaders) for seeing their cultural task as one of drawing a line between religion and adat, and for using it to sort out the permitted and the forbidden (van Halsema 1995: 93). Instead, write two of these supporters, "the church in the present phase of her existence and in her new position as a majority church has less difficulty with adat than in the period when she was a minority church and adat was still the 'property' of the marapu worshippers" (Holtrop and Vel 1995: 239). The focus now should be on the "sense-giving frameworks" of different religions and "the meaning of life on the *underside* of society" (Holtrop and Vel 1995: 240).[20]

---

20. Already in the first half of the twentieth century, missionaries such as Maurice Leenhardt in Melanesia (Clifford 1982: 89) and Louis Onvlee (1973a) in the Indies had expressed their worries about the loss of meaning among the people they missionized. And as early as 1920, W. H. R. Rivers was writing in a missionary journal that, in "undermining its ritual and beliefs, [the missionary] was at the same time . . . destroying all that gave coherence and meaning to the social fabric" (quoted in Beidelman 1982: 133).

Yet one might argue still that these forms of accommodation are made possible by an emphasis on meaningfulness and an occlusion of concrete activity that depend on the dematerialization of both culture and religion, however redefined. This dematerialization occurs at the level of both general principles and specific strategies. The first means treating the essential function of culture as providing ultimate values at the expense of particular demands, desires, habits, disciplines, practices, or techniques. The second follows from the first, by treating cultural forms as expressions of essentially abstract meanings. This is what allows the church, for instance, to translate the marapu blessing of "cool water" *(wai maringu)* into a metaphor for Christian salvation (Holtrop and Vel 1995: 242; Onvlee 1973b: 204 ff; see also Onvlee 1973e). "Water" as a metaphor is distinct from the material that flows, has specific sources, and produces causal effects. The former, in effect, need not be water at all.

The dematerialization of religion is of more than academic interest. In the first place, when religion is made primarily into a matter of concepts, it converges with the idea of disenchantment as definitive of secular modernity. Rendered a matter of private belief and cognition, religion becomes something that might be enchanted or not, whose objects might turn out to be real or unreal, and whose subjects may be reasoning well or poorly. If religion is defined in this way, the advances of science—seen as a matter of better reasoning and more realistic ideas—can be taken to lead directly to its diminishment. Thus the treatment of religion in terms of *cognitive* difference, in effect, *historicizes* it. And indeed, as I discuss in the next chapter, moral narratives of modernity are sometimes told in a way that portrays religion in general, and the more material forms of religion in particular, as anachronisms.

In addition, dematerialization shapes the ways that religion and culture have been distinguished. As in many other postcolonial nations, the political and institutional task of sorting out custom and religion (Indonesian, *agama*) still governs the cultural politics of outer-island Indonesia today.[21] The ethnographic literature has increased in scope and, one hopes, sophistication, but in many societies the fundamental categories of practical action have changed little. The irony is only slightly lessened, in the postcolonial context, by the fact that the concept of animism—which in Tylor's hands arose from a project meant to fold religion within culture—was, in

21. See, for instance, Aragon 2000; Kipp 1990; Kipp and Rodgers 1987; Rodgers 1981; Rutherford 2003; Spyer 2000. The issues arise in somewhat different ways for Muslims; see Bowen 2003.

the mission field, often placed in the service of an overarching religion to which culture would become subordinate. The idea of animism was to help separate that which is religious, hence universal, from the cultural, hence particular. In the context of this semiotic ideology, the distinction is also one between religion as the domain of immaterial beliefs, and culture as the domain of concrete expressions. The localization of religion would thus mean the subordination of cultural forms as merely the particular vehicles for universal but abstract meanings—they would be more or less arbitrary signifiers for signifieds of ultimate significance.

It may be that the Calvinist theological project in its various forms was shielded from some of the potentially destructive implications of Tylorian anthropology by stressing a certain semiotic ideology. This ideology drew a sharp distinction between signs and the things of which they are signs, between expressions of belief which are found in the material world shared with the scientist, and the beliefs themselves, which are not. By dematerializing religion, the missionaries may (however unwittingly) have been saving both their own claims to rationality and their faith. In the process, they contributed to the semiotic distinctions that underwrote the ongoing effort to define and distinguish the specific domain of the cultural. To the extent that the concept of religion continues to presuppose these distinctions, it remains, at least in part, an heir to this Victorian project and its troubles.

Each mission field created scenes of encounter in which concepts such as religion and culture were found useful or reformulated, given practical form, and challenged. Cumulatively over the nineteenth and twentieth centuries, these scenes contributed to the emerging portrayal of modernity and to the terms by which those who were viewed as nonmoderns were to be understood—and often understood themselves. In the historical context in which the Indies were missionized, the possibility of conversion seems to have depended on a semiotic ideology to a large extent shared by Protestants and proponents of more secular modernities. By taking the material forms of speech and practice to operate at a subordinate realm distinct from that of more abstract meanings and intentions, missionaries could hope to separate out religion from culture. They could also hope to foster local adaptations of Christianity without serious consequences. That is, regardless of their external form, local Christianities would retain their inner essence and, so abstracted, remain immune to history. Yet, of course, they could not—at least from the mundane perspective from which this book must be written—remain immune to history.

4   Conversion's Histories

It may perhaps be censured as an impertinent criticism, . . .
to find fault with words and names that have obtained in
the world; and yet possibly it may not be amiss to offer new
ones when the old are apt to lead men into mistakes.

JOHN LOCKE, *The Second Treatise of Government*,
chapter 6, paragraph 52

[T]he beginner . . . has assimilated the spirit of the new
language and can produce freely in it only when he moves
in it without remembering the old and forgets in it his
ancestral tongue.

KARL MARX, "The Eighteenth Brumaire of Louis Bonaparte"

Even for those who insist that divine truth is eternal, radical conversion can
foster a heightened sense of history. But this sense of history can take as
many forms as there are kinds of Christianity. Some people, like Urapmin
Pentecostalists, may experience the rush of events as a "sloping temporal
order in which people are forever pitched forward" (Robbins 2004a: 164).
That rush may be bearing them to the imminent end of time itself (Schieffelin 2002: S5). Others may constantly seek evidence in the world around
them of the eternal iteration of biblical events (Crapanzano 2000; Frei
1974; Harding 2000). Converts may identify the temporality of individual
transformation with that of whole societies, or sharply distinguish the two
(Meyer 1998). In this chapter I look at some problems that arise concerning the strong sense of historical agency that is common to many projects
of proselytization. As T. O. Beidelman observes, "Missionary views about
the process of conversion ultimately amount to a theory of social change"
(1982: 16). More forcefully, in many cases missionaries and converts alike
have been endowed with "a sense of the portentous, a heroic sense of making history—of precipitating *events*" (Errington and Gewertz 1995: 108).

Epigraphs: John Locke, *The Second Treatise of Government,* ed. with introduction
by Thomas P. Peardon (Indianapolis: Bobbs-Merrill, 1952), p. 30; Karl Marx, The
Eighteenth Brumaire of Louis Bonaparte, in *The Marx-Engels Reader,* ed. Robert C.
Tucker, 2nd ed. (New York: W. W. Norton, 1978), 595.

For many evangelists, these are events whose outcome is supposed to change the very nature of history itself, they are "a contest," as J. D. Y. Peel writes of British missionaries' efforts among the Yoruba, "between rival narratives or schemes for how individuals and communities should project themselves in time" (1995: 600). Perhaps the sharpest sense of urgency is that of the premillennialist, since, as one missionary in Papua New Guinea stated to his followers, "neither you nor they will have long to remain" (quoted in Schieffelin 2002: S5).

By "sense of history" here, I refer primarily to perceived transitions between past, present, and future. It involves questions about the kinds of agent that produce or hinder transition, about the continuities or ruptures that result from their actions, and about the projected future. The sense of history, however, is not a matter of imagination or memory in the abstract. It is produced through concrete practices, texts, and material things whose historical implications—the conclusions people draw from them and the actions they encourage or inhibit—depend on specific semiotic ideologies. Therefore, in this chapter I move from broader questions about the sense of historical transition to more specific ones about how perceptions of continuity and rupture are mediated by semiotic ideologies. In the chapter that follows it, I turn to the conversion of one Sumbanese elder whom I call Umbu Neka, to show some of the paradoxical effects of his discursive efforts to ensure continuity in some domains and effect transformation in others.

In the previous chapter, we saw that attempts to distinguish between religion and culture could end up seeking in culture something of value that persists after people have taken on the new religion. But to the extent that culture is understood in terms of the persistence of the past, it can also remain a source of trouble. Missionization is often seen as an effort to wrest individuals from particular social worlds in order to cast them—or entire societies—into a translocal community of coreligionists. Even ethnically identified churches usually see themselves, in some sense, as part of a larger order of the faithful. This has consequences for the individuals' location in time as well as space. As the West African theologian Lamin Sanneh writes, "[P]articular Christian translation projects have helped to create an overarching series of cultural experiences, with hitherto obscure cultural systems being thrust into the general stream of universal history" (1989: 2). Sanneh's words, with their echo of Hegel, seem to portray culture as a site of particularity that it is the work of history to overcome. Theologically viewed, history may be universal because it culminates in salvation. But Sanneh is also pointing to a more mundane dimension to the story, religious globalization. And indeed, as we have seen above, Christians in places like Indonesia, Melanesia, and West Africa are learning to place themselves in a history that includes ancient Israel, as well as, in many cases, the national homeland of those who missionized them.[1] I have already suggested that people have often found Christianity's power to lie in its apparent placelessness. They may also discover in Christianity a way to enter into a vastly expanded historical narrative.

But in many places this triumphalist understanding of history is chronically threatened by the habits, ideas, and values associated with "local culture," a threat that may provoke renewed efforts at semiotic purification. In this chapter, I discuss some of the dilemmas posed for Christians when they wrestle with what looks like the stubborn persistence of a non-Christian past. I suggest in particular that some dilemmas emerge from certain narratives of modernity and their constructions of the idea of historical agency and from the disappointments this idea can produce. For if conversion has historical implications, then history has moral implications. Thus we may expect to find parallel dilemmas facing other people who are committed to exercising historical agency in quite different, nonreligious, contexts. The dilemmas reflect the convergence of the challenges posed by the persistence of the past for religious converts, with the moral narrative of modernity. To illustrate this point, I start with a discussion of Dipesh Chakrabarty's reading, within a postcolonial context, of some of Karl Marx's remarks about history. I then juxtapose that discussion with the way the past and future are presented in Dutch missionary writing. The juxtaposition is meant to bring out some dimensions of the question of historical agency: Who can change the world? How does the past impose itself on our ability to change the world? How can we know that the past does not actually persist, in some different guise, and that the world has not changed after all?

The persistence of the past, of course, presses on the living from all sorts of directions and in any number of ways, from economics to institutions,

---

1. In the 1990s, Sumbanese Christians asked me about the Israel that appears in news reports, puzzled since they knew that the Israelites of the Old Testament had long since become Christian. A photo of the teacher-training school on Sumba in the 1920s shows the walls covered with maps of the eastern Mediterranean (Krijger 1927: 148). Both cases suggest ways in which the lands of the Bible are becoming part of the Sumbanese imaginary. It may be an example of the absurdity of colonialism that textbooks in colonial West Africa taught: "Our ancestors were the Gauls." But surely the absurdity lies less in the spurious nature of the genealogy than in the denial of citizenship. After all, generations of upper-class British public school boys were, in effect, taught that *their* ancestors were the Greeks and Romans, and they seem to have made the most of it.

from kinship roles to bodily habits, from technology to architecture. But religious transformation poses special challenges. For example, how exactly do invisible beings such as ancestral spirits—or demons—actually persist? Or conversely, how do we know they have been vanquished? The effort to grapple with these questions can be especially revealing of the semiotic ideologies on which people draw. Part 2 of this book explores this claim in detail. But first, in the last section of this chapter, I sketch out some of the relevant dimensions of the problem by drawing on recent accounts of Christianity's encounter with pre-Christian spirits in four contexts: Spanish Catholicism in the early colonial Americas and in the colonial Philippines, the Salvation Army's Methodism in twentieth-century highland Indonesia, and Pentecostalism in contemporary Ghana. These sketches will show some of the effects that differences of semiotic ideology can have on people's perceptions of historical transition and its possible agents.

A NIGHTMARE ON THE BRAIN OF THE LIVING

Historical imaginations face toward both the past and the future. The dilemma that the past may pose for the future is famously captured by Marx's remark in "The Eighteenth Brumaire": "The tradition of all the dead generations weighs like a nightmare on the brain of the living" (Marx 1964: 595). Chakrabarty proposes that this claim has a specifically modern character, which he points to by asking, "[W]hy 'nightmare'?" (2000: 245). The answer, he says, lies in one strand running through Enlightenment understandings of freedom. This is the idea that political freedom requires the exercise of reason. If this is so, the persistence of tradition, taken to be rooted in the contingent past and not in reason, seems (at least for the Indian intellectuals of whom Chakrabarty writes) to challenge the very possibilities of freedom itself. For tradition seems to stand in the way of the full exercise of reason.[2] This is one inflection of the moral narrative of modernity as the emergence of human autonomy.

2. Chakrabarty identifies this position with Locke. More exactly, Locke writes that even the free agent is subject to the law, which guides the free agent to "his proper interest." But one is subject to the law only by virtue of being able to understand it through reason: "Thus we are born free as we are born rational" (1952: 32). This is why children must be guided by their parents until they reach the age of reason, an idea whose echoes are surely heard in later colonial and postcolonial forms of governance.

According to Chakrabarty, this understanding of freedom creates an impasse because "the new can be imagined and expressed only through a language made out of the languages already available. Political action is thus loaded with the risk that what was meant to be a break from the past . . . could end up looking like a return of the dead" (2000: 245).[3] The persistence of language from the past does not necessarily mean that one's actions are wholly determined by the past, nor need it lead to a call for complete rupture from it. Rather, it suggests that one cannot know in advance and for certain how much power the language of the past will continue to exert over one's actions in the present. This is, in part, a function of semiotic ideology. As I noted at the end of chapter 2, when people act, they necessarily do so by means of particular semiotic forms. Since those semiotic forms circulate in public, they bear the marks of their social embeddedness and historical depth. The very materiality of those publicly circulating semiotic forms can seem (depending on one's assumptions) to be the vehicle for social constraints on one's freedom of action. The more one thinks true agency depends on autonomy, the more the existing semiotic forms may seem to undermine that autonomy and threaten one's agency. Hence the sense of paradox to which Judith Butler refers, in the passage I quoted in the introduction—the sense of paradox that arises if one's agency depends upon discourse one has not chosen (1997: 2). And to the extent that concrete semiotic forms are thought to serve the experience of external constraint, then it is likely that freedom will seem to demand more transparency and greater abstraction. In some cases, materiality itself may seem to be part of the problem.

One question that may then arise is, Why should "the languages already available" be identified with social constraint and the persistent past? Could they not instead reflect one's moral obligations to coevals or to eternal truth? Or might they reveal the resistance offered by spirits, or the innate limitations of humans as actors in the face of natural or historical determinations? To answer this, I draw on Chakrabarty's account of the idea of anachronism, because it brings out some revealing parallels between the universal history told by the progressive, on the one hand, and by the Christian proselytizer, on the other.

3. But however this may be a problem for Indian readers of Marx, according to "The Eighteenth Brumaire" itself, once the bourgeois revolution succeeded, it could put away the Roman costumes it had worn. The implication seems to be that, in the case of successful revolution, the haunting of the past will turn out to have been only so much stagecraft. I thank Sonja Luehrmann for pointing this out to me.

Chakrabarty argues that there is a fundamental contradiction between the universalizing pretensions of progressivist thought and its parochial origins in the European Enlightenment. The contradiction becomes especially apparent in the postcolonial world, where the progressivist intellectual confronts "radical heterogeneity" (2000: 46), in the form of local social realities that cannot be fitted into any overarching narrative of modernity without doing some violence to those realities. In the South Asian world of which Chakrabarty writes, Marx's "dead generations" of the past" would include such things as the power of kinship structures, certain oral traditions, social hierarchies of birth, nonmonetary forms of exchange, personalistic modes of domination, and even purportedly obsolete medical and agricultural techniques. But it is not these to which Chakrabarty primarily directs his attention, for the difficulties posed by the past for the future are perhaps most sharply embodied in the form of communities for whom the gods and spirits, who are supposed to have been banished from modernity, are real. The existence of people who include nonhumans among the agents in their world can seem especially threatening to the modern idea of agency. Viewed within the narrative of modern progress, he suggests, the existence of such people can only be understood as anachronistic. They cannot in any serious sense be our coevals. In Chakrabarty's view, anachronism is a particular mode of objectification that is produced by modern historical consciousness, a denial of the contemporaneity of those whom this consciousness sees as irrational (2000: 238–39). Anachronism, in this sense, bears echoes of the Tylorian view of culture discussed in the previous chapter, in its nonrational character and potential to remain in the form of survivals. Modes of agency and kinds of temporality that are at variance with those of modernity may have a past, but, it would seem, they have no future.

Chakrabarty's reading of Marx implies that an understanding of history as progress hinges on assumptions about the nature of agency (for instance, it demands at least a degree of autonomy from custom) and about who really exercises it (humans, not gods). Given these assumptions about agency, then religion, or at least the kinds of religion that have not been subject to purification, can pose fundamental challenges to one's hopes for progress. But the intuition of living within a universal forward-looking movement through time is not confined to European philosophy, progressivist politics, academic history, or the propagandists of modernity. As Sanneh's words quoted above might suggest, religious proselytization may end up drawing on a basic narrative structure similar to that of the secular progressive, in which human actions contribute to an ever more universal history.[4] In the next section, I bring out a few aspects of history as it has been portrayed by Dutch Calvinist missionaries. I then briefly juxtapose work done in four other mission fields in order to show some ways in which the persistence of gods and spirits can confound the historical progress implied by radical conversion.

"ONE DOES NOT FORGET, THE WORK IS SO HARD!"

In 1896, the Middelburg Synod of the neo-orthodox Reformed Churches in the Netherlands called for a mission to the island of Sumba, under the direction of the Mission of the Reformed Churches in the Netherlands (Zending der Gereformeerde Kerken in Nederland). Over the course of the nineteenth century, a number of European and American mission societies had been established independently of particular congregations or even denominations. But the Reformed Churches rejected this model on the grounds that it had no scriptural precedent, and that the apostolic mission—and by implication, Christ's agency as the first evangelist—was transmitted legitimately only through churches. Therefore, the Zending der Gereformeerde Kerken in Nederland sought out specific congregations to sponsor each particular mission field, and in 1902 the incipient mission project was placed in the hands of the three northeastern provinces of Groningen, Drenthe, and Overijssel, who soon afterward send out their first resident missionary. In later years, the dates of these two foundational events (understood within the chronological conventions familiar in secular European contexts) provided occasions for the missionaries and their supporters to publish books of retrospection and self-questioning. A brief comparison between two books, *Tot Dankbaarheid Genoopt* (*Compelled to Thankfulness*, Meijering et al. 1927) and *De Zending Voorbij* (*Beyond the*

---

4. This certainly does not mean that a religious and secular history will always recognize the same events as relevant or even as events. They also impose their own frames of relevance on historical narrative. One of the most traumatic events in twentieth-century Indonesian history was the massacre and terror that swept Suharto's New Order regime to power in 1965–1966. Although these events were relatively muted in Sumba, there was some violence and certainly much fear, and Christians were in the thick of it. But in the history of the Catholic parish of Waingapu, East Sumba (Waingapu 1978), one reads only of baptisms and the ordination of a new pastor. Even under the self-censoring conditions of the period when this was written, this is a striking omission.

Mission, van Halsema et al. 1995), is illuminating.[5] On the one hand, they concerned the same project, the Sumba mission of the northeastern provinces. They were insider perspectives, written by and about the participants for a very small audience in a closely engaged community—mostly contributors to the mission—to whom the story matters quite directly. The tone of address to the reader is relatively intimate and at times exhortatory. On the other hand, the books were produced at two distinct historical moments (one in the heyday of Dutch colonial power in the Indies, the other forty years after Indonesian independence) and express different visions of the mission, in different situations for the Protestant communities they describe. Yet they both display a struggle between the secularist time presupposed by the canonical forms of history-writing, and the divine narrative implicit in their project of evangelization.

In 1927, the Zending der Gereformeerde Kerken in Nederland's mission to Sumba had little to show for its efforts. For an island of perhaps two hundred thousand, there were four mission posts and a mission school population of, at most, two thousand. In the introduction, the tone of the writing is somewhat defensive. After giving these figures, the missionary, speaking in a distinctively Dutch voice, remarks, "But luckily the friends of our mission are still not affected by the American spirit of the 'biggest' library, the 'biggest' building, the 'biggest' city, the 'biggest' ship. They are less susceptible to the enchantment of numbers. They know that faith and patience are needed, and can wait for God to give the kingdom growth in His time" (Colijn 1927: 12).

The invocation of divine time is reinforced with that of divine agency: Theirs "is the ploughing, the sowing, the irrigating and the weeding; God himself gives the growth" (Colijn 1927: 12).[6] Yet "one does not forget, the work is so hard!" and so the question arises, Would it make more sense to concentrate the mission's forces elsewhere? In contrast to Sumba, where the population is thin, scattered, and linguistically fragmented, Java is

5. Peter van Rooden has pointed out to me (personal communication) that the more recent title is perhaps purposely ambiguous, since *De Zending Voorbij* can also be translated as "The Mission Is Over."

6. The allusion is to 1 Corinthians 3, but the imagery of irrigation and the need for divine agency is overdetermined in a place as drought-prone as Sumba. A booklet published on the twenty-fifth anniversary of a Roman Catholic parish on the island was titled *Waingapu from Desert Path to Path of Life*. References in the text to a desert brought to bloom similarly spoke of humans as tools in God's hand (Waingapu 1978: 3). Many missionaries and other visitors often commented on the resemblance between the arid plains of east Sumba and their pastoralists, and the lands and people of the Old Testament.

large, densely populated, and linguistically unified. In response to practical considerations, the author again subordinates human to divine agency:

> [O]n examination, we have not *chosen* our mission field. It was dealt to us. It was God's scheme that conveyed us to Central Java. It was His scheme too that led us to Sumba. Were one to set down and calculate, carefully to compare the pros and cons, setting the burdens and difficulties against one another beforehand, and make a choice, one would lose one's enthusiasm before even one missionary was sent out to his work.
> We *are* on Java.
> We *are* on Sumba.
> We are called by God to work there with all our faith. (Colijn 1927: 12–13, emphases in the original)

This movement between divine and human agency may reflect immediate frustrations, but it does so in ways that recall Calvinism's doctrinal distinctions (noted in chapter 2) between the more distant determinism of predestination and the more immediate tasks that fall under providence. The doctrine of predestination ultimately does not allow humans to decline the tasks to which they have been divinely assigned. Yet there are clear limits to the efficacy of human action, and in a stubborn case like Sumba more rhetorical support for the faith, at the very least, is needed. Faced with so much frustration and difficulty, the Zending der Gereformeerde Kerken in Nederland and its supporters had to be reminded that divine agency works on a divine scale of time: "Christendom was already known in our own land at the time of the Roman empire. Already by the year 300, Trier and Keulen were bishops' seats. Servaas preached 50 years later in the area of Maastricht. A good 250 years after that, work began among the Frisians, and still, some 150 years further on, Bonifacius was murdered at Dokkum by the *heathen* Frisians" (Colijn 1927: 13, emphasis in the original).

The reference to the early missionization of the Lowlanders is exemplary in several respects. It vastly expands the scale of time in order to assist in the displacement of agency from those most immediately concerned: "If our zest for labor were only to endure so that we could behold the ripe fruit of our work ourselves, then there would not be much zest for work left. The apostles beheld only the rudiments of the fruit of their work, and we too work not for the immediate outcome, but in obedience to the command to propagate the Gospel of the Kingdom to all the world" (Colijn 1927: 13). The answer to the frustrations of the moment and the call of practicality is a vast expansion of time, of space (all the world), and of agency (divine and human). This expansion of the most relevant context depends, moreover, on the tacit work of analogy built into the very presuppositions of the evangelizing mission. We are like the early apostles. Moreover, the Sumbanese are like our own ancestors, our past is their present—but, mutatis mutandis, our present is their future. So, were logic to trump politics, once Protestant the Sumbanese should be like us. It is precisely this problem that becomes a quandary for the postcolonial church, as expressed in the second of the mission histories.

Bearing the telling title *Beyond the Mission*, the second volume was devoted primarily to the period after 1942, when Japanese occupation brought an end to direct Dutch control and led to the creation of the autonomous Christian Church of Sumba (Gereja Kristen Sumba). The authors wrestle with the church's history, viewed from the more ecumenical and this-worldly orientation of their time. At the heart of the problems they faced was the "growing need for the revising of the missionary task, or rather, the missionary shape of the church" (van Halsema et al. 1995: vii).

The problem is both practical and conceptual. In practical terms, after the Japanese occupation the Sumbanese church was never again formally under foreign control. Yet, given their ongoing close personal, institutional, and financial ties, the question persisted, What now should be the relationship between the Dutch and Sumbanese Protestants? As in the earlier commemoration book, the effort returns to the first apostles and to early efforts to shape the church as an evangelizing movement to convert foreign peoples. Given this defining background, the book asks, what is the church if not missionary? More specifically, how is the church of the 1990s to deal with its colonial past? The book begins with a military metaphor and ends with extensive quotations from a West African theologian. The militancy of the early mission is captured by a hymn sung at mission gatherings:

THE SUMBA SONG
Close the ranks, oh you churches of the North
Eyes on the King, who leads His hosts
Fight for His Kingdom and bear witness resolutely
Of His mercy and His majesty!
Sumba shall shout for Christ the King:
"Glory be to Christ *my* King!"[7]

This was the cry of a stern church born in the nineteenth-century reaction against the liberalization of the Dutch Reformed Church. Its leader, Abraham Kuyper (see chapter 3), setting himself against humanism, laid out an explicitly theocentric principle for missions of the Reformed Churches. On

7. Van der Kooi 1987: 329, emphasis in the original.

that principle, the most important motive for the Zending der Gereformeerde Kerken in Nederland would be glorification of and obedience to God, to which other goals, such as education, technological development, and health care, had to be subordinate. According to the theocentric principle, all other religions were falsifications of revelation, and forms of superstition and idolatry (Reenders 1995: 6). At the same time, in accordance with the extremely localistic insistence on congregational autonomy that marked the neo-orthodox Reformed Churches, Kuyper insisted that the new churches should stand directly under Lord Jesus and not be subordinated to the mission church that had founded them. It followed, moreover, that Western forms of liturgy should not be imposed on local churches (van Halsema 1995: 7–8). The point is exemplified in "The Sumba Song," which ends with Sumba itself shouting for Christ. But notice that two other agents are implied in the earlier lines, the Dutch "churches of the North" (that is, Groningen, Drenthe, and Overijssel) and "Christ the King." Only after the combined action of these two would the Sumbanese themselves come into their own. In the context of this hymn, the churches are the self-addressed first person, the Sumbanese a distant object of third-person reference.

More generally, the two principles, of unique revelation and local autonomy, did not sit well together. The contradiction concerns the nature of locality and its relations both to the universal-truth claims of the church and to the globalizing history implicit in the project of evangelization. In practice, given the risk that locals would distort the message (as the mission church understood it), the presumed demands of revelation tended to win out over the principle of local autonomy.

Although the Dutch were unable during the colonial era to bring themselves to grant even modest forms of autonomy to Sumbanese congregations, they did continually wrestle with localization in the form of cultural accommodation.[8] One of the main ways in which the universal church and local culture were to be reconciled, as I discussed in the previous chapter, was through the idea that cultures are distinct from religions and, thus, consist of mostly permissible practices, in contrast to the forbidden ones of false religion. In many cases, moreover, the essence of culture came to be seen as lying at the level of meanings. This meant that the particular concrete forms

8. Even this effort was one-sided. As the Sumbanese theologian F. D. Wellem remarks, he was unable to find a single writing by a Sumbanese in his search through the mission journals (2004: 7). The linguist and Bible translator Louis Onvlee did work closely with the Sumbanese nobleman Umbu Hina Kapita, but Kapita (1965, 1976a, 1976b) did not really begin his own publishing career till after the Dutch colonial period had ended.

those meanings took might turn out to be not essential. The same meanings could take different forms. In such a view, the concrete semiotic forms identified with culture existed at a plane distinct from the more abstract meanings they express.[9] Once those meanings were identified, such as verbal references to "cool water" and the practices they referred to (such as sprinkling water in rites to "cool" the effects of transgression), they could be used to convey more general meanings, like "blessing," "salvation," and "good" (an issue to which I return in part 2). In different cultural contexts, then, these "same" meanings could be translated into other words and other practices. Such meanings as this allow the calibration across cultural differences that makes translation possible. Under the right conditions, this semiotic ideology can lend support to a particular sense of history. For if the quest for appropriate local forms suggests that multiple localities may have passed through multiple histories, the ultimate outcome of those histories—and their very translatability—tends toward a unified narrative. In this respect, of course, the evangelizing mission participates in the universal histories of the nineteenth-century European imaginary associated with nationalism and progress. But it does so in distinctive ways.

"THE DECEASED DO NOT RETURN"

By the end of the twentieth century, the theocentric motive had been played down by many of those associated with the Dutch mission to Sumba in favor of education, health care, economic and technological development, women's rights, and the promotion of democratic institutions (Vel 1994). Yet the same fundamental problems persist: the urge to respect and preserve local forms and the underlying values they express, working against the more general demands of progress. In this light, it would seem that missionaries face a problem similar to that faced by the progressive historians described by Chakrabarty above. In both cases, self-conscious agents of social transformation grapple with underlying contradictions between the universal presuppositions of progress and respect for the self-determination of local subjects (who may not only remain "anachronistic" but even reject the kinds of agency presupposed by that very principle of self-determination).

9. Notice that this can find support in the older tradition of iconoclasm, which I mentioned in chapter 2. As Hans Belting (1994) shows, one outcome of iconoclasm was a reconceptualization of images as signs of invisible beings instead of material presences in their own right.

Beyond the Mission attempts to reconcile the two principles of progress and local self-determination through a striking interpretation of local agency. Sumbanese Protestants exercise their agency through the creation of the "new village" *(paraingu bidi)*.[10]

> Contextualization [of Christianity manifests] itself as a reconstruction of the *paraingu* (village). That is itself not a restoration; the deceased do not return, and now other men live in the *paraingu* and other customs hold. The *paraingu*—and therewith the church of Sumba—is once and for all a part of a larger context, that of Indonesia, and again of Asia. . . . But as a *paraingu bidi*, the church of Sumba has become part of a worldwide *paraingu bidi* of churches and Christians, and its history has been inserted into a worldwide history in which from its beginning the names of Abraham, Isaac, and Jacob, Sara, Rebecca, and Rachel were recalled and which culminated in the history of Jesus Christ. . . . With this too it comes about that their own history is tested by that of others, who also were tested by the history from Abraham to Christ.
> (Holtrop and Vel 1995: 246, italics and parentheses in the original)

"The deceased do not return." With this remark, the late-twentieth-century concern with the localization of Christianity and the value of local cultures is meshed with a distinct sense of evangelical victory. This sense of unidirectionality is a leitmotif in mainstream evangelism, expressed by a different author in the same volume: "We can never, after Pentecost, go back to life and culture that is untouched by the Holy Ghost" (van Halsema 1995: 93). In the context of a historical retrospection, this is a striking conflation of mundane and divine temporalities.

But linear time is not necessarily secular time, and both mundane and divine histories, in this view, are unidirectional. And both may have to contend with threats. In the case of mundane history, the threats arise from the continued existence of anachronisms. In the case of divine temporality, the threats may not be anachronisms but rather personal backsliding and social regression to renewed interactions with pre-Christian spirits. The historical logic is perhaps best exemplified by Joel Robbins's observation drawn from his research with Pentecostals in New Guinea: the Urapmin people are still

---

10. The use of this very expression, a coinage in Kambera, the major language of East Sumba, already exerts pressure on Sumbanese semantics. *Paraingu* usually refers to a village with deep ancestral roots. A paraingu is distinguished from, and in certain ways granted higher status than, other kinds of settlements, such as satellite villages, garden hamlets, or market towns, by the marks of that historical depth, such as stone tombs, named house sites, inalienable valuables, and altars (see Forth 1981; Kapita 1976a, Keane 1997c). In this contrastive set, paraingu is defined precisely by *not* being new.

tempted to sacrifice to nature spirits, but they know this is sin. The reason is that any *present-day* sacrifice in effect denies the fact that Jesus Christ was the *final* sacrifice (2004a: 180). Despite the differences between Calvinist and Pentecostal views, there is an important similarity. In both cases, it is not secular rationality or progressive politics that creates linear history and the sense of anachronism, it is theology. Yet the result converges with, and may in the event become hard to distinguish from, the unidirectionality usually identified with secular time (see, for example, Anderson 1983).

The remark "the deceased do not return" conveys a powerful sense of the pastness of the past. It portrays any alternative to Protestant Christianity—including that represented by the large number of unconverted Sumbanese—as anachronism, if not eventually impossible altogether. But the victory is not merely that of the Dutch missionary over the local forces of paganism. It is portrayed as a victory for *local* agency. The late-twentieth-century Dutch writers set themselves apart from the earlier missionaries in their self-conscious rejection of the colonial ethos. Moreover, they seem to have found a solution to the problem of the denial of coevalness: Dutch and Sumbanese converge in a Christian future. There is an overarching history, that of the faith, into which all other histories can be absorbed. Sumbanese find their place within a larger historical narrative by taking charge of their own world, wresting it from the dead hand of the past. Sumbanese paganism is of the past, as are all paganisms sooner or later: they belong to the deceased. It is the "other men," those who now live in Sumba, who actively join the universal history of the church. The act of acknowledging the agency of Sumbanese is inseparable from the triumphalist narrative of Christianization.

But this acknowledgment depends on rendering the dead generations truly dead. This depends on silencing the languages they have bequeathed to the living, or, rather, it depends on confining them to the cultural domain that one is enjoined to respect and even preserve. Obviously this is no simple matter. For instance, conversion must be sincere. What does this mean? I discuss the concept and practices of sincerity in detail in part 2 of this book. But for the moment, we can assume that sincere conversion involves at least the expectation that the convert must be the proximate agent of her or his own conversion, even if the ultimate agent is God. One corollary of this expectation is that the words by which converts commit themselves must reveal their inner intentions. The writers of the more recent of the two memoirs, *Beyond the Mission*, are acutely aware of the complexities this involves. They report that in 1987, for instance, the leaders of a middle school in the central Sumbanese district of Lawonda determined that all children must have a religion, one of the five legally recognized by the Indonesian state, in order to graduate. In practical terms, in this district, this could only be the Gereja Kristen Sumba. The church's rules for the baptism of children hold that the parents must answer the catechismal questions at baptism on their behalf. But if those parents are marapu followers, they cannot take responsibility for their children. So in this case the schoolchildren were simply asked to declare themselves, and, seeing that they had no option, twenty new members entered the Gereja Kristen Sumba on a single Sunday (Holtrop and Vel 1995: 233). The Dutch authors comment that it is not for them, but for the Sumbanese, to say how they should regulate church admission. And Sumbanese agency in this matter is determined by distinct sociocultural principles: as the authors observe, "[I]f we compare Sumbanese society to the Dutch, one of the more notable differences is that individualism is greater in the Netherlands than in Sumba. In Sumbanese social organization one is always, first of all, part of a certain group, . . . and any new undertaking is up to the elders" (Holtrop and Vel 1995: 234).

Yet, Holtrop and Vel add that this says nothing about the religious aspect of the converts' motives, and they point out that church membership has direct consequences for the relative positions of local political factions. The authors' circumspect regard for the autonomy of Sumbanese agency and for local cultural values sits uncomfortably with their hopes that the individual conversions will be sincere. This is a familiar question across the postcolonial world. But there is another aspect to consider, the implications for histories of the future and the persistence of the past. If these children were not fully free in their decision to enter the church, there is no guarantee that their conversion was sincere. Perhaps their baptism was mere form and underneath they remain followers of the marapu. If this is so, how can we know, in the end, that the spirits of the dead do not persist after all? If the children speak like Christians, might this turn out to mean that the marapu live on for them, even in their words but under different names?[11] How do we know that Christian words or Christian acts really express a Christian spirit? The problem of transformation and persistence turns out to be thoroughly entangled with that of translation.

On the one hand, then, the conversion of Sumba takes its place as one instance of what seems in the end to be a unitary and ultimately irresistible (but hardly secular) history into which all histories will flow. If this is the case, anything that resists will indeed be, in Chakrabarty's terms, mere

11. Note that this is the reverse of the argument many Sumbanese evangelists make, that ritual couplets and other words traditionally thought to refer to marapu actually refer to God (see chapter 3).

anachronism. On the other hand, unlike other universal histories, Holtrop and Vel's reference to the *paraingu bidi* celebrates not the relentless external forces of divine intervention (or at least not this alone), and not materialist determination, but rather immediate human agency. And this agency is manifested both in historical transformations and in the persistence of local identity, both in the newness of the reconstructed *paraingu* and in the insistence that, in the end, the result remains Sumbanese.

But what does it mean to say that the future remains Sumbanese? And how, in concrete terms, does such an understanding of history become, for Sumbanese Protestant Christians at least, a possible way of acting in the world? My interest is in all the work that goes into cobbling together that narrative of victory, all that seems to remain beyond it, and the material, semiotic, and practical conditions for both. In the case of religious conversion, these questions tend to bear on the problem of what to make of the persistence and disappearance of agents that had once been powerful in people's lives.

Joel Robbins remarks that there has been a strong tendency among anthropologists, when writing about religious conversion, to emphasize "localization, indigenization, and syncretism" (2003: 221). And indeed, a leitmotif runs through anthropological writing about colonial and postcolonial Christian communities, stating that the image of a past lives on in disguise, at a depth, or under translation; that past spirits continue, "[h]idden under the surface of village Christianity" (Barker 1990: 8); and that what has developed is "split-level" religion (Whiteman 1983: 345). Robbins suggests the anthropologists' emphasis on continuity is due to a general professional bias built into the very concept of culture, since it assumes people can see the world only through received categories. Although several decades of anthropological debates have shaken the dominance of that concept of culture within the profession, the older view does cast a long shadow. And this emphasis on continuities is not restricted to anthropologists. As I have suggested, the concept of culture that became common among missionaries stressed persistence. And one common mission strategy was to foster some sense of cultural continuity, even amid religious transformation.

But then missionaries and converts, as well as other interested parties such as development agencies and government officials, are faced with potentially enormous difficulties: do apparently innocent social or cultural forms smuggle spirits or demons from the past into the present? Given this question, not all religious groups accept the innocence of existing social or cultural forms. Ghanaian Pentecostals, for instance, adamantly reject the state's call to celebrate "cultural heritage," since that heritage is inseparable from demonic spirits (Meyer 1998). All sorts of new rituals, currencies, narratives, clothing styles, food prohibitions, architectural styles, domestic arrangements, and other forms and practices can help sharpen the sense of discontinuity in time, creating a clear boundary between then and now (see Comaroff and Comaroff 1991, 1997). As Bambi Schieffelin (2000, 2002) has shown in research with American fundamentalist missionaries and their converts, the process of conversion can introduce new speech genres, grammatical and lexical innovations, and even patterns of verbal interaction. In the situation she analyzes, these changes reinforce the fundamentalist sense of time at several levels. They help reinforce both the punctate divisions of clock and calendar, and an overarching sense of history built on sharp oppositions between ignorant past and enlightened present, and between present decisions and the millennial future. Through alterations that saturate everyday talk, speakers are inculcated with new temporal sensibilities (compare Hoskins 1993).

The persistence of the spirits is hardly the only issue that Christians face, but it does bring to the fore some of the problems posed by existing semiotic materials for those who attempt to act upon history. As Robbins remarks, "[J]udgments of continuity tend to depend on underlying judgments of similarity" (2003: 228). The same could be said for judgments of discontinuity. In either case, such judgments are guided by semiotic ideologies, which determine the words, actions, institutions, and objects that will count as "the same" and as "different." As Chakrabarty suggests, it is in the languages—meant both figuratively and literally—which the deceased gave to the living that they *do* threaten to return.

TRANSLATING ANACHRONISM

Religious proselytizing and reform movements raise some basic questions about historical change and its agents: Are the dead still among us? If so, in what particular shapes are they manifest? How do they impinge on our actions and on the future toward which our actions aim? Is their presence among us benign or not? There is, of course, as much variation in how missionaries and converts understand the past and present as there are denominations. Although many missions seek threads of cultural continuity, Pentecostalism emphasizes the sense of rupture from the past (Engelke 2004a; Meyer 1998; Robbins 2004a). It is surely relevant that Pentecostalism also takes the reality, and thus the threat, of those spirits, who are now believed to have in fact been agents of Satan, more seriously that many of the denominations that encourage cultural continuity. But the need for religious evangelists and reformers to come to terms with at least one aspect of the past—tradition—has presented itself across a wide range of circumstances. Protestant groups, for example, usually distinguish themselves markedly from Roman Catholicism and Eastern Orthodoxy in their views of tradition. The difference hearkens back to Luther's doctrine of *sola scriptura*, which maintained that the Bible is the only doctrinal authority, unmediated either by tradition or the teachings of the church. But Christian conversion has raised questions about the status of tradition since Saint Paul preached to the Gentiles, who had not previously been governed by Mosaic law. A key text for subsequent discussions is Saint Paul's Romans 2:14: "For when the Gentiles, which have not the law, do by nature the things contained in the law, these, having not the law, are a law unto themselves." On the one hand, Jewish law still applied to those who had been circumcised prior to their conversion to the new moral order. On the other hand, the concept of grace made the universal truth of Christianity available to Gentiles without requiring them to adhere to Mosaic law.

The distinction leads to theological debates that go far beyond the scope of this book. Here I simply want to observe that, to the extent that religious authority draws on concepts of revelation, practices of proselytization, or individual conversion experiences, it may find tradition to be a problem that requires some kind of solution. Variations on the problem of tradition may arise in very different contexts. For example, the reform movements that arose in western Europe in the twelfth century attacked past social custom for intervening between humans and God (Constable 1996: 142–43, 262). In the Byzantine church, debates over iconoclasm centered on the proper role of customary, as opposed to scriptural, mandate (Pelikan 1990). And the question of tradition or law, and its relation to grace and revelation, was especially prominent with the Protestant Reformation. Of course each of these debates took place within distinct social, political, and theological circumstances. And each gave rise to new, enduring forms of external discipline. I mention them here in order to situate the problems faced by colonial missions in a larger context by suggesting that certain of their difficulties were not unique to their particular circumstances, however variable the relevant dimensions of contrast in any instance may be. One reason these problems recur may be because the project of proselytization can, in some circumstances, encourage a sharp conceptual distinction between inner faith and external forms of regulation, even if the proselytizers' concrete practices confound it.

When the skeptical view of law or tradition predominates, the social can be understood as both exterior to, and a constraint on, the agent. Recall John Milton's attack on the *Book of Common Prayer* that I quoted at the beginning of this book. The failings he sees in the prayer book are several, but among them is the fact that its very character as a text—being both fixed and material in form—embodies the imposition of *other people* on the freedom of the individual conscience. This is a crucial political and moral subtext to the problem of semiotic form. For this model of agency, the concrete exteriority of semiotic form seems both to impose itself upon otherwise free agents and to be the vehicle by which social others constrain the individual. (To be sure, rarely do *all* exterior forms seem to be an imposition on that agency, and much of my argument is concerned with tracing out just what forms are believed to impose constraints.) As I proposed in chapter 2, this is one reason why the narrative of modernity as the liberation of agency sometimes gives rise to demands for greater abstraction.

But when viewed as a question of historical transformation, the social may be experienced not just as the pressure of one's contemporaries but also as the dead hand of custom. The two may be indistinguishable, since the pressure to adhere to custom is so often brought to bear by one's contemporaries—rulers demanding obeisance, kinfolk expecting reciprocity, neighbors gossiping about propriety, brothers guarding the honor of sisters. A sense of the past may even be reinforced and sharpened by concrete efforts to break away from those contemporaries. As Birgit Meyer shows, Ghanaian Pentecostals place a strong emphasis on discontinuity. They insist that you "make a complete break with your past" (1998: 316). But for all their efforts, they feel that the past continues to hold them in its grip. In fact, Meyers argues that their very efforts to break from the past actually help constitute it more vividly for their imagination. The deliverance rituals they hold to exorcize the devil turn on attempts to untie their links to the past, which take the form, above all, of bonds with other people, especially family members. The struggle for liberation against the *past* requires a struggle against *social others*. And the past, in the narrative of religious conversion as much as in that of secular modernity, is the world of alien gods and those who maintain relations with them.[12]

The apparent persistence of the past took especially dramatic shape for many Europeans in the colonial world when they faced practices that

---

12. As I noted in chapter 1, if secular modernists see religion per se to be that anachronistic force, then by a kind of fractal recursivity Christians can see "pagans" in the same way (Irvine and Gal 2000).

seemed to be religious, but which lacked at least some of the things they thought defined a real religion, such as an explicit moral code, scriptures, salvation, an afterlife, ecclesiastical institutions, or a supreme god. One possibility was to deny that a given society even possessed religion at all. But other understandings were more common. As we saw in the last chapter, Tylorian anthropology invited one to see nonscriptural religions as survivals of past and, perhaps, formerly more complete religious systems. But what pathways lead from their past to present states? Stern Calvinists like Abraham Kuyper saw these nonscriptural religions as the result of postlapsarian regression and the effects of satanic delusion. Less severe missionaries like Albert Kruyt took them to be evidence of a historical progression toward a Christian future, preliminary steps toward enlightenment. Identifying the true character of the non-Christian spirits therefore had consequences for the perceived historical possibilities for any given society of potential converts. Semiotic ideologies played a role in determining whether missionaries found the most effective strategies to require coercion or persuasion, physical force or verbal discourses, material display or spiritual disciplining.

Since spirits were identified in talk and action—which were as variable as the languages and rituals that missionaries encountered—identifying them called for some principles by which apparently disparate entities could be reduced to a knowable, and known, set of categories. That is, the encounter between Christian and alien spirit worlds required strategies of translation.[13] Variations on these themes recur throughout mission history. Here I turn to four cases, two involving early Roman Catholic missions, and two among nineteenth- and twentieth-century Protestants.

THE SUBSTANCE OF SPIRITS

In the Americas until the early seventeenth century, some Spaniards considered it possible that Inca deities were the expression of a real, if limited, religious understanding. If this were the case, imperfect conversion could still be understood as a partial access to a truth shared among religions and among different historical epochs. Bartolomé de las Casas drew on the asser-

---

13. They also, of course, required direct suppression. Schieffelin found that many Kaluli vocabulary items associated with the spirits that she had recorded in the 1970s were, by the 1990s, considered by the now-fundamentalist Christians to be wrong or were no longer used (2002: S9). Entire lexical domains had shrunk. It had simply become impossible to talk about the past.

tion in Aristotle's *Nichomachean Ethics* that all humans have an innate capacity for virtue and knowledge. If this is so, he concluded, they must have the ability to know God, and therefore Indian religions held a certain theological truth (MacCormack 1991: 205–13). Garcilaso de la Vega came to similar conclusions from Platonic sources. According to the historian Sabine MacCormack, "Because, in a Platonic universe, concepts of deity are innate in man, the vagaries of imagination are not central to the question of how god can be known. Garcilaso thus insisted that Inca religion must be understood as a necessary step toward Christianity" (1991: 12). But the idea that all humans have some access to divine truth could cut two ways. Thus some Spanish theologians held that the Decalogue was natural law binding on all humans regardless of whether it had been promulgated to them. From this they concluded that, if some peoples have departed from the monotheism ordained by the Ten Commandments, it must be because they made a pact with the devil (MacCormack 1991: 40). This darker view of the Andeans gave way to an even more pessimistic one, for their religion "came to be seen no longer as an approach, however limited, to religious understanding, but as a set of superstitions the Indians were unable to shed because, thanks to their perceived cultural backwardness and lack of intellectual talent, they were and remained victims of demonic frauds and delusions" (1991: 8). The sheer violence of the conversion efforts in the colonial Andes is well known. Obviously that violence cannot be reduced to single causes; but surely such pessimism would have been unlikely to lead to earnest efforts at persuasion that were characteristic of later missions, such as that of the Dutch Calvinists on Sumba.[14]

In these early colonial interpretations of American religions, we can see aspects of the problems of historical continuity across apparent difference that would recur in later mission encounters elsewhere. The ways in which people understand and respond to problems of continuity and difference depend, in part, on the semiotic ideologies available to them. For instance, the problem of demonic delusion in early Spanish America drew on a tradition grounded in Aquinas's reading of Aristotle, which held that transubstantiation exploits the distinction between accident and substance.

---

14. As is well known, the Spaniards in the Americas drew on parallels to their experiences in Spain. Kathryn Woolard (2002) has shown that competing language ideologies (were linguistic differences set at the time of Babel, or were they the result of historical processes?) bore on such questions as whether Moorish converts to Christianity could be transformed or were marked by differences so immutable that they should be expelled from the peninsula instead. Language ideologies played a key role in the emergence of racial and nationalist ideologies.

That is, the eucharistic elements are bread and wine in accident, but they are Christ in substance. But if accident could appear so different from actual substance, what other results were possible? Could not the devil likewise "exploit this disjuncture between accidents and substance, appearance and reality, in the material universe" (MacCormack 1991: 28)? From late antiquity onward, many Christians thought demons (substance) dwelt in statues of Greek and Roman deities (accident). These theories were reiterated by the Spaniards who desecrated Inca temples in the sixteenth century. As a result, Christianity and its competitors came to be seen as radically different, and imperfect conversion might be hiding satanic belief in disguise.

As is well known, to be in a position to judge such things as the depth of *others'* conversion is one of the defining characteristics of everyday colonial power relations. But mutatis mutandis, the problem arises on the other side of the power differential as well. What are those who have converted to Christianity *themselves* to make of their former gods? For converts to Christianity, the problem of the past is compounded as they take on both the past of the Christian church and that of their own pre-Christian forebears— or as they construct even their living neighbors as anachronistic remnants of the past.[15] As I noted earlier, Sumbanese congregations often resisted Dutch efforts to introduce Sumbanese gongs, songs, or even words into the liturgy on the grounds that these might bring the marapu back to mind. The apparent persistence of spirits, or of people for whom those spirits matter, involves questions such as the proper identity of the spirits, their modes of existence, and the nature of their efficacy or its lack. Whatever else they may be, these are also fundamentally semiotic problems. For in what does the persistence of an invisible being consist apart from its embodiment in ways of acting or in talk about it? Even if one were to insist that spirits actually do exist, and are not merely beliefs or delusions, then at least the grouping of beings together within one or another set of categories—to say, for instance, that the ancestor spirits are in fact agents of the Christian devil— remains a linguistic issue, whatever else it may be. This is brought clearly to the fore when it is claimed, as is often the case in scholarly or polemical ref-

---

15. The Spaniards had already confronted a related problem of persistence and translation in the case of Islamic and Jewish conversion on the Iberian Peninsula: were there still Islamic or Jewish ideas hidden within apparently Christian words and practices? Their specific religious and political problem, in a sense, has antecedents in the first apostolic missions: Is following the law any indication of the true condition of one's heart? If so, what is the precise nature of the relationship between external acts and inner states? If not, what then is the proper status of the law?

erences to so-called syncretism, that the spirits have been translated into new terminology, that new actions are the same as old ones in different guise—claims that depend on assumptions about semiotic equivalence.[16]

FROM MATERIAL PRESENCE TO OBJECT OF BELIEF

One way that boundaries between religions are produced is by suppressing or transforming material manifestations of the spirit world. An important precedent was set for Roman Catholic missions by Pope Gregory I in his letter to Augustine of Canterbury in 601 C.E.: "the idol temples . . . should by no means be destroyed, but only the idols in them. Take holy water and sprinkle it in these shrines, build altars, and place relics . . . in them. . . . When this people see their shrines are not destroyed, they will be able to banish error from their hearts and be more ready to come to the places they are familiar with, but now recognizing and worshiping the true God" (quoted in Pelikan 2003: 312). This passage seems to assume people's attachments are to phenomenal places and things, whose sheer material continuity would override any immaterial meanings, values, or other attributions. That is, material relics and shrines can be given new meanings and functions, and so physical continuity would be an effective mission strategy. Other missions, however, insisted on destruction. This might be due to a perceived psychological effect—say, that material forms would never shake their pre-Christian associations. Or it might follow from the cosmological claim that things really are media for the exercise of satanic agency. Or destruction might be called for because *any* materialization of the divine at all would undermine the properly spiritual and immaterial understanding of the objects of faith.[17]

In practical terms, at least, the destruction of shrines, the extirpation of rites, and the suppression of priesthoods reorient discursive and other ritual activities. They may also induce transformations in the semiotic ideology that motivates, justifies, and gives shape to those activities. According

16. The concept of syncretism, in its common, pejorative sense, usually includes an implicit temporal dimension. What the purist sees as syncretistic elements are commonly understood in historical terms as so many remnants or effects of incomplete conversion (see Stewart and Shaw 1994). Syncretism thus implies the persistence of something anachronistic.

17. Missionary thinking about non-Christian objects often drew on much earlier debates over iconoclasm, which led some to treat visual images as material signs of immaterial referents (Belting 1994; Koerner 2004). I discuss materiality and abstraction in more detail below, especially in chapters 8, 9, and 10.

to MacCormack, the elimination of material objects under Spanish rule forced Andeans to reformulate and clarify theological concepts such as the persistence of a spirit's identity and activities when the material component was gone (1991: 408–11). Notice this is not simply a question of translation or of shifting semantic domains. Rather, the very semiotic character of religion changed. To be sure, the change involved the revision of concepts, such as what is a spirit, and what is its place in the new pantheon that includes, for instance, Jesus, saints, the Virgin Mary, and so forth. But equally important, there seems to have been a change in the semiotic ideology mediating between concept and practice. For instance, if there are no shrines or representations, where and how does a spirit manifest itself? If spirits are not manifest or have no location, what must people do to contact them? If Mac-Cormack is right, the loss of material forms seems to have forced Andeans to reconceptualize the gods in new, more abstract terms. Thus the very abstraction of the spirits was produced in response to a material circumstance, the destruction of objective forms. This abstraction does not seem to have been the Spaniards' original motive, although in other mission fields the insistence on dematerializing the divine would have been precisely the purpose. And, as the cases discussed in part 2 of this book show, the attack on materializations are especially fraught when people who attempt purification confront what they take to be the anachronistic persistence of false agents. But first we must consider the semiotics of persistence in light of the historical imagination.

THE HARDNESS OF WORDS

Different strategies for handling alien spirits can presuppose different semiotic ideologies. If talk of alien spirits is the result of conceptual error, for instance, then it is making use of words that have no proper referents. If those things that people call spirits are actually the products of diabolic deception, then the referents exist but have been misnamed and require retranslation—they must be called the demons that they really are. Similarly, if natural religion is the product of an original true religious revelation that has been distorted, again retranslation is called for—spirits must be called by their true names, in the appropriate vocabulary of Christianity. Finally, insofar as spirits and Gods are not usually of interest unless one can do more than talk *about* them—unless, that is, they allow or require one to act in certain ways and not others—then the linguistic issue becomes inseparable from other dimensions of action.

MacCormack says that Iberian strategies of translation in the early colonial Americas attempted to impose a Spanish vocabulary of contempt on Andean religion. Religious practitioners, for instance, became wizards *(brujos)*, sorcerers *(hechiceros)*, imposters *(embusteros)*, and so forth. Translation was supposed to effect contempt by identifying formerly neutral referents with *other* referents and, thus, by implication, showing that they shared with them an essential meaning hidden behind their former lexical distinctiveness. MacCormack, however, concludes that the Andeans were not likely to be aware of the meaning that was supposed to be produced by this lexical conjunction of sets (words for Andean ritualists and those for Spanish sorcerers and frauds), and that they appropriated the words for their own purposes, preserving a stable set of referents (1991: 406–7). In this analysis, Andeans were able to retain much of their original religious world. This is because they detached the Spanish words from their original denotations and reattached them to others.

If MacCormack's description is right, it does imply that an important element of religious continuity was semantics. After all, the Andean temples and public ritual institutions had been destroyed. Note as well that such a semantic strategy presupposes at least the absence of a linguistic ideology that insists (like, say, Islamic views of Arabic) on there being an inherent link between linguistic form and conceptual sense. By leaving open the possibility that, under the new appellations, a pagan world persists—whether as beings, ideas, activities, or values—lexical translation can threaten the Christian project of conversion. In various forms, this is a threat that would recur again and again in mission encounters.

One solution to this threat is to undertake translation strategies that would raise barriers between languages. Rather than incorporating local referents into existing categories, one could attempt to secure the link between Spanish words and Christian denotations by insisting that those words could not be translated into the local language. According to Vicente Rafael, the early Spanish mission in the Philippines took to leaving certain words, such as Dios, Virgen, and Cruz untranslated lest translation lead to the identification of pagan with Christian denotations (1993).[18] In Rafael's

---

18. For Roman Catholicism at the time, the retention of scriptural Latin was a specifically doctrinal matter reaffirmed in the Council of Trent in opposition to the Reformation's use of vernacular translations of scripture (the Roman Catholic Church did allow the use of vernacular languages for other ecclesiastical purposes). One reason was to preserve a uniform language for all Catholics (see Trent, session 22, "Doctrine on the Sacrifice of the Mass," chapter 8; session 22, "Canons on the

interpretation, the appearance of such words in the midst of a flow of their own language challenged the speaker of Tagalog "to distinguish between terms that had indigenous referents and terms whose meanings lay outside of what could be said in Tagalog. Thus the presence of Latin and Castilian terms in Tagalog opened up for the natives the possibility of finding in their language something that resisted translation" (1993: 111). This interpretation draws attention to what could be called the phenomenological palpability of semiotic forms—their hardness, as it were—regardless of whether they are semantically transparent. The refusal to translate did not lead to a more secure relationship between word and denotation. Rather, by suppressing semantics, this strategy brought semiotic form to the foreground. As a result, Rafael suggests, the Tagalog were able to treat Spanish religious vocabulary and names such as *Mary* as cult objects (1993: 120). By maintaining the barrier between languages, such words contributed to the treatment of language as an object, which is a common resource for the production of ritual power (Keane 1997b, 2004).

In the Tagalog case, the power of such bits of religious language depends on rendering them semantically opaque. But that opacity is of a distinctive sort, since its efficacy for hearers depends on their perception that certain words bear indexical links to identifiably "foreign" sources. According to Rafael, "The appeal of and to Christianity on the part of Spaniards and native converts alike had to do precisely with the fact that fragments of it remained irreducibly foreign to both. Such fragments, . . . served to signal an 'outside' that lent itself to being located, appropriated, and valorized in different ways by the rulers and the ruled" (1993: 6). Resistance to colonialism, in Rafael's view, depended on maintaining a clear distinction between an interior (Tagalog) and something exterior to it (Spanish).

Sacrifice of the Mass," canon 9; Session 24, "Decree on Reformation," chapter 7, in Tanner 1990). But, as suggested by the use of Spanish as well as Latin words in the Philippines, there are more general linguistic problems. Birgit Meyer writes that German Pietist missionaries in nineteenth-century Ghana mistakenly thought that "the chosen Ewe terms denoted the content they put into them. [But for] Ewe Christians the terms' old meanings did not totally disappear but continued to form part of the terms. One and the same term would thus have different meanings for missionaries and the Ewe Christians" (1999: 81). Recognizing this possibility in early-twentieth-century Sumba, the Calvinist Zending der Gereformeerde Kerken in Nederland rejected the missionary Lambooy's proposal to translate the word *God* into Sumbanese languages by using the indigenous word for "ancestor spirit," *marapu.*

But, as Rafael's example makes evident, linguistic boundaries are not simply objective facts: they require semiotic maintenance (Gal and Woolard 2001; Irvine and Gal 2000). This is especially the case where languages interact over long periods of time. In places like island Southeast Asia, long subject to linguistic flows from a wide range of sources, the appropriation of the power of foreign words is a common strategy. For instance, in Indonesia's Sulawesi highlands, the Tobaku took on Arabic vocabulary from lowland Muslims in the context of ancestral ritual and continued to use it after they became followers of the Salvation Army. These words included *baraka* for "divine power," *seta* (Arabic, *shaitan*) for "malevolent spirit," *ji'i* (Arabic, *jinn*) to denote a particular kind of peripatetic malevolent spirit, and Alatala (Arabic, Allah Ta'ala) for the Christian God (Aragon 2000: 172–74). If, however, the power of Arabic words depends on their perceived foreignness, then once they have entered into local circulation, it takes work to *keep* them foreign. Otherwise, such words become like any other loan words and rapidly lose the sense of difference. At the very least, some defamiliarization strategies, such as retaining "foreign" pronunciation, are required. If it is the very foreignness of new linguistic elements that makes them effective, that foreignness must be continually reconstructed: after all, the terminology of the church will not, presumably, be alien to someone who attended catechism classes and grew up surrounded by Christians and their practices in the same way it was to those of an earlier generation, confronting it for the first time. The story of conversion, whether in the colonial world or after, needs an account of subsequent generations as much as one of "first contact."

CLAIMING AND DISCLAIMING THE LANGUAGES OF THE DEAD

In the early twenty-first century, many societies lay vigorous claim to their Christianity and, simultaneously, insist on their status as possessors of a distinctive culture with deep historical roots. Their claim to being good Christians implies they share a religion recognizable to those whom they would hold to be coreligionists. This means they have entered the universal history of the church, at least to the extent that they should have left potentially anachronistic and localistic spirits in the past. Those for whom anachronism is a threat may insist that social practices be purified of any traces of persistent paganism or hybridity. Yet most communities do not attempt to live on a concrete, day-to-day basis only in the terms given by a universal religion alone. After all, Christian scripture remains silent on most problems, from planting the fields to investing profits, from child rearing to medical treatment. If these were cosmologically or morally neutral questions of technique, as they were for most Euro-Americans, this silence would be unimportant. But where spirits were once potentially implicated in every sort of practice, there is always the possibility that even an apparently harmless detail might afford an opening to paganism. Sumbanese, for example, cannot assume the religious innocence even of such things as what knots are used to tie the house beams, how one names a newborn or handles cats, which words one uses while hunting, or in which sequence rice fields are planted. In each of these cases, the traditional procedures are prompted by assumptions about spirit agents, their effects on the living, and vice versa. Even the simple, everyday social sharing of betel nut may be problematic for Protestants. Giving and receiving betel is commonly understood to potentially have effects on the person's spirit (Anakalangese, *dewa;* see Keane 1997c: 202 ff; Onvlee 1973c). More generally, in practical terms, morality remains embedded in everyday social relations, entangled with all the habits, desires, anxieties, and sheer willfulness they involve. The claims of everyday morality may exist in tension with even the most earnest effort to be a good Christian (see Robbins 2004a).

Any supposed cultural continuity—regardless of whether it confronts an apparent rupture such as radical conversion or not—requires not just criteria for identity among differences of time, place, and semiotic form but also someone *for whom* they are criteria. Consider, for instance, the Tobaku people of highland Sulawesi, Indonesia, who converted to Salvation Army Methodism over the course of the twentieth century. By the late twentieth century in Indonesia, when Lorraine Aragon wrote about them, the political viability of minority communities sometimes hinged on assertions of traditional identity. In this context, there were good political reasons for them to claim cultural continuity with their ancestors.[19] Since this is a *cultural* identity, it cannot consist only of territorial stability, demographic

---

19. Under the motto "Unity in Diversity," the Indonesian state has pushed both the assimilation of ethnic groups to a national standard and the celebration of cultural heritage (see Pemberton 1994). To oversimplify a complex history, smaller, weaker groups sometimes fare better under assimilationist policies if they can make strong claims to cultural persistence; in some cases, these claims have direct consequences for their ability to defend their rights to land (see George 1996; Kuipers 1998; Tsing 1993). For an insightful discussion of an attempt by Sumbanese to situate themselves within the national historical narrative, see Hoskins 1993: chap. 11.

continuity, or even the survival of their language. Like many Indonesians, Tobaku may rest such claims on adat, but the outside observer—whether sympathetic or skeptical—might find this to be superficial and seek something deeper. If culture is inseparable from cosmology, to assert cultural continuity would seem to require a religious component. Yet most Tobaku claim to be orthodox and even "fanatical Christians" (Indonesian, *Kristen fanatik*). Given the power of Muslim majorities nearby, and their own uncertain social standing as rural highlanders, their claim to be part of global Christendom may be politically as crucial as their cultural persistence. Both claims, to their membership in a larger religious community and the depth of their local roots, depend not just on themselves but also on being recognizable to outsiders (Clifford 1988; Povinelli 2002).

Between local persistence and global identifications, Tobaku are caught in a dilemma. Like many anthropologists elsewhere, Lorraine Aragon argues that Tobaku retain cosmological continuity with their ancestors. That means they retain their cultural identity. Yet she also wants to respect their claim to be good Christians, which seems to require a cosmological rupture from the world of those ancestors. Since the spirits and their actions thoroughly pervaded the ancestral world, it is not sufficient to say that only the religion has changed, and nothing else. To reconcile the two demands—respect for their claims to cultural persistence and to being good Christians—Aragon bases the asserted continuity on the idea of functional replacement. Salvation Army ministers, for instance, took on the authority of ancestral founder spirits and, in some cases, replaced shamans. Protestant Christian ceremonies substituted for pre-Christian rituals. This analysis is consistent both with a great deal of anthropological writing on conversion and with common missionary strategies in the twentieth century. But what does it mean to say that something is the "same" under such replacements? These functional replacements seem to depend on another, conceptual level, with language as its model. For example, "highlanders have transposed and relabeled their pre-Christian deities to conform to missionary-supplied categories such as God, Jesus, the Holy Spirit, and Satan" (Aragon 2000: 30). New labels replace older ones, but in this account they continue to refer to the same thing. What they refer to must therefore exist in a domain separate from the words themselves.

The problem is to identify exactly what is remaining constant, given manifest change. According to Aragon, ideas attached to the words "Owner of the Land" have been transferred to "God"; those of "ritual transgression" have become "sin" (2000: 186–87). As a result, "[t]he reformulation of deity categories in the Lulawi highlands is less a change in deities' and ancestors' expected behavior than in their titles and individuality" (2000: 174). But it seems that, in the past, pre-Christian Tobaku spirits were not the object of much speculation or very clear conceptualization, apart from the requirements they imposed on human actions. More than a change of labels is involved. If Aragon is right, then once reconceptualized in Protestant terms, spirits become part of a world in which not only are there new objects (Jesus, Holy Communion, Bibles, churches) and practices (recitation of creeds, weekly church services, grace), but also the very existence of clear, knowable, spiritual entities is itself new. The spirit world has become a domain of "beliefs." In this respect, the shift in the semiotic status of spirits resembles that which took place in the Andes, as they became discrete objects of conceptual representation. The argument for persistence depends on a notion of translation that itself requires new kinds of semiotic ideology, in which words and the things they denote exist in distinct planes. In the dominant ideology assumed by twentieth-century Europeans, these planes are linked by social conventions.[20]

There seem to be several underlying models for translation at play here. Among the most recurrent models are those that link word and conceptual representation, and public act and private interpretation. This linkage depends on a specific linguistic ideology, the so-called arbitrariness of the sign or, more accurately, the unmotivated character of the relationship between words and the objects they may be used to denote. For only under this assumption, or something close to it, does it make sense to think that new words could apply to old referents with no consequential change. Yet even denotation depends on more than the relationship between the word and the object of denotation, since it is also a function of relations among linguistic terms. So there is another aspect of this language ideology. For straight adaptation to function best, one should assume that the referents are stable independently of any particular human signifying system—as they would be were they all to derive from a single divine source.

For some people, like the Protestant Ewe of Ghana as described by Birgit Meyer (1999, 2004), the old spirits *do* exist. One factor that seems to have played into this perception of the past was the translation strategy of the German Pietist missionaries, who began their work there in 1847. They held that Ewe were among the descendants of Ham, who, having once

---

20. Versions of the claim that words depend on social convention are found very early in Western history. But the "arbitrariness" doctrine of the sign becomes securely part of widespread common sense within the representational economies characteristic of the nineteenth- and twentieth-century worlds from which Protestant missionaries came (see Aarsleff 1982; Bauman and Briggs 2003).

known the true God, later fell into Satan worship (Meyer 1999: 57–58). It follows from the Pietists' view of history that ancestral spirits were really the same demonic beings also known to Christian cosmology. This may have encouraged the Pietists' strategy of using existing Ewe vocabulary to translate certain Christian concepts. Given this implied ontological continuity, questions of persistence turn on correct identifications between spirits and Christian vocabulary and the proper actions these identifications entail. Through what Meyer (1999) describes as "diabolisation," Ewe came to accept this identification of their ancestral spirits with the demons. Among the consequences, as the Pietist missionaries found to their disappointment, was that Ewe were not convinced of their sinfulness. Rather, drawing on the earlier cosmology and its way of distributing agency among beings in the world, they saw sin as something one endured, since its ultimate agent was Satan.

But this did not mean the world was unchanged for Christian converts. Ewe Christians came to see demons manifested in the persistence, despite their conversion, of such things as sexual and monetary temptations, religious backsliding, and the malevolence of other people. Unlike the unconverted, however, Ewe Pietists did not have recourse to older means of dealing with misfortune, such as sacrifices or exorcism. In this context, part of the appeal of Pentecostalism, which began to compete successfully with Pietism in the twentieth century, lay in that fact that it took demons seriously and, unlike Pietism, provided ways of expressing their reality through possession and ways of dealing with them through deliverance rituals. Meyer writes that "[b]y creating room for the expression of the satanic in the context of deliverance, Pentecostals are allowed to enact otherwise forbidden or muted aspects of themselves" (1999: 211). The result is that in practice they are continuously brought back into contact with what they have been trying to leave behind.

In contrast to the Pietist model of conversion as a linear, once-and-for-all rupture with the past, this experience is accepted within a Pentecostal model of ongoing struggle. Ewe see religious backsliding as a return to the demons. According to Meyer:

> One characteristic feature of Pentecostalism is its successful incorporation of local ideas and practices pertaining to old gods, witchcraft, and new spirits. . . . In contrast to the orthodox mission churches, which regarded such local ideas as irrational "superstitions" to be left behind by converts, or at least to be overcome by education, Pentecostal churches took these views as a point of departure. In Pentecostal deliverance sessions, for example, the exorcism of demons holds a central

place. . . . In short, to a very large extent, Pentecostalism's popularity stems from the fact that it takes seriously popular views about spirits. (2004: 96)[21]

But these views about spirits are not simply the persistence of the past. Rather, they are *representations* of that past, "reifications of 'traditional religion' in terms of diabolization" (Meyer 2004: 98). Thus, what could look like mere Ewe conservatism or cultural persistence, Meyer shows to be the outcome of active, self-conscious engagement with pressing difficulties in the present. Persistence is an activity. The past, as portrayed in these representations, is more a product of the urban Protestant imagination than of something like villagers' stubborn resistance to change. And, in Meyer's analysis, the apparent persistence of the past is prompted by contemporary, and often specifically Christian, dilemmas. One of the most important things demons do is help explain why the dreams of the good life promised by modernity do not fully materialize (2004: 103).

For Ewe Pentecostals, the existence of demons can challenge a linear model of history at both the macro level of social change and the micro level of individual experience. In this respect, Ewe may find that the past, in the form of demonic spirits, weighs upon the brains of the living much like Marx's "nightmare." In both cases, the apparent persistence of the past threatens the future toward which one is striving. The future that is threatened by the past need not be the one envisioned by Marx, of course. It might be Christian salvation, or simply the good life promised by modernity. But what the political radical, the religious convert, and, say, the Ewe migrant to the city share is this: each experiences the past through his or her expectations of the future. And each may see in the weight of the past an explanation for the failures of human agency in the present.

When Rafael says that the Tagalog treated Spanish religious vocabulary as so many cult objects, he concludes that the Tagalog dealt with Christian divine beings as if they were ancestral spirits. In effect, his analysis of words presupposes some notion of functional equivalence or analogy, that certain ways of acting, such as Catholic confession, are in some important respect *the same* as others, such as offerings given to ancestral spirits. But what transcultural metalanguage of actions would allow us to calibrate functions across such different practical and conceptual contexts? One way to answer this question is to ask *for whom* apparently different religious

---

21. The phenomenon is ubiquitous and as far-flung as Fiji (Tomlinson 2004) and across Melanesia, where, for instance, "Christian practices [were] a ritual antidote to the dangers that emanate from the traditional spirit world" (White 1991: 107).

practices *count as* "the same," what permits and encourages people's perception of identity across instances, and how that perception is produced. In contrast to Tobaku Methodists, for whom the continuity an outside observer sees may not be apparent or desirable, Ewe Pentecostals discover continuity where the outsider observer might deny it exists.

Clearly the tradition of the dead generations is only a nightmare for certain people with certain kinds of expectations. After all, many people find the ability to identity with their ancestors, and to wield the materials of tradition, to be a source of power and value. Others look to the future as a continuous unfolding or development out of a past rich with possibilities. Why, then, should the past seem to be a threat? There are, of course, as many answers to this question as there are histories. What I have been concerned with in this chapter is some of the problems faced in the attempt to construct a moral narrative of progress, a persuasive sense of victory, for projects of self-conscious transformation such as that of radical religious conversion. The narrative of progress, as Chakrabarty suggests, constructs certain kinds of difference as anachronism. Given such transformative projects, the apparent persistence of past semiotic forms—traditions, languages, objects—can seem to pose serious challenges to the agency of the living. They threaten that agency by introducing alternative agents or otherwise undermining the sureness of living people's own powers. If the narrative of progress is one of secular modernity, then the very persistence of religion itself may seem to threaten the agency that properly belongs to humans, by displacing it onto God—as if it were a kind of opium, in another of Marx's famous comments. If the narrative of progress is that of the religious reformer or proselytizer, then the existence of false gods, demons, and fetishes among the unconverted—and perhaps in disguise among the apparently converted—can have a similar effect.

To be sure, God may be the ultimate agent, but as the Dutch missionaries I discussed above realized, divine agency still requires humans not just as its vehicles but also as purposeful agents in their own right. Those Calvinist writings reveal one point of intersection between the more secular moral narrative of modernity and that borne by many projects of proselytization. That missionaries are self-conscious agents of secular history · despite their acknowledgment of a divine scheme is not necessarily paradoxical. The Dutch authors suggest that, only when humans realize the agency which is proper to them, wresting it from the false agents to which they had imputed it, will the many local histories flow into a universal one.

The sense of history, to the extent that this means perceptions of transformation or persistence and the trajectories into the future they imply, depends on an ability to identify certain aspects of the present as either the same or as different from things as they were supposed to have been in the past. Yet in some sense even the most stable or conservative of societies forms a Heraclitean world, since—unless one were to insist on a perfectly repetitive cosmology—one never steps into exactly the same river twice. Moreover, as Chakrabarty's critique of the very idea of anachronism suggests, we should not even assume there is a single river. The perception of continuity or persistence from the past into the present is mediated by semiotic ideology, which tells us, for instance, that these words are translations of those ones, these actions are equivalent to those, this object is like that one. Perceptions of continuity are inseparable from concepts of change and the stances toward the future they make possible. But these concepts and stances do not exist merely as so many thought worlds. They are embodied in the particular forms available for action, and in the semiotic ideologies that mediate between the forms that actions take and their consequences. Given their potential for distinct kinds of historical motion, the semiotic ideologies, the practical actions, and the specific forms those actions take may pull in quite different directions from one another.

PART II

Fetishisms

General meeting of the missionaries on Sumba, circa 1925. From M. Meijering et al., eds., *Tot Dankbaarheid Genoopt: Gedenkboek ter Gelegenheid van de 25-Jarigen Zendingsarbeid op Soemba vanwege de Gereformeerde Kerken in Groningen, Drente en Overijsel* (Kampen, Netherlands: J. H. Kok, 1927).

5   Umbu Neka's Conversion

The Pauline model of conversion takes the ultimate unit of Christian salvation to be the individual.[1] From this perspective, the conversion of nations depends, in the end, on the multiplied capacity of the individual to step outside of certain demands of kinship and aspects of custom, to elude the hand of the past. However much the ultimate source of such acts is divine in origin, and the final outcome takes place at the level of sweeping historical forces, it is most often understood in some version of personal choice. As a scholar of Dutch Calvinist missionaries puts it: "[T]he possibility of God's revelation in the events of everyday life elevates those events, and our lives, to the order of some grander plan or design. Here, too, is the space where human agency operates, because despite God's omnipotence, humans remain responsible for the correct response, liable for their decisions or indecisiveness" (Kipp 1990: 22–23). But if social transformation is more than the aggregation of discrete individual changes, it depends on some forms of mediation. One crucial point of articulation between individuals and larger orders of change lies in the publicly circulating semiotic forms available to them, what in the previous chapter I called, following Chakrabarty, the languages of the dead.

1. The emphasis on the individual conversion is especially characteristic of the post-eighteenth-century missions, which took the public/private distinction for granted. It was not necessarily found in earlier missions (van Rooden 1996). For general claims about the individualism implicit in Christian ideas about salvation, see Burridge 1979; Dumont 1986; Troeltsch 1931; notable exemplifications of the claim include Clifford 1982; Comaroff 1985; Pels 1999; Viswanathan 1998. For individualization of Sumbanese Christians, seen through changes in naming practices, see Kuipers 1998.

In this chapter I turn to one man's response to divine intervention, to show how his appropriation of existing semiotic forms mediates between personal conversion and the experience of history-making. After a brief sketch of the history of Christianity on Sumba, I turn to a series of orations performed in the district of Anakalang, on the occasion of Umbu Neka's conversion in 1986 from ancestral ritual, in which he had played a central role, to the Calvinism of the Christian Church of Sumba. I argue that Umbu Neka was a man who accepted the claim that cultural forms of speech, dance, song, and exchange have remained unchanged since earliest times and, more important, that they have retained their powers. It was this seemingly conservative claim that made it possible for him to act by means of those public media in his active efforts to effect, if not invent, a future. On closer examination, we will see that, in his oratorical performance, denotations pull in one direction, pragmatic entailments pull in another, semiotic ideologies clash, and his creative intentionality is divided between them. The outcome exemplifies the consequences of the modernist work of purification, as reformers attempt to distinguish between the surface form of expressions and inner, immaterial intentions and to separate words from things.

DUTCH CALVINISM ON SUMBA

Sumba was incorporated into Dutch rule early in the twentieth century, in the final burst of colonial expansion that filled out the borders of what is now Indonesia. Located off the main trade routes, drought prone, thinly settled, agriculturally marginal, and lacking a politically threatening Islamic presence, Sumba held little to attract the ambitious, greedy, or geopolitically inclined and remained the province of a handful of administrators and missionaries.[2] Dutch policy forbade competition among different religious missions in a single region, and Sumba became the domain of the neo-orthodox Reformed Churches.[3] As noted in the previous chapter, the northern Dutch

2. The sandalwood for which Sumba was once known was pretty much depleted by the nineteenth century. By then, the only other significant export was horses. Sumba had been subject to sporadic raids by slavers from other islands before the slave trade was suppressed by the Dutch in the nineteenth century. In 1930, at the height of the colonial presence in West Sumba, the census reports a population of 32 Europeans and 107,877 Sumbanese (*Volkstelling* 1930: 123, 137, 173).

3. In 1929 an exception to this monopoly was granted to the Catholic order Societas Verbi Divini (since replaced by the German Redemptorists) on the grounds

congregations of Groningen, Drenthe, and Overijssel took on responsibility for the Sumba mission (Zending der Gereformeerde Kerken in Nederland) in 1902 (van den End 1987: 7).[4] Two years later, Douwe Klaas Wielenga, a twenty-four-year-old with formal training in theology, missiology, and Malay, settled with his wife, Margaretha, in Kambaniru, near the port town of Waingapu.[5] Within the first three years, their house was torched twice and Wielenga himself was seriously wounded in a spear attack, but the family remained on the island until 1921. Another missionary arrived in 1909, and there gradually followed a small cohort of preachers, schoolteachers, nurses, and medics distributed among five or six mission outposts. One of the most influential voices in shaping Dutch understanding of Sumbanese society was that of the linguist Louis Onvlee, who had a doctorate from Kuyper's Free University. He was sent to Sumba as a Bible translator, worked there from 1926 to 1947 (interrupted by internment under the

---

that there were still some Sumbanese who had been baptized by a short-lived Catholic mission in West Sumba from 1885 to 1893 (Haripranata 1984). Despite the strong objections of some local officials (see, for example, Waitz 1933: 41), they were allowed to operate but initially were restricted to a limited number of places. More recent additions include small congregations of ethnic Chinese town dwellers who have joined the American-based evangelical Bethel Church.

4. The loosely affiliated group calling itself the Reformed Churches was an offshoot of a conservative secession from the dominant Hervormde Kerk led by Abraham Kuyper (see chapter 3). By 1899, the Reformed Churches claimed 8.18 percent of the Dutch population, the Hervormde Kerk 48.61 percent. The Reformed Churches (which underwent a complex series of factional divisions and reunifications) had their strongest base among artisans, small farmers, skilled laborers, and small tradesmen (Wintle 1987: 3, 59). One of the main distinguishing features of this movement was its rejection of a centralized church hierarchy in favor of small, self-governing congregations, hence the plural form of the name. Their missiology stressed the glorification of God, to which lay work such as health care and education was subordinate; the autonomy of local congregations; the rejection of independent mission organizations in favor of church congregations; the rejection of any forms of coercion; and an emphasis on the converting of individuals within the context of their communities (see Willem 2004: 110–16). The latter point tended to lead to a focus on converting elites and to efforts to preserve cultural norms (see chapter 3); also, in contrast to some missions, the Reformed Churches did not try to found their own Christian villages apart from the rest of society.

5. The Reformed Churches had sent a few missionaries to Sumba starting in 1887, but their mandate was confined to coastal communities of migrants from neighboring Savu. The Reformed Churches sent a total of twenty-seven missionaries to Sumba between 1902 and 1990 (Willem 2004: 117). For the history of the missions to Sumba, see Deputaten 1965; Haripranata 1984; Kapita 1965, 1976b; Luijendijk 1946; May et al. 1982; Meijering et al. 1927; *Rapport inzake de Zending op Soemba* 1965; Rot-van der Gaast and van Halsema 1984; Webb 1986a; van den End 1987; van Halsema 1987, 1995; Wellem 2004; Wielenga 1926. See also Hoskins 1993; Kuipers 1998.

Japanese occupation) and 1951 to 1955, and returned to Amsterdam to found the anthropology program at his former university in 1956. The time committed by most ethnographers to the societies with which they work pales by comparison to that of some of these missionaries (P. J. Luijendijk, for example, lived on Sumba for about twenty-six years). Among these early missionaries, Wielenga and Onvlee stand out for their ethnographic interests and prolific writings. Wielenga wrote essays for the mission's journal as well as several local-color novels. These remain invaluable sources of ethnographic information, as do Onvlee's essays and his East Sumbanese dictionary and the Indonesian-language writings of his Sumbanese assistant, Umbu Hina Kapita.

As the missionaries quoted in the previous chapter make apparent, the mission was not a quick success.[6] By 1932, there were only 755 adult members of the Reformed Churches in West Sumba, out of a population of approximately 107,800 (Waitz 1933). The central Sumbanese district of Anakalang, where I did my fieldwork, received its first resident minister, Pieter Johan Luijendijk, and his wife, Jannetje, in 1933. The Luijendijks had the prospective wives of evangelists and schoolteachers live in their household, so they could teach these women housekeeping, health care, and Malay as part of an ongoing association of the church with modernity, the reordering of the domestic sphere, and nation-oriented education. Many of the first converts were children raised and educated in that household. Nevertheless, by 1946, Anakalang had only 180 baptized church members out of a population of over 22,000 (Luijendijk 1946). This slow pace resulted from Sumbanese resistance as well as the limited number of missionary workers and the highly demanding conditions for conversion set by neo-orthodox doctrine.[7] Despite the largely populist character of their following, the Reformed Churches required their missionaries to hold university degrees, unlike many other Indies missions. Emphasizing voluntary and informed conversion, the missions, and until recently, the Sumbanese church that succeeded it, admitted converts only after long doctrinal training and rigorous

6. Accounts differ as to when the first baptism occurred, ranging from 1915 (Webb 1986a: 20) to 1928 (Deputaten 1965: 44).

7. This slow and careful progress can be contrasted to more exuberant activities elsewhere: a single missionary of the Protestant Church of the Indies claimed to have baptized 5,000 persons on his first brief visits to Mamasa, Sulawesi (Bigalke 1981: 143). In recent years, the pace in Sumba has quickened considerably. In the 1980s, I heard of one mass baptism involving more than 100 people, and one report from around the same time claims 10,001 were baptized across West Sumba in two months (van Halsema 1987: 7).

examinations in the Heidelberg Catechism. Even as regulations were slightly loosened, the prevailing rationalistic scrupulousness of many of its leaders may have contributed to the slow rate of conversion.

Practical operations were taken over by Sumbanese and other Indonesians after the Japanese occupiers interned the Dutch in 1942. In 1947, as the nation was winning its independence, the Sumbanese were formally vested with control of the church, and the Christian Church of Sumba (Gereja Kristen Sumba) was formed (Kapita 1965: 45–46; van den End 1987: 34). But the Gereja Kristen Sumba retains close financial and advisory ties with the Netherlands to this day, and there have been small numbers of Dutch medical and technical advisors affiliated with the Reformed Churches during most of this period (van Halsema 1995; Vel 1994).

More rapid conversion to Calvinist and Catholic churches on Sumba began only after the attempted coup in Jakarta and subsequent nationwide killings of 1965–1966, when nonadherence to a legally recognized religion was taken to be synonymous with communism.[8] This generation of converts was not always marked by religious enthusiasm or doctrinal purity. In villages where Christians came to dominate numerically, however, the religion became the presupposed background in which subsequent generations came of age: for them, the doctrines seemed less strange or foreign, and their own Christianity not the result of personal conversion per se. Although the "stealing" by one church of those already converted by another has been rare (and strongly discouraged by local officials on the grounds that it would be politically destabilizing), in the 1980s and 1990s there was growing competition over the remaining unconverted.[9] By the end of that period, more aggressive evangelization, especially by groups of young Christians, was contributing to the rapid increase in converts in more isolated hamlets.

Although Catholics compete with Protestants for the remaining unconverted and are the object of some enthusiastic interdenominational back-

8. Sumba was marginal to the national political scene. Nonetheless, there was a handful of killings at this time, largely, it seems, by the military, and a general atmosphere of fear. In the 1980s, some individuals categorized as being "implicated" in the Communist Party were still under close watch by local authorities. For a brief sketch of the situation on Sumba, see Webb 1986b.

9. As the Suharto regime fell in 1998, there was one violent outbreak between Protestants and Catholics in Waingapu, Sumba's largest town. The participants, however, may have seen their affiliations as much in ethnic terms as religious. Although there are Catholic enclaves on Sumba, the Protestant church dominates, and many Sumbanese think of Catholicism as the religion of people from neighboring islands such as Flores.

biting, the most important contrast by the end of the 1990s, across most of the island, remained that between marapu followers and Gereja Kristen Sumba Calvinists. Ancestral ritualists formed a majority across most of the island in the 1970s and in some places have remained so—their presence a constant reminder of the historical recentness of the church. Only in the 1980s and 1990s did the Gereja Kristen Sumba become really assured of its eventual dominance over the ancestral ritualists and smaller groups of Catholics and Pentecostals (Islam having made no significant inroad among Sumbanese).[10] One important factor in the perceived modernity of Protestantism, especially in recent years, is state religious policy. Although Indonesia is largely Muslim today, the postindependence state has always accorded formal recognition to Protestantism, Catholicism, Hinduism, and Buddhism. In the last decades of the twentieth century, the state increasingly treated membership in one of these religions as a condition for citizenship by, for instance, requiring it of civil servants and insisting that an affiliation be declared on identity cards. In some parts of Indonesia, this, along with the strong church presence in schools and development projects, had the effect of identifying Christianity either with the state or with the West—or both. In either case, Christianity is commonly associated with modernity.

The state's national ideology (Pancasila) declares Indonesians to be monotheistic believers (Kipp and Rodgers 1987; see Bowen 1993; Geertz 1973; Hefner 1985, 1993). All others are relegated to the politically suspect position of those who "do not yet have a religion" (Indonesian, *belum beragama*), or the more neutral census category "other" (Indonesian, *lain*). Into the latter fell 63.6 percent of West Sumba's population of 262,813, according to the 1986 census (Kantor Statistik 1987). Such figures, of course, reflect neither the numbers of practicing Christians who had not yet taken the step of baptism, nor those among the baptized who continued to join in ancestral rituals.

The context of conversion in Sumba differs in one important respect from elsewhere in Christian Indonesia. In most of Indonesia, Islam, the dominant religion in some form or another, establishes the terms of oppo-

---

10. Under Dutch colonial policy, Christian missions were discouraged in the Islamic heartlands of the Indies but permitted in regions where Islam had not taken hold. As a result, certain areas such as the province in which Sumba is located, Nusa Tenggara Timur, are now predominantly Christian. Many Indonesians of Chinese descent are also church members. On Christianity in Indonesia, see Aragon 2000; Kipp 1990, 1993; Kipp and Rodgers 1987; van Klinken 2003; Rutherford 2003; Schrauwers 2000; Spyer 1996, 2000; Steedly 1993; Tsing 1993.

sition by which others define themselves. Although Sumbanese are sensitive to the domination of Islam in the nation as a whole, Muslim presence on the island itself is largely confined to officials, soldiers, and traders, mostly localized in two or three small towns. Practitioners of marapu ritual, still a majority in West Sumba in the 1980s, found themselves a minority within a province (Nusa Tenggara Timur) that is dominated by Christians. The strongest pan-Sumbanese institution is the increasingly assertive Gereja Kristen Sumba, whose members see one of their most immediate challenges to be the power of Catholics in the provincial government.

If religious difference is not primarily a matter of ethnic difference, neither at the moment does it clearly follow class or geographical lines. Here I can speak most precisely about Anakalang, where I carried out fieldwork in the 1980s and 1990s. In Anakalang, it is not unusual to find families in which one brother is Protestant, one Catholic, and yet another a marapu follower.[11] Occasionally a husband and wife have different affiliations, although Christian families are reluctant to let their affines, to whom they are linked by strong exchange and ceremonial obligations, remain outside the fold. Once a person has entered one or the other church, he or she is assumed to have declared an allegiance once and for all; theoretically, one crosses the historical divide between pagan and Christian only once.[12] This results in a certain tension between Catholic and Protestant, for while marapu followers can be treated as a pool of potential Christians, a Christian of one denomination is lost to the other.

In general, by the 1980s and 1990s, religious difference was not a major divisive element. Anakalangese, regardless of religious affiliation, coexisted more or less easily on a daily basis. Christians and non-Christians lived in the same villages, cooperated in working the same fields, were not usually forbidden to intermarry, and perhaps most important, participated equally in the compelling social obligations of feasting, marriage negotiations, and funerals. Nevertheless, with half the population Christian and half not, religious difference was an undercurrent that might break through most

---

11. *Marapu* refers to the spirits of the earliest ancestors. The term has come into general use in Sumba to refer to the entire ritual system and its practitioners. I use the term *follower* with some hesitation. Ancestor ritualists do not follow spirits as one follows a prophet, but they do speak of performing rites as "following" *(keri, padutungu)* the "tracks" *(wewi)* left by the ancestors.

12. In fact, people do occasionally return to the marapu, especially in response to serious illness or other crises. A person who changes too often, however, especially among different Christian churches, is scorned as being feckless and is likely to be excluded from positions of responsibility.

effectively where it was least guarded against. One largely invisible point of difference was between Calvinist and marapu-oriented semiotic ideologies. This point of difference was usually invisible because, outside explicitly religious contexts such as church services, semiotic forms in the hands of Christians did not seem to differ much from those in the hands of marapu followers.

LOSS AND REPRESENTABILITY

The first recorded Dutch visit to Anakalang was in 1910; by 1912, a "king" (Indonesian, *raja*) had been appointed, one of some dozen-odd raja to be appointed over the various societies or "domains" (Dutch, *landschappen*) of the island (Witkamp 1912). In this first generation of colonial indirect rule, the authority of the various raja in West Sumba was limited, for it lacked any solid foundation in the acephalous social structure of autonomous and competitive clans. The colonial officials, perhaps disappointed by an implicit comparison with the impressive courts they had experienced elsewhere in the Indies, tended to take a cynical view of the rulers they had established. The ruler of Anakalang was among the least respected of them all, making "absolutely no lordly impression at all with his bony diminutive stature and his mumbling chirping voice" (Wielenga 1912: 150; see also Lansz 1919). In subsequent generations, matters changed somewhat, depending in part on the skills of specific rulers and variations in local societies. The third raja of Anakalang, Umbu Sappy Pateduk, took office in 1927. Working hard to establish his position, he founded the village of Kaḅoduku as a sort of capital and revived certain lapsed rituals (Riekerk 1941). By the time of his death in 1953, the family power and wealth was well established and his son, Umbu Remu Samapatty, went from being raja to become the first regent (Indonesian, *bupati*) of West Sumba. Other members of the family continue to hold high positions in Sumba and as Sumbanese representatives in the national capital, Jakarta, to this day.

This colonial background has two implications for the present relationship of Anakalangese to the past. One concerns the recentness of the creation of the raja and his kingdom. The rise and fall of the kingdom of Anakalang took five short generations, its origins hardly lost in the mists of the past. Even the most partisan defenders of the legitimacy of the raja clan cannot overlook the fact that the kingdom was a Dutch invention. This provides contemporary Anakalangese with an example from recent experience that distant ancestors are not the only ones who may stand at the origins of things. The rise of the raja clan to dominance in local politics and ritual practice can be dated back to the actions of men who are still remembered. This suggests that those who are alive today may also take on ancestral stature as founders of new forms of order. In order to be recognized as an ancestor-like founder, however, the person who claims to be one must appear to be realizing a capacity for ancestral status that is already latent in the nature of ritual practices.

This was what the third raja, Umbu Sappy Pateduk, was doing when he strove to restore lapsed annual rites and when he moved his seat from the ancestral village of Lai Tarung to the newly founded Kaboduku. In an apparent effort to give substance to the new position of raja, one that before his time had lacked credibility in Anakalang, he set out to act as an ancestor, that is, as founder of a new order. In addition to making important marriage alliances and enriching himself, this meant fulfilling the potential already embodied in the rituals of house building and village clearing. In founding the village of Kaboduku, Umbu Sappy Pateduk initiated a long sequence of ritual obligations centered on the rituals for cleansing the village site and building houses and tombs. The force of these founding actions is seen in the fact that, some thirty years after Umbu Sappy Pateduk's death, the people of Kaboduku still felt the weight of those rites that remain unfulfilled.

The second implication of the colonial background concerns the concepts of "custom" (Indonesian, *adat*), "culture" (Indonesian, *kebudayaan*) and "tradition" (Indonesian, *tradisi*), which are influenced by European definitions (see chapter 3) and Indonesian state policies that presuppose them. In the local version of a nationwide development, Anakalangese, like other people on Sumba, are coming to perceive themselves as possessors of a culture largely understood not as ways of acting but as something to be known and described (chapter 9; see also Keane 1997a). Culture is represented, on the one hand, as a stable and bounded body of knowledge that a person might master discursively and, on the other, as practices no longer alive and complete but partially lost. This contrast between verbalized knowledge and practice derives not only from historical circumstances: it also has sources in Sumbanese idioms of loss and lament, in a general European nostalgia for stable, archaic traditions (itself conjoined with specific requirements of indirect rule), and in recent national pressures to domesticate local differences in the interest of order (Pemberton 1994).

Local idioms both of ritual speech and everyday etiquette stress loss, depletion, and lament. Even in the first decades of the Dutch period, Sumbanese were claiming that in the past the rains were always abundant, in contrast to contemporary conditions of periodic drought (Onvlee 1973g: 115). A Dutch administrator noted, "The populace treasures up an extraordinarily pretty recollection of this [past] marapu, it carries them to the time when the 'Company' [i.e., the Dutch] was not yet here, a time overflowing with milk and honey, a time without calamities, without sickness, without heavy duties, without tax reckoning" (Waitz 1933: 9). Without the colonial sarcasm, this expresses a distinct historical imagination in which the sense of a depleted present appears to be too pervasive and too enduring to be a simple response to empirical circumstances. The comparison of the world before the Dutch to that after their arrival parallels a more general comparison of the ancestors to the living. This comparison articulates in turn with strong Anakalangese norms of modesty as well as self-protection. For example, one does not directly draw attention to one's wealth or knowledge. The negotiation of exchanges is also necessarily pervaded by claims of ignorance and poverty. Speech addressed to the spirits resonates with the same idiom. It is accepted that mistakes in ritual are bound to happen, and one hedges one's ritual speech with disclaimers and requests that mediating spirits correct one's mistakes before passing the message on to the greater forces.

These disclaimers and requests, however, are not necessarily false modesty or hollow forms of etiquette. They often reflect a recognition that the formal complexity and order of ritual life stand out against empirical shortcomings. One instance of this is the common way of describing ancestral villages. Normally a person will enumerate all the house sites (yili uma), regardless of whether a house has actually stood on the site in anyone's memory. When talking about such things as empty house sites, people often use the opposed terms mema and jiawa. Mema, meaning "original" or "the way things have always been," is contrasted to jiawa, "foreign." Jiawa identifies the modern era (Indonesian, masa moderen) and Christianity. Note that with the word tana (literally, "land," "place," or "a distinct region"), the concept of a temporal epoch takes a spatial form. In the mid–twentieth century, Onvlee wrote (referring to the Weyewan language of western Sumba), "Tana mema is the familiar, the accustomed, original world wherein one feels or felt oneself at home and wherein one knows how to behave. Contrasted to this is tana dawa the foreign world" (1973g: 114). He adds that old Sumbanese say the dawa has rendered "powerless our customs, one might say, our very lives. Kàba, faint, tasteless, powerless, what can, e.g., be said of a medicine that no longer works, its power has gone, or of the ndewa [spirit] of a man who has been publicly shamed" (1973g: 115–16). By the late twentieth century, jiawa had been identified in folk etymology with the name *Java*, the seat of political power in post-Independence Indonesia, but the term itself has a much wider range and be applied to the Dutch bearers of Christianity and the present Indonesian government.[13]

In the context of talk about villages, mema not only means "old" but also distinguishes what is "true" but empirically (and contingently) absent from what is present. The house sites, whether empty or occupied, are conceptually permanent components of the "ancestral village" *(paraingu)* that constitutes the ritual center of a "clan" *(kabisu).* The low status "branch villages" *(kalebu gàlu)* remain subordinate in status to the ancestral villages from which they descended until they have themselves obtained altars, tombs, and inalienable valuables and the founding rituals have been performed. The formation of ancestral villages is usually thought of as having been completed once and for all in the time of the ancestors: house sites are empty in reference to houses that once were, not in anticipation of houses yet to come. Nevertheless, in practice some branch villages do, over time, achieve such ritual completion and thereby gain the status of ancestral village. One of the chief means by which Umbu Sappy Pateduk asserted his position as founder of a new era of kingship was by setting into motion such a ritual completion. As a result, the ancestral village of Lai Tarung, in which only three houses were standing in the 1980s, began to give way to the village of Kaboduku founded only some sixty years before.

People in Anakalang often insist that only the ancestors knew the complete and correct rites and histories; all that is left is remnant knowledge. The presence of the spirits is itself manifest in traces *(tada,* literally, "proof," "sign," or "mark") left behind. In addition to house sites, ritual procedures, and the words of prayers and histories, these consist of stone tombs and, most significant, inalienable valuables (literally, "the marapu's portion," *tagu marapu)* "replacing" *(pahèpangu)* the lost body of the ancestor. Such traces are commonly referred to as "shadows" *(mawu):* what we can know is "the shadow on the dry land, the reflection in the water" *(mawu ta mara, ninu ta wai).* "Shadows" are metonymically linked to referents that are more complete, often of higher rank, and temporally prior to them. This shadow relation is likewise mapped on the land as ancestral villages spawn

13. Etymologically, jiawa seems to come from a root meaning "outside" or "far." Westerners are termed "white foreigners" *(jiawa kaka).* Long pants (in opposition to Sumbanese cloth) are "foreign clothing" *(kalabi jiawa),* the road is "foreign rice-field dike" *(kamotu jiawa),* government office work is distinguished from traditional duties as "foreign duty" *(dihi jiawa),* and recently introduced ceremonies, such as wedding receptions, are "foreign custom" *(na pata jiawa).*

garden settlements, which are less complete and of lower status because they lack tombs, fixed house sites, and certain altars.

A similar perception of the present as a depleted version of the past is found in the prevailing attitude toward change in ritual practices. Such change is most often expressed in terms of addition and subtraction. Anakalangese actively worry more about people adding to ritual procedures, which they often identify with illegitimate status competition. On the other hand, subtraction—for example, performance of only a portion of the appropriate sacrifices for a certain event—accords with conventional laments of depletion. Incomplete rites are common due to economic and logistical constraints. The result is that rituals may vary according to the economic capacities and rank of the participants and therefore constitute a hierarchy from simpler to more elaborate versions. Simplified rites confirm the value and stability of the complete versions that sponsors are unable to accomplish. The ability to add to rites, like the ability to create new villages, challenges the prevailing perception that the present, as a trace, is in a subordinate relationship to the more complete past.

One common way of expressing the notion of loss and traces is in the claim that a "book" was left behind on Bali by the ancestors in their trek toward Sumba (compare Kammerer 1990). It is for this reason, some say, that the Balinese have such famous and elaborate cultural displays while the Sumbanese remain in obscurity. Two comments that Anakalangese made about this book reflect divergent ways of understanding the nostalgia for lost order. One ritual specialist *(ratu)* told me that, had that book not been lost, the Sumbanese would now be able to make more efficacious rites and more realistic carvings. The concern of a Christian village head was that, had the book been preserved, the rules would be unchangeable. His perspective was somewhat more "modern," as it echoes the government's views of "tradition" as ideally immutable. Note that the practitioner's primary focus is on what must be done and how correctly to do it, while the village head's interest is the reproduction of a stable order. There is another aspect of the village head's perspective as well, which reflects the influence of central government policies and his personal ties to promoters of tourism on the island. He told me that he must know his traditions so that he would be able to answer if someone were to ask him what they were. The fact that he was a practicing Christian was not at issue. His concern was with answering questions; at this point, then, he was seeing tradition much more as a kind of knowledge that can be mastered, formulated, and spoken of than as a source of ways to act in and on the world independently of the discourses about tradition themselves.

Although increasing numbers of Anakalangese, Christians and marapu followers alike, say that "the foreign marapu has won," this assertion involves a way of formulating history that preserves the idea of marapu at the same time that it vanquishes marapu ritual, or at least its core practical modalities. It was my strong impression that only the most orthodox Christians among the people I knew in 1980s and 1990s seriously challenged the reality of the spirits. Rather, what was at issue was the power of the spirits relative to the Christian God and the relative efficacy or economics of the rituals they demand. It has, for example, become common for both Christians and non-Christians to draw analogies between the world of the Old Testament and marapu practices, such as the making of burnt offerings, food taboos, and the importance of cattle. Drawing parallels like this goes back to the fact that many missionaries sought as scholars to uncover a natural monotheism of native peoples (see chapter 3), and they used the Old Testament comparison as a rhetorical strategy in their preaching. At present, the analogy has been adopted by many Anakalangese. Comparing marapu practices to the Old Testament grants them great status, for antiquity, synonymous with the ancestral, is in Anakalang an important source of value and authority. One ratu made explicit the value of precedence in evaluating religions when he told me that, after the marapu people, it was the Catholics who should be ranked second, for Luther's "protest" was quite recent.[14]

The language of temporal precedence is equivocal, however, for it can go along with the notion of temporal epochs. It locates the spirits in a segregated past. In this perception of history, the precedence of the spirits is acknowledged in the very act of displacing them. The displacement evokes a theme of loss. Many modernist Christians may on occasion speak in nostalgic tones of the spirits—one Protestant minister told me it is a pity that, once all the old men die, no one will know the rites anymore. He reminisced to me how he himself, when a child, had taken pride in being the one to hold out the chickens for sacrifice. This is of course the sort of nostalgia that confirms one is on the side of destiny, that, in the words of the Dutch quoted in chapter 4, the deceased do not return. But it is reinforced in the ritualist's defensive lament, which contrasts the empirical shortcomings of

14. This characterization of Luther seems to be rhetorically motivated in another way as well. Many Anakalangese, with strong support from bearers of the state's ideology in Suharto's New Order regime, tended to see "protest" (Indonesian, *protes*), whether Lutheran or that of contemporary politics, in purely negative terms.

the present to the more perfect lost order known to the ancestors. These laments in turn resonate with the obligatory complaint of poverty demanded by the etiquette of exchange. Remnant traces of the marapu past provide a contrast that highlights the powers of Christianity and the state. The contrast sharpens the visibility of difference that makes it possible to speak of a new historical epoch, the "free age" (Indonesian, *masa merdeka*), which is sharply delineated from, yet devolves out of, the past.

INTO THE FOREIGN LAND

By the last quarter of the twentieth century, people in Anakalang could represent Christianity as either a radical departure from the past or as the legitimate successor to their earlier religion. In actual practice, Anakalangese sometimes claim that everything is different, that "the land is foreign now" *(na tana jiawa yayi)*, and that "the foreign ancestor spirit has won" *(taluneka na marapu jiawa)*. Anakalangese, however, also commonly speak of the present in contrast to a past distinguished from it by greater wealth, ritual correctness, and possession of stable social hierarchy. This perception stresses an essential continuity with the past, marked only by degrees of loss, and it implies that the difference is merely quantitative. "Tradition" is one way of talking about or against this juxtaposition of past and present.

The appeal to tradition commonly involves a claim that present acts repeat those of the past. Yet this apparent repetition can bring about reevaluations and transformations of those very procedures. More specifically, to enact rituals in the present context often has the effect of changing the stuff of tradition from a set of ways of acting to a fixed body of knowledge (see chapter 9). As a fixed body of knowledge, tradition is something that, potentially, can be repeatedly displayed, without external effects or internal changes. If it is associated with the past, that past will no longer impinge on the present through the obligations the living owe to demanding and dangerous ancestral spirits. Rather, the past in which tradition is located comes to be perceived as lying on the other side of a boundary that cannot be crossed: the past has no effect on the present, and conversely, the living present may speak *of* but cannot speak *to* or by means of the ancestral past.

Although Anakalangese Christians and marapu followers tend to agree on the precedence of ancestor worship, and to see themselves at an historical juncture, these general perceptions are available for the competing interpretations and strategies of rivalrous and political factions and individuals. I turn now to a highly public assertion of historical agency. It is both unusual and exemplary, and it draws on the rhetorical modes of performance largely restricted to male elders of fairly high standing, and on claims about subjective experience that can be more widely, if covertly, distributed.

In 1986, a man I call Umbu Neka, an elderly ratu (ritual specialist) from Kaboduku and close kinsman of the late raja Umbu Sappy Pateduk, planned to enter the Sumbanese Christian Church. He was deeply knowledgeable about local history, myth, and ritual and had also held a number of positions in local government. With an astute eye for historical resonances, to say nothing of a flair for self-promotion, Umbu Neka set his baptism for Indonesia's national Independence Day, August 17. This alignment of personal transformation with the national narrative is especially striking in Sumba, where the coming of Christianity has tended to play a role in the historical imagination and the idea of modernity far larger than that of the nationalist narratives for which independence from colonial rule is the defining moment. This is in part due to the relative distance of national events, compared to the immediacy of the missionaries and the intimacy of their impact. It is reinforced by the sense of identification Sumbanese Christians have with their Dutch coreligionists—the story of liberation from colonial rule is far less appealing to those who feel this has stranded them in a nation of Muslims. Umbu Neka's choice suggests that the relations between the two parallel historical narratives may be undergoing some recalibration. His own attempt to align the personal event of conversion and the larger historical orders of national triumph and global salvation would contribute to this.

The night before his baptism was to be held, Umbu Neka staged a *yaiwo* in the ritual dance plaza of Kaboduku. Yaiwo is a performance that should last continuously from sundown to sunrise.[15] A single man sits at the edge of the plaza, singing to the accompaniment of gongs and drums. In the plaza, a line of young men dances exuberantly to this music, brandishing swords and shields and occasionally yelling. Women who are watching from the edges of the plaza respond to their yells with ululations. Periodically, the music and dance are interrupted by a long loud cry from the sidelines by a man announcing his intention to speak. The music falls silent and the

15. For a detailed analysis of the yaiwo and other genres, and of the authority of ritual form on which these remarks rest, see Keane 1997c, where I mention this event briefly. Closely related genres from neighboring parts of Sumba are described in Hoskins 1988 and Kuipers 1990.

dancers retire to the sidelines so he may do so. Yaiwo orations are impro-vised compositions made up of conventional parallelistic couplets. Over the course of the night, several orators, usually older men, will participate, and their speeches tend to be in dialogue with the other speeches. Dialogue is also formally built into the oration itself, since each orator marks segments of his speech by crying out, "Oh yaiwo singer!" *(O ma yaiwo)*, to which another man replies, "Go ahead!" When the speaker finishes, the music and dance resume, the singer begins again, his song consisting of quotations from or allusions to the orator's words. In the marapu rituals that were the normal context for yaiwo performances, the singer's function is to pass those words along to the spirits. The marapu register their response to those words through augury, using the entrails of chickens or the livers of pigs, horses, or water buffalo that are offered and slaughtered at the beginning and end of the event (see Kuipers 1990: 99–107). Christians, of course, are supposed to reject this interpretation of the song and to avoid the auguries. The same oration, for them, functions within a representational economy different from that of marapu followers.

Significant individual conversion narratives seem to be rare in Anakalang. Umbu Neka, however, insistently claimed, in both private con-versations and public oratory, to have been led to the church by neither education nor persuasion, but by a visionary calling. In his account, after years of resisting the importunities of preachers and kinfolk, he had been summoned by a voice out of the darkness during a serious illness. His story was striking in its apparent individualism and subjective content. More commonly, Anakalangese conversion narratives dwell on rather mundane or rational matters, rather than startling claims about new insights or lives transformed. They typically portray entering the church as an act appro-priate for educated persons, as an acknowledgment of the power of the gov-ernment, the modern epoch, or one's kin, or as a more rational, economic mode of life in which one eschews the expense of sacrifices.

Although Umbu Neka stressed the uniqueness of his conversion, his oratory contained an important theme that would be familiar to most of his listeners. In the act of representing himself as entering "onto a different path" *(ta lara hekaya)*, he claimed for himself a founding relationship to that path. The image of the path is resonant in Anakalang, for it refers to the correct way, worn by constant, repetitive, undeviating passage from the time of the ancestors. Correct ceremonial procedures, the "trodden path, crossing way" *(lara li, ada pala)*, contrast with straying into the shrubs and thorns. In historical narratives, known as the "path taken by the ancestors" *(lara li marapu)*, there is another important feature: the path of the ancestors is delineated by the marks and traces they left behind. These may be the scraps of knowledge and rules by which their descendants attempt to follow them. But when the path is traced across space as well as time, they are also concrete signs: the tip of a spear here, a broken tomb there, small gardens in distant parts of the island. In this semiotic ideology, the signs that have been left behind are not only fragments of a former whole but are also marked for rank. The gardens, for example, are said to this day to be tended by the descendants of slaves or dependents who had been left there by the ancestors to guard them.

In the present case, not only did Umbu Neka point *forward* to a path that he claimed ran forward from his conversion, but he also left *behind* his own sign, a successor priest, who was marked as inferior in rank, exemplary yet marginal, as befits the "shadow" of an ancestor. In representing conversion this way, Umbu Neka followed a model for action that makes innovation possible—and he was able to do so precisely because, implicitly, for him the oratory of marapu ritual remained a way of acting on the world, not merely the display of a fixed body of knowledge. Indeed, his way of representing his conversion made great claims. He represented himself not as merely another of a growing number of converts. Instead, through his orations and the ritual ending of his relations with the spirits, he demanded public recognition of the founding character of his actions, that his move to Christianity was in some sense a powerful act that reshaped the world much as the ancestors were able to reshape the world.

To claim such a foundational role is to situate oneself at the beginning of a new "path," just as the ancestors too are found at the origins of the various historical paths that lead to present-day arrangements. Claims like this can succeed only if other people are willing to acknowledge them—they are contentious and risk being denied. This risk is perhaps proof of the continued vitality of Anakalangese oration in the last decades of the twentieth century. Umbu Neka was not able to take the authority of his claim for granted, for it might not necessarily be accepted by others. Others were able to make contending claims of their own. This is what happened within months of Umbu Neka's baptism, for example, when a marapu priest from another clan held his own oratorical event, fiercely attacking the Christians, implicitly putting forth his own claims based on the role of his own father in rebuilding several ritual houses. In either case, the risk was that the speaker would not obtain the recognition necessary to make his novel act foundational. His actions would then turn out to be simply idiosyncratic or antisocial, to be called "individualistic" (Indonesian, *individualis*), a strongly negative term. This was, in fact, the accusation made against Umbu Neka by that fellow priest: "Who is he to think he received direct word from God? Why even Moses didn't see God. Does he say he's been summoned with a letter?"

Umbu Neka's accuser brought to light a crucial distinction between marapu and Calvinist semiotic ideologies. The Protestant concepts of grace and revelation support practices such as prayer spoken by an individual, using words of his or her own choosing, that is addressed directly to God. The concepts and the practices that follow from them deny the principle of mediation that defines Sumbanese dealings with marapu. I discuss the implications of the Christian challenge to verbal mediation in the chapters that follow. But the heart of the distinction is summarized by the somewhat casuistical reasoning of some marapu ritualists who have been listening to Christians: Sure, there is a Creator God, but how do you reach him?[16] God created Adam and Eve, and we descended from them. We cannot reach God directly. Even if it were possible, it would be arrogant to try. We go by way of that trail of ancestors which leads from him to us. This is why we speak in the language those ancestors gave us, the couplets of ritual speech, and follow the proper ritual forms. We speak to them in their words, not our own.

What Umbu Neka's accuser focused on is the hubris of someone—like the Christians—who claims an unmediated relationship to the invisible world of spirits. But there are other implications as well. The explicit intentions of the speeches in Umbu Neka's yaiwo were to inform the spirits of the change in religions and to introduce them to the priest who would succeed him, whom I call Umbu Ndongu, another kinsman of the raja, but by a low-ranking wife. Early in his opening speeches, Umbu Neka introduced himself by declaring his foundational position as the senior priest, the one who passes on the priesthood to a successor, "who switches the water sluice, who replaces the house" *(ma hailuya na soka, ma hèpaya na uma)*. Addressing the spirit of his kinsman, the late raja, he linked himself to this greater authority who had made him a priest: "Earlier, I received the pot-rests on the head, earlier I received the burdens on the shoulder" *(Waiga ḍuku kayisa ḍa kaliangu ta katiku, waiga ḍuku kayisa ḍa daitu ta kaḅaki).*[17] In this introductory segment, Umbu Neka established his authority as speaker, priest, and sponsor identified with the greater interests of the clan. He drew the parallel between the role of the ancestor and his own role: just

16. Neither Sumbanese nor Indonesian pronouns are marked for gender, but in view of the conservatism of the Reformed Churches Calvinists, I am probably justified in treating God as male.

17. Pot-rests help balance water pots carried on the head, a task normally restricted to women. Many couplets pair male and female elements, which helps convey a sense of completeness and correctness in Sumbanese aesthetics.

as that ancestor had bequeathed the office to him, so he would bequeath the same office to his chosen successor. By invoking the role of his late kinsman, the raja Umbu Sappy Pateduk, as rebuilder of fallen houses and founder of the village of Kaboduku, Umbu Neka was also claiming ancestral status for the actions of the raja, whose authority he clearly sought to appropriate. Having set the context for the ritual, he then described himself: "I go babbling as a child, I go decrepit with age" *(Laugika ta kajokalu lakawa, laugika ta nokulu kaweḍa)*, a conventional description of old age. His approach to the matter at hand was, following convention, indirect; he spoke not as an apostate but as a retiree.

Closing the first speech, he brought in figures that represented the irrevocable passage of time and the diminished present. He referred to Lai Tarung, the ritual center for his clan set, now mostly abandoned due to the move to the late raja's village of Kaboduku. He contrasted its present state with its former liveliness, which in turn was likened to that of the original village of the first ancestors. In Lai Tarung now, unlike in the past, "there is not even the pecking of chicks, there is not even the lapping of pigs at the trough" *(da aimangu na ma katakaru patituk, da aimangu na ma kabogaru pajàba)*. Already, before the explicit theme of conversion was introduced, the contrast of past and present was emphasized. This contrast rhetorically supported Umbu Neka's attempt to situate his conversion at the border between two epochs.

Another recurrent theme was sounded in the lines "I would just reach the tip of the wood, I would just cover over the soil" *(Ku supukadiyaka ta ai, ku pinukadika ta tana)*. This is a conventional expression of the obligation to complete unfinished rites. In this case, Umbu Neka referred to ritually completing the village of Kaboduku that was founded by the raja Umbu Sappy Pateduk. This village had an immense tomb, but not the other defining features of a clan center, such as a stone monolith next to the tomb, a Great House, and purification rites. As long as these were lacking, the raja's founding act was incomplete and the remains of the former ritual center, Lai Tarung, persisted as a reminder of a general state of deferral and depletion. Umbu Neka drew on temporal imagery both in defense of his own conversion and against the accusation of having abandoned his responsibilities before their fulfillment. The meaning of his own conversion was underlined as he affirmed the continuing legitimacy of ritual obligation. Here the cultural theme was mobilized to contribute to the sense of temporal boundedness.

The structure of his oration affirmed the contrast between the ideal past order and present-day remnants. Approaching by steps the actual place and time of his oration, he began by naming the primordial ancestral village, moving then to its later successor, Lai Tarung, the village that had gone into decline since the raja founded Kaboduku. Only then did he refer to Kaboduku, where the crucial purification rites, monolith, and Great House remained unaccomplished. The sequence of images reflected the common Anakalangese perception that the closer one is to the temporal and spatial present, the greater the manifest incompletion and imperfection. It was a lack, however, that in this instance referred both backward and forward in time: Lai Tarung half abandoned, Kaboduku half completed.

Umbu Neka then explained that the last requests of the raja had committed him to completing his works by adding the monolith, the Great House, and the purification rite. The bounded temporality here was delimited in two senses, for it was not only a past that had to be closed off but specifically one defined as a prototypical founding event. By founding the village and raising the tomb, the raja had attempted to constitute himself as prototypical ancestor. Dying before the completion of his task, he asked Umbu Neka to carry on for him, with words that Umbu Neka now quoted: "I leave behind the rear end unraised, I depart leaving the feet unlifted" (Pakamodu kídi dijakugu, pawisi sàda wèrugu). Repeating the theme of temporal boundedness, Umbu Neka then referred to his baptism to occur the following day:

At daybreak on the land,	Na wehangu na tana
I arrive at the hand that summons me	tomagika ta ma lima pakawaikuga
at the rising of dawn;	na hunga na hadei
I arrive at the eye that winks at me.	tomagika ta ma mata pakabadukuga.

The closing lines of the speech reasserted the continuity of the priestly line, assuring that Kaboduku would be completed

as long as they are my fellow piglets of one sow,	mali wawi oli baidigusa duda
as long as they are my fellow chicks of one hen,	mali manu oli inadigusa duda
as there are they who switch the sluice,	ba aija da ma sailuya na soka
as there are they who replace the house.	ba aija da ma sèpaya na uma.

The presence in the speeches of the late raja, Umbu Sappy Pateduk, in the character of a ritual founder, was strong. He was the one who had maintained the continuity of tradition passed on by the first ancestor, "he who scooped up the first rainwater, he who followed the tracks of the ancient pig" *(na ma haika na wai kawunga urangu, na ma kanukaya na wewi wawi)*. Umbu Sappy Pateduk represented both continuity from the ancestors and the capacity to reproduce their deeds with a new beginning, the latter culminating in the founding of the very village, Kaboduku, in which Umbu Neka now spoke. By implication, his kinsman Umbu Neka could tap the same capacity. The founder Umbu Sappy Pateduk was also the last of a generation. He was described as "the remaining ember" *(na kajupu patuni)*, reinforcing the delineation of temporal boundedness. The image of the last glowing ember in the hearth evoked not only the dying down of a fire but also the source of new fire, since a common sight in the village was that of a child sent from one house to another with a coconut shell to carry back embers for starting up the hearth fire again. This image, then, provided assurance that the minimal conditions for achieved continuity remained, despite the strong countertheme of temporal boundedness. Although the convert had crossed a border, like a territorial boundary, both sides remained present, *if* segregated.

But was continuity really maintained? Umbu Ndongu, the successor priest, made his own speeches in response to Umbu Neka, a reflexive complaint about the event itself that exposed the contradiction at the heart of the whole rite. In Anakalangese ritual there are two minimal prerequisites for all formal communication, whether among humans or, for non-Christians, with the spirit world. One is the use of ritual speech. The other is the grounding of that speech in prestations, offerings or sacrifices, known as the "material" *(dati)* that serves as the "base" *(lata)* for the words. Words, no matter how proper, if not spoken on the "base" of materials, risk going astray and having their intentions lost (Keane 1997c, chapter 3). Christians, however, are forbidden to make sacrifices, so in Umbu Neka's yaiwo ritual, the guests were fed with pigs that had been slaughtered without being offered to the spirits with prayers. This killing of animals without prayers is believed by marapu followers not only to threaten successful communication with the spirits but also to be an example of the greed of Christians, who kill animals for no reason other than their meat (see chapter 8). Moreover, shifting the full weight of the event's performative efficacy onto the oratory has consequences for the implied agents as well. Ritual agency still remains distributed, since there are several orators. But if the animals are slaughtered merely to feed the guests, and not as sacrifices, the people who had raised, obtained, and brought the animals no longer have a direct role in the real action. Moreover, once the dead animal is treated only as meat, it no longer plays a speaking part in its own right. That is, the divinatory examination of liver or entrails has been eliminated and, with it, the only way that the spirits can respond directly to the orators. Dialogue has been replaced by monologue. As I have suggested, the difference in semiotic ideologies has implications for the representational economies in which talk, killing, eating, and obligation function. As Christians chip away at the traditional forms of mediation, they are seen by many other Anakalangese to be making exaggerated claims for their own personal agency.

Umbu Ndongu took aim at precisely this point. Without sacrificial offerings of betel, meat, and rice—the base required of any offering—he said, "there is no material for them [i.e., the spirits] to listen with, for them to receive us with" *(da aimangu bahana na parangu waida, na pakayi waidada)*. As a result, "there's no path, it's already mixed up, eh?" *(ya da aimangu lara, pakariwangunapa)*. So in this ritual, there was no leave-taking: "Before we enter another path, let us finish this one" *(Manga di tama ta lara hangi higapakinya na lara ya)*. He too insisted on the importance of temporal boundedness and the creation of an ending.[18]

Umbu Ndongu had made explicit an important point. By seemingly reproducing the traditional rites, Umbu Neka in fact transformed them, making the spoken part central and removing the crucial sacrifices, thereby ignoring the potential anger of the spirits. Yet when Umbu Neka mobilized the imagery of closure in a new context, he was able to present himself as simply carrying on life as usual. In vain did Umbu Ndongu, the weaker successor, protest that the emperor had no clothes. Umbu Neka had gone a long way toward successfully constituting himself as a new epoch's founder, to whom future generations might refer their own acts. At the same time, his very use of ritual transformed it into a diminished form of action, one that lacked supernatural consequences.

18. Umbu Ndongu was not merely acting as a stickler for proper form. Not surprisingly, there was also a political subtext to his intervention, a dispute over a rice field that was supposed to go with the ratu's office. As the proceedings of the American Congress do, Anakalangese rituals provide an opportunity to filibuster, publicly holding up the procedures, in order to make a point. But Umbu Ndongu's intervention, whatever the ulterior motives, could serve this function only by using a logic that others would accept. And indeed, as was to become clear in my conversations with people over the months that followed, whatever people thought of his claims to the rice field, most of them recognized the legitimacy of his criticism of words spoken without a base of offerings.

AUTHORITY, THE RECOGNIZABLE,
AND THE UNREPEATABLE

Umbu Neka claimed that God had intervened in his own life to induce his conversion to Christianity. In this respect, the ultimate agent of his conversion lay beyond himself. Yet Umbu Neka also sought to claim authorship of his conversion, indeed, of the transformation of Anakalangese society overall. He did so by appropriating the most authoritative modes of action available to him, staging a yaiwo ritual and forming around his conversion the greatest possible public. The authority of the semiotic forms of the yaiwo (oratory with parallel couplets, formalized dialogue, gongs, dances, and offerings) derives from their capacity to index the persistence of the past within the present. These forms are purportedly derived from, and addressed to, forebears whose genealogical antecedence and superordinate position is manifested in their invisibility. That invisibility puts practical demands on semiotic form: the living must act in ways the dead can recognize (see Keane 1997c). But the purpose of these acts is not to hold onto or reproduce the past. Rather, it is to draw on the greatest powers the living have at their command, in their orientation to the future. This is not a future constituted as a rupture from the past, as Chakrabarty suggests it is for the historicist imagination, but a distinct mode of temporality. Umbu Neka's authority depends on a mode of objectification that linguistic anthropologists call entextualization. Through the palpability of form, his utterances are "aligned to the already-said and anticipate the to-be-said" (Bauman and Briggs 2003: 319). In order to draw on the power of the past, the orator takes advantage of the materiality of the yaiwo as a speech genre: the insistent repetitions of linguistic form, the special qualities of the oratorical voice, the sound of drums and gongs, everything that contributes to giving his acts a sensible distance from the present moment and makes them recognizable as instances of an ancestral mode of action.

Whether or not events such as Umbu Neka's yaiwo retain their power to affect the spirit world, they do serve as a way for people to negotiate and redefine the historical moment and their relationship to it. Oratorical dialogues provide occasions for people to demand recognition of their version of events and for others either to grant or deny these demands. Through such public interactions, mutually acknowledged meanings and relations are affirmed or dissolved. A year after his ritual, Umbu Neka boasted to me that it was only after he converted that everyone else began to enter Christianity. In fact this was a highly subjective claim. Conversion has been an ongoing process, with occasional periods of greater acceleration. To define a point at which it "begins" requires arbitrary boundaries of precisely the sort constituted by a "founding act." By holding his yaiwo, Umbu Neka put forward a claim that, thereafter, conversions were to be held to date from, and repeat, his own conversion. Meanwhile, he left behind on his former path the diminished traces of his presence, in the person of the lowly successor priest. While Umbu Neka was in a special position of influence, he was not alone in his sense of historical moment and desire to make useful sense of it. Indeed, if his claim to be founder of a new epoch comes to be accepted, this will be not only because of his status but also because the rhetoric of his orations made sense to his listeners. The public world of Anakalang is contentious enough that individual assertions like Umbu Neka's are perhaps never wholly subject to agreement. When I last saw Umbu Neka in 1993, shortly before his death, his claims were generally accepted at least within his sizable and influential clan. This does not mean they would ever become entirely canonical. What is more important, however, is what his effort reveals. He had formulated the difference between past and present deeds in a way that allowed him to imply that he was essentially only repeating what had happened before, in the time of the ancestors, as he, by further implication, claimed similar ancestral status for himself. This effort was one most Anakalangese would have found admirable. At the very least, they would have recognized the morality to which it appealed and the semiotic ideology it implied.

Yet if the act of conversion was represented in forms that imply an underlying continuity, so too this apparent continuity carried a reenvisioned present into the remembered past. Umbu Neka's ritual arose from a model for action that enabled his conversion to be significant and recognizable as foundational like the deeds of an ancestor. If his claims are accepted, the identity between present and past that he implied will become that much more established and able to circulate across the public world of Anakalang, if not beyond. Anakalangese will be able to say that the new epoch grew out of the old, and that Umbu Neka stood at the source of the path leading from one to the other. At the same time, he followed a model for innovation already implicit in the capacity of ancestors to be founders. Although his own way of using authoritative oratory was novel, in that it promoted words at the expense of offerings, he used oratory because it remained for him a powerful means of action. The transformation of a "traditional" way of acting exemplified by Umbu Neka's conversion ritual was possible because Umbu Neka still responded (if with covert selectivity) to models for action grounded in the world of marapu followers. Although he explicitly evoked differences between past and present, he did so in ways that implicitly affirmed their continuity, as in his use of formal oratory to speak to the spirits. Conversely, it is where he evoked continuity, in his use of ritual forms of address for the spirits, that he pragmatically introduced change, separating speech from sacrifice. Umbu Neka still had the authority to act with and within the forms provided by marapu ritual. Ironically, one outcome of his exercise of this authority was to widen the practical gap between ancestors and the living to suggest, through the omission of offerings, that the living no longer needed to fear the dead. To the extent that ancestral action is located on the far side of this gap, such authority will become scarce. To the extent that ritual and its language become stabilized and relocated in an unrepeatable past, no one may legitimately act and innovate with them. An unrepeatable past of this sort (although other outcomes may yet emerge) is knowable as a canon of words, a possession that people may display as an emblem of their "traditional" identity, but one, perhaps, no longer permitting them to act upon the world.

LANGUAGES PAST AND FUTURE

The point of this story certainly does not lie in its typicality. After all, Umbu Neka spoke with the secure authority of a senior male of high rank at a time when Christian and marapu adherents were nearly balanced. But his performance makes especially visible some key issues. First, when Umbu Neka wanted to speak with authority, he turned to existing genres, the available semiotic modalities of action; in Chakrabarty's words, he wielded "a language made out of the languages already available" (2000: 245). His case was only an extreme instance of two more general points, that the speech genres constrained him but also offered him raw materials with which to work. The persistence of generic forms gave his actions a distinctive historicity. Second, if this suggests a certain drag on innovative possibility, the reverse is also apparent. When Umbu Neka was most conservative in intent, his actions were the most transformative. And, third, the key moment in this transformation was a function of Christian modes of purification, the insistence both that sacrifice be eliminated and that words cease to serve many of their ritual functions, such as engaging one in dialogue with marapu or performing consequential actions in the world by virtue of the powers conveyed by their ancestral forms—what Christians might call "magic."

As I asked in the previous chapter, if spirits and deities exist in discourse, then what does it mean to say that the same spirit is still there once its name has been translated into a new language and used in new ways of speaking? In the case of the early Catholic Tagalog, if we accept Rafael's interpretation, signifiers are semiotically hard: that is, foreign words are capable of remaining alien presences in the midst of local discourse. But their hardness is subject to the work that people do upon existing semiotic forms over time. The transformation of these linguistic and performance forms by means of which—and the objects with respect to which, and the persons on behalf of whom—these words are spoken involve far more than denotations and concepts. In the early colonial Andes, for instance, the loss of material forms led to a greater emphasis on denotation and the conceptual properties of the spirit world. In twentieth-century highland Sulawesi, Tobaku use terms taken from Arabic that have retained a certain linguistic shape, but whose pragmatic function and semantic configuration are distinctive due to their place in the context of local discourses. In each case, semiotic forms have become part of the context to which people actively respond and the raw materials upon which they more or less purposively work. For the world of possible agents, these semiotic modalities are one dimension of the conditions referred to in Marx's observation (too often, perhaps, taken as a mere truism) that "men make their history[;] . . . they do not make it under circumstances chosen by themselves" (1978: 595).

As I suggested in chapter 4, if we want to say that the spirits still exist but under different names, or more generally, to say that anything cultural endures, we must be alert to the particular textual moments in which they are manifested and recontextualized. For translation occurs within the dynamic of entextualization. This means that translation begins with particular texts (stretches of discourse and, by extension, other forms of repeatable action) manifested as text artifacts (actual written objects, events of speaking, or recognizable actions) embedded in specific social and historical contexts (Silverstein 2003; Silverstein and Urban 1996). The process of translation eventually results in yet other texts and text artifacts, in other contexts. To call this multidimensional transformation of contexts "translation" depends on being able to claim some crucial identity between these different texts and actions. Since the contexts, text artifacts, and acts are manifestly different, semiotic ideology plays a crucial role in determining what counts as significant continuity and how people will experience it as real continuity.

Umbu Neka's yaiwo performance made an explicit claim about difference (I have entered a new religion) and an implicit one about continuity (The language of the ancestors is still a viable medium for the assertion of authority). If, as Chakrabarty says, the new can work only with existing languages, these languages are not merely conservative in character and do not merely reproduce anachronisms. Conversely, the most earnest claims to be setting out on new ventures, even to be entering into a universal history—whether these be narratives of modernity or of global salvation—must take on *specific* semiotic forms. What looks like the localization of Christianity may be, above all, one perspective on the conflicting outcomes of the semiotic form in motion. One aspect of this motion is purification: in his yaiwo, Umbu Neka attempted to put the spirits in the past by separating words from things, thereby stripping their language of some of their agency. In this respect, his was a small instance of the greater efforts at purification that characterize the evangelical project.

6 Fetishism and the Word

In the previous chapter I gave one example of how words and things serve as media for action yet also resist people's efforts to master and transform them. There are many ways to understand that resistance to human efforts. A Calvinist might see the ultimate source of resistance to human agency to be the will of God. From this perspective, the limits to human capacities are inseparable from the very sources of human freedom, since both have roots in the Creation, Temptation, and Fall. One way this postlapsarian condition is experienced is in the problems that words and things pose for Calvinist semiotic ideology, as I sketched out in chapter 2.

But of course the conundrums of agency are hardly confined to religious believers. For one thing, divine will is not the only source of the limits people may themselves impose on their actions. Even atheists, for instance, may attempt to submit themselves to the rule of law, the compelling force of logic, an aesthetic discipline, the demands of economic rationality, scientific truth, adherence to tradition, or ideals of justice. Or they may have submission imposed on them: recall the "iron cage" that Weber said had been forged by the modern economic order (1958: 181). But these constraints are easily cast as external to the human subject. They can be seen as having been chosen by that subject and, thus, as not bearing directly on, the inherent nature of the agency that chooses. Or they may be seen as conditions that might be altered given the right circumstances. It can be more troubling, for some concepts of human freedom, to find that the very media of action themselves impose limits on human agency. In a strong form of this view, any recalcitrance of semiotic form might be seen as a resistance to human actions. Recall again Judith Butler's reference to "a discourse we never chose . . . that, paradoxically, initiates and sustains our agency" (1997: 2). One source for the experience of externality and limits is the materiality of the semiotic forms by means of which people act.

At this point I look more closely at certain moments in the missionary encounter that bring the concept of agency and its complex, sometimes paradoxical, involvement with semiotic form into sharper focus. I argue that religious conversion can involve the introduction of a new semiotic ideology that transforms the conceptual and practical relations among words, things, and persons. For purposes of analysis and exposition, the next three chapters treat words and things separately (chapters 6 and 7 concentrate on words, chapter 8 on things). But the overarching argument of these three chapters is that such a distinction is in some important respects artificial, since words, things, and persons are mutually implicated in a representational economy, and ideological and practical changes in one have consequences for the others.

In this chapter I look at how agency is expressed in differences among the powers that people impute to spoken words and the kinds of subjects to which they attribute the authorship of words. As I argued in chapter 1, to think about agency, at least in its most robust forms, seems to demand an account of the conscious agent. But in order to be truly conscious, one might surmise, this agent must be conscious of the fact of agency itself. Such self-knowledge seems to be demanded, at least by any description of action that would separate intended from unintended consequences, and that would take into consideration what actors themselves expect of *other* actors as they guide their own actions. Yet if the particular forms and objects of consciousness are historical and cultural products, so too must be the concept of agency that mediates the agent's self-consciousness. Seeking out agency, then, includes looking for the historical construction of the idea of agency itself.

If agency, in some sense, depends on self-consciousness, only rarely does that self-consciousness take the form of an explicit theory of agency. Yet we may still ask, in any instance, to what kind of subject do people think agency properly belongs? The semiotic forms that mediate agency may give us access to the understandings implicit in modes of action. In this chapter and the next, I look at language—both as a set of practices and as an object of reflection—as an especially useful source of insight. There are both theoretical and ethnographically specific reasons to look at agency by way of language. For one thing, the semiotically and pragmatically complex character of language is such that speakers can refer to explicit beliefs about action, while their speech practices embody tacit, and possibly divergent, assumptions about the nature of action. And in the encounter on Sumba, both Dutch Calvinists and marapu followers place special weight on the powers and forms of language. Since language is simultaneously intimately bound up with the subjectivity of its speakers and consists of linguistic forms and pragmatic conventions not fully of speakers' own making, it is more than simply one medium of action among others. Although much of what I have to say applies to the speech of everyday conversation, the discussion here is restricted to words addressed to the spirit world. In the special but highly valued genre of prayer, different views of language and its speakers take some of their most sharply defined, and thus most visible, forms.

If I were to thoroughly discuss agency and language, I would have to pay close attention to the tacit understandings embedded in everything from legal institutions to gossip to linguistic structure (see Ahearn 2001; Duranti 2004). The ramifications lead in many directions. John Calvin, for instance, attacks the making of vows, partly on the grounds that they impose on the vow maker an external bondage that goes against "the blessing of liberty which God has conferred upon us" (1949: bk. 4, chap. 13, para. 3). In this chapter, however, my focus is narrower. I look primarily at how people address invisible spirits, how they talk about the powers and value of the speech with which they do so, and what the implications are for the presumed nature of the persons who do the speaking. It is in these special circumstances that questions of what human action is, what means are available to it, and what it can hope to achieve are brought most sharply, and in most general terms, to people's awareness.

By focusing on human interactions with the spirit world and their moral consequences, I am also confining myself in another respect. As I noted in the introduction, I often simplify the story by portraying it as if it were a clear-cut encounter between two sides. I make use of this dichotomization in order to render certain distinctions more visible. The dichotomization is reinforced by the dynamics of colonial missionization and the postcolonial memory. But opposition so simple is also problematic, a point to which I return at various junctures. Earlier I suggested that Sumbanese and Dutch Calvinists were likely to see themselves aligned against secular Europeans, and both Christian and non-Christian Sumbanese may identify with the Dutch against Islamic Indonesians. Internal differences also emerge among the Dutch Calvinists themselves. At the end of this chapter, I challenge the dichotomy from a different angle, suggesting that insofar as both sides of the encounter are responding to similar semiotic possibilities, each is vulnerable to the other's accusation of fetishism.

Despite this qualification, the missionary encounter is especially illuminating. First, religious conversion was one of the chief problems worrying Sumbanese at the time of my fieldwork in the 1980s and 1990s. Their memories of colonialism, perceptions of what they call modernity (Indonesian, *masa moderen*), and interactions with the Indonesian state are dominated by the experience of religious change. Second, over the course of this century, missionary activity and religious conversion have been a constant inducement to self-revelation and reflection. Missionization almost always demands an enormous amount of talk. Much of that talk is explanation and justification. Scholars of colonialism are perhaps most familiar with the explanations most obviously associated with power differences, such as Western missionaries explaining their potential converts to other Westerners, which is the stuff of official reports, Sunday newspaper supplements, fundraising brochures, and ethnographies. But preachers, converts, and the unconverted are also compelled to explain themselves to others, and to explain others to themselves. They are often the prime audience for their own self-justifications. And both theological inclination and practical realities drive Calvinist adherents continually to explain themselves, compelling marapu followers to explain themselves as well.

Finally, the high value that Protestant conversion places on human powers of self-transformation contributes to, or shares in, a defining feature of Euro-American views of modernity. That is, modernity can be characterized in part as bearing "a vision of the world as potentially open to transformation from within" (Cascardi 1992: 6). At the very least, Protestant conversion provides a clear and influential model of the powers of transformation of both persons and society. In this respect, it brings to the fore a theme I stressed in the earlier chapters: Protestant notions of agency and its subject play a central role in the moral narrative of modernity.

THE MISSIONARY'S FETISHIST

The question of how to correctly understand and locate agency animates some of the most fraught debates of the missionary encounter. The possession of agency is a defining feature by which missionaries distinguish subjects from objects, an ontological distinction with practical entailments for both morality and political economy. In particular, in Dutch eyes it is the pagan's inappropriate ascription of agency to nonhuman subjects that underlies the dangerous errors condemned under various labels, which I treat as part of a general category of fetishism. Moreover, although the theological supports behind the word *fetishism* may have faded from the academic scene, much of contemporary academic and political talk about agency continues to incorporate some of the assumptions about authenticity and liberation found in Christian discourse about paganism.

As William Pietz (1985, 1987) has pointed out, talk about fetishism—whether religious, Marxist, or Freudian—arises in the encounter between an observer and some sort of Other (see also Ellen 1988; Sebeok 1991). To impute fetishism to others is to set in motion a comparison, as an observer recognizes that someone else is attributing false value to objects. In Pietz's words: "The fetish is situated in the space of cultural revolution, as the place where the truth of the object as fetish is revealed" (1985: 11). It is this view of fetishism that interests me here: To speak of fetishism is by implication to assert that one views the desires and acts of others with a clear eye. Moreover, one often views those desires with a historicized and historicizing eye, one from which the scales have fallen. It is thus no accident that fetish discourse commonly attends narratives of modernity.

The discourse of fetishism, in its several varieties, is concerned in part with the true distinction between subjects and objects. This is evident in the colonial and postcolonial encounter between Dutch Calvinists and marapu followers. Over the course of this century, both historical circumstances and theological beliefs were such that the Dutch Calvinists were not in a position to force Sumbanese to convert and had to rely heavily on persuasion, even in the heyday of Dutch colonial power. The unconverted were in turn increasingly prompted to talk back, something that has continually put me in the midst of long and animated discussions. Much of this talk concerns the proper nature of the human subject. Viewed as a precipitate of the encounter itself, the discourse of fetishism provides a glimpse of the process by which the character of subject and object are constructed or challenged.

In 1909, for example, the recently arrived Dutch missionary D. K. Wielenga wrote, "The primitives confound that which is a fruit of the imagination with the reality, the objective with the subjective, the outer phenomena with their own spirit life" (1909a: 332). Wielenga drew here on a commonplace distinction between inner and outer, immaterial and material. But the issue is not simply a question of knowledge and error. Talk about fetishism is especially concerned with the misattribution of agency, responsibility, and desires to objects, to what the observer knows to be mere dead matter. Moreover, what seems to lend to the imputation of fetishism its extra charge is the sense not only that others are mistaken but also that their error is both seductive and dangerous. By ascribing agency to things that in truth lack it, they thereby deny, perhaps even rob, the agency of those who properly possess it (whether these are humans, God, or both). For this reason, the missionary's work of demystification entails liberation, restoring to natives the agency they have given away. Bringing others to true consciousness, in this view, is a critical step in their real development as agents—a logic whose echoes we can still hear in the ethical concerns of much contemporary anthropology.

ADDRESSING THE INVISIBLE

For reasons that will become apparent shortly, much of the debate about agency and fetishism dwells on the proper use of language in dealings with the spirit world.[1] Although speech is important in both marapu and Protestant worship, it plays distinct roles, given the differing assumptions about the agency of speakers and hearers manifest in questions of authorship and voice. The words that should emanate from the sincere individual speaker in Protestant prayer contrast to the highly formal and supposedly fixed canon of couplets used in Sumbanese oratory and marapu ritual. Like Umbu Neka, whose oratory I discussed in the previous chapter, most contemporary Sumbanese place enormous value on ritual speech, which they accept as having been handed down unchanged from the ancestors. The value, efficacy, and authority of Sumbanese ritual speech lie to an important degree in its formal characteristics. Many of these characteristics promote the textual dimension of language, those aspects of language that are most detachable from particular speakers and the immediate social, temporal, and physical context of speaking.[2] By doing so, they help impart to speech and its speak-

1. This was an important strand in Protestantism from the start. Even Luther, whose position was less radical than that of Ulrich Zwingli or Calvin, complained of "the kind of babbling and bellowing that used to pass for prayers in the church" under Catholicism (quoted in Pelikan 2003: 165).

2. The textual dimension of language is promoted by such devices as repetitiveness and highly formalized poetic structure (Silverstein and Urban 1996). In terms of explicit belief, these devices display the fact that ritual speech follows unchanging forms mandated by the ancestors. In semiotic terms, these devices, along with the elaborate stylization and distribution of participant roles, emphasize the separation between words and the intentions of particular speakers and can contribute to the sense that what they say is self-evident (DuBois 1986). Another important way in which ritual speech is entextualized is by suppressing deictics, those elements of language whose reference is oriented to the specific speech context. These include the pronouns that indicate speaker and addressee, and words like *here* and *there*, and *now* and *then*, which presuppose knowledge of the time and place in which they are uttered. For a discussion of entextualization in ritual speech, see Kuipers 1990; Bauman and Briggs 1990; and Keane 1997b, 2004.

ers the authority of an ancestral medium that arises far from the here and now. To speak in this medium is to display one's detachment from personal and factional interests (see Kuipers 1990). Full command of ritual speech in performance indexes the speaker's legitimacy as someone who has received words by a series of links over the generations back to their primordial originators. Ultimately, ritual speech also enables its users to lay claim to a form of agency that transcends the spatial and temporal limits of the individual, mortal body (see Keane 1997c).

The value of these ritual couplets lies, to an important degree, in their capacity to portray their speaker as someone who is *not* their author or the agent of the actions they perform. To the extent that the individual agency of the speaker does become apparent—when performance slips—the ancestral origins and thus effectiveness of this speech are in doubt. This model of language embodies a broader set of assumptions about the nature of authority and the practices of power. In the case of Sumbanese ritual speech, the signs of power are conceived to be generated by a source that remains distinct from the bodily individuals who wield them. It is part of the formal character of this speech to make that conception persuasive and available to the experience of both listeners and speakers. At the same time, this conception of power shapes the formal character of speech and forges it into the most effective means of acting in a world of invisible agents.

This view of language stands in contrast to certain elements of some especially pervasive, commonsense Euro-American understandings of how language works. The debate over speech practices in Sumba involves two aspects of these understandings in particular: namely, the central role it accords speakers' intentions and the kinds of functions it understands language to serve. The first of these, the intentionalistic model, was expressed at least as early as Saint Augustine (Asad 1993: 154n28). An important modern formulation of the place of intentions in meaning was given by the philosopher H. P. Grice (1957). In this view, linguistic signs work by virtue of the speaker's intention to communicate and by virtue of their being understood by the hearer to reflect such an intention. That is, for you to properly communicate with me, I must impute to you not only an intention to communicate to me but also an intention to get me to recognize that intention. By implication, then, my communicative act is mediated by the recipient's underlying assumptions about language. But as will become apparent, Sumbanese and many other ethnographic counterexamples suggest that—by privileging individual intentions, in tandem with the denotational functions of language, in his account of conversationalists' default assumptions—Grice has laid out a specifically Western language ideology (see criticisms in Duranti 1993; Hanks 1996).

The second relevant aspect of Western language ideology provoked by Sumbanese practices concerns language function. Several linguists have argued that, for purposes of communication, speakers of European languages tend to see the normal function of language as reference and predication (Silverstein 1979). This commonsense view of language stresses its capacity to point to things in the world and to speak about them in ways that are essentially true or false; and this view locates that ability in the semantics of individual words. But contrasting language ideologies exist, as pointed out some time ago when Michelle Rosaldo (1982) argued that the Ilongot of the northern Philippines see language first and foremost as a means of uttering directives. Indeed, the West also offers a wide range of alternative views of language, including mystical, magical, and poetic ones. Within analytic philosophy itself, Ludwig Wittgenstein (1953) and J. L. Austin (1955) offered substantial challenges to the reference and predication view. But the two strands to which I am pointing here have played a dominant role, especially in self-conscious efforts to analyze, evaluate, and regulate language use.

EFFECTIVE SPEAKING

Implicit in the practices of Sumbanese ritual speech are assumptions about how language works that differ markedly from the notion that it is primarily a medium for the making of propositions. Sumbanese ritual speech is supposed to carry out efficacious actions.[3] The contrast was well expressed by the missionary and linguist Louis Onvlee. Puzzling over how best to translate the Dutch word *bidden* (to pray), he wrote:

> I think of the word with which we render our "to pray," viz. *parengena li'i*, which literally means to make someone hear the word, direct the word to, a word that is indeed used in this sense in daily speech. . . . [But] once I went along when summoned for the killing of a chicken, [and] one of the officiants was told to *parengeni li'i na manu*, in other

---

3. When discussing a given expression in ritual speech, Anakalangese rarely discuss reference or denotation, that is, "What does it say" *(Gana wina)*. Rather, they are more likely to be interested in the appropriate circumstances for using it and in the possible social, material, or spiritual effects of using it, asking, "Where does it strike?" *(Beya na pinya pawanana?)*.

words, make the chicken hear the word, in order that by and by the chicken intestines should then speak what the forefathers mean to say, to be able to serve as [an] oracle.[4] And in another context, regarding what was "hot," and thus [ritually] perilous, and ought to be cooled, they said *parengengge li'i ne we'e*, make the water hear the word, thus "talk about" the water so that it indeed shall be able "to cool." And thus I am here in the neighborhood of the magical word, which confers coercive power onto that over which the word is spoken. And now we use this word in another connection and say *parengeni li'i Mjori*, to make the Lord hear the word. Shall this word continually be clear for those who hear it? (1973f: 202)

In this passage, Onvlee accurately describes a central component of Sumbanese ritual speech practice—noting that it has the formal structure of dialogue—and, along with this, the implicit ideology that dialogue produces material effects. The mistranslation of *to pray* is important because of the way it leads irrevocably from speech practices to mistaken views of agency, views of the kinds of beings that inhabit the world, and, ultimately, views of the morality of certain ways of interacting with the divine. The mistranslation of *to pray* arises from distinct views of the purposive uses of language. The errors immanent in Sumbanese marapu prayer, according to Onvlee, are threefold. By addressing the chicken, marapu prayer treats as an agent that which ontologically lacks agency. In cooling that which is hot, it falsely attributes efficacy to words. Finally, it incites the speaker to coerce the listener. In doing so, marapu prayer tempts mere humans to commit lèse-majesté with respect to the spirit world and, by implication, divinity.

Language ideologies are linked to concepts of the speaking subject and the nature of action. For this reason Protestant theology is scandalized by marapu ritual practices—not only because they differ in their commitments to particular theories of language, but also because of the wider implications, both ontological and moral. In the quotations to which I now turn, we can see that, when Dutch Calvinists look at marapu prayer, they counterpose the sincerity of Christian prayer as expressions that arise from individual and internal sources against what they take to be a fetishistic displacement of agency onto objectified forms. This is a two-way street: marapu followers in turn attribute to the isolated speaker of Protestant

---

4. This refers to the fact (discussed in chapter 5) that marapu prayers must always be spoken over some kind of material offering. Not only does the offering initiate material exchange with the spirit world, but it also serves as a medium of communication. Spirits cannot speak with words, but they reply with physical signs to those who address them. These are found during the preparation of the sacrifice by inspecting the entrails of the chicken or the liver of larger animals.

prayer an excessive willfulness, a hubris that is at once dangerous and ineffective. Over the course of these debates, which accompany changes in speech practices, each group expresses distinct concepts of language, action, and the nature of the speaking subject.

As Lionel Trilling points out, the development of the concept of sincerity is linked to that of "society," as something that is separate from, and can become a discursive object for, the free individual (1972: 26; see also Fliegelman 1993). Thus, the Protestant anxiety about the apparent insincerity of pagans seems to imply a linked concern with the apparent domination of the Sumbanese individual by the rules of society: note that the ancestral mandates that shape religious practice are inseparable from those that shape society. In European eyes, the marapu follower is subject not only to devils but also to the imperious dictates of inflexible traditional custom, such as marriage rules, forms of etiquette, and the system of ceremonial exchange. As I discussed in chapters 1 and 3, the idea that the fulfillment of human agency entails freedom from custom and other aspects of society is at the heart of certain moral narratives of modernity.

Missionary practice is often shaped by the referential model of language function. The initial task of a proselytizing religion is, after all, to teach a basic version of doctrine, usually encapsulated in the creed (see chapter 2), and to fill that education out by preaching the Gospel, commonly contextualizing it within local daily life. For Dutch Calvinists, such preaching can work only by virtue of denotations.[5] It must not seek to effect consequences directly, which would be magical. In its austerity and caution about syncretism, Calvinist preaching does not even have recourse to the passions, as in the ecstasy of the evangelical camp meeting or what the missionaries see as the seductions of Catholic ritual. Preaching can only convey true statements about the world and hope thereby to persuade.

INTERIOR AND EXTERIOR

What are the implications of these contrasting language ideologies for their respective understandings of the speaking subject? In Calvinists' critiques,

5. Thus, the enormous amount of careful attention Dutch missionaries paid to questions of translation. See, for example, Lambooy 1930, 1937; Onvlee 1973h, 1973b, 1973f, 1973d, 1973e; Pol 1931; compare Steedly 1996; Fabian 1986. Note that the question of translation tends to focus on the rendering of the discrete word, which Western language ideology often takes to be the primary locus of linguistic meaning (in contrast to sentences, grammatical structures, illocutionary effects, or larger discourse units).

idolaters (among whom they often include Catholics) confuse or conflate exterior and interior. This confusion underlies the terrible dread that is supposed to pervade heathen life because all evil arises from agents external to the human subject. As Wielenga explains, "The characteristic oppression of [the marapu-follower's] religious spirit- and soul-veneration is fear. . . . He feels himself always surrounded with threats" (1923: 224). To counteract this, Wielenga continued, the preacher must explain that "the human's soul, the human's life principle, thus sits *in* the person. . . . [I]t is inner, invisible. The wise Creator has so placed the soul that there is no danger from external, material things" (1923: 224–25, emphasis in the original). This means that the sermonizer must present a model of interiority explicitly distinguished from the subject's investment in physical objects and other external agents.

Against the external agents so feared by pagans, Protestants often counterpose sincere speech. For them, speech arises from within and is itself immaterial. It thus manifests the presence of the real spiritual locus of the individual will (Niesel 1956: 212–26), something carried to one logical conclusion in the Quaker institution of silent meeting, which rejects all but the most spontaneous words as inauthentic (Bauman 1983).[6] Much as pagan fetishism embodies a profound misunderstanding of which attributes properly belong to material objects, and which pertain to human subjects, so too with language. Thus, today Sumbanese Calvinists insist on the importance of shutting one's eyes while praying, something that continued to puzzle marapu followers in some of our conversations in 1993. The Calvinists' insistence on this point has become a prominent part of their public image. For instance, it was this that one marapu follower, who was hostile to the Christians, picked out when he asked me, "What are they afraid of?" answering his own question sardonically, "Maybe they're afraid their sins are visible!"

What is at stake for Sumbanese Calvinists? A church warden explained to me that you close your eyes so that your speech will come from the heart. He contrasted this to Catholics, who must keep their eyes open in order to read the prayer book. We might hear in this an echo of Milton's attack on the prayer book quoted in the introduction. Pointedly the warden compared Catholics to marapu followers, adding that Catholic practices

6. To be sure, the faithful may be opening themselves to the words God is speaking *through* them, but in the Quaker case this takes the form of inward seeking and the elimination of any influences from fixed texts, social conventions, or other forms perceived as exterior to the speaker in this world.

verge on idolatry, with their statues of the Virgin. Note that, by including Catholicism in his remarks, he was making an explicit association between the fetishizing displacement of idol worship and that of reciting the written word. Another person put it to me this way: "As for marapu followers, they don't even pay attention during the prayers, as long as they have their priest doing the job for them. They don't concentrate as we do, but just chat away." In a sermon I recorded, the minister drew these contrasts in order to characterize sincere prayer, saying: "Yes, as for Catholicism, there are often formulae. Can't skip over or go contrary to the way of praying. Have to follow exactly. . . . Like in Islam, for example, it has to be so many times. We are not taught like this. It's not enough, just five times. If we breathe, we don't just do it five times. Breathing goes on and on, doesn't it?" Notice here the rhetorical effects of the image of breath. This image denies the discreteness of the act of speaking and assimilates it to other constant bodily processes. Constant rather than framed, ordinary rather than elevated, intimate rather than detachable, the speech of Protestant faith is identified with the full presence of the everyday, physical locus of the individuated subject.

This view of formulae expresses another aspect implicit in Onvlee's criticism of marapu prayer, "to make someone hear the word," which I quoted above. It concerns the meaning of *li'i* (word), which denotes both the couplets used in ritual speech and, by metonymy, the original commitment between the ancestors and their descendants. The couplets are spoken in rites that fulfill the commitment, and in principle the less those couplets deviate from the original words of the ancestors, the more complete the fulfillment. The authority of any given performance rests precisely in the fact that the words neither originate with the speaker, nor display themselves as conveying a set of propositions.

As the minister's comments about the idolatry of the Virgin suggest, Calvinist criticisms of inauthentic prayer (whether marapu, Catholic, or Islamic) view it as being similar to the fetishized object. Like the spirits it addresses, it stands outside the subject, and to it the subject surrenders the real capacity to act. By contrast, authentic speech must originate within the speaker, guided by intentions and referring to a world beyond itself. Onvlee insisted that the church must be careful not to destroy the moral fabric of society by dismantling its ritual practices. Instead, the forms of these practices should be preserved, but their performative *effects* reframed to strengthen their voluntaristic yet disinterested character. For example, the ceremonial feast could be reinterpreted, in Onvlee's words, as "no longer a necessity but a gift. Not in order to influence but to thank; not 'supaja' [Indonesian, 'in order'] but 'sebab' [Indonesian, 'because']" (1973h: 156–57).

Notice three things about this brief quotation. First, agency is restored to humans, who previously had been in thrall to ancestral mandates.[7] Second, the ritual activity that results is itself no longer agentive in any strong sense: it has lost its place in a world of causation and been reconfigured as a form of expression that refers to other sites of action. And third, even material practices such as the slaughtering of animals, distribution of meat, cooking and commensality turn out to be displaced forms of speech, so many ways of saying "thank you." Thanks come after the fact, referring to outcomes brought about only by the speaker's bodily efforts and the autonomous workings of God. By insistently denying the power of words, Calvinists affirm that humans are endowed with a free will and are thus liberated from the tyranny of fetishes and capricious spirits. At the same time, they are faced with the risk that this very freedom will produce purely self-interested, instrumental action (whose forms would proliferate, see chapter 10). In the process, Calvinists also deny the agency of marapu followers for whom the words are a source of, or point of access to, power.

LANGUAGE AND ITS TEMPTATIONS

When they attack magical or ritualized language, the missionaries and their converts tell us a familiar story, much like the one I sketched in chapter 1: The progress of salvation is one of growing self-recognition, as humans cast off their attachment to false, external idols. In the process, they come to recognize their existing inner resources and capacity for self-transformation, which allows them actively to develop the individual conscience. This story ultimately not only pertains to Protestant conversion but also supports a

---

7. On the one hand, marapu followers are endowed with some degree of agency, and on the other, Calvinists see God as the ultimate agent. Onvlee's view of the difference, as I see it, lies in how he understands ritual traditions to function. Calvinists fulfill God's will through the free exercise of that agency proper to them, which requires that they recognize their freedom to act within their proper sphere. By contrast, marapu followers take the rules of marapu ritual to be imposed upon them from outside. Therefore, their agency is confined to following rules. Since, in the missionary view, many followers do not recognize their freedom, they are therefore incapable of serving God's will. As Elizabeth Povinelli (2002) points out, some legal systems similarly define traditional culture or religion by its supposedly compulsory character. The unintended consequence is to force people who exert agency into the category of those who lack traditional culture.

common narrative of modernity, as a process of increasing individualization, interiorization, and, by many accounts, eventual secularization.

But there is a complication in this narrative. This can be seen in another debate between marapu followers and Calvinists. In the eyes of missionaries, pagans manifest a double error, a confusion between the agency proper to humans and that proper to divinity. The marapu followers' view of human beings imputes to them both too much and too little agency. On the one hand, according to Wielenga, "[t]he human ego is thus the center of his religion" because the pagan wants ritual to bring about material benefits. On the other hand, such is the pagan's fatalism, Wielenga continued, that "the greatest stumbling block in the path of personal consciousness of sin is that he denies his human responsibility. That deprives him of all personal sense of guilt. He is firmly certain that he has come into the world with all his virtues and all his vices. These a man cannot alter" (1923: 222–23).

Within the spirit world itself, a similar confusion about agency can be found. Sumbanese attribute too little agency to the deity and too much to the ancestors. According to Wielenga, "A highest Being that has created all exists only in faint recollection. . . . [A] man on earth takes no account of him. High above the clouds he sits enthroned in inaccessible distance" (1909a: 334–35). The agency possessed by the ancestors deprives *both* humans *and* God of that which is properly theirs. Therefore, Wielenga proposed that the preacher tell them, before anything else, that "it is not evil arbitrariness and angry envy of the spirits that determines men's lot, but the almighty and all omnipresent power of God. . . . [L]eaves and grass, rain and drought, fruitful and unfruitful years, food and drink, health and illness, wealth and poverty and all things come to us not by chance but from His fatherly hand" (1923: 220).

This distinction among kinds of agency means that the Protestant subject provides an ambivalent origin for actions. In addition to the human interior, there is another locus of agency, namely God, along with the mediator, Christ. The story of creation and the insistence on the continuing activity of the Lord in the contemporary world impose a critical limit on the extent of human agency. In this respect, Protestants are more like their marapu interlocutors than like their own, ontologically more materialist and religiously skeptical or liberal contemporaries in early-twentieth-century Europe.

Despite the centrality of individual intentions and authenticity in Protestant language ideology (or, indeed, as a historical and logical precondition for that centrality), there is an important qualification, for language is in some ways exterior to its speaker. Therefore, however much one might wish to find in words the true locus of the spirit, language cannot entirely guarantee the autonomy of the subject. This is due to its material embodiment in sounds or writing and its social character. Words have some degree of existence outside both the speaker and listener. After all, since we hear ourselves speak, our words once uttered come to us much as the words of others. Our words also come to us from others ontogenetically: we learn a language that exists prior to our own utterances. In speaking, we display the extent to which others have entered into our own words (Bakhtin 1981; Lucy 1993). These aspects of language thus can seem to pose obstacles to sincere prayer, if, as in the view of many Protestants, it is defined by its origin in the individual speaker. If we could guarantee the divinity of those words, this might not present a problem for religious practice. Likewise, if social others were vehicles for a tradition that transmits divine truth, this would not present a problem. But to the extent that language is social in origin, and the social is seen as a force exterior to and independent of core aspects of the individual subject, then it might reveal, at least potentially, the incipient insincerity that threatens to intervene between speaker and the divine addressee. It may be impossible to eschew language altogether, but the worry does manifest itself in the ways of marking or constraining speech developed across a wide range of religious reform movements (see Keane 1997b). In the Christian tradition alone, Quakers in meeting must remain silent until moved by the Inner Light to speak (Bauman 1993), Pentecostals reproduce the moment of Pentecost by speaking in tongues that resemble no human language (Robbins 2004a), and Zimbabwe's Friday Apostolics refuse to read scripture at all (Engelke 2004b).

Although the Dutch Calvinists did not take their concern about this problem to the extremes of those groups, they did demand that worship be spontaneous enough to forego the use of written prayers or memorized formulae. Yet at the heart of their faith remained one overwhelmingly ulterior source of words, the Holy Gospel. In 1957, Onvlee offered the following reflections on a lifetime of linguistic research and Bible translation:

> After our return from Indonesia someone asked me to speak about how you translate a Bible. To this I answered: You do not do that, I do not do that, we do not do that. Human beings do not do that. Yes, indeed, men are really occupied with it, and human activity is really involved in it. Languages must be investigated and known, as far as this is possible; a text and understanding must be established, and there must be translation from one language to another. And that all ought to occur in responsible ways; linguistics and philology and exegesis ought necessarily to contribute, and not only these. But to translate the Bible . . .

[ellipses in the original] It is with this as with all work in God's king-
dom[,] and good understanding will say this with all our work. . . .
[O]ne investigates and explains, and another is engaged in rendering
(Dutch, *overzetting*), but it is God who translates (Dutch, *vertaalt*) the
Bible. (1973f: 197)[8]

The language of the Bible, of course, is different from the authentic
speech of the person who prays, as Onvlee went on to observe: "What, now,
can men say in words? All that which in one way or another falls in the circle of our thoughts and our experience. But what was spoken here [in the
Bible] has arisen in no man's heart. How can human language be the bearer
thereof?" (1973f: 198). Onvlee's reflections suggest that in at least one
respect biblical language resembles that of Sumbanese ritual speech. Its
authority lies precisely in the fact that it does not derive from mortal
speakers and they are not its authors. That is, they are the agents of a principal: they give voice to words that must be understood to derive from a
source that lies beyond experience.

The existence of words that emanate from a distant, divine source opens
up a possibility on which many Sumbanese seize immediately—that the
Christians' book itself could be fetishized as a site of or access point for
agency that lies beyond the human subject. Onvlee recalls:

> On a certain day one of our acquaintances came running in to us, ask-
> ing if we could look in the Book for him. On inquiry, it appeared that
> his son was working in the government office in the administrative
> center of Waingapu, thus outside the sphere of Sumbanese life. Now he
> had received news that his son was sick and so would like to know if he
> would recover, and what should be done to bring it about. Therefore he
> asked us to look in the book. He had thus assimilated the word *zurata*
> (letter or book) to a related word (of his), viz. *urata*, which means line,
> also the line of the hand and the line in a chicken entrail or pig liver
> which is inspected in communicating with the dead in the spear-
> divination, from which one can know the word and wishes of the
> dead. (1973f: 201–2)

According to Onvlee, the man's confusion (which was not idiosyncratic; see
Lambooy 1927: 82) here was twofold—he was self-interested where he

---

8. *Overzetting* and *vertaalt* both refer to translation. By juxtaposing them here,
Onvlee presumably means to bring out their contrasting senses, which reflect the
more general Calvinist distinction between divine and human agency. *Overzetting*
refers more narrowly to the hands-on work of rendering a translation, and *vertaalt*
has the broader connotation of making its meaning available to the world. I thank
Peter van Rooden and Patricia Spyer for discussing this passage with me.

should be otherworldly, and he misconstrued the functions of language and thus the nature of material signs. The anxious father here sought from the Bible not statements about the truth of the world but directives for efficacious action in this world.

Five decades after the colonial period of Onvlee's recollections, the authority of scripture, and by extension, of the written word more generally, remains a central concern for Sumbanese, both Christian and marapu.[9] Some Sumbanese seize on the centrality of writing in the Protestant Church to justify their reluctance to convert, explaining that, being unable to read, they must remain marapu followers. Although many Sumbanese take the lack of a scripture as one defining feature of marapu ritual, others seek to ground their authority in alternative forms of writing. Like the father in Onvlee's anecdote, many people today identify the divinatory reading of intestines as "the Sumbanese book." Others claim for themselves an equivalent to the authority of the book, some marapu ritualists asserting that their knowledge too is a form of writing. For example, to gloss the expression "there is the ancestral track," one told me that "this means it's like we take a piece of paper, then put down lines, we give our performance direction." Still others directly resist the authority of the written word. A recalcitrant marapu follower, complaining of the aggressive efforts of young local evangelists, told me, "How I surprise them! When the proselytizers come to my house and open that book to read to me, I tell them to listen first, then I tell them what I know about the origins and Babel."[10] Yet another priest said, "But those Christians, all they have is a book. This book can be destroyed, or again its handiwork can fade." In contrast, marapu followers argue, they have a more secure evidential base for their links to the ancestors, the gold and tombs that remain to this day, and that the links by means of which they inherited the valuables parallel those along which ancestral words have been transmitted.

The lack of an ancestral book does not prevent Sumbanese from trying to take advantage of the powers latent in books as sources of words exterior

9. If anything, this concern is accentuated by state religious policies, by which only scriptural religions are legally recognized (Kipp and Rodgers 1987). Sumbanese views of writing tend to associate the authority of religion with that of the state (see Keane 1997a).

10. Certain biblical stories have had wide word-of-mouth circulation, and at least one ritual expert related the story of Adam and Eve to me as a Sumbanese origin myth. Among other things, this exemplifies the power of a text to detach itself from any context of origin and become available for reattachment to, and for the creation of, new contexts.

to the speaker. Some, as Onvlee observed, use the Bible as a tool of divination. In this, Sumbanese are simply discovering a possibility that the authority and materiality of the written divine word seem always to have contained. Keith Thomas, for example, points out that, throughout the Middle Ages and into the Reformation, "[a]ny prayer or piece of the Scriptures might have a mystical power waiting to be tapped. The Bible could be an instrument of divination, which opened at random would guarantee one's fate" (1971: 45). In one respect, such divination is simply an appeal to a source of words whose authority is superior to that of ordinary humans. But this use of the Bible takes advantage of a more general characteristic of divination, which, as the linguist John DuBois (1993) has argued, constructs aleatory mechanisms precisely in order to suppress the existing intentionality of persons. Thus, the appeal to a nonhuman source of words acts to efface or momentarily bracket human agency. As I have suggested above, this is the active mode of one side of the discourse of fetishism: To ascribe agency to one locus is simultaneously to deny it to another. In using the Bible for divination, Sumbanese seem to mobilize the latent possibilities afforded by the very distance of the Calvinist's divine agent—as if they seek agency, but not exactly to claim it for themselves.[11]

WILLFULNESS OR AGENCY?

Dutch Calvinists in Sumba counterpoise the sincerity of expressions arising from individual and internal sources against what they take to be marapu rituals' fetishistic displacement of agency onto objectified verbal formulae. For them, a mistaken view of language is inseparable from a mistaken understanding of the human subject. Of particular concern to them is wrong speech that forms an obstacle on the way to achieving an interior state of grace. As Wielenga writes:

> [W]henever one has a bad understanding of "redemption," then it is also a given that one has a bad understanding of "thankfulness." He

---

11. To speak of effacement may, I think mistakenly, tempt one to conclude that local constructions of agency merely dissemble the real agency that humans actually know they possess or induce false consciousness. To consciously efface or bracket one's own agency, however, can also be a way of deferring to the agency one imputes to others, including denizens of the spirit world. For example, Sumbanese purposely do this in nonverbal ways by creating situations in which they will "accidentally" lose spiritually powerful objects that are too dangerous to get rid of intentionally (see Keane 1997c: 92, 251n34, and chapters 1 and 9 for the more general discussion of power).

shall answer the question: how shall I be thankful to God for such redemption?—thank and love God. Words and nothing but words. And it turns out that the thankfulness stands in acknowledging that he *says* thanks. Only seldom shall he convert it into a deed both saying and doing: I am your servant and will do work for you. His heathen religion has cost him much, many pecuniary and material sacrifices. . . . [In marapu ritual,] a removal of guilt must "be purchased," for all must be "paid for." But a Christian "*asks*" forgiveness, receives it, and "*says*" his thankfulness. (1923: 223, emphases in original)

The lack of interiority is mutually implicated with the misuse of words. If words are deeds, a view Wielenga imputes to marapu followers, they would be sufficient in themselves. But if words are only supplementary to deeds, something closer to Wielenga's own view, they lie external to the subject and so in themselves remain unbound to the subject's condition and acts. Inauthentic speech is then inseparable from materialism, going hand in hand with the corruption that conflates economic exchange (the purchase of an indulgence) with spiritual effects (forgiveness). Wielenga's view of speech, in its very appeal to interiority, recognizes the ambiguously external character of language, which needs some additional resources if it is to be bound to inner states and outer works.

But each side in the encounter between Calvinists and marapu followers finds the other to be in error. Dwelling on different loci of agency, Calvinist and marapu followers alike accuse each other of willfulness and lack of deference to the world of invisible beings. Thus, for their part, marapu followers frequently accuse Calvinists of hubris in seeking to address the deity directly. Marapu followers see their ritual forms, in contrast to the direct address to which Calvinist prayer aspires, not as insincere but as deferential. The performers insist that the words they utter are not their own, and that they dare address only intermediary spirits, not the ultimate powers.

In this light, marapu followers commonly attribute to the isolated speaker of Calvinist prayer an excessive willfulness that is at once dangerous and ineffective. According to these critics, it is precisely the Christians' refusal to attribute the warrants claimed by the speaking subject to the exteriority provided by language that renders them suspect. That is, through its efforts at sincerity and spontaneity, Christian prayer seems to deny that language and its powers originate beyond the individual speaker. To marapu followers, this means an illegitimate transfer of responsibility from the invisible world of spirits to the fleshly domain of the living. Looking at the individual assertiveness embodied in Christian practices, marapu followers are unimpressed by doctrinal claims of respect for the Lord. Conversely, attending to the deluded character of fetishism, colonial missionaries were similarly unimpressed by marapu followers' understandings of agency and overlooked the persuasiveness, authority, and delegated nature of ritual couplets. To be sure, there is a predictable cultural and political clash going on here, but I suggest there is something else involved as well. Both sides have to contend with a lingering doubt: For marapu followers, it is about the presence of the invisible spirits; for Christians, the presence of sincere intentions in the worshipper. What both sides share is that neither, in practice, treats the subject as fully autonomous and self-present.

The potential for dispute or confusion about the locus of agency and the authorship of words is perhaps inescapable. The Calvinist mission seeks to fix and stabilize the agency and authorship that most matter, distributing them between the interiority of speaking subjects and the distant site occupied by God. The Protestant genealogy of the version of authenticity and agency I have sketched here suggests that those who use these words should be alert to the assumptions they bear. Both marapu followers and missionaries share a fundamental understanding of authority. Its human bearers should not be known or even know themselves to be the ultimate sources of agency. This authority is most legitimate, persuasive, and efficacious when the agency it manifests seems most to arise from somewhere else. What worries marapu followers and Protestants, both Dutch and Sumbanese, about each other is not entirely that the other "displaces" agency away from living human beings. Rather, it is that the nonhuman site at which they find agency is the wrong one.

The discourse of fetishism, whether theological, Marxist, or Freudian, harbors a promise of liberation linked to self-consciousness. As part of a broader concern for agency, it is especially evident in the current anthropological reworkings of Marx's assertion that human beings make themselves, even if not under conditions of their own choosing (1978: 595). But however fundamental their differences, marapu and Calvinist discourses coincide at one critical point. Neither accepts the proposition that human beings simply make themselves, and both impose significant limits on human agency—locating it not just in Marx's dead weight of the past but with other, nonhuman agents altogether. Indeed, both Calvinists and marapu followers might doubt any vision of fully self-present agency freed altogether from the possibility of what others might describe as fetishism. If we take seriously the ways in which the actions of subjects are mediated by objective forms like those of speech, we might ask whether anyone's practices could altogether escape some sort of charge of fetishism.

This is part of the puzzle for the well-intentioned interlocutor: If the agency of others is predicated in part on their own beliefs and on the notions of agency immanent in their practices, how are we, if, for example, we are secular scholars, to reconcile their attribution of agency to divine subjects with our desire that they recognize that agency lies within their own hands? And, to the extent that the value Western scholars place on self-transformation is itself a product of our own genealogy, what does it mean for us to insist on the self-transforming powers of others? As we seek to grant agency to historical subjects, we might ask ourselves not only what agency is and where to find it but also under what terms, and with what entailments, it must be accepted. We must also be prepared to recognize that the paradoxes of agency, such as the vulnerability to some charge like "fetishism," apply to us as well as others.

7 Modern Sincerity

The purposeful effort to become "modern," as a moral project, can resemble that of religious conversion in certain respects. Both projects often propose to transform people by disabusing them of earlier errors and abstracting them from the constraints of former social entanglements. An examination of how this is supposed to happen, and the risks this project may involve, offers insights into some of the practices by which human subjects are, and are not, constituted. In this chapter I look at the subject proposed by conversion to Calvinism from the perspective of the norm of sincerity. I situate this norm within the context of what I call the moral narrative of modernity. The moral narrative helps make sense of the work of purification when this work takes the form of an effort to distinguish the human subject from that which might threaten its relative autonomy.

As in the previous chapter, I focus on changes in religious practices and semiotic ideologies. Whereas in that chapter I focused on the uses of words and the challenges that words can seem to pose to human agency, given certain semiotic ideologies, in this chapter I shift to the people who speak. I begin with a brief discussion of the effort to reform the subject by redefining its distinction from objects such as material goods (a topic I examine from another angle in chapter 8). I then turn to the normative ideal of sincerity in speech as another component of this reform.

CONVERSION'S SUBJECTS AND THEIR OBJECTS

Sumbanese Calvinists face some recognizable problems raised by attempts to produce and sustain a relatively autonomous subject. The trouble is partly due to the clash between the presumed immateriality of that subject and the inescapably social and material character of those representational practices by which that ideal autonomy is made inhabitable. As a form of self-understanding, the subject is likely to require some contrastive terms—those objects against which its distinctiveness can be defined. It is the work of purification to sustain that contrast.

By *objects* I mean not only material things but also institutions, rituals, social others, and the language one shares with those others. For instance, we need look no further than familiar, sometimes trivial anxieties about plagiarism, quotation, cliché and originality, truth telling, keeping one's word, mimicry, and finding one's own voice to find hints of how thoroughly language can trouble the boundaries of the subject. This linguistic trouble with boundaries, the sense that heteroglossia (Bakhtin 1981) might pose a threat is, however, hardly confined to minor questions of style and everyday ethics. Religious traditions abound with worries about the slippery, corrupting, or deceiving effects of language (and signs, more generally) and efforts to control them (Keane 1997b). In many cases, these worries, and the efforts at purification they engender, center on the perceived external and material or objectlike character of language. Some early English Protestants, such as the Quakers, for instance, considered rhetorically elaborate styles of language to be "fleshly" distortions of God's truth (Bauman 1983). Their insistence on plain style and even silence seems to have been, at least in part, a response to an intuition that language *is* external to that spiritual component defining what is most valuable in the human person, that which would transcend the material world.[1] To the extent that their worries about fleshly language articulate with their worries about other aspects of the "external" world, like showy clothing, forms of etiquette, liturgical rites, architectural ornament, or religious icons, those worries reveal how such words and things are part of a representational economy.[2]

---

1. One may worry about the externality of language and yet not make rhetoric the precise focus of that worry. Any number of aspects of linguistic structure, language use, and discursive context may come under scrutiny. Consider, for example, the passage I quote at the beginning of this book, in which John Milton speaks as a committed Puritan. Certainly his poetry shows no fear of elaborate rhetoric. Rather, he is vehemently opposed to the use of fixed, published prayers. At the opposite doctrinal extreme, the Council of Trent (Tanner 1990) attacked the Protestant use of vernaculars, in part because its members were worried about the disunities introduced by linguistic variability. Latin was meant, among other things, to be a bulwark against the corruptibility of ordinary speech.

2. A concern with the materiality of language is pervasive in many religious traditions but has particular force in the more ascetic kinds of Protestantism. See, for instance, the Primitive Baptists of Appalachia, whose concern for authentic

As I show in this chapter, language ideology may be linked to ideas about material goods through their respective implications for the presumed nature of the human subject.

The seventeenth-century Quakers may have been extreme, but they were certainly not alone in their reformist interest in words and their relation to the material and social world. As I mentioned earlier, their contemporaries, the scientists who founded the Royal Society, promoted a "naked, natural way of speaking" (quoted in Bauman 1983: 2; also see Bauman and Briggs 2003, chapter 1). They aspired to language so transparent that it would do no more than refer to those things intended by its speaker and, thus, would serve as a proper vehicle for objectivity. The convergence of Protestant morality and scientific objectivity at a particular historical moment, in a similar language ideology, would seem to be no accident. In their conjunction, we can see themes that have come to be characteristic of some common ideas about the proposed subject of modernity. Briefly put, this is the subject whose distinction from the domain of objects is produced not only in the norm of sincerity but also in its sharp distinction from material goods and in a related aversion to the supposed excesses of ritual, idolatry, and even courtesy—an aversion that the historian Peter Burke has suggested is characteristic of modern Europe (1987: 13, 224).

As I argued in chapter 4, a focus on proselytization and conversion has played a crucial role in the historical self-definition of Protestantism as having produced a rupture with false or merely obsolete traditions, or as having brought the unsaved into a new historical trajectory. For sects that consider backsliding a perpetual threat, conversion anew is demanded even of those born into the church. In conceptual terms, the aspirations of conversion give rise to a host of commonplace ideas and assumptions about iconoclasm, spirituality and materialism, conscience, agency, worldliness, and transcendence.

Nineteenth- and early-twentieth-century Christian missionaries across the colonial world often thought they were confronting varieties of animism and fetishism. That is, the unenlightened were confused about the true distinctions among humans, things, and divinity: they imputed spirit

---

speech focuses on material forms. They do not permit preachers to write their sermons before preaching them and consider even the Bible to be a dead letter unless the spirit is present (Peacock and Tyson 1989: 122–26). In Zimbabwe, the Friday Apostolics eschew the Bible altogether, seeking their faith "live and direct" (Engelke 2004b). For some general implications of the rejection of rhetoric in the contemporary United States, see Crapanzano 2000.

to dead matter, divine agency to ordinary creatures, and so forth. In effect, when the missionaries attacked animal sacrifice, the worship of carvings, or magical language, they took the side of science—at times unwittingly, at others purposefully—in disenchanting some part of the world. The transformation of the human subject would seem to be inseparable from the redefining of its distinction from the world of objects. The task of bringing converts to a proper understanding of their spiritual nature required convincing them that rocks, trees, animals, or in some cases, even words were not similarly endowed.

This is an important point to bear in mind about purification: it does not eliminate one side of the opposition but, rather, seeks to establish a clear boundary and restore all things to their proper sides of it. Even the most spiritual person may not so much deny materiality as seek to confine it to its proper place in the world. In this respect, proponents of contemporary forms of religious purification such as the neo-orthodox Calvinism of Abraham Kuyper (see chapter 3) may claim their religion can easily coexist with science. Perhaps in this light we can understand the exchange between Maurice Leenhardt, an early French Protestant missionary ethnographer in Melanesia, and one of his early converts. According to Leenhardt, when he said, "In short, what we've brought into your thinking is the notion of spirit," his convert replied, "Spirit? Bah! We've always known about the spirits. What you brought was the body" (Clifford 1982: 172). Dematerialization of the human spirit simultaneously produces an objectification of those things to which it is opposed.

To be sure, there is enormous, and growing, variety among kinds of Protestantism. Certainly neither antimaterialism nor an emphasis on the speaker's own voice, is found in all cases. Indeed, some of the most popular forms of evangelical Christianity today, such as Pentecostalism, various televangelisms, and the prosperity gospel, may be seen in part as reactions *against* earlier more austere doctrines (Coleman 2000; Harding 2000; Robbins 2004b). Orthodox Calvinism, at any rate, is no longer on the religious front lines. But it can give us insights into the kinds of Protestantism that have most influenced those secular habits of thought and action associated with the moral narrative of modernity as it circulated in the nineteenth century and first half of the twentieth century. That influence was not necessarily overt. As I argued in chapters 1 and 2, the global proselytization of Protestant ideas, moral values, and practices has made the associated semiotic ideologies available to all sorts of people in ways that more esoteric concerns of literature, philosophy, political thought, and science have not.

Mainstream Protestants such as the Dutch Calvinists normally considered "mere" ritual form to be insufficient for salvation or the inculcation of moral virtues. The liturgical and everyday practices they developed were supposed to provide concrete ways of inhabiting new kinds of personhood. One aspect of this personhood was a certain vision of language and its speakers, embodied in the norm of sincerity.

An obvious objection at this point is that many of the claims I make for Protestantism—such as an anxious concern to distinguish subject from object, the associated critiques of materialism and language, and the urge for sincere and inner-directed conversion on the part of even the most humble believers—are characteristic of a wide range of contemporary religions, such as Islam (Eickelman 2000) and Buddhism (Gombrich and Obeyesekere 1988). But first, where the insistence on inwardness has been found in the pre-Reformation and non-Christian world, it was typically confined to elites or religious virtuosi. Second, as I argued in chapter 1, these religious characteristics seem to be spreading, partly in response to the pressures of the contemporaneous globalizations of Protestantism, the nation-state form, and other institutions of modernity (Asad 1993; van der Veer and Lehmann 1999). As a friend who was raised as an urban, educated Greek Orthodox individual remarked to me, "We are *all* Protestants now." If so, one might speak of a world-historical configuration that exceeds particular doctrinal identifications. But it is Protestantism above all that has staked its claims to a distinctive identity in having first articulated these particular concerns as a *historical* intervention. Like other reform movements, it looked backward to a purer past; but it also helped define, and identified itself with, the new era.

I take modernity here to be a term of self-description in a narrative of moral progress. And as I have noted, it is only one among several competing visions of modernity. Among the more dystopian are those that portray modernity as alienating people from their true selves, dividing what was once whole, subjecting humans to machines or impersonal institutions, producing mass societies, and giving rise to new forms of authoritarianism and oppression. But the moral narrative of modernity that concerns me here is part of a purposeful project. It involves the cultivation of and high value given to individual agency, and inwardness, the goal of individual self-creation, and, paralleling these in the domain of the social, the devaluation of tradition in the name of historical progress. At the heart of this vision of modernity is the work of purification that aims to abstract the self from material and social entanglements.

SINCERITY AS A MORAL NORM

One component of this vision of the self is the normative ideal of sincerity in speech. The concept of sincerity is particularly interesting here because it forges links among language, social interaction, personal character, freedom, and regimes of truth. The moral value of sincerity is also interesting because it is part of the taken-for-granted background of the world in which I write this book. Euro-American travelers and anthropological fieldworkers in unfamiliar social contexts frequently discover that some of their most disorienting moments arise amid ordinary interactions when they no longer feel they can intuit whether other people "mean what they say." They may find themselves even more disturbed by talk that must be purchased, that is treated as a burden to be taken on by others, that patently refuses to answer the question being asked, that seems to parrot someone else's words, or that simply seems unbelievable.[3] It should be no surprise that there is enormous variation in ways of speaking across societies. But why should this variation be troubling? One reason is that it may run against deep-seated intuitions that endow differences in speaking styles with a moral dimension. Such intuitions guide our evaluations of other persons and may hint at their evaluations of us as well. In the Euro-American West, sincerity has, of course, played an important role in philosophical analyses of language, such as those by J. L. Austin (1955) and Paul Grice (1975). But the moral dimensions are perhaps better revealed in ordinary interactions and instincts. Consider my own immediate surroundings in an American university: when we mistrust another's intentions, or value a free press, or insist that students do their own work, or favor a politics in which people find their own voices, or merely sign our writings, we are likely to be drawing on tacit norms of sincerity.

In the second half of this chapter, I argue that the idea and practices of sincerity reveal certain core dilemmas for the self-conscious project of becoming a certain kind of modern subject. Radical religious conversion char-

---

3. Linguistic anthropology is full of examples, but two classic articles are especially useful. Judith Irvine's "When Talk Isn't Cheap" (1989) analyzes the multiple dimensions along which language is be articulated with political economy, and Charles Briggs's "Learning How to Ask" (1984) shows how naive it can be to simply ask a straightforward question and expect a straightforward answer. The results can be more than embarrassment or confusion. For example, as Elizabeth Povinelli shows, serious political consequences may arise when Anglo-Australian advocates for Aborigines find themselves baffled by "unbelievable" ways of talking that do not adhere to either the interactive or judicial norms familiar to them (2002, chapter 6).

acteristically demands changes in assumptions about material things and language. For the Calvinists on Sumba, one target of reform is the way words and things are implicated in a general condition of human sociability. To the extent that words and things circulate among persons, requiring acceptance or uptake by them, the very conditions for people's objectification, self-knowledge, and identity necessarily involve other persons. For those Protestants who try to foster and authorize (relatively) more socially autonomous selves, the better to be open to divine grace, this embeddedness may pose a threat. But to the extent that even the project of transcending the carnal world requires some material activity, this embeddedness is an inescapable condition of semiotic practice. In this chapter, therefore, I discuss two topics: first, the Calvinist dimensions of certain ideas about the modern subject, and, second, the ways that semiotic ideologies form links and distinctions among language, material things, and persons. Thus, what can be called "Protestant" about the modern subject is a function of how a particular semiotic ideology articulates these links. To show that this semiotic ideology has a material as well as linguistic character, I look at the problem of material goods before turning to sincerity in speech. I then return to material goods in chapter 8.

INTERIORITY, SOCIALITY, AND MATERIAL VALUES

Protestant conversion invokes an ambivalent historicity. On mission frontiers, as in triumphant church histories, it often marks a specific moment of historic rupture across an entire social world (see chapters 4 and 5). But for many Protestant sects, conversion can never be assured. At the individual level, it entails an ongoing process of self-examination, potential backsliding, and reform. In the 1980s and 1990s, for example, the emerging Protestant majority on the island of Sumba in eastern Indonesia experienced conversion at both levels.

Activists of the Gereja Kristen Sumba (Christian Church of Sumba) combined a sharp awareness of historical rupture with wary alertness to individual weakness and the persistent temptations of ancestral spirits. In Sumba, the latter temptations were prompted in particular by the vicissitudes of marriage exchange. In the 1990s, Sumbanese marriage exchanges were still politically salient, socially consequential, very expensive, and hard to disentangle completely from the powers of the spirits who are commonly supposed to underwrite them. Although there is considerable local variation across the island, Sumbanese marriage exchanges, in general, mediate the gift of blood (thus of life and spiritual protection) from the bride's lineage to her husband's, creating a debt that forms the basis of a larger political and kinship alliance. Entering into marriage exchange, the husband's lineage draws on as many supporters as necessary to give "male" valuables of cattle, horses, and gold to the wife's lineage and their supporters, who reciprocate with the "female" valuables of cloth, pigs, and ivory. The resulting chains of debt have wide-reaching economic, political, and ritual consequences, and the core alliance creates obligations and informal ties over several generations.

One of the chief problems that ceremonial marriage exchange commonly poses for reformers in Sumba and elsewhere is its apparently misplaced materialism. Ever since Marcel Mauss (1990) argued that the gift is binding on the recipient because it is an extension of the giver, ceremonial exchange has commonly been understood to act by virtue of identification between persons and things. For Mauss, the extension of the giver's personality to things was characteristic of archaic societies, whose particular moral character was lost as the modern world came to disarticulate persons from a more objectlike world. The intuition that modernity is characterized by a certain way of distinguishing subjects and objects is persistent. As I discussed in the introduction, Bruno Latour (1993) asserts that this very refusal to recognize "hybrids," which threaten to blur the distinction between persons and things, defines the modern. It should therefore not be surprising if observers from the Euro-American West, whether conservative missionaries or progressive feminists, have often felt what Gayle Rubin (1975) dubbed the "traffic in women" to be a scandal because it seems to dehumanize the subject. On the one hand, it is indisputable that the articulation of persons and objects in exchange has commonly mediated, and sometimes obfuscated, profound relations of domination, not only of women by men, but also of juniors by seniors and the poor by the rich. On the other hand, as an intuitive response, the Euro-American's sense of scandal is sometimes provoked by more problematic ontological assumptions. The first of these is a tendency to assume that the equivalence between persons and things in ceremonial exchange is similar to the alienating effects of commodity exchange. The second assumption is that the value of the human is defined in its distinctiveness from, and superiority to, the material world. The former assumption shows its origins in capitalism, the latter in Protestant notions of transcendence. In conjunction, each lends support to the other.

In fact, people who engage in marriage exchanges usually take them to exemplify rather than threaten the distinctiveness of human self-worth. Thus, one elderly Sumbanese woman was shocked when I told her that

Americans do not carry out marriage exchanges. To her, this meant we thought ourselves no better than animals in all their sexual promiscuity, something demonstrated by our anarchic freedom from both ancestral regulations and material obligations to our immediate and affinal kin. Sumbanese marriage exchanges are, at the very least, a vigorous working through of the implications that people are, or should be, embedded in social relations with others (both living and dead), and that these relations are inseparable from their material entailments. The social, in some important respects, *is made possible* by the material. Thus the material manifests sociality, not simply as a conventional symbol of social values, but also by virtue of its causal role in constituting social relations. I depend on others for the things I give to you. Therefore the things I give to you are indexical of the presence of other persons. Thus a challenge to materiality entails a challenge to sociality and vice versa.

THE SPIRIT OF THE THING

Sumbanese express this sense of embeddedness and the work needed to sustain it with reference to the palpable effects of exchanges on the spirit (dewa) of persons. In the vocabulary common to many Sumbanese, one man told me (like many marapu followers today, he used the vocabulary of Christian monotheism), "If we push away good fortune [in exchange], it's not a fellow human whom we push away, but God. So he withdraws [his support]." The efficacy of one's dewa both affects and is also affected by exchanges and extends to any and all of the material conditions of production and micropolitics that lie behind exchange, from drought and disease to feuding. Thus each particular exchange takes its place in a career, a trajectory of success or failure, of strengthening or weakening ties to others, as the outcomes of exchange record the state of one's dewa (Keane 1997c, chapter 8).

Ceremonial exchange thus raises serious difficulties for Sumbanese Protestants. Few are willing to reject exchange out of hand, for even the best Protestants, if they possess but a shred of respectability, are enmeshed in exchange politics, obligations to kin, relations of dependence or patronage, and so forth. Yet if they take their Christianity (and their modernity) seriously—and most do—they cannot accept the world of ancestor spirits and rituals at its foundations. Those who celebrate modernity and economic rationality must have some explanation of the respective values of ceremonial exchange and its alternatives, both economic (such as purchase and sale) and ritual (such as church weddings). For example, exchange valuables should have no alternative destination as sacrificial offerings, and the outcomes of exchange should have no interpretive or practical bearing on the self's relations to ancestral spirits or its future powers.

This is where Protestant discourses of interiority and materialism come into play, helping to express shifting distinctions between subject and object. An especially pressing question that Sumbanese Protestants, along with other Christians, must often face is: What value is transacted in marriage exchange? The general response is exemplified by this excerpt from an essay by a high school student, published in a provincial newspaper in 1997:

> Bridewealth in the form of traditional valuables like ivory, gold, buf-
> falo, is at base only a symbol in order to raise a woman's value and dig-
> nity. Demands for bridewealth show that a woman must be honored,
> valued. . . . Bridewealth is only a symbol of the woman's self-respect.
> . . . It is proper that bridewealth be retained, on the basis of its essence
> as a symbol of woman's own value and dignity—and not tend toward
> business or "trade" in daughters. On the part of women themselves, the
> most important problem is as far as possible that she be able to guard
> her self-respect so that the demand for bridewealth, which is to be dis-
> cussed by her family, doesn't put her to shame. One should value one-
> self by way of one's patterns of thinking, attitude, and praiseworthy
> behavior, before one is valued by others, especially the groom, by way
> of the bridewealth that will be discussed.[4] (Witin 1997)

As in many anthropological analyses of exchange, here the author assumes a clear opposition and hierarchical relation between material and social values (see Polanyi 1944: 46). The author dematerializes exchange to treat material objects as being merely signs of an immaterial value to which they are subordinate (the bride's dignity, not the buffalo, is supposed to be of value in this exchange—her dignity cannot "stand for" the buffalo as the buffalo "stands for" her).

There are several things to observe about this article. First, the subject is supposed to be clearly separated from its objects. To the extent that these objects are alienable, they have lost that integral relationship to their own-ers and transactors that helped define the Maussian gift. The relationship

---

4. The essay appeared on the equivalent of the op-ed page. It is an instance of a common genre of journalism in the region, in which people struggle to rationalize tradition, adjudicating between state and local pressures to modernize, on the one hand, and anxieties about the moral perils of abandoning tradition, on the other. The same essay also attempts to reconcile exchange with the companionate mar-riage associated with freedom, rationality, and individualism. The author is a Catholic from the island of Flores, but the ideas are thoroughly conventional among young Sumbanese Protestants, especially those with some church school education.

has instead become one of representation—the object stands *for* the person on the condition that they stand *apart*. In effect, objects act much like the linguistic sign as described by Saussure: their significance determined by social convention and their material substance having only an arbitrary relation to that significance. Second, in the process, the exchange value of those objects is supposed to be abstracted fully from any causal articulation with concrete practices and material forms. Not just the labor but also the social ties, political efforts, and ancestral powers that lie behind one's ability to obtain goods for exchange should cease to have any bearing on the meaning of those goods. Instead, they take their place in the world of alienable commodities and abstract value (see chapter 10).

As Marx remarked, there is a good fit between the abstract values presumed by commodity production and "Christianity with its *cultus* of abstract man, more especially in its bourgeois developments, Protestantism, Deism, &c." (1967a: 79). In both cases, he argues, the concrete comes to be subordinated to the abstract. In Marx's sardonic comparison to the elevation of spirit over the carnal individual, "just as the sheep's nature of the Christian is shown in his resemblance to the Lamb of God," so too it is only the abstract human labor represented by linen that makes it exchangeable for a coat (1967a: 52). From Georg Simmel's less sardonic perspective, "Money is really that form of property that most effectively liberates the individual from the unifying bonds that extend from other objects of possession" and thereby becomes a foundation for individual freedom (1990: 354). In the case of the Christian reinterpretation of marriage exchange, the separation of the person from things, and of concrete things from their symbolic value, entails a dematerialization of the person (who comes to be defined by "value and dignity" as well as, presumably, by an immortal soul) and concomitant despiritualization (and subordination) of the material object. Only in these terms may persons and things properly be brought into relation with one another.

Finally, the high school author shifts the focus of the exchange from the groups who enter into it to the individual bride, whose spiritualization is implicitly bound up with her social separation from social bonds—facilitated, it seems, by the treatment of exchange as a circulation of signs.[5] The individualism of modern ideas of marriage is, of course, well recognized in Euro-American history as well as elsewhere (and it is a common theme in early-twentieth-century Indonesian novels). Note, then, how the shift in the understanding of material goods reinforces the shift in focus to the indi-

---

5. I am grateful for the astute comments of Danilyn Rutherford on this point.

vidual. For the kinds of self-consciously modern Christians represented by
the quotation here, the bearing of goods on the formation of social persons,
where material utility ought not to be at issue, should be merely symbolic.
As prestations thus shift in their commonly understood semiotic status
from being indexes (which causally link signs to their referents) to arbitrary
and conventional symbols, they seem increasingly to be under the control
of, and direct expression of, autonomous human intentions. Circulating as
a sign of respect for tradition or for the bride, for example, the marriage
prestation of cloth, ornaments, or cattle becomes the bearer of messages. The
recognizable and legitimate costs and material consequences of exchange
become increasingly reduced to the status of incidentals.

In this context we can see that changes in how people view material
objects articulate with changing assumptions about language. The messages sent in marriage exchanges are being understood in terms of the
intentions of the sign users. So too, speakers' words are taking their meaning from intentions and the objects of reference, rather than, say, their aesthetic or magical power, the flawless repetition of ancestral words, or dialogues leading to convergence between different speakers. As a result, a
Protestant who wants to account for the value those objects hold for the
subject is left with little but the desires of a willful (individual) subject as
its source. In non-Christian views of Sumbanese exchange, people manipulate objects of value in deference to ancestors, the ultimate agents of ceremonial action, whose agency is manifested in long-term material consequences. But when Sumbanese Protestants deny that the materiality of
objects is meaningful, they are transforming the representational economy
in which they circulate, rendering them into signs wielded by relatively
abstract sign users, and pointing to invisible and abstract values such as
"social solidarity," "tradition," or "self-worth." This change in one part of
a representational economy shows how the modern subject must be the
source of its own value, standing apart from ancestral agents, social others,
and material things. Behind these signs stand the abstract subjects whose
intentions they express. But where do these subjects stand?

SINCERITY AS A METADISCOURSE

The subject, to the extent it aspires to modernity, as I have been describing
it, seeks to act as the source of its own authority.[6] In many Protestant ver-

---

6. Of course in some sense one defers to the agency of God. But in practice, most
mainstream Protestant groups have historically tended to treat divine agency as an

sions, at least, this source cannot be the physical body, material goods, or social standing, but instead is the character and condition identified with its own interiority. And crucial to the concept of interiority, and the practices that promote it, is language. To make sense of this, I turn for a moment to the notion of sincerity, beginning with its underpinnings in familiar, common English-language ways of talking. That is, I want to bring out an implicit semiotic ideology that seems to be embodied in widespread commonsense understandings of sincerity and its moral implications. Against this background, I then return to Sumba to illustrate how the materiality of semiotic practices is both condition for *and* constraint on the possibility of becoming one kind of person rather than another.[7]

As Lionel Trilling (1972) puts it, sincerity is a way of characterizing a relationship between words and interior states. To be sincere, in this respect, is to utter words that can be taken primarily to express underlying beliefs or intentions.[8] Carrying Trilling's observation further, we can call sincerity a metadiscursive term. As such, it is a component of linguistic ideology, that

---

assumed background against which the person acts or seeks divine sources for the radical assertion of the individual's own agency (see Troeltsch 1958: 61). In either case, the actual consequences tend toward an emphasis on individual agency. Note that in many cases even the original Calvinist emphasis on predestination eventually faded (Troeltsch 1931: 690).

7. The idea of semiotic practice should keep us alert to both the semiotic-pragmatic requirements for and limits to possible transformations of the subject. If the "individuality" of the "Western self"—what E. Valentine Daniel has called "the impossible world of the Cartesian cogito" (1996: 189)—has been overdrawn (compare Battaglia 1995), this is no doubt in part because of the clash between ideologies and the constraints of semiotic-pragmatic possibilities. What is imaginable exceeds the range of what is possible.

8. Nondiscursive actions are sincere only insofar as they can be translated into discourse or be treated as some sort of signification. A smile or a gift is insincere if we find a mismatch between the smile or gift and the invisible feelings we conventionally expect to produce them. That is, we treat them as external signs of an interior state. I am aware this narrows the definition of sincerity, making it too cramped to include internal states of single-mindedness or purity (see, for example, Hampshire 1971; Walker 1978). One might respond to this model at two levels: One would be along the lines exemplified by Sartre's classic critique of the demand for sincerity as an act of bad faith, its fulfillment impossible: "Total, constant sincerity as a constant effort to adhere to oneself is by nature a constant effort to dissociate oneself from oneself" through an act of self-objectification (1956: 65)—a sharp doubting, perhaps, of the possibilities for what Dennett (1976) calls "second order desires." Another, more ethnographic response would be to argue that a full-fledged and explicit concept of sincerity cannot be disentangled from the speech practices by which it could be pragmatically internalized and which would give public evidence for it.

is, of local assumptions about how language functions.[9] This ideology posits a specific sort of relationship between speech and its imputed sources in the speaker's self: Sincere speech aims to make that interior state relatively visible. Sincere speech adds and subtracts nothing in words that was not already there in thought. This is linked to the historical emergence of language ideologies that stress the referential and predicational functions of language over, say, social pragmatics such as indexing social deference—to say nothing of language that produces supposedly "magical" effects.

The idea of sincerity is therefore also associated with the understanding of "religion" that centers on truthful propositions rather than, for example, ritual activities or bodily disciplines. It also seems to propose a hierarchical relation between words and thoughts, since the thought seems to come first and thereby determines and imposes a limit on the words. The concept of sincerity thus seems to assume a clear distinction between words and thought, as parallel discourses (interior and exterior), such that they either could or could not match up. Should they indeed match up, language would thereby become transparent, nothing significant would remain of the material forms or social origins of words, allowing the unmediated thought to reveal itself. Moreover, as linguistic ideology, the concept of sincerity also seeks the *authority* of words in that relationship of matching. To take words as insincere is to at least cast some doubt on them. If I characterize your praise or promise as insincere, I am suggesting that I take the thought to hold primacy over the word, discrediting the latter. Moreover, sincerity seeks to locate the authority for words in the speaker as a distinct and self-possessed self as the responsible party (Rosaldo 1982).

Insofar as the concept of sincerity assumes that words could reflect inner states, it involves us in the linguistic questions about intentionality. Insincerity typically involves an intentional divergence between expression and thought: this, for example, would be the difference between a lie and an error. What about the reverse: can one be unintentionally sincere? I suppose it might be possible to think of examples of unintentional sincerity

9. Everyday assumptions find formal expression in two of the most important approaches to linguistic action in analytic philosophy. Austin (1955) makes sincerity one of the conditions for a successful performative. Grice (1975) says sincerity is one of the "conversational maxims" that are part of everyone's default assumptions that allow them to interpret other people's words. Certainly Grice did not think speech is always intended to be sincere. Speakers purposely violate maxims all the time. Rather, it is the effort to make sense of such violations that invites the listener to draw inferences about what the speaker really meant. It remains, however, an empirical question how general sincerity is even as a maxim.

(would a Freudian slip count?), but the heart of the concept lies elsewhere. As I understand it, sincerity is not just a matter of imputed alignment between expression and interior state but also a product of one's desire to make one's expressions aligned in this way. That is, sincerity says something not just about speech, or about speech and thought, but also something about the character of the speaker. This is why one also hears of persons, and not just particular acts of speaking, being described as sincere. As Trilling observes, sincerity in its fullest form demands "arduous effort" (1972: 6). Words taken as sincere therefore index that effort.

Thus, the concept of sincerity seems to link ideas about language to moral questions. I think we should take the concept of sincerity to be inseparable from some kind of judgment—it is hard to make sense of a neutral concept of sincerity. And the speaker's efforts at producing sincere expressions would likewise seem to be a function of that judgment. The concept of sincerity weds metadiscourse with the sphere of moral evaluation. It is a guide to the linkage between linguistic ideology and other cultural values. And this leads me to the third aspect of the concept of sincerity: it is interactive. For, in being sincere, I am not only producing words that reveal my interior state but am producing them *for you;* I am making myself (as an inner self) available for you in the form of external, publicly available expressions.[10] At the same time, the words I make available to you, to the extent they are sincere, display their freedom from any external compulsion: I do not say them merely out of deference to you, nor am I parroting the words of someone else, for instance. Certainly my words are not my own invention, and, as Jonathan Culler remarks somewhere, even "I love you" begins as quotation. Sincerity involves the effort to display to you a connection between those words and my inner self, and to ensure that for you those words do not fall back into the status of quotation. For doubts can remain that they are "mere words." Thus sincerity is a kind of public accountability to others for one's words with reference to one's self. And it is in this aspect that sincerity most evidently cannot be understood as only conceptual, since the interactive dimension presupposes concrete practices.

10. One might compare this to Sweetser's claims (1987) that, for English speakers, the immorality of lying consists not just in its untruthfulness but also in abusing the addressee. In broader and more historical terms, Charles Taylor (1989) defines the "inwardness" that he finds characteristic of the modern self in terms of what one is able to hold back from others. And holding back implies one could have done otherwise, could have expressed oneself more fully, in contrast to, say, the notion that human interiors are fundamentally opaque, a view that, for instance, Annette Weiner (1983) attributes to Trobrianders. For a contrasting morality concerning the expression of publicly shared sentiments, see Appadurai 1990.

But there remains a hierarchy in which the self is the ultimate foundation, since it is an accountability that presupposes a self that knows itself. To be sincere, for words to match thoughts, those thoughts must be no more ambiguous or opaque than the words that express them. Moreover, both thoughts and words must be fully under the control of the speaking self. It doesn't seem to make sense, for example, to speak of the sincerity of dialogues as such, apart from the sincerity of each respective participant separately.

Now obviously one should not project this account of an English or American (or perhaps even more local) ideology too far.[11] Rather, I offer it here as a way of provoking two sets of ethnographic questions: First, as an element of a metadiscursive vocabulary, what linguistic ideology does the concept of sincerity (or any of its relatives) presuppose? And what specific ways of speaking does it envision? What does it assume about the normal relations between speakers and speech? Second, as an element of a cultural value system, what is the moral load of the concept of sincerity? What does it assume about the value and authority of the relations between speakers, their speech, and other persons? What does it say about the self and its relations to others?

These are separate sets of questions, in part because it is at least possible that historically one could change and not the other: Members of a given society, for example, might maintain a certain view of language and its speakers but alter how they evaluate them. This is precisely the sort of thing that might happen in a case of religious conversion, to the extent that the relatively tacit, pragmatic assumptions underlying interaction are less susceptible to intentional, self-conscious, ideologically motivated change than are explicit moral and ideological evaluations.

SINCERITY AS FREEDOM

As Trilling (1972) argues, the semantic and moral load carried by the concept of sincerity for contemporary speakers of English bears strong traces

---

11. The most usual terms for *sincerity* in Sumba seem to be the Indonesian *tulus* and the Arabic loanword incorporated into Indonesian, *ikhlas,* and, in limited contexts, the indigenous *wali atingu,* "from the heart" (literally, "liver"). Importantly, these are perhaps most commonly used to refer to the participants in an exchange who give generously without having to be forced. Clearly this usage is different from the linguistic ideology I depict here. I take this to manifest a persistent Sumbanese understanding of the relationship between persons and material things, against which some Protestants are consciously exerting themselves.

of a religious genealogy in which Protestantism plays an important role. Or, at least, the implicit individualism, the specific ways of distrusting language, and the authority granted to interior states all find especially strong and influential expression in those strands of popular thought associated with the Protestant Reformation and its effects on Euro-American cultural and political formations (Burke 1987). Moreover, in many parts of the colonial and postcolonial world, this particular concept of sincerity, as formulated by Protestant churches, has often had its most direct impact on non-Western ways of thinking about language, selves, and interaction. For people to take sincerity as a measure of one another entails certain views of language. But this concept cannot remain at the level of belief alone: there must be some practical means of taking it up.

Recall Asad's claim that the universalizing definitions of religion characteristic of ideologies of modernity have shifted attention from power and practices to beliefs or, as he puts it, to sets of propositions that command assent (1993). Even this shift itself depends on the existence of certain kinds of concrete practices. This is both because propositions themselves depend on the materiality of semiotic mediation and because (as Blaise Pascal recognized long ago) this second-order understanding—according to which, belief statements are the heart of religion—requires some embodiment in a concrete semiotic and pragmatic form if it is to be a plausible and possible way of "having" a religion. At the same time, Asad is right to point out how strongly this embodiment has often been denied, which leads me back again to the question of modernity and transcendence.

One of the critical obstacles with which Calvinist missionaries and converts have had to contend in Sumba is the power of local discourse pragmatics and their underlying assumptions. For example, as I showed in the previous chapter, Sumbanese Protestants are concerned about the problem of authentic speech in prayer. They are highly critical of both Sumbanese ancestral ritual, which makes use of formulaic couplets supposed to have been handed down unchanged from the first people, and Catholic ceremonies, in which people rely on printed prayer books. By contrast, Calvinists believe prayers should come from the heart, spontaneous and truly felt; that is, they should be sincere. But the problem is that these words remain in the form of human language. And so, to the extent that words always bear some trace of their origins (in society or wherever one imagines particular languages to come from), beyond the individual speaker, they seem to challenge the ideal that one should claim one's own words. It turns out to be difficult even for purportedly spontaneous speech to abolish all traces of its externality to the speaker.

At issue is the autonomy of the human subject in contrast to the world of objects. To the extent that language is experienced as originating (at least ontogenetically) outside and circulating beyond the speaker, it can seem to confuse the distinction between interior and exterior or challenge the individual's control over that distinction. But the stakes appear in slightly different terms for those who may be less theologically inclined. For many ordinary Protestant converts, sincerity is inseparable from other aspects of agency and autonomy that are functions of modernity's promise of more concrete and immediate forms of freedom. First, as Marcel Mauss observes, the "gift" includes not just material goods but also "acts of politeness" (1990: 5). One implication is that, as goods come to be distinguished from persons, so do certain forms of social interaction. Etiquette, for instance, may come to seem external to the actor, a matter of "mere form," and may even appear to be an external constraint on one's agency. Thus, as both Asad (1996) and Taylor (1989) have pointed out, sincerity emerges in European discourses as part of an account of how the individual's interiority is the chief site of that which might elude political coercion. By extension, sincere speech is that which is compelled by nothing that might lie "outside" the speaker, whether that be, for example, political authority, written texts, or social conventions.

For example, in Sumba the act of Christian conversion gives, among other things, substance to the idea that, upon entering modernity (Indonesian, *masa moderen*), one enters the free (or liberated or independent) age (Indonesian, *masa merdeka*). The church, that is, offers a concrete way of understanding of the word *freedom* (Indonesian, *kemerdekaan*, from "free," *merdeka*) that identifies the postcolonial era across Indonesia and situates that understanding in the supranational, world-historical context of a transcendent church. In particular, this freedom is expressed in releasing oneself from the ritual obligations imposed by ancestral mandates in order to join a voluntary organization in response to consultation with one's own conscience—a freedom that also acts as the guarantee of one's sincerity.[12] Or, at least, this is how public ceremonies stage the acts of entering the church and reconfirming one's faith. Indeed, this very willfulness is precisely one of the things that the recalcitrant nonconverts complain of, in contrast to their assertions that they remain faithful to an often oppres-

---

12. In this respect, to take religious conversion as paradigmatic of the historical and personal advent of freedom would seem to support Zygmunt Bauman's 1988 assertion that the concept of freedom implies release from a prior and inferior condition of nonfreedom.

sively demanding ancestral order. Being voluntary—as people around the globe have found variously to their distress and delight—church membership can cut across and undermine the ties of marriage, siblingship, villages, and clans, challenging the authority of ancestors, elders, and in some cases, males. In the process, as some Sumbanese explicitly recognize, the practices of adult baptism and confirmation provide ways by which one can flamboyantly insert oneself as a newborn subject into a particular historical trajectory, declaring oneself to be part of the modern or rejecting it. This is what Umbu Neka was doing when he staged the oratorical event on the occasion of his baptism (see chapter 5). Indeed, one thing these performances enact is the very fact of change itself and its positive evaluation, which is a defining feature of Protestant modernity.

CONVERSION AND THE PERFORMANCE OF SINCERITY

One small yet telling step into Protestant modernity is the taking of a Christian name (or, for those who practice infant baptism, its bestowal). The national identity card requires a personal name in a form the state will recognize. Increasingly, that name is the one assumed in baptism rather than given in clan rituals, bestowed as teknonyms and nicknames, or assumed by adults as they ceremonially change their status (Keane 1997c: 129–33). A friend of mine, whom I will call Edy, explained the virtue of Christian names this way: "Kids," he said, "change their names all the time. You might be called 'Jon' at home and 'Lord Jon' at school. Later you might decide to be called something else. Only the baptismal name is permanent, because it's registered 'up there.'" Note here the tension between willfulness and inscription. Edy portrays the social existence of Sumbanese names as being prone to the vagaries of individual whim and local interactions. Yet the Christian name itself is the mark of a voluntary act of self-transformation.[13] And it is precisely this apparent assertion of one's own will that scandalizes many non-Christians, who themselves are supposed to displace the agency of naming through divinatory procedures that put the matter into ancestral hands. So how can Edy claim the Christian name is permanent? In two respects, it seems. First, in theological terms, the stability of individual identity is a function of some sort of transcendent plane of record keeping, "up there," where Edy gestured, in heaven. And second, in concrete terms, that

13. As Kuipers (1998) observes, Christian names are less categorical than Sumbanese non-Christian ones and facilitate certain modes of individualization, such as census taking.

transcendent record is embodied in visible forms of inscription: the Bible, from which the names are taken, the birth and death certificates, the marriage registry, the church rolls, the school enrollment lists, and the national identity card. Now, we might argue that the notion of heavenly record-keeping transcendentalizes the disciplinary apparatuses of the state. Certainly these inscription practices are an important point of articulation between the person's religious and civil status. But for someone like Edy, the relations are reversed, for what makes these state practices possible is the prior existence of the heavenly record book. His perception captures how both state and church work to resolve the semiotic problem of making a transcendent and abstract authority work in concrete terms that can become part of ordinary experience.

Given Protestant notions of self-transformation, baptism cannot in itself be sufficient to make one a Christian, for that would be a kind of magic—good enough for Catholics and other heathens, perhaps. And this brings me back to the problem of sincerity as contingent upon practices. Adults must confirm their true faith in a public performance, one of an endless series of socially grounded affirmations. And such confirmations are themselves a discursive pedagogy, as they work to transform individuals, in Susan Harding's astute observation, from listeners into sincere speakers of the language of faith (2000).

The confirmation of faith involves standing before the congregation while the minister delivers a sermon (Indonesian, *chotbah*). The sermon is a distinctive and highly authoritative kind of speech event that, while unprecedented in pre-Christian Sumba, is strikingly parallel in form to the speeches (Indonesian, *pidato*) by which the Indonesian state periodically addresses its subjects. Like the speech, the sermon is pedagogical or exhortatory in nature. It aims to instruct and improve its listener through the disembodied authority of the public official as the representative of an abstract entity. One of the most prominent formal properties of the Sumbanese sermon is that it is broken into short, evenly spaced segments by direct address to the congregation. Like the speech, the sermon uses a highly marked form of address, most often (literally) "fathers, mothers, and siblings" (Indonesian, *bapak-bapak, ibu-ibu, dan saudara-saudara*), through which the listener is repeatedly constructed as the abstract addressee of national language. The sermon itself takes a linguistic form that provides the speaker with an authority deriving from beyond the here and now. It makes use of a linguistic style far from everyday speech. In the excerpt quoted below, we will see that the minister, at one moment, addresses the congregation on behalf of the Lord and then, in the next, addresses the Lord on behalf of the congregation. His pronoun use marks the minister as one with the congregation as he faces the Lord; then he shifts to a different pronoun as he gives voice to the Lord's words. Spoken prayer and quotations from the Bible offer a wide range of registers and voices, oscillating between transcendence and immediacy. And almost all of this is carried out not in the local languages of Sumba (which everyone present would understand) but in the national language (which not all members of the congregation are likely to understand easily), as if anyone in the nation might potentially be eavesdropping.

The resemblance between sermon and governmental speech is underscored by the similar spatial configurations in which they occur (podium facing rows of benches, the very rectilinearity of the audience's disposition), the peculiar public they command, and, as it happens, their insistence on cash over goods in kind. Let me briefly observe how strange this emergent kind of public feels to most Sumbanese. This was clearly expressed by a woman I will call Ina, when once we were talking about the feeling of embarrassment (Anakalangese, *maké*). By way of example, she told me this is how she feels when she goes into the church, which she does almost every Sunday. Now, Ina is not prone to timidity. One of the most highborn Sumbanese women I know, she is also a tough character. "What," I asked her, "is embarrassing about entering the church?" "There are all these people you don't know," she replied. She feels them looking at her. As an aristocrat, she rarely goes to the market (a relatively recent institution in Sumba), so the church is virtually the only space in which she finds herself among other people who are not gathered together because of specific ritual or kinship ties. Even if she recognizes most of the people she sees, she has the uncomfortable experience of being in public. And this is a certain kind of public. To the extent that Gereja Kristen Sumba churches are not supposed to be structured by social hierarchies (the seating in the pews, for instance, is not formally sorted out by social rank or gender), each person in church is exposed to the gaze of others, who, at least in their capacity as fellow congregants, stand notionally on an equal footing. Thus, being in public, she finds herself exposed as an individual: her rank, clan, marital identity, and so forth are all stripped away by both congregation and, perhaps, the eye of divinity. This is the very model of the abstract disinterested person that Michael Warner (2002) has claimed is presupposed by the modern public sphere. What, then, could be more public than a Protestant church?

I now turn to the public confirmation of faith. Typical of such performances is one I recorded in August 1993. A minor local official with a wife and several children set out to regularize his union and, in the process, take a crucial step in "following the age" (Indonesian, *ikut zaman*) with a church marriage. First, the official had to confirm his faith in front of the congregation, but most of the talking was done by the minister. Here, for instance, in a characteristic moment in the framing sermon, we hear the voice of the church articulated by a single speaker (the minister), delivering itself to a split addressee: the official himself (as a single individual) and the congregation. At this moment the minister addresses the audience in Indonesian by naming the authority on whose part he speaks:

> We [using the inclusive *kita*] are called . . . and at this moment we are called to implement the announcement of the Parish Council in successively implementing various kinds of activities. And the first opportunity we are called to implement the carrying out of is the declaration of the confession of faith by the brother whose name has already been mentioned in the announcement, and we all are invited to follow him. And, before that, we are invited to listen to the reading of the declaration, which is connected with the aforementioned activity. Beloved brethren, congregation of God, at today's hour of religious service, there is a brother of ours who desires to acknowledge and declare his belief before God and before his congregation here. He has requested, and been received in an ecclesiastical manner, to become a member with full responsibility in the congregation of God. He has been cultivated and educated [Indonesian, *dibina dan dididik*] to take a change of faith, and promised this to his parents when he was baptized while still small.

The action to take place here makes explicit reference to a bureaucracy with all the appropriate forms of proper procedure. These include the preliminary announcement of the upcoming event and the retrospective reference to those announcements, thus assuring the listener that what now occurs follows the rules and is not unexpected. In pragmatic terms, the minister's authority is immanent in the rational procedures of the church, as well as in the formal Indonesian language he wields and the pedagogy alluded to by the words "cultivated and educated" (which also have strong associations with state discourses). The minister continues:

> The regulations [Indonesian, *tata tertib*; another expression associated with the state] for the confession of faith are bestowed by our Lord Jesus Christ, who always accompanies his community and helps us hold fast to the promise bestowed by God from generation to generation. So that our brother's confession of faith be evident before God and before the congregation, I invite him to stand before God and declare his faith to answer the questions that I am about to submit. I will read the questions in their entirety, and then I will give him an opportunity to

answer them. The first: Do you believe that the teaching of this Bible and the twelve articles of the confession of apostolic faith is teaching that is true and perfect for the purpose of your salvation? . . . Do you believe, acknowledge, and promise?

Here the official replies, "I believe, acknowledge, and promise." And the minister tells him, "Therefore you have become a member with full responsibility in the holy congregation of God."[14] The minister then turns the man to face the congregation and tells them to receive him as a friend and sing a hymn.

The congregation here serves as a single collective witness. To the extent that the sermon is addressed to the man who stands before them, this witness overhears the summoning of an individual conscience. The church ceremony enacts a scene in which each individual member's conscience is subject to the overhearing of others. Each is kept true to his or her own conscience by this repetitious recalling of the moment of his or her own summoning by the church. Indeed, one of the formal promises is to listen to the advice and warnings of the vestry.

The sermon is supposed to address the listener's conscience. This doctrinal stress on interiority works in tension with the highly formalistic procedure that enacts not evidence of belief per se—there is no testimony, no cries of anguish or exultation here—but rather the discourse of belief. The church summons the man here to give an accounting of himself. He must reply in the language of belief. What interests me about this scene is precisely its schematic quality, its formality, its lack of apparent psychology. Nothing requires us to assume any belief on the part of the official who stands in front of the congregation. What is important here is rather that the one affirming his faith understands that he must stand ready to give an account of himself in the language of belief: he must at least be able to say, "I believe," if summoned to do so by the church. Such practices give concrete expression to Asad's notion that religion, as a concept linked to the modern, centers on propositions sincerely assented to. This initial performance opens up a lifetime of further practices (recitations of creeds, prayer meetings, Bible-reading groups, the education of children, and so forth) that similarly stress concepts of referential truth, belief, and sincere speech.

14. The other three commitments are to believe that salvation lies only with Christ, to spread the Word, and to accept the authority and supervision of the congregation and its elders. Two of these are thus affirmations of belief, and two are promises regarding future behavior.

The congregation is also constituted as those before whom this profession is witnessed. They form the public who provide the warrants for such acts of self-accounting. Indeed, they are owed such an accounting of this man's invisible interior state of belief. And they are given the risk and responsibility in the future to call him to account *if* his acts should stray from this declaration of interiority. His sense of responsibility is not his alone; it is mirrored in that of the community.

Here two historically and ethnographically distinct pathways converge, and with them come two explanations. On the one hand, this church ceremony remains within the parameters of certain interactive norms and conventions of Sumbanese society that limit the acceptable expressions available to the sincere conscience in locally specified ways. The church service, for all its appeal to both bureaucratic rationality and the language of interiority and belief, also responds to persistent Sumbanese intuitions about how to act in the world. Long-standing assumptions embedded in the pragmatics of performance in Sumba require public recognition of the self in formalized interactions, as elaborated in everything from marriage negotiations to any dealings with the ancestral spirits (see Keane 1997c). As my experiences with the highly formulaic nature of more intimate family and village-based prayer and Bible study groups also suggest, even sincere speech, if it is to have any authority for Sumbanese, must take the form of a public performance and demand a public affirmation.

On the other hand, in this context and in certain respects, Sumbanese expectations can find something familiar and acceptable in the performance styles produced by the doctrinal requirements of the Reformed Churches' neo-orthodoxy. For the congregation is supposed to monitor its members continually in formal professions of faith. As Weber points out (1946), for many Protestant sects this monitoring is a logical outcome of the combined emphasis on freedom and sincerity. Because membership in the church is supposed to be voluntary, nothing guarantees in advance that individuals are morally upright and genuine in their faith. Therefore they are on constant probation and subject to the ongoing scrutiny of other members. In neo-orthodox Calvinism, this scrutiny requires repeated public affirmations of faith. Their formality reflects a doctrinal suspicion of emotion (Troeltsch 1931: 589) and assumes a sharp distinction between the spiritual and material worlds, such that one should not expect external signs to be automatic expressions of internal states. (And, in Indonesia, it is no doubt reinforced by a tendency to associate formality with the state's version of modernity as well.) This is one of many possible resolutions of the general semiotic problem of making transcendence available in practical terms. In this respect, the apparent disjuncture between the idea of sincere belief and the formality with which it is expressed is not simply a matter of an incomplete or "syncretic" transition from "traditional" to "modern" Sumba. Given this semiotic overdetermination, it may be impossible to fully disarticulate these two sources for this performance style.

Public performance is, of course, a highly marked kind of event and involves specific sorts of speech genres. In reflecting on these public objectifications of the believing self, offered for the recognition of others, we should ask not just who has sincerity but also when it should appear, when it should *count*. For Sumbanese Protestants, the demand for the performance of sincerity is most evident at weddings and funerals. It is as if one should enact one's moral subjecthood and the freedom that sincerity should express at moments when one's being embedded in the world of other people is most apparent. Obviously we are not justified in concluding from events like this that *no* other expectations of, or concepts of, sincerity might exist across the full spectrum of interactive contexts offered by Sumbanese life. We may remain in doubt as to the exact psychological transformations under way, but at least we should attend to the most salient model available the manifest transformation in representational economy and the means *it* offers for the production and constant reaffirmation of the norm of the sincere self.

TRANSCENDENCE, MEDIATION, AND MATERIALITY

If a representational economy involves relations among such things as language ideology, habits of interpreting material things, explicit religious doctrines, and tacit expectations of interaction, there is no reason in principle to assume they all snuggle harmoniously together. However much semiotic ideology may strive to regiment them, explicit discourses, tacit expectations, ordinary habits, and extraordinary disciplines are subject to different causal and logical pressures, with different temporalities. And in circumstances of dramatic historical transformation, we should expect to find a clash between semiotic ideology and religious doctrine, between the presuppositions of speech pragmatics and explicit, public concepts. At the same time, if we talk about different kinds of selves, we cannot ignore the possibility that clashes—between the tacit and the explicit, among different speech genres, and among presupposable selves, or, for that matter, between the workings of exchanges and the meanings of the objects that flow through them—are, in fact, commonplace or at least an always lurking potential. Moreover, if doctrines of purification propose an escape from semiotic mediation altogether, those clashes must be unavoidable, thus confounding some of the higher ambitions for the autonomous, sincere subject that modernity names.

The problems raised by the examples of ceremonial exchange and the performance of conversion mentioned in this chapter have two things in common. One is that they both concern conflicting assumptions about the human subject that emerge in changes in its material mediations and objectifications. The second is that these conflicts ideologically align Protestant Christianity with the idea of modernity, referential language (as expressed in the values of transparency and truth), and the signifying practices that underlie abstract value (as expressed in money and commodities) in opposition to paganism, the past, performative and magical language, and ceremonial exchange. In this highly simplified conceptual alignment, the categories "Protestantism" and "modernity" and, one might add, "capitalism" (see chapter 10) point to different aspects of the processes that abstract the subject from its material and social entanglements in the name of freedom and authenticity. It is in this that we can see one suppressed link between modernist views of language and things, on the one hand, and the more theological concerns expressed by Protestant and other religious reformers, on the other: the value of freedom and abstraction lies, at least in part, in their offer of transcendence. Gifts symbolic of intentions, words true to the heart and to the world of referents, actions taken without deference to other persons, and the abstract value represented by money are the quotidian forms of such transcendence.

To the extent that freedom is defined as the elimination of semiotic form and the social others it indexes, however, it becomes unattainable. The subject cannot free itself from objectification, it cannot eliminate bodies, sociality, or the multitude of ways in which even self-knowledge is mediated by words, things, and social others. It cannot even be sincere without publicly recognizable, socially indexical, materially embodied forms of speech. People misunderstand something crucial if they imagine that semiotic form is only an exterior constraint on what would otherwise be free action directed from an ultimately disembodied interior. Put in other terms, the work of purification cannot fully succeed. Whether one focuses on people in their actions or in their modes of knowing, one will find they are dynamically involved in a full-fledged representational economy in which the various ways that words and things circulate have not only logical implications but also causal consequences for one another.

8 Materialism, Missionaries, and Modern Subjects

> Sound contrition and brokenness of heart brings a strange
> and a sudden alteration into the world, varies the price and
> value of things beyond imagination, . . . makes the things
> appear as they are.
>
> THOMAS HOOKER, *Application of Redemption*

> In the realm of ends everything has either a *price* or a
> *dignity*. Whatever has a price can be replaced by something
> else as its equivalent; on the other hand, whatever is above
> all price, and therefore admits of no equivalent, has a
> dignity.
>
> IMMANUEL KANT, *Foundations of the Metaphysics of Morals*

When Calvinists encounter ancestral ritual in eastern Indonesia, they recurrently wrestle with problems of material value and that which is "above price," the human subject. The dilemmas posed for Calvinists by sacrifice, sacralia, and other forms of "idolatry" cast into sharp relief the ambivalent relations between Protestant spirit and material economy. As I argued in chapter 4, since overseas evangelization often overlays a contrast of present and past upon a parallel contrast of here and there, it also introduces a historical dimension into the relations of spirit and matter. The comparisons induced by religious conversion—like those arising in other colonial, ethnographic, or home-grown reformist contexts—provide a site for interpretive and evaluative reflection on culture as well as cosmos, reflection animated by a sense of moral and mortal consequences. The missionary seeks to change the convert's self-consciousness so that, in Thomas Hooker's words, things may "appear as they are." Evangelism is thus, in

---

Epigraphs: Thomas Hooker, *Application of Redemption*, excerpted in Perry Miller and Thomas H. Johnson, eds., *The Puritans* (New York: American Book Company, 1938), 312; Immanuel Kant, *Foundations of the Metaphysics of Morals and What Is Enlightenment?* trans. Lewis White Beck (Indianapolis: Bobbs-Merrill, 1959), 53.

part, an assault on the explicit contents of what is construed as false knowledge. But the church also seeks to transform local practices, with implications that may exceed the range of explicit doctrine. As I have argued in the previous chapters, central to the Christianization of twentieth-century Sumba is the work of purification, an effort to correct what appears to the missionary to be an illicit conflation of words, things, and persons. This process of disentangling is critical for the constitution of a modern subject (in at least some recensions) and its place within an emergent political economy. The process, however, can be a matter of ongoing and sometimes heated dispute, even among missionaries of the same church.

Two sets of practices in particular serve in Sumba as potent synecdoches for the transformations of value and the subject, and they occasion a high degree of controversy. The previous two chapters focus on language; this one examines some of the difficulties missionaries face when they seek to delimit the functions and meanings of material objects. Again, the central problem is the aporia that are encountered in the work of purification as an attempt to distinguish and stabilize the differences among signs, objects, and subjects and to assign each its proper values within a stable representational economy. The material object seems to have been an especially destabilizing element in this cluster and continues to trouble economic rationalizers and the development-oriented activists of both state and non-state organizations, as well as some who simply hope for the inculcation of a recognizable liberal subject. The problems faced by the work of purification help cast into relief the dimensions of a representational economy within which matters as seemingly disparate as the distribution of meat at feasts and the closing of eyes in prayer have entailments for each other, and may have serious moral and even political consequences.

THE OTHER'S ERROR

The difficulties posed for the church by Sumbanese uses of valuable objects and animals are manifold. In practical terms, valuables circulate in a complex network of expensive exchanges that so pervades social and economic life as to resist direct efforts at reform.[1] But these material practices also

1. Regardless of the participants' religious affiliations, highly formalized and often very expensive exchanges involving gold, cloth, metal items, ivory, pigs, horses, and buffalo are critical to Sumbanese social relations, local status politics, and economic organization. In the eastern part of the island, the focal point is marriage exchange, while in much of West Sumba competitive feasting takes center

seem to raise in some observers a degree of anxiety that exceeds mere practical considerations, and which arises at the intersection of theological iconoclasm with the founding assumptions of a modern political economy.[2] Traditions of iconoclasm—whether Christian, humanist, or Marxist—tend to view "fetishistic" or "idolatrous" practices with both contempt, as the mistaken and inappropriate elevation of inferior signs, and fear, as a threat to the powers and autonomy of the human subject (Mitchell 1986).[3] Such practices are especially problematic given their peculiar location at politically and emotionally fraught sites of conjuncture. As I have discussed in the previous two chapters, the concept of fetish arises in a comparative context, as an observer's response to seeing *other* people attribute false values to objects. Such discourses of fetishism and idolatry are marked by their doubleness: they require both a fetishist and an outside observer in whose eyes the fetishist is trapped in misrecognition. This approach draws attention to the critical or anxious responses that this doubleness induces. While Marx appropriates the language of religion ironically to speak of political economy, we can follow his trope back to the questions of belief and value in which it originates, for, whether a matter of false gods or commodities, "fetish discourse always posits this double consciousness of absorbed credulity and degraded or distanced incredulity" (Pietz 1985: 14). But fetish

---

stage. Across the island, the principles of exchange dominate even the minutiae of everyday interactions (Onvlee 1973a, 1973c). Sacrifices, inalienable possessions, and other ritually potent objects take much of their power from their contrast to the flow of exchange valuables (Keane 1997c: chapter 8).

2. In Weber's account (1958), Protestantism eschews "idolatry of the flesh" because the sensuous is the point of entry for corruption. For Kant, the distinction between things and humans is between means and ends (1956: 53). Objects can have a price insofar as they are interchangeable with other objects in relation to an end that lies beyond them, while humans are ends in themselves.

3. In discussing Marx, Mitchell draws on Max Müller: While the idol is considered by its worshipper to be a *symbol* of something else, the fetish is seen as itself supernatural (Mitchell 1986: 190). Note that this implies an epistemological distinction, for while the outsider might see *both* as varieties of false practice, the *practitioner* cannot in good faith do so. The so-called fetishist or idolater, who might agree with the outsider as to the symbolic status of the idol, is in principle excluded from a position that would recognize the fetish as no more than a fetish. In the following discussion, I do not attempt to distinguish between these two concepts. My interest is in the entire complex of problems raised for Christians by non-Christian uses of material objects. Both missionary and indigenous discourses slide from one to the other view of non-Christian practices, as predisposition and strategic advantage dictate. For *fetish* as a technical term, the standard Dutch definition in the early twentieth century was that given by the missionary ethnographer A. C. Kruyt (see chapter 3), who defines it as the attribution of powerful "soul substance" *(zielstof)* to unusual objects (1906: 199–201).

discourse is seldom complacent in its incredulity. It is precisely because material things seem to be endowed with objective, culture-free values, in the
eyes of both the bearers of a capitalist political economy and adherents of
religious totalizations, that the encounter with others who evaluate things
differently can be so troubling.[4]

When I lived on Sumba, despite my efforts at diplomatic neutrality I
was often the recipient of partisan complaints about religious difference. A
particularly long and vehement discussion arose in 1993, on my return
visit to the village of Prai Bakul, an important center of marapu ritual. I sat
on the veranda with several men as they brought me up to date on what
had happened after I left in 1987. They were especially proud of the fact
that one of their ratu (ritual specialists) had recently been elected head of
the local unit of government, the desa. This success, they boasted, was a
tribute to the superior powers of their ancestor. The desa head added that
none of his new colleagues bothered him about religion, since, after all,
though each had his or her own faith (an interpretation that is not, as it
happens, officially sanctioned), all shared a single direction. After a while,
however, the conversation took a less complacent turn, as the desa head left
and Umbu Delu began this complaint:

> How can those Christians claim to face God directly, and tell us our
> own drum was only made with human hands?[5] And they keep coming

4. Given the role of emotions and subjectivity in much of the classic literature
of conversion, for writers as different as John Bunyan and William James, this focus
may seem excessively intellectualist. It has been my experience, however, that,
when both Christian and non-Christian Sumbanese talk about conversion, they are
usually undramatic, rational, and rarely touch on emotional questions—in part, a
reflection of a general Sumbanese reticence about most forms of emotional expression and lack of interest the language of interiority. The style of missionization also
contributes to this rationalism. Describing the missions of the Reformed Church
(Hervormde Kerk) in Sumatra in the late nineteenth century, Kipp writes, "[E]ntry
into this community . . . was not an emotional rebirth but a rational process. Converts expressed a desire to be Christians, were schooled in basic understandings,
examined, and then baptized" (1990: 23). Missionaries were taught to preach "without the use of dogmatic terms such as sin, conversion, regeneration, redemption,
atonement, and others of a similar kind" (Brouwer 1912: 232). If anything, this
style was probably even stronger in Sumba, since it was evangelized by the mission
of the more self-consciously neo-orthodox Reformed Churches, which, alone of all
the mission groups, required its missionaries to have university degrees (Brouwer
1912: 226; van den End 1987: 27). On the vocabulary of emotions among contemporary Sumbanese Christians, see Kuipers 1998.

5. He refers to a large drum that hangs in his clan's ancestral house and bears
the same name as the founding ancestor. This and the gold referred to later in the

to my house to plague me. But after all, how do we get to God, anyway? God created Adam and Eve. They in turn had Cain and Abel. Now, they had children in turn, and so on—how many centuries before arriving at my father? My father is in front. But now these Christians say, "It's only God that we face." But if not by way of my father, then how? . . . Christians say, "Only God: besides that there's nothing." Indeed, God made Adam and Eve, all of humanity. God ordered them to replace God. Cain and Abel, he handed it on to them after Adam and Eve were old. It descends down to our parents. So the right comes from God to us—so we're God now. But Christians say, "That's useless."

At this point, Umbu Hiwa, a ratu in his fifties (and nephew of an early convert and Protestant minister), took over, asserting his authority to speak of ritual knowledge and imposing his own canon of discursive coherence on the conversation:

According to tradition, this ancestor was an ordinary human. We give rice and chicken to his spirit—not to gold, but to the ancestral spirit. We have gold so that he's there, as a reminder that our ancestor was rich. The gold is in the house so we remember the spirit of our ancestor. It's like when you write things down in your book there, so you remember.

Here Umbu Delu interrupted:

But *that* thing [i.e., the church] I call a subtle colonizer [Indonesian, *penjajah halus*]—*every* day you pay money. Give money to the minister, to the congregation. They say, "If you don't give money, it's not under the command of God." If you don't give them money, they won't read from their book. Pay that money. It's as if we buy it. But what are we buying? What we hear all our lives. It's the same too if we're sick— pay first. . . . Even if you pay, you'll still be dead in the end. When are we going to see the proof? They talk about hell—there's no proof of hell. The minister says whoever doesn't follow Christianity will go to hell. I was already a Christian once, but they made me pay every day. Plus tithes every year. So I left the church.

I asked:

What about the expense of sacrifices?

---

conversation are both components of the "marapu's portion" *(tagu marapu)*, inalienable valuables said to have been brought to the present location by the ancestors after their wanderings and normally kept hidden in ancestral houses. They are handled only during occasional rituals, and then only while those who handle them adhere to strict rules and prohibitions.

Umbu Delu replied:

> That's only once a year, and if there doesn't happen to be any, we give areca and betel, [and] it's alright. But if there's no money in front of the minister, it's for nothing.

Umbu Hiwa intervened again:

> Let's compare religions. As for our proof, you can already see it—there's that gold. But the Christians don't have any proof. All they have is that book. . . . That's where we have our strength—we didn't make that gold. Each one of these houses has its gold, the replacement of the name of the ones who brought it, so there's a sign that they really came here. But these Christians, all they have is a book. This book can be destroyed, or again its handiwork can fade.[6] But as for the tomb of [our ancestor], we can see it with our own eyes, we don't have to go far. . . . It's not easy to look at God, if it weren't for our ancestor who's at the side of God. We don't know God's place, only our ancestor does. We're not saying God doesn't exist—he exists [points upward]. We say so, so do the Christians. . . . But *they*, they only *talk*, they say, "These are my sins," while *we* use *materials*—*like* our ancestors did: they'd say, "Give me a buffalo."

Then, having made his point, he reasserted the norm of acceptance, that there's really no difference, only the fact that humans have different opinions. Given that Prai Bakul is the center of a strongly marapu enclave, there was a certain element of self-confidence mixed in with the resentment. But similar notes were sounded elsewhere—for example, in the talk of Umbu Dingu, who, having returned to the marapu after his first wife died when still young, now saw himself as the holdout in his village after several waves of mass baptism:

> It's like when you come here to visit: we roll out the mat for you to sit on. That's the base. That's what our gold is. It's just dead matter, but to say the name of God, you need a base. . . . Now, those Christians say we make stones into God, but that's not so. The stone altar is where we

6. His point, as I understand it, is that the reason the presence of gold in the house serves as a proof *(tada)* of the ancestor is, first, because it could have come from nowhere else, and second, because its very persistence forms a direct link to that ancestral source. The sheer materiality of gold, in semiotic terms, makes it a presupposing index of a lineage of transmission that connects it to its origin. The contrast to the Bible is a bit more obscure, but he seems to be saying that books, as physical objects, are extremely fragile and will not last (which is certainly true, given the climate and storage conditions in most Sumbanese villages). I suspect he is also thinking that, in contrast to individual, named gold valuables, books, by their replicability, cannot be indexical of any particular link to a point of origin.

meet. It's like if I promise to meet you, we need to have someplace to meet, right? How can we meet if there's no sign? . . . The Psalm says God exists everywhere—in the house, on the veranda, in the forest. Well, if this is so, how come when we pray [in these places] they tell us it's Satan? Take the Owner of the Land [Mangu Tana]. Like when you arrive at someone's house and you call out [the greeting] "Hey, house owner!" [*O mangu uma!*]—who's that? It's the person who made the house! So too, the Owner of the Land is the Creator. . . . The ancestors didn't know God because they didn't have the Bible. Only a Bible that isn't read, isn't written; that is, only gold. Now they say when we pray at the spring we're praying to Satan. But it wasn't Satan who made that spring, it's God. So if we take water from the spring, why not give thanks? *We* didn't make that spring! So too in the secret room [i.e., the bedroom], they say it's wrong to pray there. But what goes on in that room is not the work of our own hands, such that children come to be created in the womb of women.

These conversations bring up many of the most prominent leitmotifs when marapu followers talk about religions (I'll turn to the Christian side of the story in a moment). They do not challenge the truth-claims of Christianity—indeed, they cite the Old Testament in their own defense. The conflict lies instead in the nature of practices and their interpretation, involving both criticism of Christian and defense of marapu ritual procedures. The challenge to Christians given above touches on three issues: mediation, language, and money. The defense of the marapu cites norms of deference, claims of realism and symbolism, and the rhetoric of the state. One possible resolution cites a concept of functional equivalence among religious practices that implicitly seeks to lay claim to a relativistic interpretation of religion and (against most available evidence), state policy.

The appeal to relativism seems to have three sources. One is the sociological specificity of ritual powers, such as clan ancestors, commonly found outside the totalizing claims of "world religions." Thus, in Africa, Dr. Livingston attributed to a Kwena "rain doctor" an appeal for mutual respect: as we don't despise your knowledge, you shouldn't despise ours (Comaroff and Comaroff 1991: 210). A second source might be the direct influence of the Dutch. As I discussed in chapter 3, their training early in this century included the principle, albeit for strategic ends, that "a missionary must learn to respect the national and spiritual life of other peoples" (Brouwer 1912: 237), and several missionaries developed a strong interest in ethnography. One elderly ratu, when marshaling for me his many arguments against the strong pressure being put on him to convert, claimed that no less an authority than the missionary and Bible translator Louis Onvlee himself had told him never to abandon his faith. A third source seems to be a very selective reading of state ideology, which speaks of religious tolerance. This last source is especially problematic, since marapu ritual is not officially recognized as a religion, and there is considerable dispute as to whether it sufficiently recognizes a single God ever to appeal its standing with authorities.

The note of humility with which Umbu Dingu closed is characteristic of the Sumbanese sense of contrast between a depleted present and past plentitude (see chapter 5). He was implicitly contrasting his own modest stance with the arrogance displayed by Christians in both their strong knowledge claims and liturgical practice. So, too, Umbu Delu started off by speaking of the Christian presumption in claiming to face God directly, rather than through the mediation of ancestors. The problem is in part a matter of knowledge: as Umbu Hiwa put it, we don't know where God is located. Christians lack a form of proof for their claims as convincing as the possession by marapu followers of material remnants of the ancestors. This is more than an epistemological dilemma, however. It is a statement about hubris. After all, marapu followers do not challenge other Christian claims to knowledge, accepting the additions to ancestral history apparently provided by the Old Testament (for example, many people, even those most embittered and alienated by the new state of affairs, speak of ancestral valuables as coming from Babel). But the claim to be able to address God directly is a form of arrogance at variance with every expectation of respectful behavior in Sumba. Umbu Hiwa reflected this, saying that, unlike Christians, "we don't say his name." Or, as someone else put it to me in the heavily laden terms of state rationality (and echoing the logic of the man who complained about Umbu Neka's claim to have received his revelation directly from God, which I mentioned in chapter 5), "After all, you don't communicate directly with the president in Jakarta, do you? You go through the desa head, the district head, the regent, and the governor." What Umbu Delu and Umbu Hiwa were claiming for themselves was greater refinement, shown in their respect for deferential mediation.

The nature of this mediation is critical. In addition to seeking to face God directly, Christians just use talk: that is, they make no offerings. One sign of the arrogance of Christians is that they eat meat without prayers of invocation—they kill, marapu followers often say, simply in order to eat meat. Doing so is triply vulgar, as it emphasizes the materiality of the animal, the willfulness of the action, and the lack of self-control in the face of desires or appetites (see chapter 10). In contrast, deference is expressed by displacement. Marapu rituals, however much those who perform them may seek desirable ends, such as wealth and fertility, are enacted as inescapable obligations arising from an origin beyond the wishes and intentions of the participants. The value of displacement is also embodied in ancestral valuables. This is why Umbu Delu was offended by the Christian claim that the drum named for the ancestor was made by human hands. The contrast between the God-given, or natural, and human production has long been a defining tenet of Christian attacks on idolatry.[7] One response to Christian attacks is to insist that the present drum (despite periodic ritual renewals) is consubstantial with that left by the ancestors. Note that Umbu Dingu took up the argument of idolatry and implicitly turned it back on the Christians: we give thanks for that which was palpably not our own production. This echoes Christian claims that we owe thanks to God as the source of everything—and it transforms the nature of marapu prayer from interactive request or cajolement to an expression of thanks. But a second attack on idolatry is that it mistakes the very nature of objects and, by worshipping them, takes them to be subjects. Umbu Hiwa and Umbu Dingu, both sophisticated apologists, had ready responses: they essentially accused the Christians of error, of mistaking symbols for substances. At least at the level of explicit propositions, they claimed to agree with the Protestant distinction between material and spiritual and asserted that objects of marapu ritual are material signs of immaterial substances.[8]

Umbu Delu's economic complaint (which others also stress) is especially interesting, because one of the recurrent claims by *Christians* is that marapu ritual is wasteful. About twenty years before that conversation, one of the first Anakalangese to be ordained had composed a song with a line that ran, "What good is prayer, the marapu words? [They] just use up the little

7. Pietz traces the word *fetish* back to the *factitius* of early Christian theology, whose referents include both superstitious materialism (versus the immateriality of spirit) and the willful alteration of the natural body (1987: 26). When Augustine, speaking of the defeat of desire, contrasts the chaste person to the eunuch, he argues that only the former truly embodies a virtuous soul. The difference lies in the expression of the (immaterial) will as opposed to merely material operations (Pietz 1987: 28).

8. As I show in detail elsewhere, the actual practices of marapu offering and sacrifice cannot be reduced to a simple distinction between material expression and immaterial meaning (Keane 1997c: especially chapters 3, 7, and 8). The ritual meaning of objects includes ideas about the effects of objects on human spirits (dewa). These effects in turn are inseparable from the practical consequences of the social and political economies within which the objects and their transactors are embedded. I think Umbu Hiwa and Umbu Dingu understood this very well but also realized that the wiser rhetorical strategy was to work within the terms offered by Christians.

chicks." In a similar vein, one man justified to me his baptism in the mid-1960s in terms of neither truth nor ethics but practical expense. He figured the cash given to the church came out to less than all the chickens and pigs he sacrificed in his rice fields each year. Pak Pendeta, a retired minister, one of the first to go through the off-island Dutch theological school system, told me, in speaking of his evangelical efforts in the 1940s and 1950s:

> I'd ask them, why are they afraid of the marapu? Because they created us, and if we don't respect them, we'll get sick. I'd tell them, "Yes, that's true, we must be afraid. We're afraid because we can't *see* him. So the ancestors used gold, gongs, spears; those humans—they became signs that Lord God is there, like a king or a ratu. People fear them because of their power. So now we don't need to pray. God doesn't want us to bring chickens anymore. God sent me so you can return to God—not that wood, not that rock. What saves us isn't wood, rock, cattle, but Lord Jesus.

He, like early missionaries, sees non-Christians as living in a state of constant fear. His representation of material media is similar to those of Umbu Hiwa and Umbu Dingu in one respect: he sees them as replacements for something absent—that is, as representatives and signs of something else. It is only because that something else has no manifest form that material objects are needed. But now, with an encompassing account carried in the words of the Bible, these substitutes are no longer necessary.

DEVIL WORSHIP AND MISRECOGNITION

The interwoven themes of economy and of signs mistaken for real things (and vice versa) play their roles in a contemporary context of burgeoning state power, an ideology of development, and the accompanying pressures for rationalization of markets and institutions. They are also shaped, however, by church policies and terms of debate dating back to the early years of the mission. Confronted with what looked to some like a living Old Testament world, the Dutch were often greatly at odds among themselves as to how to interpret and respond to Sumbanese ritual practice. Much of their interest was in a perennial problem in Christian theology, the role of material objects in religion, brought to focus by the practical need to make decisions about the distribution of offerings. Practical need was, however, already anticipated by prior scriptural knowledge, as expressed by one of the mission deputies:

The wretchedness of paganism comes from the abominations which they commit and "the fear of the dead, with servitude to whom they are subjected all their lives" (Hebr. 2: 15). That wretchedness comes out more deeply in what the Scripture teaches us about the way in which the poor heathen seeks comfort and deliverance. For he brings offerings which he supposes he offers to the gods and actually he offers them to devils. The Sumbanese know of the one great God, who rests and to whom little service is shown; moreover, he knows of deceased ancestors, who exercise great influence on the lives of men.[9] He divides these into good and evil; the good intends well-being for their descendants and confers on them only favors, the evil bestows perdition upon men; they avenge themselves for the evil that was done to them in their earthly lives and for negligence of their memory. Now the Sumbanese seek to satisfy these evil spirits through offerings. Their idol-worship is therefore direct devil-worship. . . . The God of truth receives there not the least honor; there is likewise no recourse to be had to the only Helper in their need. In one word: that in the midst of all pagan wretchedness, this is the greatest, that one has no helper. Poor pagan! (Dijkstra 1987: 122–23)

As in current debates, the problem here is not entirely one of truth. The European missionary seems to find himself in the same universe as the Sumbanese, one that can indeed be identified in Old Testament prototypes. By Dijkstra's account, both European and Sumbanese know of God, and it seems both know of other invisible beings as well. Since the Sumbanese err not in their intentions but in misidentifying the recipient, the issue is not whether invisible beings populate the world but what their real natures are. The pathetic condition of the pagan is twofold: a matter of confusing devils with gods, and the resultant life of fear without help.[10] The practical outcome of false identification is misdirected practice: offerings have the wrong destination (a destination of whose existence Dijkstra seems to be in no doubt).

9. The reference here is to the distinction between a vaguely conceived creator and the spirits of ancestors who actually intervene in human affairs, and who are thus the recipients of most prayers and offerings.

10. The theme of fear persists to the present, as can be seen in Pak Pendeta's comments given above. One former marapu ritual specialist, who entered the Roman Catholic church between my first and second periods of fieldwork on Sumba, said somewhat scornfully of another priest who refused to convert that the man was afraid of lighting. He added, "Now that we have that metal [lightning rods] to put on top of buildings, we don't need to fear the marapu any longer." His remark echoes a long-standing theme in Western narratives of secularizing modernity.

A more self-consciously scientific spirit presents itself in the report of a visit to West Sumba after some fifteen years of missionization:

> Lumbu Langa had a long time ago removed the marapu-stones [i.e., altars] from his garden, and as his maize was no less than that of his neighbors, he therein knew that it is evident that things go just as well without offerings. . . . And now the conclusion is obvious. Making offerings yields nothing, but is merely harmful, the misery of chickens and buffalo. And so as time goes by one becomes detached from the marapu. Naturally that says nothing about the positive, only that the old was broken. But it is indeed still the time to bring the Gospel. There exists the risk that otherwise men become indifferent, that they let go of the old without desiring the new. (Colenbrander 1987b: 218–19)

By presenting the Sumbanese as born scientists stumbling across an empirical demonstration, Colenbrander's narrative implies that they are following a natural relationship of causality between active subjects and an objective world. In this respect, his view of religious spirituality reproduces the objectivism of contemporary European natural science. He also implies that the offering mediates nothing—it is reducible to its material form, chickens and buffalo, and thus to the economic calculation of losses. In addition, his worry reveals another important theme, that of functional equivalents. He can imagine a world without any belief at all and sees in the new religion a functional substitute for something absent. Compare the view of the influential missionary Kruyt, who warns against acting too harshly against what he sees as a necessary first stage of "superstitious Christianity," lest the missionary, "by attempting to drive the people to be more spiritual that they are capable of being may promote their becoming free-thinkers and atheists" (1924: 271–72). Like Colenbrander, Kruyt imagines the loss of a set of beliefs, if not replaced with another, leads to some sort of a null set. However, to equate this absence with free thought seems to require an additional supposition, which might lie in his description of heathens as fundamentally materialistic (1924: 266) and, thus, perhaps, in particular danger of sliding into a Western style of materialism.[11]

In theological terms, an especially disturbing dimension of material offerings is the fact that they can be interpreted economically, still an important issue today. They are subject to diversion into alternative uses and value frameworks (Appadurai 1986a; Thomas 1991). In contrast to verbal performances, their semantic meaning and social value are relatively

---

11. This was not an uncommon fear among missionaries; see, for instance, Beidelman 1982: 116, 211; Kipp 1990: 230.

underdetermined (see Keane 2003c). Furthermore, unlimited by clear distinctions between religious and secular action, the expenditure of sacrifices threatens, in the eyes of missionaries, to become indefinitely excessive. This is brought out when D. K. Wielenga, writing for a mission-society journal, seeks an elevating comparison for the Sumbanese (and quietly assumes for himself the position of the apostle):

> "You men of Athens, I perceive, are in every respect like religious men," so Paul was once forced to exclaim, seeing the "civilized" Athens so full of altars of numerous gods and goddesses that they had built one there for the unknown God himself, as they were afraid to have forgotten one, whose wrath they might then unwittingly bear. And in Sumba, the "uncivilized" land, one stumbles, as it were, over the numerous offering stones. For he too is "in every respect like religious men." . . . So the men of Athens reach out the hand to the "poor uncivilized Sumbanese." . . . A Sumbanese, however, has quite little self-confidence. From his birth to his death, he lives in animistic dependence. Even the most simple and everyday actions are supposed to be dependent on the will of the supernatural powers. It is then also astonishing, the number of offering stones that one comes upon everywhere, different in structure and different in intention. One not only offers under all green trees and on all high hills, but also at each house and at each village and in each garden. (1910: 72–73)

Like Dijkstra, Wielenga emphasizes the affectual dimension, portraying a fearful native more deserving of pity than scorn. His real interest, however, is ethnographic, and he devotes the bulk of the article from which this is taken to describing marapu ritual, giving a wealth of detail that fleshes out the trope of excess with which he closes: "And so one has offering stones for the fish in the sea and the birds in the air and the wild animals in the fields and the forests. One stumbles over the offering stones. Poor Sumba, so sunken in idolatry and spirit worship!" (1910: 99).[12]

Whereas for Dijkstra the offering involves real intercourse with real others who are misidentified, for Wielenga the sacrifice is a material waste predicated on false ideas—there is no real recipient, only objective matter. A third view, the logical underpinnings of which were already implied by Colenbrander, becomes over time increasingly central: offerings have no recipient, but they serve symbolic or social functions. The ambiguous status

---

12. Note that, in early Christian theology, the quality of excess is a defining feature of *superstitio*, which refers to "that religious sensibility which produced exaggerated or excessive, and hence superfluous, cult practices" (Pietz 1987: 29).

of material media provides the occasion for some evangelical irony in Wie-lenga's account of a reconnaissance trip to West Sumba. There, he watches the sacrifice of a rooster. After the prayers have been said and the bird plucked,

> [t]he children came back and brought along a tuft of the tail feathers. Umbu Pandji took it and stuck it above us in the roof amidst the alang-alang [thatching material]. That was for the *Marapu* of the house, that was his share of the slain animal. At which feathers he can see that one had not forgotten him.
>
> "If I were the Marapu in this house here, I would rather the flesh than the feathers," I said.
>
> "*What* did my lord say?"
>
> "Well, that the *Marapu* here is already quite soon contented. We men will presently eat the flesh, and he must be lucky with but a tuft of feathers. Even the dogs are yet better off, for they still get the little bones and the pigs under the house will devour the intestines. No, you fellows trifle a bit with the Marapu!"
>
> "But still he sees our goodwill; we have given to him, haven't we?"
>
> "But when you brought a chicken to the king this morning and asked him for a favor, what did you do then? Perhaps the same thing, hastily killed and then put some feathers on a plate and gave them to Umbu Timba, while taking the meat yourselves. I should certainly like to see the face of the raja then. I think that he would prettily abuse you and fling the plate with the feathers at your head."
>
> "That is rather natural, but with our *Marapu* it is somewhat differ-ent. He is content with this. Such is the custom of old days here. It is a sign [Dutch, *teeken*] that the guests have not forgotten him, the spirit of the house." (1908: 172–73, italics in the original)

The play of irony here lies in taking literally the materiality of the offer-ing—that what the marapu seek, for example, is actual gain and not ges-tures of deference—which provokes the response by Umbu Pandji that the offering is merely a sign. Wielenga, at least as he presents his tactics to the Dutch reader of a missionary periodical, represents the Sumbanese as involved in two possible forms of misrecognition. In Socratic style, he wishes to cast doubt on the ritual by displaying himself as mistaking a sign for the real thing.[13] He does not challenge the reality of the marapu but

---

13. In playing with the distinction between sign and substance, he is, of course, echoing a central concern of iconoclasm (see Belting 1994; Koerner 2004). The prob-lem recurs not only between Christian and pagan and then between Protestant and Catholic, but even within the Reformation. Protestantism challenged the mediating

rather the appropriateness of the medium. At the same time, his irony is directed at the materialism of Sumbanese desires: In Wielenga's account, Sumbanese imagine marapu to be as covetous as they are themselves. This inappropriateness, however, is itself predicated on a greater misrecognition of lesser spirits for higher ones.

THE PROBLEM OF MEAT

It is relatively easy for converts to abandon altars and cease making offerings to gold, since in their apparently religious character they seem readily distinguishable from practical functions. Meat is another matter, because, as food (unlike the token portions in Holy Communion), it is hard to categorize as lacking immediate practicality, and because, as the medium of social feasting, it is difficult for people to escape the practices in which it plays a role. This gives rise to probably the most contentious and long-lived debate in the course of Sumbanese conversion, concerning the policy to adopt toward sacrificial meat.

Large-scale sacrifice and commensality occupy an important part of Sumbanese ritual and social life. Most rituals require the killing and eating of at least a chicken or two, and at some events, such as funerals, scores of buffalo are dramatically slaughtered in the village plaza for distribution among many hundreds of guests. Despite occasional government interventions in the 1980s and 1990s, in parts of West Sumba the feasting season is the stage for vigorous status competition. In major feasts, meat is distributed both raw and cooked, the latter consumed on the spot, the former apportioned among guests to take home. Hosts make great efforts to assure

---

powers claimed by the Catholic Church, in part by denying the act of transubstantiation within the Mass. Luther still stressed the materiality of the Eucharist, writing, "It is the greatest idiocy to say 'the bread means or is a symbol of the body he gave for us.' . . . [Y]ou won't chew or slurp him like the cabbage or soup on your table unless he will it. He has now become incomprehensible; you can't touch him even if he is in your bread—unless, that is, he binds himself to you and summons you to a special table with his word and with his word points out to you the bread you should eat. This he does in the Last Supper" (quoted in Mack 1992: 21). For Calvin, whose position lies between that of Luther and the even greater iconoclasm of Zwingli (Niesel 1956: 215–24), the material ingredients of the sacrament have no inherent efficacy but serve as outward signs of the verbal promise made by Christ: "If the visible symbols are offered without the Word, they are not only powerless and dead but even harmful jugglery" (*Corpus Reformatorum*, quoted in Niesel 1956: 213). The Word does not in itself require embodiment, but, in the face of the weaknesses of human faith, the tangibility of material things helps provide certainty.

that everyone is given a share, and to be overlooked or to refuse one's portion are equally sharp offenses. To demand of converts that they withdraw from this commensality is to threaten their participation in society altogether. In the early days of the mission, this did not seem to be a problem; in fact, what seemed to be in question was whether the Sumbanese would *permit* the Christians to take part:

> Also [the missionary W.] POS tried to penetrate more and more into Sumbanese life, although little was said of a direct mission campaign. So he told of a "prayer time" which was held by them and which he attended. . . . First, with certain ceremonies, the Marapu were given offerings consisting of cooked rice, roasted hens, buffalo meat, and betel with areca-nut. . . . It happens there very "informally" and they had no objection that the missionary also attended this ceremony. He himself was permitted to participate in the meal, which consisted of the offerings presented. (Wielenga 1926: 112)

According to Wielenga, however, when Colenbrander mentioned this event in a report, "a sister of the congregation in the fatherland" criticized this eating of sacrifices and a long controversy ensued. In arguing their cases, the partisans were in part concerned with questions of strategy but also encountered the ambiguous status of material signs.

In 1914, Wielenga, who had been working in East Sumba, published an article called "On the Eating of Flesh Offered to Idols" (see van den End 1987: 196). He argued in pragmatic terms that the missionary should be permitted to eat sacrificial meat in order to maintain good relations with the Sumbanese. So important was feasting there that to refuse to participate would be to cut oneself off from them. The following year, L. P. Krijger, who ran the West Sumba mission from 1912 to 1922 (van den End 1987: 16–17), announced that he had forbidden his native evangelists to eat sacrifices. This public controversy led to a special assembly of missionaries in 1917. The key texts for this and all subsequent discussion of the issue were 1 Corinthians 8 and 10, in which Saint Paul warns against the temptations presented by others' idolatry:

> But I say, that the things which the Gentiles sacrifice, they sacrifice to devils, and not to God: and I would not that ye should have fellowship with devils. Ye cannot drink the cup of the Lord and the cup of devils: ye cannot be partakers of the Lord's table, and of the table of the devils. . . . If any of them that believe not bid you to a feast, and ye be disposed to go; whatsoever is set before you, eat, asking no question for conscience sake. But if any man say unto you, This is offered in sacrifice unto idols, eat not for his sake that shewed it, and for conscience sake: for the earth is the Lord's, and the fullness thereof: Conscience, I

say, not thine own, but of the other: for why is my liberty judged of another man's conscience? . . . Give none offence, neither to the Jews, nor to the Gentiles, nor to the church of God. (1 Corinthians 10:20–21, 27–29, 32, King James version)

The problem is not any effect of meat itself, which is merely objective matter and bears no inherent consequences (1 Corinthians 8:8). Rather, the problem is the effect of being seen eating the meat of idolaters *by others*. Other people, especially recent or potential converts, lacking the knowledge that one has oneself, may succumb to temptation, their religious resolve weakened by the missionary's own misconstrued example.

The assembly was inconclusive, as opinions were split and the matter left to case-by-case decisions (van den End 1987: 196). Meat continued to introduce a remarkable element of instability into mission practice; nearly a generation later, a different pair of missionaries replayed the initial conflict. Again, the debate reveals an interaction between theological interpretation and ethnographic contexts: the more tolerant view in each case is taken by the missionary with experience in East Sumba, where the competitive politics of meat are less pronounced. By 1930, converts in West Sumba were subject to discipline for accepting meat sent to them at home from a marapu feast, an act that was permitted in East Sumba. Justifying the prohibition, W. van Dijk, who had taken over in West Sumba in 1932, cited 1 Corinthians to the effect that eating sacrificial meat must be shunned as a snare for new Christians, lest they be gathered back into the circle of idol worshippers (van den End 1987: 344n1). Objecting to this was P. J. Lambooy, based in East Sumba from 1924 to 1948 (van den End 1987: 17).

In 1932, when both men were on leave, they were called before the Board of Deputies to discuss the matter, but again the board remained divided. Shortly thereafter, Lambooy defended himself to the deputies. What Paul criticizes, he asserted, is participation in a sacramental communion with a god or goddess, through which the communicant receives new life.

> In Sumba, the killing and eating of animals has an entirely different meaning. There it is a food given to the deceased ancestors. Materialistic as the heathen is in his religion, he thinks of his deceased as still wanting nourishment. . . . At the end of the feast the praying priest may eat up [the liver presented to the dead]. The rest of the animal is divided among those present. This last food is not having a communion with the ancestors through eating. The communion is only practiced through being present at the feast. . . . It is therefore not desirable for our Christians to go to the feasts and to participate in them. (Lambooy 1987a: 345)

He set participation in the feast itself in sharp contrast to the meat sent home with the guests after the same feast: "Therein is rightly expressed a demonstration of friendship or fellowship, but this has no meaning of sacramental communion with idols" (Lambooy 1987a: 346). To forbid Sumbanese to eat meat that has been brought to the house "would be a great insult. One holds this as the breaking of all bonds and friendship," a strategic error, "to the great detriment of the spreading of God's Kingdom in Sumba." Instead, one must sort out religious and secular functions—something that Lambooy, anticipating later policies, attempted to perform by mapping different intentions directly onto different pieces of meat.

In the face of this continued controversy, the deputies asked Colenbrander, who had returned to the Netherlands, to undertake a biblical exegesis. His report supports Lambooy, but by drawing in part on a somewhat different principle: apparently following the libertarian strain in the neo-orthodox Calvinist views of government (Wintle 1987: 59–60), he asserted that to restrict the eating of meat would be too interventionist: "One must make distinctions between the meat at the offering meal itself and the meat that comes from it. . . . The former is obviously forbidden both for the risk that it will be an offense for another and for the risk of exposing oneself to the danger of a sphere where the evil power prevails" (J. F. Colenbrander 1987a: 357). In principle, there is nothing wrong in receiving this meat at home, however—that remains a matter for the individual conscience. He goes on to compare this meat to the Holy Communion, for no one objects to giving leftover bread and wine to the poor or sick, "because it is felt there is no longer the least connection with the table of the Lord." In conclusion, having drawn a sharp distinction between matter and spirit, he returns to the overriding principle: "One must also in the Missionfield not go further than what the Lord said in His Word, not to rob the freedom which the Lord granted. In certain respects it is easier only to set this rule, that one should never eat any meat with which some pagan act has taken place. But then that would be a rule which God's Word does not give" (Colenbrander 1987a: 357). Indeed, if persons were left free to deal with the dilemma, they would be forced to reflect on their actions. This antiregulatory stance, therefore, is not only a matter of principle in its own right but serves as a means to further the development of self-consciousness. The pressure exerted by *practices* can, as it were, induce effects in the *subject*.

Yet in the end, the restrictive view won out, in a resolution delivered by a Special Assembly of Missionaries in 1934:

A Christian, through the accepting and eating of meat brought to the house that comes from animals slain according to pagan *adat*, of which he knows the source, has objective communion with the worship of the devil. Moreover, the accepting and eating of meat as mentioned above is (a) unworthy of the Christian, (b) dangerous for the Christian and the young Christian congregation, (c) contrary to the commandment of brotherly love. Also on the ground of all these considerations, the accepting and eating of such flesh is in conflict with God's Word, for which reason . . . our Christians must hate and eschew such a thing from the heart. (Special Assembly 1987: 369)

This policy, which even van Dijk remarked was "really very harsh" (van den End 1987: 344n1), seems to reflect the increasingly isolated position of S. J. P. Goossens, who by 1939 broke with the church altogether and joined the Freed Church (Vrij Gemaakte Kerk) (Kapita 1965: 31–32). Indeed, the policy remained unworkable without either Christian withdrawal from social intercourse altogether or the cooperation of marapu followers. The former path was finally taken by Goossens's schismatics, who established a closed compound in which not only the eating of sacrificial meat but also all other material media of sociability—tobacco, coffee, and betel—were eliminated. The latter path has become common as marapu followers find their numbers shrinking and thus become increasingly dependent on Christian support in rituals and other exchange events. By the 1980s, Anakalangese sponsors of large marapu rituals often set aside specified animals to be omitted from the offering prayers so they could be fed to the Christian visitors. In the latter case, such a move from offering to food helps sustain the social dynamics of reciprocity even while shifting the ontological grounds on which it had been predicated.

The course of this debate replays problems found, under the rubric of idolatry, in Christianity's encounter with paganism from the start and in Protestantism's challenge to Catholicism as well.[14] More specifically, I address three points here: the difficulty Christians encounter in clarifying the distinction between performative language and material object, the problem of social functionalism, and the ambivalently modern models of economic matter that result.

14. Early Dutch Calvinist travelers explicitly identified African fetishes with Catholic sacramental objects (Pietz 1987: 89). In contemporary Sumba, many Protestants claim that images of the Virgin Mary are no better than the gold and offering stones of marapu ritual; some also claim that the foundations of Catholic churches are strengthened with the buried corpses of sacrificed children (a version of a rather widespread belief in Southeast Asia).

EXCHANGE VALUE, USE VALUE, AND SPIRIT

If the notion of economic rationality presupposes a subject that has a clear understanding of material objects, then religious confusion over objects implies an earlier, irrational economy.[15] That marapu followers are to be seen as lost in economic irrationality is abundantly clear from missionary perspectives and some Sumbanese representations of the past as well.[16] A typical passage comes from Wielenga's first visit to West Sumba. While it does not directly address ancestral ritual, the episode is revealing for the light it casts on the problem of value. Wielenga has arrived at a small port, where he meets Umbu Dong, a noble from the interior:

> He was a still inexperienced nature-child, his many years notwith-standing. A true child of the hills, gullible before the cunning Endenese [Muslim traders]. And now he was in the process of doing so-called "business." He wanted to sell a month's worth of accumulated yellow dye-wood. He had already earlier received some goods as an "advance" but now would settle up. . . . And so, how many bunches would he provide? He had some thousand bundles lying above in the hills. And what now will he get for the thousand bundles? Our Umbu at this named: a chopping knife with an ivory handle, three rolls of white material, one roll of black material, one mamuli, and some more. We wrote it all down and came to the high assessment of about f. 90. Thus he must provide a thousand bundles of wood for f. 90 of goods. Now four bundles are the same as one *pikol,* the same as f. 4. That is according to Bartjes thus f. 1000. (Wielenga 1908: 257–58)

This is, of course, a familiar scene in colonial literature, in which the native is characterized by the inability to know the true value of things. The scare quotes that frame "business" and "advance" portray the activity itself as

---

15. The concept of fetish was first formulated by early travelers to West Africa, for whom the most prominent aspect of value-bearing objects was "the impersonality of their mode of being and operating and their perceived transcultural significance" (Pietz 1987: 40). That is, the practical value of a gun or a bolt of cloth is the same regardless of what you believe about them—one aspect of the impersonality of goods against which Mauss (1990) defines gift exchange. The shared rationality of objective utility would seem as well to provide a foundation on which translation across radical linguistic and cosmological differences might be established.

16. In missionary writings, the economics of sacrifice seems to have evoked much less discussion than the spiritual dimensions. In contrast, today the state is more concerned with the economics of Sumbanese practices. Feasting is seen as a serious problem of waste, and several efforts have been made to limit it (Kuipers 1998; compare Volkman 1985).

mere mimicry of the real thing, a stock figure in colonial perceptions (Bhabha 1994a). Anakalangese today sometimes still represent their own ancestors as economically foolish. I have been told that in the past people bartered like quantities for like, regardless of differences of quality. A sack of maize went for an equal-size sack of coffee. With such remarks, Anakalangese portray the past as a time in which people were taken in by the very materiality of things (a point I return to in chapter 10).

At the same time, while portrayed as unschooled in economic calculation, the Sumbanese also appear to be thoroughly materialistic. For one thing, heathens ask the spirits for wealth. While the missionary must accept a certain amount of magical thinking in the early stages of Christianization as only natural, notes Kruyt, he must "deal severely with such demonstrations when he notices that the aim is to get personal benefit therefrom" (1924: 275). This is not merely a matter of means and ends; it has consequences for the very character of the subject. For example, when Wielenga tells the raja of Napu of the Ten Commandments, the latter responds that he already knows them:

> But when I said to him it would be good if you were to begin then with leaving these bad things behind, he asserted that it would not be possible. "For the human is so evil! How many buffalo have I already not been obliged to kill and how many offerings have I already not brought. But yet I go at it once again. Yes, a bad deed costs much, but luckily I am rich." He thus would say: Ah, when I but confess my fault to the gods and placate them with an offering, then it shall still turn out well. With paying and with gifts one comes far in this world, but also in the next. (1909b: 41)

Here a perverse political economy stands in the way of moral redemption, for as long as one can buy one's way out, one requires no interior transformation (and here Wielenga was surely aware of the parallel to Calvinist views of the penitential economy of medieval Roman Catholicism). The link between the materialism of the Sumbanese and their inability to know the true value of things lies in this conflation of that which is properly material—namely, objects and that which pertains to the immaterial soul.

Indeed, even the effort to give a sympathetic portrait of marapu life tends to present a political economy, if not of misplaced value, then at least of excess. For example, Oe. H. Kapita, a writer of Indonesian-language ethnographies who had long served as the Sumbanese assistant to the missionary linguist Onvlee, describes traditional Sumbanese life as a total cultural system. Children are trained from the beginning to serve the marapu, the purpose of marriage is to produce a next generation for the marapu, the work of planting and herding all aim to provide offerings: "It may be said that in all efforts of the Sumbanese, the principal goal is in order to get offering materials for Marapu" (Kapita 1976b: 102–4). Omitting any other function, such as keeping oneself fed, providing oneself with descendants, or acquiring power, Kapita writes as if, in sorting out material and spiritual worlds, the latter must either be everywhere or nowhere. But the Sumbanese stand accused of excess in opposing directions, for they at once recognize too many spirits in too many places, and, reflecting Colenbrander's worries that they might turn into free thinkers, are too materialistic.

In self-conscious contrast to this seemingly irrational past, the contemporary Gereja Kristen Sumba aspires in its financial operations to the fully rational procedures of a well-controlled institutional operation. Umbu Delu's complaint was to that extent accurate: Money is everywhere in church activities.[17] The ubiquity of cash and the economic calculation it suggests are, if anything, highlighted by the manner in which cash is collected—unlike ceremonial exchange, which is theatrically displayed, church collections are at once public and yet veiled. The black cloth collection sacks passed each Sunday in church are designed to conceal the donor's hand as it reaches in to drop a coin or bill. When collections are made at home, during prayer meetings or wedding parties, people are always careful to circulate a plate covered with a piece of cloth, under which the donor slips a discreet hand; sometimes the cash is further hidden in an envelope. And yet these transactions are then exposed in a public accounting in the starkest economic terms. In the announcements before the beginning of each church service, a member of the vestry reads off that week's accounting, giving the totals received in each collection sack and at each household gathering, naming the household heads in question. This may well serve as a public disciplining and incitement; it also situates the church within an order of rational calculation at odds with the deferential mediations of ceremonial exchange. The act of giving, which takes center stage in exchange, is suppressed in favor of the totaling of outcomes. Dwelling on final sums displays the usefulness and convertibility of cash into resources, a sharp contrast to the ways exchange plays down use in favor of conventional symbolism, social bonds, and performativity. As the agent that renders accounts and the recipient of multiple donations, the church transcends any particular claims that the bonds of giving might impose.

---

17. Cash is still hard to come by in much of Sumba; see chapter 10 for more about money.

DILEMMAS OF FUNCTIONALISM

To suppose that the media of pagan ritual themselves carry some sort of potency that threatens the convert risks crediting the putative content of pagan beliefs. Although the prohibition on eating sacrificial meat always threatens to slip from serving as a bulwark against the weakness of others into an acknowledgement of the power of the spirits themselves, as the Calvinist separation of material and spiritual takes hold the missionaries allow themselves to reevaluate the nature of ritual. The groundwork for a functionalist reinterpretation of Sumbanese practice was already laid, both in governmental policies of indirect rule (see, for example, Riekerk 1934; Waitz 1933) and in the ethnographic training of missionaries (Brouwer 1912; Kruyt 1936).

Like missionaries elsewhere, those on Sumba weighed strategies for the "recreation or renewal" (*recreactie of vernieuwing* [Lambooy 1987b: 341]) of local practices against the risks of syncretism:

> The giving of food to the dead and the mortuary-feasts can be renewed in a commemoration speech on New Year's Eve. Harvest feasts become thanksgiving days. On the social terrain lie practices such as contribution to the pagan priests, which becomes transposed into contributions to the church and the poor. . . . In funerals, animals may rightly be killed but only those which are necessary to provide food for those in attendance. The custom among the Sumbanese, to bring home the meat given to the spirits, is transposed into support for the poor. (Lambooy 1987b: 342)

To "renew" means several things. One is to continue a material practice but reframe it in speech. Another is to redirect the flow of material goods to a recognizably practical function, such as feeding the guests at a funeral. In the first instance, the materiality of things is to be suppressed in favor of their reframing as symbolic expressions of something else, an immaterial intention. In the latter case, their materiality is to be pushed to the foreground at the expense of any other interpretations. Both require vigilance against the propensity of objects to acquire unwanted meanings and effects.[18] It is perhaps only in charity for the poor that an economic function (useful goods for those in need) and immaterial intention (the embodiment of an ethical spirit) can be combined.

It was the most ethnographically oriented of the missionaries, writing at a time when the eventual victory of the church was assured, who faced

---

18. On the general problem of controlling the meaning or even practical function of material objects, see Keane 2003c.

most directly the dilemmas of functionalism. Louis Onvlee was trained as a field linguist and Bible translator. In a lecture given in the Netherlands in 1969, after his long residence in Sumba, he returned to the question of sacrificial meat, commenting that nowhere has it led to more discussion than in Sumba (1973h: 144). His approach was to ask what it meant to accept meat in Sumbanese society. The overriding principle, he said, is this: "[O]ne kills no animal without reason. Ideally, killing only because of the desire to eat meat does not occur" (1973h: 145). Thus, the first step toward a relativistic understanding of meat was to foreground intentionality over mere matter. This intentionality could be described in terms of functions, which Onvlee organized in relation to contexts in which meat played a role: when receiving guests, when participating in collective labor, at funerals, and in religious feasts. The analytic task, echoing that faced by the earlier generations discussed in chapter 3, was to separate out social (thus religiously neutral) from religious (thus pagan) functions. Although Onvlee portrayed these contexts as a progression from social to religious function, he observed that, even in the first type, "host and guest both stand in relation to the invisible part of society" (1973h: 146), and even the funeral, during which the animal was sacrificed to accompany the deceased to the afterworld, had the economic function of creating debts that guaranteed future contributions and the social one of affirming status. For a guest to receive inadequate acknowledgment in the distribution of meat was shaming. Here Onvlee made a curious aside, in an uncharacteristic departure from his careful ethnographic relativism: "As if I should be embarrassed for meat!" (1973h: 147)—a remark that seemed to force itself out, as if to say that, despite all his scholarly efforts, the sheer materiality of this social medium became suddenly too much for him to accept.

The real meaning of meat, Onvlee asserted, was located in both general social functions and specific intentions expressed in the words of the invocation. But, invoking Durkheim, Onvlee assumed that "culture is an integrated coherent whole; each part is understood to be in this whole and each alteration works on this whole (1973h: 133). As a result, *all* meat is a kind of offering, and all transactions of flesh, living or dead, have social functions (1973h: 148); thus, to forbid the accepting of sacrifices is to induce social isolation. In opposition to the 1934 prohibition against accepting meat, Onvlee wished to distinguish between rituals with religious functions and those that foregrounded the social and economic motive (1973h: 149–50). Yet the very holism of culture that he presumed in fact rendered this distinction problematic. This is evident in the final section of the lecture, a discussion of feasting, in which he proposed that commensality of some sort be retained as a sort of functional equivalent of what had been lost. Like Colenbrander, he was concerned that conversion "creates here an emptiness which asks to be filled" (1973h: 156).

Refunctionalized, material objects become forms of symbolic expression rather than media through which actions are performed; they become more representation than practice. By reframing the rite, the voluntaristic yet disinterested character of action can be strengthened. The words quoted in chapter 6 are apposite here: "The feast then is no longer a necessity but a gift" that expresses one's thanks (Onvlee 1973h: 156–57). What this suggests is that, in order for the will to be properly located, it must be clearly distinguished from the material objects that serve as its media, as well as from its orientation toward simple material gain. One way to do this is to restructure what had been itself a form of *action* into an *expression* that responds to the actions of an other.

Yet what is most striking in the rhetorical structure of this concluding segment of the lecture is the repetition, five times on a single page, of the assertion "The world wherein one lives has become fundamentally other." This refrain suggests a sense of loss greater than the somewhat insubstantial hope that new functional equivalents can be found. In this moment of rhetorical flourish, Onvlee appears most strongly to recognize the implications of his holistic view of culture. He expressed this sense of loss in the face of modernity in another essay about cattle (1973a, 1980). This quotes verses supposed to have been sung by a lord's horses when he sold them for export in the late nineteenth century (1973a: 12–15), voicing Onvlee's own lament at modern forms of alienation in words attributed to the very possessions themselves. Here Onvlee, in certain respects an intellectual heir of Mauss, stressed inalienability, not to excoriate economic irrationality, but to celebrate an integrated premodern world. Archaic modes of inalienability, however, have consequences for the subject's capacity to act, for "[a] person cannot do whatever he pleases with his possessions. Possessions have their rules and prohibitions *(hida hàrina)*, and breaking these rules is dangerous because possessions react to such trespasses. A person may be the master of his possessions, but his possessions exert an influence on him to which he must respond" (1980: 203). The power of objects, as it were, extracts something from the subject, much as the horror of idolatry is that it will drain the humanity of its practitioner (Mitchell 1986: 190). Things, insofar as their nature is misconstrued by the non-Christian, impose unwarranted limits to human freedom.

The article closed on a note of lament:

Possessions on Sumba . . . must be seen in terms of broad social and religious relationships. These relationships are now breaking down. . . . As the Sumbanese come increasingly to regard their possessions in an economic sense, I can only hope that they will view these goods in the proper context, without which these possessions could become a dangerous and threatening power. I can only hope that the Sumbanese people will find a new control over their possessions—one that will provide a new context and a new respect. (Onvlee 1980: 206–7)

Here the theme of the willful subject and the threat posed by the material object has, in a sense, come full circle. It is no longer idolatry that threatens the humanity of the ritualist but something that starts to look like a commodity fetishism supplanting social relations.

The Christian's assurance of victory permits a moment of nostalgia for a holistic world. This nostalgia seems as well to express a more troubling recognition, that the secular world of economic calculation emerges precisely from the very separation of subject and object for which the mission has striven. If "primitive" fetishism threatens the subject by attributing agency to possessions—recall Wielenga's comment that the Sumbanese, lacking self-confidence, live in animistic dependence (1910: 72)—the emerging economic regime threatens to awaken in objects dangerous new powers as commodities.

As the conversations above suggest, the remaining marapu followers also resist the transformed role of objects. When they accuse Christians, who slaughter without offering prayers, of self-centered greed for meat, they are portraying a parallel alienation in which self-assertive subjects set objects into free circulation, unconstrained by ancestral obligation. Dwelling on different loci of agency, Christians and marapu followers alike accuse each other of willfulness and lack of deference. Looking at the individual assertiveness embodied in Christian practices, marapu followers are unimpressed by doctrinal claims of respect for the Lord. Convinced of the deluded character of fetishism (and holding a stake in existing political hierarchies), colonial missionaries are similarly unimpressed by marapu followers' understandings of agency and overlook the ways in which valuable objects articulate a spiritual model of power with a mundane political economy, material quantities with spiritual qualities.

PERSONAL INTENTIONS AND UNSPEAKABLE THINGS

The entanglement of marapu and Christian discourses reflects the double problem that missionization faces, especially when it is internal to a single society. The church must now ask both how it can win over the unconverted and how, once converted, the converts should behave. Nonetheless, the problems faced by marapu followers and Christians differ in characteristic ways. Christian talk about heathen practices displays anxieties beneath the ·self-assurance, while marapu followers are continually put in the defensive position of responding and rationalizing. Although marapu followers retain their most important practices, the need to justify themselves has forced them increasingly to assume the dualistic and functionalist terms presumed by Christian discourse. When Umbu Pandji defended himself against Wielenga's challenge over giving only feathers to the marapu, he was already accepting a distinction between the material and the symbolic. The same distinction persists when marapu followers speak of ancestral gold as being a mat, reminder, proof, or site for meeting the spirits. Marapu followers also seek to appropriate the language of functional equivalents (the purification ratu is like Christ, chicken entrails are like the scripture) but, in doing so, leave themselves vulnerable to the claim voiced by Pak Pendeta, that Christianity provides a more encompassing language into which their local speech can be translated. Conversely, the practical economy of material practices continues to entangle Christians in operations, such as marriage exchange and feasting, whose presuppositions and economic requirements exceed the limits of doctrine—indeed, of what can be put into words at all.

A final anecdote, not from Sumba but from a feasting society on Sulawesi, an island to the north, captures the dilemmas encountered in the attempt to specify the meanings of material objects. Torajan Christians, balking at having to present the customary shoulder cut of meat to the headmen, offered instead to give him a different cut of meat on the grounds that the shoulder cut was pagan, but the substitute gift still bore the *secular* display of deference. The headmen complained to the Dutch authorities, and finally the governor, considering it riskier to alienate the elite than offend the converts, ruled that, as long as the chiefs would swear to receive the meat merely as an honorific, the practice could continue (Bigalke 1981: 233–34).

These Christians saw the logic of functional equivalence along two dimensions, for as food, one cut of meat is pretty much equivalent to another, and as a symbolic gesture, one act of giving may be equivalent to another. But, imputed intentions aside, neither objects nor gestures were equivalent for the chiefs in material or symbolic terms. The case cannot be resolved by separating the economy of material things from the intentionality of immaterial human subjects. The meat is not reducible to either a material good or a symbolic expression. Now consider the governor's effort to fix the meaning of the act through an oath, which supposes the verbal oath to exhaustively and accurately represent the speaker's beliefs and the meanings of the transaction. Even if that model of speech were adequate, it still fails to acknowledge the character of material exchange. The oath is meant to bring the intentions of the recipient into line with the already stated intentions of the donors, but this works only if the performative act itself has no meaning beyond the respective intentions. Yet the original objections of both donors and recipients, which emphasize the actual cut of meat, suggest that the effects of the gift cannot be fully grounded in individual purposes.[19] Leaving aside the matter of what the governor had called "pagan symbolism" (apparently an expression reflecting the Dutch assumption that objects merely express immaterial meanings—which, as statements, can thus can be evaluated as true or false), the governor's solution still fails to take seriously the fact of the meat itself. In supposing that the intentions of donor and recipient could fully constrain the meaning of the gift, the oath solution overlooks both the economy by which the meat actually enters into circulation and the fact that the gift is embedded in a social field that exceeds individual interpretations and goals. The difficulty that "pagan" exchange presents is, in part, that the value of things cannot be established by appeal to desires, uses, or intentions, and these in turn cannot be fully defined by what can be said.

Pietz argues that the concept of fetish arises at points at which contrasting value systems meet and the obviousness of the distinction between immaterial and material things is challenged. The Christian missionaries attempted to control the semantic and economic underdetermination of objects by pinning down their functions and meanings and assuring that these can always be put into words. Thus, Lambooy tried to map different functions, sacred and secular, directly onto different pieces of meat. Following reasoning similar to that of the governor for the Toraja, Goossens and, later, many contemporary Sumbanese tried to situate the function in performative speech, to prohibit the meat over which the invocation is spoken. To an extent, this attempt reflected actual ritual pragmatics, in which the powers of words and things are complementary and mutually dependent. But these solutions sought to carry out the work of purification by isolat-

19. Insofar as even purely verbal performatives are public acts that always bear a socially conventional dimension that permits them to be used "out of context" or "insincerely," they cannot be fully and conclusively grounded in the intentions of the individual speaker (Derrida 1982).

ing the offering from the full performance, the economy, and the exercises of power of which it is part. Moreover, the solutions reflected, and ultimately helped reproduce, a representational economy in which words and things are radically unconnected, and in which the range of ties between persons and possessions is obscured. In this model, objects bear obvious and universal uses yet lack meaning or certain kinds of power, while the purpose of words is limited to expressing intentions located within the speaking subject. This reflects a modern subject's position in the world of circulating and useful things, but it has not succeeded in containing the elusive ability of words and things to carry both values and meanings that exceed the purposes of their transactors.

PART III

Purifications

Women posing in front of the Gereja Kristen Sumba church in Waibakul, Anakalang, West Sumba, 1986. Photo taken at their request, by Webb Keane.

9 Text, Act, Objectifications

In part 2 of this book, I showed how Calvinist missionaries tried to draw the boundaries between subject and object. I argued that missionary encounters like these, and the cluster of anxieties and accusations to which they give rise, the discourse of fetishism, can be understood as part of the work of purification. With this chapter and the next, I turn to some contemporary outcomes of the process beyond the immediate concerns of the mission. These concern areas of Sumbanese life—poetic performance and financial transactions—that were not at the heart of the evangelizing effort. They do, however, show the broad effects of Protestant conversion (in conjunction, to be sure, with schools, state institutions, markets, and so forth), and the emerging semiotic ideologies that attend it, within a larger representational economy. A look at the creation of a cultural text, in this chapter, and the handling of money, in the next, will put many readers in somewhat familiar territory. Both chapters describe processes that have often been taken to define modernity. This chapter describes a process of textual objectification, the following one a process of economic abstraction. Both also show the consequences these processes have for how Sumbanese understand agency and for their possibilities for action. But these processes do not simply indicate a fall from some prior state of wholeness, immediacy, or concreteness into a modern condition of fragmentation, alienation, or abstraction. Rather, they build on and respond to aspects of semiotic form that are already available in, and modes of objectification that are motivated by, earlier Sumbanese forms of action.

This chapter concerns the textual form that an object of knowledge can take. The particular context is the speaking of words that had formerly been addressed to marapu as they appear within the emergent frame of culture. The latter context is one in which a Christian speaker can retain most of the text from marapu rituals while denying that they have any consequences.

The formal properties of those words were originally designed in response to the problem of engaging with invisible spirit agents, the marapu. For Calvinists, such agents are supposed to have been eliminated from the scene. The objectification of language in the form of text that results is a function of a redistribution of the agents and agency that are supposed to animate the world.

The relationship between discursive form and objectification is, of course, hardly a new question. Foucault's concept of discourse centers on the idea that its possible objects—what does or does not readily lend itself to being talked about—are functions of particular historical moments (1972). As he stressed, not all things are unspeakable because they are in some way suppressed. New epistemes bring into being new objects of discourse, such as "multiple personality disorder," the subject of Ian Hacking's careful exemplification of this process (1995). Some possible objects of discourse are simply invisible because they are part of the apparently natural surround that everyone knows so intuitively that no one needs to, or even could, put them into words, what Bourdieu (1977) called *doxa*. Epistemological crises or political struggles may challenge the boundaries of the unspoken. In response to challenges to the taken-for-granted, orthodoxies and other officializing ways of talk may emerge. Bourdieu criticized ethnographers for taking at face value the officializing talk that schematized social and cultural things at the expense of unspoken practical know-how. We have become justifiably suspicious of cultural schemata and textual self-representations. They seem to be instances of the kind of objectification I discuss in the introduction, effects of that modernizing episteme that aims to see and yet not be seen, so that local worlds may become "picture-like and legible . . . readable like a book" (Mitchell 1988: 33).

I begin with the observation that what looks like discursive objectification can have sources other than just the disciplines, routines, and institutions associated with modernity. One source is people's ability to produce and to reflect on the entextualization always inherent in language. Speech about practice is itself a form of practice. This means that any instance of metalanguage is itself a form of language and thus, potentially, the object of further reflexivity (Lucy 1993; Silverstein 1979; Urban 1996). Nor is this a question of language alone; as Gregory Bateson (1972) suggested long ago, recursiveness and the vulnerability to reinterpretation are fundamental to the capacity for social interaction. This suggests that one modality of objectification—a capacity to stand back from a textual object—is likely to be historically and culturally ubiquitous.

Language ideologies articulate linguistic forms and pragmatic functions with social institutions, modes of action, and beliefs about the world, within representational economies, all of which are subject to historical transformation. For instance, such economies are the focus of the missionaries' work of purification described in the previous chapters. In this chapter, I look at the shifting status of talk as people reflect on what they know and do, and suggest that there is more than one position from which to view a "picturelike" world.

Across Sumba and much of Indonesia, an exemplary focus of reflexive talk is the "traditional house," which people commonly treat as an interpretive key to local culture and identity. My interest here is in accounting for its ready availability for *talk* about cultural meanings. I do so by looking at how it is constructed as a verbal object in ritual. The semiotic form this talk takes is shaped by the demands imposed by the primary actions it mediates, and thus by the social institutions, by ontology, and by the semiotic problems they pose. When institutions and ontologies change, as under conversion to Christianity, so do the practices, problems, and language ideologies they entail. At the same time, as people draw on available semiotic resources, such as the words of ritual, they often recontextualize them. That is, the text retains a certain hard semiotic form within a changing representational economy. Here I describe one result, a facility in talking about the house as an object laden with a wealth of cultural meanings that, however, seems to exist independently of speakers and contexts. Such representations work in part by invoking the authority and apparent concreteness of both the words and the things to which they refer. They select and take advantage of *already existing* features of ritual speech that make it susceptible to new ways of treating it as a source of stable texts.

The resulting accounts of the traditional house and its meanings can be misleading in two respects. Because these accounts draw on genres of speech that Anakalangese associate with the past, both the talk and the house itself can appear to be timeless artifacts that express a fully readable culture that lies apart from speakers' own actions. Conversely, because representations of the house have many of the schematizing and abstract features of talk addressed to outsiders, a skeptical anthropologist might assume that these representations are nothing more than "invented traditions" (Hobsbawm and Ranger 1983) or the peculiar effect of Western or academic knowledge. To pose the matter in terms of such simple alternatives threatens to restrict our view of people's verbal resources to an unrealistically narrow range of possibilities.

HOUSE STRUCTURE AS A PARADIGM OF
CULTURAL ORDER

In my first week on Sumba, being a student of culture, I was presented with a remarkable nine-page typescript account of "Sumbanese culture" written in Indonesian (Wohangara 1985). The author was a Christian and a retired civil servant who lived in Waingapu, the largest town on the island—a market and administrative center and home to a mix of ethnicities uncharacteristic of most of Sumba, all of which may help explain the cosmopolitan nature of the document. Clearly embodying the serious reflections of a speculative intellect, the typescript covers many of the topics favored by other Indonesian-language synoptic treatments of culture and tradition, such as the ancestral treks and rules for marriage and for burial.[1] One striking feature of this work is the prominence it gives to the house: "[The] 4 central pillars . . . [are] named according to their respective functions as the Four Principles of the Sumbanese people . . . that form a basis for ordering the way of life of Sumbanese people throughout life." These pillars are identified with "godliness," "marriage," "prosperity," and "life and death," with the four compass points, and with the entranceways to the ancestor village. Here in a nutshell are the basic treatments: parts of the house are metonymically linked to cultural principles, and the whole is a diagram of village structure and larger world. Through such alignments, the author portrays the house as a schematic structure and microcosm, as both a practical ground and a conceptual outline for an entire moral and cultural order.

Examples of this treatment of the house could be multiplied. In many casual conversations, people offered me unprompted exegeses of the meaning of the house. The simplest version divides the distinctive bamboo, wood, and thatch house into three levels, corresponding to the worlds of spirits in the attic under the high-peaked roof, humans in the raised living platform, and animals beneath the floor (see at right). Finer discriminations produce five levels, which, some told me, parallel the five-point state ideology (Pancasila), and additional homologies such as the parts of the human body.

That Anakalangese, at least in speaking with outsiders, may take this model as a key to an entire culture is suggested by two anecdotes with

1. While the paper was typed for me and also addressed to me, the care with which it was thought out suggests that the basic text had been prepared beforehand, though for what audience I cannot say; D. H. Wohangara apparently also wrote a paper on marriage rules (1963), probably for a conference on customary law convened by the regency government. I therefore offer this as no more than a particularly apposite illustration of how easily one encounters schematic descriptions of Sumbanese culture, and how central the house is in them.

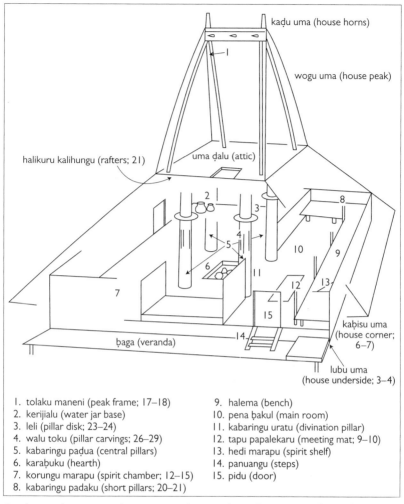

kaḍu uma (house horns)

wogu uma (house peak)

halikuru kalihungu (rafters; 21)

uma ḍalu (attic)

kaḅisu uma (house corner; 6–7)

ḅaga (veranda)

lubu uma (house underside; 3–4)

1. tolaku maneni (peak frame; 17–18)
2. kerijialu (water jar base)
3. leli (pillar disk; 23–24)
4. walu toku (pillar carvings; 26–29)
5. kabaringu paḍua (central pillars)
6. karaḅuku (hearth)
7. korungu marapu (spirit chamber; 12–15)
8. kabaringu padaku (short pillars; 20–21)

9. halema (bench)
10. pena ḅakul (main room)
11. kabaringu uratu (divination pillar)
12. tapu papalekaru (meeting mat; 9–10)
13. hedi marapu (spirit shelf)
14. panuangu (steps)
15. pidu (door)

Sumbanese house. Numbers in parentheses indicate lines in ritual text that refer to that part of the house. Artist: Bill Nelson.

which, as a searcher after such knowledge myself, I was often entertained (and perhaps admonished). The first concerns a Sumbanese boy who was sent to Java to study. There he was interviewed by the authorities, who asked, "What does your father do?" "He's a herdsman." "What do you eat?" "Maize and tubers." Basic matters of production and consumption disposed of, the clincher was his ability to schematize the house: "Where do you live?" "In a three-level house: the top contains our food, the middle the humans, and underneath, the cattle." A second anecdote concerns a Dutch student who had undertaken fieldwork in Anakalang several years before I did, but who had never completed his dissertation. One version of his fate is that he failed his exam back in Holland, being unable to describe the house levels when asked to do so by his professors.

The house, as a structure that embodies publicly known, wide-ranging categories, forms one paradigmatic referent for cultural discourse in Sumba.[2] That the house is a living space and a social concept is not sufficient to account for its verbal objectification. Furthermore, discourse is selective: it does not capture everything of interest or importance about the house.[3] To make sense of the Sumbanese facility with talk about cultural things requires an understanding of the place of such talk in a changing representational economy of speech practices and semiotic ideologies. For *all* societies produce dwellings, doubtless laden with meaning—but not everyone *talks* about the house like this society does.

The treatment of the house as an object of discourse is not simply an expression of its referent but arises in part from its place within speech practices. Talk about the house builds upon foundations laid in speech performances that *verbally* lay out the house as a formal structure, decomposed and displayed part by part. In Anakalang, these practices are shaped by certain communicative and pragmatic challenges. As these challenges become less important in a Christian world, the speech practices increasingly lend themselves to treatment as sources of texts referring to objects that seem to stand apart from the speaker.

RITUAL SPEECH AS CULTURAL TEXT

As in many parts of Indonesia, people in contemporary Sumba often treat the couplets of ritual speech both as treasured cultural artifacts in their own

2. The current prominence of the house is doubtless reinforced by its nation-wide rhetorical importance, for the state has found in architectural differences an exemplary token of safe ethnic difference. This is most evident in Taman Mini Indonesian, the national theme park outside Jakarta, where each province is represented by an oversized "traditional" house (see Anderson 1990). In a wide range of contexts, the house provides a visual emblem of cultural distinctiveness. For an early analysis of the cosmological house in Indonesia, see Cunningham 1964.

3. Formal descriptions do not, for example, tell you how to build a house or how to live in one (for a criticism of totalizing models of the house, see Ellen 1986). Talk about cultural preservation, usually by people identified with development, tends to emphasize architectural form over practices, proposing, for example, that houses located in pockets of tradition be required to have thatched rather than zinc roofs.

right and as descriptors of traditional culture. This double role is implicit in the statement by the Sumbanese ethnographer Oe. H. Kapita, that his lexicon of ritual couplets could be called a "Dictionary of Culture" (Kapita 1987: 9). Full performance of Sumbanese ritual speech addresses a spirit or human other across some sort of social or ontological difference (Keane 1997c). The gap between interlocutors imposes difficulties that require, yet permit, special communicative efforts to overcome them. Two characteristics of this gap mark the ritual speech that aims to bridge it. One is the reflexivity that makes ritual speech a way of naming the things, agents, and types of action involved in the actual event in which it occurs. The other is the formality that provides this speech with aesthetic power, textlike qualities, and ancestral character.

The first characteristic motivates a kind of abstraction that has usually been taken to characterize discourse directed at "outsiders" (Bourdieu 1977: 17). Sumbanese ritual speech has many of the properties of talk between strangers, dealing with communicative uncertainty through redundancy and constant reference to the relevant actors, events, and goals. These properties work in tandem with a poetic structure that makes speech recognizable to the spirits and gives the speakers depersonalized authority. Together, ritual speech produces a kind of objectification of language or entextualization. This is language removed from the particular intentions and personal identities of its speakers, and even from the context of time and place. As a result, it is readily treated as an object that appears to transcend particular circumstances. Entextualization is of particular interest here because it allows highly contextual speech *events* to create the effect of *texts*, building on those aspects of language that contribute to what have been treated, for quite different theoretical ends, as the "already uttered" (Bakhtin 1981) or as the writing that "supplements" speech (Derrida 1973). It thus articulates in practice aspects of language often considered analytically to be in mutual opposition.

These two characteristics underwrite the use of ritual speech as a source of objectified cultural representation. Its formality supports its treatment as a text that exists independently of, and is highly portable among, particular events, persons, contexts, or practices. These properties, however, derive from functions that are distinct from their use for reference and denotation or even as lodes of rich metaphors. Contemporary Anakalangese use ritual speech in a range of contexts and purposes with contrasting sets of presuppositions about the nature of language and its effects. These texts enter into different representational economies, in which their functions are ideologically stressed as interactive, on the one hand, and denotative, on the other. Words that provide a way of speaking *to* powerful interlocutors and inducing *responses can* also be read as text *about a* separate and self-contained world.

These two emphases can be seen in speech practices respectively associated with relatively conservative and self-consciously modernist, usually Christian, parts of Anakalangese society. To exemplify the contrast, the following section presents a brief canonical text depicting the "traditional house." It was offered to me in the descriptive mode. Its source, however, lies in ritual performances addressed to invisible spirits. Although these two discursive practices presuppose distinct social fields of action, we cannot understand the former without taking into account the social and cosmological conditions that shape the semiotic form of the text in the latter. Their textual character is in part a function of the perceived challenges of communicating with distant interlocutors, such as the dead, and of obtaining from them recognition and responses. The character of ritual words in turn facilitates their use in new contexts, supplying an emergent folkloric discourse with materials that are interesting primarily for what they denote or as a code awaiting exegesis. It should be no surprise that the speech performances that most lend themselves to entextualization are favored as lasting cultural objects.

THE HOUSE IN WORDS

About a year after Umbu Neka's baptism, discussed in chapter 5, he and I spent an afternoon in rather aimless conversation. Taking me, as usual, to be a possibly somewhat simpleminded student, he suddenly asked whether I knew about the house, and began to speak as follows, as I transcribed:

dug out site	*yili pakowa*
excavated site	*yili pataukaru*
discarded remnants	*pakabuangu kamumu*
thrown out bathwater	*pabongu wai baha*
goes up to	*deta ta*
house corner	*kabisu uma*
head of the main floor	*katiku penang*
arrives at	*tomaja ta*

unrolled mat	*tapu papalekaru*
and the offered pillows	*yeka ḍa nula pakahorungu*
stops by there at	*liya ta*
warm chamber	*koru mamutu*
the warm basket	*na bola mamutu*
head's companion pillow	*katiku oli nula*
flank's companion mat	*karasa oli tapu*
stops by	*lisa*
the attic uprights	*ḍa tolaku maneni*
crossbeam of *lagapa*	*aharu lagapa*
stop by up there at	*lisaka nau ḍeta ta*
short pillars	*kaḅaringu padaku*
encircling rafters	*halikuru kalihungu*
descend	*purungu*
to the full disk	*ta eli mangu isi*
to the fruited branch	*ta kajanga ma wua*
stops by there	*liya*
the eight pokings	*na walu toku*
the eight flutings	*na walu lara*
the sharp spear	*na ḍakut nibu*
the water cup	*na koḅa wai*

As Umbu Neka spoke, he gestured, as if to map out a series of points leading the spirit addressee upward and into the house from the village plaza (although the house in which we sat lacked the peak, altars, central hearth, and pillars). The first couplet denotes the clan's permanent house site. The succeeding couplets name the pen housing the livestock beneath the living platform (lines 3–4); the front corner (lines 6–7); the benches in the most public room of the house (lines 9–10); the interior sleeping chamber (lines 12–15); the roof beams (lines 17–18); the central posts and beams (lines 20–21); the disk-shaped shelves on the central pillars (lines 23–24); and the pillar carvings along which communications with the spirits are said to travel (lines 26–29). This was far from the first time I had heard such a recitation, and Umbu Neka was not the only one to give one to me. But was this nothing more than a product of the ethnographic encounter? Matters are not that simple.

WAYS OF TALKING ABOUT A HOUSE

Texts such as the preceding one, although they may have been summoned up and refitted for my benefit, were not merely invented for the outsider. Neither every society nor every speaker readily provides such texts—nor do they provide texts on every possible topic. If the parts of the house are common knowledge, what social conditions favor their codification as schematic objects of verbal communication? This fragment was familiar to me, as I had heard individual couplets quoted many times and had recorded longer versions. Ritual guests are received with couplets as they are verbally led up into the house to their seats—even when the encounter takes place in a townhouse or a field hut. Mortuary prayers use analogous maps to direct the deceased to the village of the dead. After a burned house has been rebuilt, a similar step-by-step enumeration summons back the spirits who fled: the divination ritual uses the words to draw the spirits' attention, and wrongs are expelled by reversing the sequence (Kuipers 1988: 106).

Today, increasing numbers of Sumbanese live in cement or stone houses with corrugated zinc roofs; even in the past, many people lived not in houses with elevated platforms and peaked roofs but in much simpler dwellings.[4] Ritual practice, however, does not require a full-fledged house: a temporary shelter can serve if the proper offerings and other performance conditions are met. Conversely, many otherwise modern houses, churches, and government buildings are given high-peaked zinc roofs to denote Sumbanese tradition, but these may serve no ritual function like that of earlier houses. In this historical moment, material forms and ritual functions are shifting their relations as distinct representational economies emerge.

SOCIAL ACTION AND SEMIOTIC DIFFICULTY

The semiotic form that produces the textual house is generated by a practical and ontological problem: effective communication with spirits is never assured. For one thing, the very *presence of* invisible beings is not certain,

---

4. In the mid-1980s, probably fewer than half the houses in Anakalang had peaked roofs.

and, once they are in attendance, it is not guaranteed that they will recognize the speakers as their proper descendants. The formal and performative characteristics of ritual speech in Sumba ultimately take shape in reference to the social actions that they mediate. Sumbanese ritual speech is preeminently a way of addressing a listener across a significant and power-laden social divide. The kind of ritual dialogue in which formal speech occurs presupposes—and helps make imaginable—difference and a distinct sort of interlocutor. The separation between participants in the speech event is represented as physical. Thus, for instance, to pray to the spirits is to be "face to face" *(pahagangu)* with them, requiring passage across a gap. Prayers direct the spirits to "descend" *(purung)* to the offering. In other situations, words are directed upward and outward. Discourse is achieved across an ontological space that is felt to make communication hard to achieve, and which it is the function of the elaborate listing of places to define. Prayers are accompanied by careful attention to any sign indicating whether their addressees have arrived in the appointed place and have heard what was said, although the clinching evidence may occur only much later, when subsequent misfortunes are attributed retrospectively to past ritual errors. Ritual encounters thus exhibit two features crucial for the discursive relationship to culture: they require people to speak to others across a sociological, physical, and even ontological divide; and this communication is represented as difficult and subject to failure.

The words that Umbu Neka used to denote a cultural artifact have their source in actions directed to ends other than description. Their purpose, when used, for example, to summon a spirit into the house, explains the order in which the parts are named, from outside to inside, bottom to top, iconically or diagrammatically reproducing the relevant action. The role of predication here is a function of the task, of the sense that it could fail, and of the delicacy of the etiquette of directing a deceased elder. The desired movements of the spirit are spelled out in step-by-step detail, for only a minimal degree of shared information about the action being undertaken can be presupposed between speaker and addressee, and no agreement on intentions can be taken for granted.[5]

The pragmatic structure of speech events, as authoritative but difficult talk across a social or ontological gap, helps explain why much of the refer-

---

5. Only the one-line directives such as "goes up to," indicate the pragmatic, and interactive, character of the text's function. These directives are not embodied in fully canonical couplets, and people often omit them, along with other contextualizing markers, when quoting cultural texts (Kuipers 1990: 60).

ential content of ritual speech consists of metalanguage that announces the purpose, context, and participants in the event. The structure of performance, its uncertainties, and its consequential nature underwrite and mobilize its powers of reference. As a result, the construction of ritual encounter supports a certain discursive objectification. In contrast to those engaged in everyday, face-to-face interaction, ritual speakers cannot assume that their interlocutors are aware of the relevant elements of the context or are even able to hear them. The medium through which they communicate is best fitted to this purpose by virtue of its ability to transcend particular contexts through the formal properties of entextualization: it is ancestral speech. The *presence* of ancestors, embodied in the actions of speakers, is evoked by foregrounding the *absence* of those human speakers from their identities as speakers of the colloquial. And participants understand the semiotic problem in terms of pragmatic outcomes. Any given performance is authorized by the commitments that link it to previous and future performances and looks toward successful or unsuccessful outcomes. Reference and predication in marapu ritual, then, are functions of how speakers understand their words to act and have effect, and of the kinds of relations between speakers and addressees they can presuppose.

SPEECH WITHOUT OBLIGATION

I have argued that the referential character of ritual speech operates in relation both to the distance assumed to lie between ritual speakers and addressees, and to speakers' beliefs about the words that can most effectively cross this distance. In contrast, a quite different relationship was enacted when Umbu Neka produced a formal description of the house, offering a nugget of cultural knowledge and displaying his own authority. In the context of our conversation, his words were to be understood primarily as referential in function, serving to point out and name the parts of the house. I was not the spirit addressee, nor was this part of a speech event responding to an obligation or demanding recognition and action. In fact, he spoke "out of context" in a breach of performance restrictions that a non-Christian would consider dangerous. His freedom to do so was a function of the categorical distinction between culture and religion, whose nineteenth-century roots I discussed in chapter 3. As elsewhere in Indonesia, performance restrictions are loosened if one's speech is thought to concern culture rather than religion, since the consequences of errors, abbreviations, or other deviations are quite different (Fox 1988: 20).

To use ritual speech without risk is made feasible by changes in the nature of practical power under increasingly coercive state rule and the ontological transfigurations brought about by Christianity. Church and state intervene in local institutions and practices in interlocking ways. The state, having already superseded the main powers of clans, continues to downplay clans' identities and discourage their actions. Through regulations, pedagogy, exhortations, events such as interdistrict sports events, and the use of the national language Indonesian as the language of authority (Keane 1997a, 2003a), it seeks to supplant them with allegiances situated within a nested hierarchy of administrative-territorial units.

Similarly, Christians, as members of a global institution, should not aim to create or fulfill specific obligations with individuated, potentially responsive ancestral agents. Enjoined from heartfelt speech in religious functions, Christians are left to see ritual speech as something different. Government policy, though demanding adherence to one of the five legally recognized world religions, encourages the preservation of local culture.[6] Non-marapu appropriations of marapu ritual speech can arise in at least two basic forms: as a display or as a cultural text in citation or exegesis. Common contexts for display include induction ceremonies for officials and cultural shows, which treat even local audiences as if they were outside spectators (Kuipers 1998).

If performance without danger reveals a shift in linguistic ideology, the second use of ritual speech, as cultural text, brings out the focus on the denoted object. This is evident in a conversation I had in 1993 with Ama ni Delu, a middle-age elementary school teacher. Proud of his evangelical efforts on behalf of the Gereja Kristen Sumba, he showed me how he used the textual house to persuasive effect:

> Who *is* at the "house corner, head of the main floor"? Why is it called that? What's there? I'll tell you, it's Satan, the tempter who caused humanity to fall. Because if you pray to marapu, look at where you go. When you stop by the head of the main floor, it never mentions the door—it goes straight up from the plaza into the room. Now who travels secretly like that, without going by the front door? It must be the tempter. And that's why he's *below* Nuku [spirit in the house peak], below the Creator. Now, if we're to believe in Jesus, we've got to go in by the door. The door is Jesus: "I am the door of truth."[7]

6. In fact, a major sponsor of the publication of cultural materials in Sumba is the church (Kapita 1976a, 1976b, 1987, n.d.).

7. Presumably an allusion to John 10:1, 9.

The logic of Ama ni Delu's rhetoric builds on the structure of the house as a set of physical relations. Like Umbu Neka, he objectifies the house by drawing on the ritual text, treating its pragmatic sequencing in terms of a spatial logic: the absence of a door in the text expresses something about the world it denotes. In this treatment, the effects of speaking the text are subordinate to the objects that it denotes, which exist independently of the performance and its effects. Of course, he does indeed speak to achieve specific effects. But this is the *persuasive* effect of an *argument* constructed around the object portrayed in the ritual text, whose force is ultimately more a matter of logical (at least ideologically) than poetic structure and semiotically grounded authority.

REFERENTIALITY AND WHAT COUNTS AS CULTURE

I have mentioned a number of ways Sumbanese objectify the house in talk, from ritual directives to written cultural synopses and casual conversations (with ethnographers, with representatives of the nation and state, and with one another). I have emphasized Umbu Neka's speech, in part because of the way it straddles the difference between ritual action and cultural text. As I showed in chapter 5, when Umbu Neka speaks, he can still assume the authority of one used to facing and engaging the spirits. In contrast to Wohangara's typescript, his recitation exhibits a lack of contextual specificity and performative force that cannot simply be attributed to the operations of, say, literacy in opposition to orality. Like the typescript, however, Umbu Neka's words were directed not at an *addressee* from whom he demands countering actions, but at an *audience*. Such an audience potentially includes a world beyond Anakalang, introducing listeners who are not able to respond in kind.

Umbu Neka's recitation was clearly distinct from an address to a spirit: his words were not embedded in the other speech performances with which his recitation should be linked, they were not predicated in earlier promises, he did not cry out the ritual name of an interlocutor, and we did not have the appropriate offering in front of us. Each of these absences was sufficient evidence that no *response* was expected. Whatever authority he might have invoked as one who knows the texts, he was not for the moment claiming to speak either as or to an ancestor. For his audience, this use of couplets posed problems less of response and outcome than of interpretation and translation. In this context, his recitation is to be evaluated primarily by its truth and completeness of reference rather than its consequences—and it is to such an evaluation that Ama ni Delu refers in identifying the door altar with Satan.

In the context of his recitation, the text that Umbu Neka offered me bore two implications. As an informative text, it denotes a referent, the symbolically laden traditional house, something existing independently of the performance and of the demand for response. As a display and transmittal of knowledge to a note-taking student of culture, it offers that referent as an exemplary cultural artifact. In both respects, however similar the words might be, it departs from speech addressed to a spirit, whose textual character and apparently schematic mapping of space reflects the need for precision in the face of the problems posed by the encounter, the cautious etiquette, and the consequentiality that these entail. The discursive object is an effect of the traces left by risk-laden interaction.

In a representational economy in which both the invisible interlocutor and the difficulty of interaction are lost, what is left is, on the one hand, a text and, on the other, an object of reference. New aspects of the object may come to the fore. One is the altered temporal dimension: because there is no event, there is no before and no after. The step-by-step description of the house does not construct a motion across space in time but rather indicates a structure that potentially is fully present (but independent of the text) and words fraught with interpretive possibilities. As a picture, the text neither evokes nor responds to possible failure. Without uncertainty and danger not at issue, the picture might be incomplete and the words semantically puzzling; but the action will not be infelicitous.

There are always things about which it is not possible, or at least reasonable, to talk. (Yet even this way of putting it risks reifying what is not being said as a thing.) The forms of talk that make some things easier to say than others, or that bring certain things into discursive existence in the first place, can be shaped by the circumstances that make such talk necessary. So it is in pedagogy, legal testimony, and practical instruction manuals. The pragmatic and poetic forms of Sumbanese ritual speech respond to particular necessities. These semiotic forms are shaped by assumptions about language and the beings that inhabit the world, within a representational economy. At the same time, the very textual dimension of ritual speech—like the materiality of physical objects—leaves it open to appropriation in new contexts, its various properties shifting in their relative utility and significance, serving new purposes. The power of speech is not that it works, in Bakhtin's terms, as either utterance or text (1986: 74), but that it can be both, as it plays its roles in different representational economies and gives rise to different modes of objectification.

10　Money Is No Object

The work of purification seeks to draw clear boundaries between persons and things. Distinctions among kinds of objects and the ways they circulate are consequential, in part because they have profound implications for the character of the humans who possess the objects and carry out transactions with them. One of the crucial points of ontological distinction is expressed in the relative political economic status of subject and object. Kant (1956) defined the human as that which has no price. At the beginning of the twenty-first century, most inhabitants of even the freest of market economies are still likely to feel that cash value stops, or should stop, where the truly human begins.[1] In the contemporary United States, amid the efflorescence of free-market ideologies, the problem of confining the scope of alienability is evident in everything from debates over patenting genes and the question of child labor to the nervousness that often attends the circulation of money within the household. These domains of moral and conceptual anxiety reflect the religious genealogies of modern semiotic ideology and its inability to ever fully complete the work of purification.

Market economies, then, do not do away with inalienables so much as they reorder the regimes of value in which they function (Carrier 1995; Zelizer 1994). And contestations over these reorderings are not simply

---

1. At the boundaries of the properly salable in the United States, we find things such as prostitution, fees charged for adopted children, the sale of body parts, and bribery. These are notable precisely for the discomfort, anxiety, or outrage they provoke. See Pietz 1997 for an insightful discussion of this problem as it was faced by the writers of liability laws for human deaths caused by machines in the early industrial age.

economic matters but are deeply concerned with the nature of persons as it is defined at the shifting boundaries between subjects and objects.

In this chapter I address the unstable meanings of money and material objects at the margins of twenty-first-century capitalism. In the process, I raise some general questions about the relations among materiality and abstraction, the values of persons and things, and the moral narrative of modernity. For the last few generations, people in Sumba have been involved in a classic confrontation between an elaborate, costly, and socially potent system of ceremonial exchange and the growing importance of money. In the previous chapters, I have discussed this in relation to sacrifices and offerings (forms of exchange with the invisible partners), feasting, and marriage exchanges. The focus has been on the question of agency and the distinctiveness of persons from things. But it is only under the work of purification that so-called economic value seems to be distinct from such things as communications with the dead or inner expressions of piety. In those chapters, my emphasis was on how Calvinists dealt with these questions. In this chapter, I turn to questions of value that emerge within the work of purification beyond what anyone involved considers to be specifically religious domains, in people's efforts to make clear distinctions between the material and immaterial. These efforts, however, reflect the same semiotic ideologies that inform the religious debates already discussed. By discussing money in this chapter and cultural texts in the next, I hope to indicate some of the wider ramifications of the clashes between semiotic ideologies after Calvinists entered the scene.

We can no longer assume, as an earlier generation of anthropologists did, that people who practice ceremonial exchange simply perceive money to be a threat to social values. It has become clear both that the advent of money may be welcomed even in so-called exchange societies and that it is not necessarily seen as inimical to the persistence of exchange (Akin and Robbins 1999). But certainly the growing availability of alternative regimes of value can give heightened visibility to certain assumptions. Faced with money and its attendant discourses about modernity, freedom, and economic rationality, Sumbanese must try to account for the value things hold for people.

I have been arguing that Protestant modernity characteristically involves a certain dematerialization of the human world, a denial of some of the ways human subjects are enmeshed with material objects. But in a world of increasingly abstract subjects, where could value come from? One common site in which to locate the sources of value is the desires of the individual person. And it is money, issued by the state and linked to state discourses about modernity, that seems most to promote these desires.

Thus, in dealing with money, people find themselves wrestling with a host of dilemmas raised by the tensions between the promises and threats of modernity.[2]

These tensions are especially prominent in local talk about materialism. As their long-term interests, immediate concerns, and discursive circumstances variously incline them, Sumbanese may portray "the modern age" (Indonesian, *masa moderen*) in terms of an increasing materialism in people's needs and economic activities—or in terms of disenchantment as people lose their primitive and fetishistic overinvestment in things such as ancestral valuables or bridewealth. New forms of production and circulation may be celebrated as bringing with them rationality and enlightenment. Conversely, money and commodities may be portrayed as corrosive agents that attack kinship, amity, spirituality, sociality, and virtue on all fronts. The relationship between modernity and "the materialist" (Indonesian, *materialis*) is a topic of anxious concern across Indonesia, whose ruling New Order regime from 1966 until the fall of President Suharto in 1998 combined an aggressive emphasis on economic development with social conservatism and political authoritarianism. By conventional measures, until the Southeast Asian economic crisis of 1997 the regime fostered rapid economic progress, although this progress may have seemed distant and of questionable value for many who lived at the geographical and political margins of the nation.

Many Sumbanese tend to see money and markets as incipient challenges to the values supposedly embodied in exchange. Government officials and development experts worry, on the one hand, that ceremonial exchange is hindering economic development, and on the other, that the demise of exchange systems will have destructive consequences for social cohesion (Iskandar and Djoeroemana 1994). Such worries are not new. As I mentioned in chapter 8, in 1952 the missionary-ethnographer Onvlee forecast that, once Sumbanese came to see their traditional valuables in economic terms, possessions would "become a dangerous and threatening power" (1973a: 26). But the distinction between inalienable and alienable may not be so clear-cut. On examination, both money and ceremonial exchange present certain difficulties to any effort to explain the value of

2. Albert O. Hirschman (1977) argues that the emergence of capitalism in the West was legitimized in part by the development of a conceptual distinction between the passions and the interests. The former were seen as destructive and irrational, the latter as subject to rational calculation. But like people in many other places where other values are being challenged by the market, most Sumbanese find calculation and rationality themselves to be antithetical to social virtue.

objects solely by appeal to their conventional sign value, mode of production, or innate ties to persons.

MEANING, VALUE, AND THE MOTION OF THINGS

Consider the following episode from a marriage negotiation I attended in 1986 in the Sumbanese district of Anakalang. Early in the initial stages of negotiation, trouble arose because the principals on the bride's side were from a neighboring district and thus unfamiliar with local procedural nuances. The bride's side initiated the exchange in the conventional way by sending over a dish on which they had placed a cloth, in order formally "to ask the purpose" of their guests' visit. The groom's side replied in an equally conventional manner by sending the dish back with a one-hundred-rupiah note (a trivial sum even on Sumba and the smallest amount available in paper form, worth less than the price of a pack of cigarettes). Across Sumba, the proper reciprocation to cloth is a gold ornament. Anakalangese generally accept units of money as a substitute. In either case, the object in the offering dish is an obligatory token that serves as a "base" to make the spoken words formal and binding. But the mother of the bride loudly rejected the note, saying the use of money in a formal exchange was inappropriate. After some discussion, the bride's party asked that the note be replaced with a five-hundred-rupiah note. At this, the spokesman from the groom's side sharply berated them, explaining that when money is placed in the dish, it must not be treated as money. It is a token, just like a gold ornament.[3] With a certain amount of grumbling, the bride's side was persuaded to accept this on the condition that it was a proper procedure and not an insult, and the negotiation proceeded.

This incident took place at the highly fraught border between money and exchange, but are the two positions really clear-cut? The bride's side seemed at first to be defending moral boundaries in a way familiar from received descriptions of spheres of exchange. From this point of view, they recognized the threat that money and the marketplace posed to traditional

---

3. Given the disproportions of value, this might sound disingenuous. But it is possible that the original connection between ornament and money was made not because both were valuables (nor because both could be ornaments, as proposed by Graeber 2001). Certain Sumbanese rituals require the use of small slivers of metal or shavings from a coin, watch, or other metal object. Judging from similar uses of metal on neighboring islands, I think their most relevant property in these contexts is that metal is hard. The substituting, in ritual contexts, of coins for ornaments of unequal exchange value derives from the ritual quality of hardness.

moral values and the solidarity of precapitalist society. But when they retreated, they asked for an increase in the face value of the money, as if the insult had not been the intrusion of money after all, but rather the low price. In this, they revealed a possibility that always exists in exchange—that symbolic tokens might slip into alternative regimes of value. For, on the one hand, exchange valuables do not necessarily possess all the properties (inalienability, personality, morality) attributed to them by the model of the gift a priori. And on the other, the status of money itself is not entirely stable: in this case it served as a formal token whose referent was confined to ceremonial exchange, yet it retained the potential for reinterpretation as cash value. In either case it was "symbolic," but its vulnerability to slippage was in part a function of its irreducible materiality. Even money shares with other objects the property of taking objective form. Thus it can cross contexts and, being semiotically underdetermined, is subject to reinterpretation.

However distinct it may be, money shares three features with other objects in their roles as social media: in both cases they are readily separated from the transactors and the context of the transaction; they are available for multiple interpretations; and throughout, they remain material objects and thus vulnerable to all that can happen to things. Being material, objects are always subject to the forces of what Grice (1957) calls "natural meaning" (signs based on causality—paper money offered because no coin was available). But as tokens within social action, they are also always subject to transformation into bearers of "nonnatural meaning" (intentional signs—paper money as an expression of low esteem). And this means the latter is always intertwined with the former. The meanings of things cannot be sharply disengaged from the ways in which they are causally embedded in the physical world. Yet, insofar as objects often *seem* to carry their values and meanings on their sleeves, as it were, they can play critical roles at the intersection between different functions.

AMBIGUOUS ATTACHMENTS

In practice, Sumbanese formal exchanges stress the representative functions of objects, play down utility, and rigorously exclude money except as a symbolic piece of metal. Nonetheless, formal exchanges are embedded within a larger political economy of both social signs and usable things, and they take some of their meaning from the way they articulate with other regimes of value. Explicit talk about "the real tradition" is one way the barriers between exchange and its alternatives are regulated. Sumbanese can point to the coexistence of exchange with markets, barter, usurious lending, and theft in order to insist on its distinctive moral value. For example, when one man tried to impress upon me the superior morality of exchange, he said that the same pig that would get you five buffalo and five horses in marriage exchange would be worth the price of only one middling buffalo and a small horse if sold. In saying this, he was drawing on market values as a way to measure the heavy weight of the obligations imposed by proper exchange.

One aspect of the comparison of exchange and its alternatives is an implicit claim about rank. Sumbanese frequently assert that market thinking is purely a recent development and (depending on the case they want to make) usually a deplorable one—that in the past, no one calculated the value of what they gave you. This is a part of the logic in talk about custom, which explicitly portrays both donors and recipients as acting not out of their own desires or willfulness but only because they are obligated by ancestral requirements. But, people say, now we live in a selfish era whose slogan is "as long as I (get mine)" *(mali nyuwa)*, an era in which people are driven by personal desires.[4] As a way of expressing and historicizing the difference between formal exchange and its alternatives, people sometimes talk about the economic irrationality of the past. As I mentioned in chapter 8, one man told me that people used to trade like quantities for like, regardless of the actual substance: one sack of maize would go for one much more expensive sack of coffee. He was suggesting that the folly of his forebears consisted in being taken in by the very materiality of things. They were unable to perform the symbolic operations embodied in money: exchange value in those days was inseparable from the things themselves. Part of the subtext here is that the ancestors' apparent folly—their lack of skill at rational calculation—is inseparable from their aristocratic disdain for haggling. The hierarchical implications of alternative regimes of value become explicit when some people observe that Sumbanese who engage in trade are usually of low rank, because, they claim, such people are naturally more

---

4. The association of modernity with desire and desire with money is explicit in many parts of Indonesia. By the 1920s, the Minangkabau of Sumatra already contrasted the cooperative character they ascribed to traditional villages with the "desirousness" (Indonesian, *hawa nafsu*) that money induces in those who "eat wages" (Indonesian, *makan gaji*) (Kahn 1993: 126). In Java, where conventionally it is women who handle money, people see both money and marketplace as stimulants to sexual and material desire (Brenner 1995; Siegel 1986; for a Western analogy, see Hirschman 1977: 9).

clever at calculation. Their freedom, it is supposed, derives from being unconstrained by a sense of honor.

Calculation implies a play on the relations between the object as a sign of something other than itself and as a source of value in itself, which is most evident at the boundaries between formal exchange and other kinds of transactions. The boundaries among kinds of transactions are permeable—if not conceptually then practically, for there are few exchange valuables that do not have some value in other contexts. For example, a horse received from Christian affines in marriage exchange can be sacrificed to marapu or sold for cash. This permeability is both a resource and a threat, insofar as a skillful or simply powerful player can take advantage of it, but the existence of alternative schemes of value bears the increasingly real potential to undermine the status claims sustained by exchange, a threat at once logical, political, and economic.

MONEY TAKES OVER?

Since Mauss, systems of exchange like those in Sumba have come to stand for everything that the economic character of modernity supposedly lacks. The contrast is not restricted to Western scholars; for people in Sumba, as in many other places, the concept of modernity and the experience of the state that attends it are inseparable from the ubiquity of money. Sumbanese often experience modernity, strive for its promises, and resist its threats by way of their dealings with money. Like many of those who have written about modernity, Sumbanese often treat money as something with its own dynamic, something that, once introduced into society, has a rapid, corrosive effect. The classic expression of this perspective remains that given by Marx, for whom money was a radical leveler, extinguishing all distinctions, because it never revealed which commodities had been transformed into it: "The circulation becomes the great social retort into which everything is thrown, to come out again as the gold-crystal" (1967a: 132). In this context, Sumbanese practices and discourses surrounding formal exchange are not simply remnants from an archaic past but are developing into strenuous and self-conscious responses to the world of money and markets. This response is both discursive, a vision of an alternative regime of value, and practical, an effort to control the circulation of value's objectified forms (compare Akin and Robbins 1999; Comaroff and Comaroff 1990; Hutchinson 1996).

Here I focus on three aspects of money: its relations to abstraction, alienation, and production. I look at money not primarily as a component of an established system of commodity circulation but rather as currency in its phenomenal and imagined forms, ways in which it appears even in the absence of a full-fledged monetary economy. I am interested, that is, in local experiences of and ideas about money. For whatever the larger political economic context, as Jane Guyer points out, money "is a vastly important reality to vast numbers of people, all but an infinitesimal number of whom have absolutely no idea of the official doctrines under which it 'makes sense,' but whose own constructions . . . are a necessary component of that 'sense' as it works out in practice" (1995: 6). People, that is, cannot *not* have ideas about why and how money is valuable. Both money's fluidity and its limits—including the extent to which people trust it—are functions of those ideas.

Sumba is a useful place from which to look at money, because, being a relatively recent arrival and still scarce, money is far less taken for granted there than in more thoroughly monetized places. Until the twentieth century, the few coins that made it to Sumba were either treated like other inalienable valuables or melted down as raw materials for ornaments.[5] It was not until the 1920s and 1930s, with Dutch encouragement, that regular markets appeared, but trade was still carried out largely by barter (Versluys 1941: 463–64). In Anakalang, the first petty traders, none of them Sumbanese, seem to have set up more permanent kiosks in the 1930s (Riekerk 1934). Beginning in 1911, the colonial government imposed a head tax, to be paid in cash (Couvreur 1914). But by the end of Dutch rule, just before the Japanese occupation, one study found that money had made little impact on local society, being used largely as a unit of value for things of small worth (Versluys 1941: 481).

Under the Indonesian state, monetization of Sumba lagged behind that of the rest of the nation, and large-scale government expenditure, the most important source of cash there, began only in the 1970s (Corner 1989: 184; Iskandar and Djoeroemana 1994: 67).[6] In the 1980s and 1990s, most Sum-

---

5. Even in parts of Indonesia where money and market production appeared much earlier than in Sumba, coins were often treated as valuables. In nineteenth-century highland Sumatra, for instance, pepper growers demanded payment only in Spanish "Carolus" dollars, whose high silver content was preferred for melting down into jewelry. Only coins with the full bust portrait of the king were acceptable for marriage payments, apparently for iconographic reasons (Steedly 1993: 90–91).

6. In the 1990s, the most important sources of money for Sumbanese were government salaries paid to minor officials and schoolteachers. Some young unmarried men and women earned wages by working for non-Sumbanese merchants, but

banese still lacked a regular cash income. Cash was required primarily for taxes, school fees, church offerings, and the purchase of items such as medicine, kerosene, cooking oil, salt, sugar, coffee, tobacco, and more occasionally, shirts, sandals, dishware, and transportation fares. Only in the most recent decade or so have the most ambitious and well-heeled families begun to send children off the island for higher education, in the hope that they will land positions in the civil service. Funds for this are usually raised piecemeal by pooling the resources of many kinfolk—usually along links built through past ceremonial exchanges. In the 1990s, off-island schooling constituted perhaps the single greatest incentive for Sumbanese to sell cattle.

Money thus plays a limited and highly marked role on Sumba. Although the Indonesian rupiah is trusted, or at least was until the economic crisis of 1997 (in contrast to money in highly inflationary economies or weak states), in Sumba it does not flow freely or pervasively. Money's purchasing power is highly constrained; labor, land, and cattle, for instance, are more easily and legitimately acquired through kinship, patronage, or exchange. Many people obtain money only for specific purposes such as paying taxes or school fees (Vel 1994: 70), and thus money runs through very tight circuits without entering into investment or credit (compare Guyer 1995: 9). When one person comes into some money, others are likely to make their claims on it; this is why some civil servants try to get themselves posted to parts of the island far from their kin. For those few people who have bank accounts, the main reason is to hide their money from others. As a result, money in Sumba does not always fully possess the properties of fluidity, impersonality, or abstraction, and, like exchange valuables, it often retains some indexical links to its sources and owners.

THE VALUE OF RENUNCIATION

Recall the use of money as a token in marriage exchange in lieu of a gold ornament. This context suggests that gold and money have more in common than simply their properties. Both take their value in part from con-

---

these wages were not sufficient to support a family. Other people engaged in petty trade in weekly markets, and a very small number sold everyday goods from tiny kiosks. Reports from across Sumba gave the percentage of the population with access to cash at between 2 and 10 percent (Hoskins 1993: 188; Vel 1994: 47). Given Sumbanese resistance to out-migration (Iskandar and Djoeroemana 1994: 57), remittance income was apparently negligible.

straints on their materiality—the concrete particularity that for Marx defined the use-value of objects is played down in favor of semiotic abstraction. This is one reason money is so often compared to the quintessential arbitrary sign: "Like money, language manifests itself in material form, but in the former as in the latter the manifestation is external to the nature of the means and does not really matter" (Coulmas 1992: 10). This negative property of money was described by Simmel as the result of a process of elimination or suppression: "It appears that even the most useful object must *renounce* its usefulness in order to function as money" (1990: 152). Only in this way can objects serve to symbolize simple quantities of value (yet the very uniformity that sustains money's abstractness has historically depended on the uniform, divisible, and durable properties of the materials out of which it is manufactured [Crump 1981: 4]).

But this renunciation is incapable of fully abolishing its alternatives: even money, for example, to the extent that it retains a material form, may take on new functions. Coins may become jewelry or bullion; as Marx puts it, "But no sooner does coin leave the mint, than it immediately finds itself on the high-road to the melting pot" (1967a: 125). Not only that, the very absence of one possibility is a critical component of the meaning of what remains: in Simmel's words: "[T]he value that money has, and that allows it to perform its function, may be determined by those other possible uses which have to be foregone. . . . The perceived value of the developed function is constituted by . . . the exclusion of all other functions" (1990: 155).

So both gold and money, when placed in the dish during formal exchange, take their value from a similar basic structure of deferred value: everyone knows that the object in the dish is convertible to other forms. The one hundred rupiahs could, of course, become money again. Gold and cloth, too, can be diverted from exchange. Indeed, their persistence as valuables can be seen as a continual refusal to allow them to return to their original state. It takes the work of ritualization to maintain the boundary between the semiotics of exchange valuables and the alternative meanings and uses that things might possess in coexisting regimes of value.

Anakalangese descriptions of their world before modernity stress the absence of abstraction and a fetishistic clinging to the materiality of things. Anakalangese accounts of the naïveté of their forebears, however, contain an important subtext. People in the past ignored differences of quality because of their nobility. They eschewed such calculations because they refused to give in to their desires. Whereas for Marx the concrete particularities of things were important as the source of their use-values (1967a: 133), the apparent empiricism that Sumbanese ascribe to exchange is a mark of people's relative *independence* from use-value. To follow ancestral rules is a demonstrative refusal to calculate utility, which can be understood only as a function of need or desire. Desire is something that separates one simultaneously from one's own best self (a loss of self-control) and from others (by attacking the moral bonds of community), and thus it threatens one's claims to high rank. By stressing the conventionalized semiotics of objects, formal exchange displays the players' imperviousness to the appeal of utility or their own wants.

The abstractness and fluidity that are supposed to characterize money appear, by contrast, to place desire in the foreground. Unlike inalienable valuables, money realizes its value neither in transaction as a social performance nor in simply being held, but only in that which it obtains in a future expenditure. To the extent that money is abstract and its uses unspecified—that is, as it is free both of particular qualities in itself and of the constraints of ancestral rules—any particular expenditure represents a choice among possible options. Therefore it seems to express, above all, the wishes of the person who spends it. And to legitimate those wishes is to challenge the principles by which people are valued and particular relations of domination sustained.

PRODUCTION

Money seems to many Sumbanese to have sources not only distant in space but also at a remove from the labor and agency of humans. In 1912, a Dutch official recounted the following conversation:

> A puzzle which our host would gladly have solved was why the "taoe djawa" (= foreign men, Europeans) came to have much money. He was asked what he thought himself. He said that in the foreign land three trees must grow, one which bears as fruit gold pieces (English pounds of which men on Sumba see much), another of silver (rijksdollars), and the third copper coins (2½ cent pieces). At a certain time, as soon as there is a need, the king or kings order a harvesting. Guilders and smaller silver coins are nothing other than unripe rijksdollars, cents still undeveloped "gobangs" (2½ cent pieces). (Witkamp 1912: 486)

If this story has a familiar ring to it (for I, at least, had to be reminded as a child that money doesn't grow on trees), it may be because it expresses widespread fantasies. When money is relatively unfamiliar, what accounts for its uncanny value? Its value seems different from that of other things, and perhaps this difference provokes the dream that money requires no more labor than the plucking of fruit from a tree, a form of production requiring the minimal intervention of human agency. (This recalls Marx's satirical remark that those who fetishize capital assume it is "a property of money to generate value and yield interest, much as it is an attribute of pear trees to bear pears" [1967b: 392].)

Money can also come to represent the state as a distant and possibly opaque place of origin. In a place like Sumba, money is one of the most pervasive forms the state takes in most people's everyday experience.[7] Money is legal tender because it is stamped with an inscription bearing the state's political authorization. The authority represented by money portrays itself on money's material substance: as Keith Hart (1986) observes, every coin or banknote carries some emblem of the state. It wears, in Marx's imagery, a "national uniform" (1967a: 125; see also Foster 1998; Shell 1982). Money is not necessarily even antisocial: like exchange, the use of money still requires trust (something made explicit on American currency, if sociopolitically obscure, by the slogan "In God We Trust"). It is just that the object of this trust has shifted from exchange partners and the ancestors to the state. To this extent, money does not so much abolish society as it institutes a different kind of society. So wherein is the distinctive difference that makes for modernity?

THE STATE OF DESIRE

Sumbanese associate money's appearance in their lives with the state in numerous ways. As in many subsistence economies, the need for money was initially produced by the state's demands for taxes. Today most money in Sumba ultimately derives from the state, either in salaries or from businesses whose income is due largely to government projects. More generally, the state has established itself as the chief promoter of capitalism and endeavored to do away with what it sees as the more irrational forms of local expenditure. Economic rationality has been the constant topic of government exhortations and directives.

What the state hopes money will come to mean may not fully determine how people understand it locally. The ways Sumbanese handle and speak

7. In fact, money's association with "the outside world" *(tana jiawa)* is reinforced by the fact that most money is directly received from and paid back to non-Sumbanese, either the state or ethnically "foreign" traders—that is, those of Chinese or Arab descent (Vel 1994: 68–69).

about money seem to be responses to a dilemma posed by the state project of development. This dilemma is that, to the extent that money's origin lies in the state, it seems to be the state that guarantees the play of individual desires. Sumbanese describe the present era with the Indonesian expression "free era" *(masa merdeka)*. In national discourse, the era of freedom, or "free era," usually refers to liberation from colonial rule. More often, for Sumbanese, the "free era" refers to a time dominated by "economic think-ing," meaning rampant individualism. Like other familiar critics of money, many Sumbanese describe the present day as a time of antisocial stinginess, a ruthless calculating of costs and benefits unconcerned with honor or rank.

Of course not everyone has the same stakes in the regimes of value and the social hierarchies that money seems to threaten. Former slaves and unmarried women, in particular, often benefit from the promise of freedom both from rank and from material dependence as reproduced in exchange (see Keane 1997c; Hoskins 1998). But even those who celebrate modernity and economic rationality must have some account of the respective values of exchange and money. This is where Christian discourses of interiority and materialism come into play, discourses that help give expression to shifting distinctions between subject and object. Talk about materialism seems to incite people to a certain dematerialization in their understandings of the world. This is evident in, for instance, the effort to treat material goods as merely symbolic. As I observed in chapter 7, marriage exchange raises new questions of value within the emergent representational economy of Sum-banese Christians, and it creates the tendency to treat exchange goods as symbols of immaterial meanings. This dematerialization underwrites the world of money, in which the subject is supposed to be clearly separated from its objects and in which value can be fully abstracted from concrete practices and material forms. Yet in seeking to account for the value those objects hold for the subject, one is left with little but the willful and desir-ing subject itself. To the extent that money is abstract, it permits a poten-tially unconstrained range of choices among purchasable items. In coming to stand for those choices, for freedom, it seems in the Sumbanese context to point toward the desires that any given choice expresses.

But who stands behind money and its promises? Here the subject encounters the state, which, by authorizing money, seems to sponsor that willfulness. Yet certainly neither the state nor (for different reasons) most Sumbanese are willing to accept the consequences with complacency. The state's efforts to control willfulness and desire (as stimulated by, for exam-ple, elections or advertising) lie beyond the scope of this chapter. Sumbanese efforts were visible in the continued power of exchange in the 1990s. Recall again the use of money as an exchange valuable in the offering dish. To use money as a material token, emphasizing the underdetermined character of its materiality, is to deny the authorizing stamp on its face. To treat money as if it were gold is to deny the ultimate power of the issuing authority in favor of the semiotic value asserted by ancestral mandate. The use of the coin does not replace material use-values with symbolic values, but rather it asserts the primacy of one authorizing origin for signs over another. It asserts the superior power of exchange to suspend use-values in favor of claims to higher value. In the process, it seeks to deny the abstractness of money. Yet it does not necessarily do so by reasserting the materiality of meaningful objects. Rather, those objects are turned into signs of invisible values such as "social solidarity," "tradition," and "self-worth."

We might compare this to the treatment of money in the church, mentioned in chapter 8. Recall that one complaint non-Christians made was that the church demands money offerings and tithes. In Umbu Delu's words, "If you don't give them money, they won't read from their book. Pay that money. It's as if we buy it." One dimension of his complaint may be resentment at an emerging set of class distinctions: those with no ready access to cash are certainly put at a disadvantage if the church refuses to accept payment in goods. But, as I argued in that chapter, Umbu Delu is also making claims about the value of persons that is produced through the deferential forms of ceremonial exchange. Those dealings are not supposed to be visibly—calculably—driven by personal desires. At the same time, the values they involve are inseparable from the sheer materiality of the goods transacted. The contrast with the handling of money in church is striking. Rather than being visibly displayed like a particular gift, the church offering is placed in a black bag or in an envelope under a cloth, as if there were something to hide. Yet all the individual transactions are eventually computed and made public at a moment separated in time from the moment of giving. They are rendered in their most abstract form, one that allows the direct comparison of quantities. As I suggested above, this displays the transformation of cash into useful resources. It also puts families into visible competition with one another. Sumbanese exchange has always had a strongly competitive character; the difference is that the church's rational calculations contribute at most only indirectly to the social bonds among the congregants.

That the church's ways of handling money display its abstract character and form a sharp contrast to the sense of honor and the social bonds created in ceremonial exchange is certainly not surprising. It is a familiar story for anthropologists, who can point to parallels in many places where money has been introduced into new contexts. What I stress here is that it is the *church* that forms a preeminent site for this display. This is not a simple matter of claiming that the church works in collusion with the state or some other purported agents of rationalization. More to the point is this: The abstraction of money makes sense within the semiotic ideology that distinguishes persons from things, immaterial meanings from material forms, souls from bodies, and signs from the world. The supplanting of ceremonial exchange with money, in the context of a moral narrative of modernity, is far more than a technical improvement or a means of achieving greater efficiency. It plays a role in the fostering of new kinds of human subjects.

The tension between the two uses of money I have discussed in this chapter is a tension between two sites of agency. In exchange, persons manipulate tokens of value in deference to the displaced agents of ancestral mandate. In commodity circulation, the state seems, unwittingly, to authorize the cleverness of desiring selves and the endless possibilities that money affords them. The individual who can buy and sell with impunity bears the warrant of the state, which itself remains invisible except in its effects, in the form of "use"-less, circulating signs of itself. This vision is, in turn, an effect of that aspect of the ideology of money that celebrates abstraction, denies social mediation, and imagines that signification offers the subject an escape from materiality. It is the semiotic vision of purification.

Afterword

Through much of this book, despite occasional qualifications, I have found it useful to speak of an encounter between two sides. On one side the Dutch, on the other the Sumbanese; on one side Calvinists, on the other marapu followers; on one side a representational economy governed by a semiotic ideology identified with modernity and purification, and on the other economies and ideologies that are quite distinct. This dichotomization is a conscious strategy of exposition rather than a reflection of the world. But in some important respects, this parsing out is right. First, in historical terms, the Dutch appeared on the scene from afar—not the first foreigners to impinge on Sumba by any means, but foreigners they were. So they took themselves to be; so the Sumbanese saw them. The violence of colonial history and the new power relations that succeeded it demand we not forget that difference. Second, in conceptual terms, however dubious various assertions about modernity may turn out to be, the idea of being modern remains a great divider among peoples, kinds of actions, desires, and hopes. And third, the missionary project of converting others must also, in some sense, take the unconverted to stand on the other side of a dichotomy. The unconverted may be in thrall to devils, or they may be bearers of an original revelation who need only take a few more steps, or they may even be those among the saved who have merely suffered some backsliding or who belong to a mistaken sect, but the proselytizer faces them across a distance that really matters. Along with the dichotomy between humans and spirits, such dichotomies and the distances they may impose between their respective terms can, under certain historical circumstances, become sources of objectification.

But here already the oppositions begin to lose their clarity. However much the proselytizer's constructions of the unconverted may vary, the very ambition to proselytize must at least presuppose a human soul that might be saved. Even the strictest Calvinists, who held that the parceling out of saved and unsaved individuals was determined from the start, still preached sermons and sent out missionaries. Those to whom they preached could not, in principle, be wholly Other. Conversely, as I have observed at various points, there were internal conflicts even among the members of the same Dutch mission. Their debates about sacrificial meat described in chapter 8, for instance, show how the work of purification could produce aporia even within a narrowly confined range of discursive possibilities. If too sharp a dichotomy risks obscuring internal differences within each "side," it also threatens to obscure the various ways the two sides coexist, live within the same world with one another, and, for that matter, with the author and readers of this book. Their very conflicts are predicated on having at least that much in common. The denial of that commonality is, in some registers, an effect of the work of purification that places self-aware human agents on one side, and fetishists in the grip of cultural and animistic compulsions on the other.

For their part, Sumbanese long resisted the universalizing claims that motivated the mission—not just claims about cosmos and salvation but also about more mundane things, such as their place in history and the real value of money. Many still resist wholeheartedly; others have found ironic modes of rapprochement that confine those universal claims to specific domains of life (churches, marketplaces, schools). Yet in pragmatic terms, most Sumbanese eventually found something they thought they could recognize in the Dutch. They made deals with them, threatened, pleaded with, and cajoled them. That is, their actions show they took the Dutch to be not entirely unknowable, and over time a variety of discursive and practical forms developed that confounded difference. This is not an essay in the problems of radical translation; suffice to say that, over time, these people called Dutch and Sumbanese found locally persuasive—that is, good enough—ways to talk and listen to one another. By this I hardly mean some sort of Habermasian ideal speech situation. Much of what I have said about language in the previous chapters should make that clear enough. By the end of the twentieth century, however, many Sumbanese had come to develop ways of agreeing that it was, after all, "religion" (along with "economics," "kinship," and "culture") that they were talking about. At that point, Sumbanese had been grafted onto a genealogy shared with the Dutch, as well as, no doubt, with most readers of this book.

To be sure, the missionary encounter took place within a project of domination, and the field of power was such that Sumbanese and Dutch were not simply coauthors. When religion and culture became relevant concepts, they could hardly shake off their European origins altogether. As that power grew over time, Sumbanese Christians increasingly found they did not have to listen to certain kinds of arguments from marapu followers. At that point, marapu were coming to be objectified in the familiar sense associated with modernity. In time, many Sumbanese found themselves able to enthusiastically take on the role of Bible teacher, sermonizer, and so forth. In the process, they have surely changed those roles; how could it be otherwise? After all, social theories of persistence and resistance aside, it is at least, as I have suggested, a Heraclitean world, and they could not have been baptized in exactly the same river as their Dutch theological forebears. But when Sumbanese tell us they are good Christians like anyone else, as when they (perhaps less frequently) tell us they are good Indonesians, we must take seriously at least that desire to be so. To demand otherwise—say, to ask that Sumbanese display superhuman powers of self-invention, that they be wholly autonomous—would be absurd. We should not make their humanity depend on possession of a degree of agency that eludes even us. Perhaps only the most radical version of a moral narrative of modernity could make such a demand.

But when I say we must take their words seriously, when, for instance, Sumbanese say they too are good Christians, this does not mean we should assume too quickly that we understand exactly what they are saying. The global circulation of seemingly familiar things like Christianity or, say, money does not eliminate the difficulties of understanding. If anything, thoughtful attention to that circulation should begin to make them seem unfamiliar. By casting the encounter in terms of representational economies, I hope to make visible certain things about the historical processes involved. First, by saying that Dutch and Sumbanese could talk to one another in good enough ways, I certainly do not have in mind deep understanding or some vague sort of ecumenical communion. Rather, I am concerned with surfaces, the extent to which Dutch and Sumbanese could step into the same semiotic shoes, as it were. These semiotic forms are preeminently linguistic, but the process could also involve sharing food, exchanging goods, swapping clothing, and entering the same architectural spaces. To be sure, colonial domination depended on constant efforts to restrict the range of possibilities. Even the Dutch propensity elsewhere in the Indies for donning clothing more appropriate to the tropical climate eventually had to be prohibited since it seemed to blur the lines between colonizer and colonized (Schulte Nordholt 1997; Keane 2005; compare Stoler 2002). But if colonial practice depended on maintaining barriers, it also required some openings in them and created new possibilities. The openings made use of hinges provided by semiotic form.

Here, what Derrida has observed of language applies to semiosis more generally. Sign forms (beyond pure indexes) are made to be repeatable out of context. They are inherently vulnerable to citation. Homi Bhabha (1994b) has drawn attention to one possibility, that mimicry becomes the vehicle for sly civility on the side of the colonized, and the occasion for anxieties on the side of the colonizer. For the missionary, the critical form this anxiety takes is this: is their conversion sincere? The nature of iterability means one can never be sure; the most earnest deeds and protestations of faith are in themselves but acting, mere words. But there is another side to the story. Citation can become use. Creeds uttered by rote can be taken to heart. Semiotic forms can become the objects of disciplinary practices aimed at absorbing them in new ways. This does not mean the forms themselves change: Sumbanese couplets recited in a display of cultural knowledge can be indistinguishable from those addressed to a spirit agency. Christian scriptures held as talismanic devices may still be read for meaning. The persistence of forms across changing representational economies is part of what makes the past seem to impinge on the present. This persistence allows people to repeat the words of ancestors as if the past were alive. It may lead others to prohibit old gong tunes or certain styles of dress, lest they summon forth spirits who would block their progress into the future. But the indeterminacy of forms also means that new prospects could emerge out of them: they point as much to possible futures as to the past (see Keane 2003a). The persistence of forms across contexts is what makes it possible for the Dutch and Sumbanese eventually to speak to one another, somehow.

To the observer, marapu worshipers and Dutch Calvinists may seem most inscrutable to one another when the observer takes them to be, essentially, the bearers of incommensurable beliefs, immaterial thoughts, and invisible intentions—that is, full masters of their respective worlds of meaning. Disembodied in this way, the categories of marapu follower and Calvinist risk coming to mean distinct thought-worlds, with no point of triangulation, so many monads that can, at most, have "impacts" on one another. There are ethical problems with this (Fabian's denial of coevalness [1983] names just one of them) but also empirical ones. For one thing, there is the familiar question of particularism: how many monads are there? If we want to describe Sumba, do we stop at language groups, dialects, idiolects? Districts, clans, villages, houses? Why not expand outward, since, after all, they are Indonesians and, some, members of Christendom too?

There is also the question of history. As I suggested in chapter 1, the globalization of religions like Christianity and Islam, their promiscuous circulation of people, texts, and identifications, cannot be grasped merely by attention to particularity and locality. This observation is not meant, however, to be an invitation to neocolonial triumphalism or humanistic universalism. The point, rather, is to acknowledge the materiality of the semiotic forms that circulate, the causal effects that materiality subjects them to, the disciplines that cultivate the users of those semiotic forms, the representational economies into which those forms enter, and the semiotic ideologies that organize and endlessly rework them and whose work they ultimately elude, as well. When Dutch and Sumbanese encountered one another, it was amid the circulation of words and things. To *dismiss* the materiality of those words and things in search of inner depths alone is to play into the work of purification.

Moreover, these forms, disciplines, and ideologies are the stuff of history just as much as heroic actions and deep structural forces are. There are moments when semiotic forms are cast up before people as objects that seem wholly external to them, and that require some kind of response. Sometimes that response means icons must be smashed, fetishes abolished, reified categories of analysis dissolved, and languages reformed. In European history, the quest for freedom based on moral autonomy underwrote one such occasion. Yet the very actions people take must, perforce, have concrete forms. Actions must be recognizable at least to those who undertake them, if not to other people as well. They must, that is, have public, semiotic form and thus be available for circulation, decontextualization, and recontextualization anew. Even the effort to spiritualize the conscience, by sharpening the distinction between immaterial subjects and material things, fosters the conditions for objectification. Purification fails not because there is an agent who resists but because actions put into play new forms, or old forms within new representational economies. If the work of purification would set those material forms wholly apart from self-aware, agentive humans who would thereby stand alone, it is a task that cannot be completed.

References

Aarsleff, Hans. 1982. *From Locke to Saussure: Essays in the Study of Language and Intellectual History.* Minneapolis: University of Minnesota Press.

Ahearn, Laura. 2001. Language and Agency. *Annual Review of Anthropology* 30: 109–37.

Akin, David, and Joel Robbins, eds. 1999. *Money and Modernity: State and Local Currencies in Melanesia.* Pittsburgh: University of Pittsburgh Press.

Anderson, Amanda. 2000. The Temptations of Aggrandized Agency: Feminist Histories and the Horizon of Modernity. *Victorian Studies* 43 (1): 43–65.

Anderson, Benedict. 1972. The Idea of Power in Javanese Culture. In *Culture and Politics in Indonesia*, ed. Claire Holt, 1–69. Ithaca, NY: Cornell University Press.

———. 1983. *Imagined Communities: Reflections on the Origin and Spread of Nationalism.* London: Verso.

———. 1990 (1973). Cartoons and Monuments: The Evolution of Political Communication under the New Order. In *Language and Power: Exploring Political Cultures in Indonesia*, 152–93. Ithaca, NY: Cornell University Press.

Appadurai, Arjun. 1986a. Introduction: Commodities and the Politics of Value. In *The Social Life of Things: Commodities in Cultural Perspective*, ed. Arjun Appadurai, 3–63. Cambridge: Cambridge University Press.

———. 1986b. Theory in Anthropology: Center and Periphery. *Comparative Studies in Society and History* 28: 356–61.

———. 1990. Topographies of the Self: Praise and Emotion in Hindu India. In *Language and the Politics of Emotion*, ed. Catherine A. Lutz and Lila Abu-Lughod, 92–112. Cambridge: Cambridge University Press.

———. 1996. *Modernity at Large: Cultural Dimensions of Globalization.* Minneapolis: University of Minnesota Press.

Aragon, Lorraine V. 2000. *Fields of the Lord: Animism, Christian Minorities, and State Development in Indonesia.* Honolulu: University of Hawai'i Press.

Asad, Talal. 1993. *Genealogies of Religion: Discipline and Reasons of Power in Christianity and Islam*. Baltimore: Johns Hopkins University Press.

———. 1996. Comments on Conversion. In *Conversion to Modernities: The Globalization of Christianity*. Ed. Peter van der Veer, 263–73. New York: Routledge.

———. 2003. *Formations of the Secular: Christianity, Islam, Modernity*. Stanford: Stanford University Press.

Austin, J. L. 1955. *How to Do Things with Words*. Cambridge: Harvard University Press.

Austin-Broos, Diane. 1997. *Jamaica Genesis: Religion and the Politics of Moral Orders*. Chicago: University of Chicago Press.

Bakhtin, Mikhail M. 1981. *The Dialogic Imagination*. Trans. Caryl Emerson and Michael Holquist. Austin: University of Texas Press.

———. 1986. *Speech Genres and Other Late Essays*. Trans. Vern W. McGee. Austin: University of Texas Press.

Barker, John, ed. 1990. *Christianity in Oceania: Ethnographic Perspectives*. Lanham, MD: University Press of America.

Barnes, R. H. 1992. A Catholic Mission and the Purification of Culture: Experiences in an Indonesian Community. *Journal of the Anthropological Society of Oxford* 23 (2): 169–80.

Bateson, Gregory. 1972 (1955). A Theory of Play and Fantasy. In *Steps to an Ecology of the Mind*, 177–93. New York: Ballantine Books.

Battaglia, Debbora, ed. 1995. *Rhetorics of Self-Making*. Berkeley: University of California Press.

Baum, Johann Wilhelm et al. 1863–1900. *Ioannis Calvin Opera quae supersunt omnia*. Brunswick, Germany: C. A. Schwetschke.

Bauman, Richard. 1983. *Let Your Words Be Few: Symbolism of Speaking and Silence among 17th-Century Quakers*. Prospect Heights, IL: Waveland Press.

Bauman, Richard, and Charles L. Briggs. 1990. Poetics and Performance as Critical Perspectives on Language and Social Life. *Annual Review of Anthropology* 19: 59–88.

———. 2003. *Voices of Modernity: Language Ideologies and the Politics of Inequality*. Cambridge: Cambridge University Press.

Bauman, Zygmunt. 1988. *Freedom*. Minneapolis: University of Minnesota Press.

Beding, P. Moses. 1978. Misa "Panca Sila": Satu Pertanggung-Jawaban. In *Waingapu Anda Waraya La Andaluri/Waingapu Jalan Pasir ke Jalan Kehidupan; 25 Tahun Paroki Waingapu*, 92–104. Ende, Indonesia: Arnoldus.

Beidelman, T. O. 1982. *Colonial Evangelism: A Socio-Historical Study of an East African Mission at the Grassroots*. Bloomington: Indiana University Press.

Belting, Hans. 1994. *Likeness and Presence: A History of the Image before the Era of Art*. Trans. Edmund Jephcott. Chicago: University of Chicago Press.

Benedict, Philip. 2002. *Christ's Churches Purely Reformed: A Social History of Calvinism.* New Haven, CT: Yale University Press.

Berman, Marshall. 1982. *All That Is Solid Melts into Air: The Experience of Modernity.* New York: Penguin.

Besnier, Niko. 1995. *Literacy, Emotion, and Authority: Reading and Writing on a Polynesian Atoll.* Cambridge: Cambridge University Press.

Beyer, Peter. 1994. *Religion and Globalization.* London: Sage.

Bhabha, Homi K. 1994a (1985). Of Mimicry and Man: The Ambivalence of Colonial Discourse. In *The Location of Culture,* 85–92. London: Routledge.

———. 1994b (1985). Sly Civility. In *The Location of Culture,* 93–101. London: Routledge.

Bigalke, Terance W. 1981. A Social History of "Tana Toraja," 1870–1965. Ph.D. diss., University of Wisconsin, Madison.

Blumenberg, Hans. 1983 (1976). *The Legitimacy of the Modern Age.* Trans. Robert M. Wallace. Cambridge: MIT Press.

Boas, Franz. 1911. Introduction to *Handbook of American Indian Languages,* 5–83. Washington: Government Printing Office.

Bourdieu, Pierre. 1977 (1972). *Outline of a Theory of Practice.* Trans. Richard Nice. Cambridge: Cambridge University Press.

Bowen, John R. 1993. *Muslims through Discourse: Religion and Ritual in Gayo Society.* Princeton: Princeton University Press.

———. 2003. *Islam, Law, and Equality in Indonesia: An Anthropology of Public Reasoning.* Cambridge: Cambridge University Press.

Brenner, Suzanne A. 1995. Why Women Rule the Roost: Rethinking Javanese Ideologies of Gender and Self-Control. In *Bewitching Women, Pious Men: Gender and Body Politics in Southeast Asia,* ed. Aihwa Ong and Michael G. Peletz, 19–50. Berkeley: University of California.

Briggs, Charles L. 1984. Learning How to Ask: Native Metacommunicative Competence and the Incompetence of Fieldworkers. *Language in Society* 13: 1–28.

Brouwer, A. M. 1912. The Preparation of Missionaries in Holland. *International Review of Missions* 1: 226-39.

Brouwer, K. J. 1951. *Dr. A. C. Kruyt Dienaar der Toradja's.* Den Haag: J. N. Voorhoeve.

Bruce, Steven B., ed. 1992. *Religion and Modernization: Sociologists and Historians Debate the Secularization Thesis.* Oxford: Oxford University Press.

Bunyan, John. 1960 (1678–1684). *The Pilgrim's Progress from This World to That Which Is to Come.* Ed. James Blanton Wharey. Oxford: Oxford University Press.

Burke, Peter. 1987. *The Historical Anthropology of Early Modern Italy: Essays on Perception and Communication.* Cambridge: Cambridge University Press.

Burridge, Kenelm. 1978. Introduction to Missionary Occasions. In *Mission, Church, and Sect in Oceania.* Association for Social Anthropology in Oceania monograph no. 6, ed. James Boutilier, Daniel T. Hughes, and Sharon W. Tiffaney, 1–30. Ann Arbor: University of Michigan Press.

———. 1979. *Someone, No One: An Essay on Individuality.* Princeton: Princeton University Press.

Burrow, J. W. 1966. *Evolution and Society: A Study in Victorian Social Theory.* London: Cambridge University Press.

Butler, Judith. 1997. *The Psychic Life of Power: Theories in Subjection.* Stanford: Stanford University Press.

Bynum, Caroline Walker. 1995. *The Resurrection of the Body in Western Christianity, 200–1336.* New York: Columbia University Press.

Calvin, John. 1949. *Institutes of the Christian Religion.* Trans. Henry Beveridge. London: James Clarke.

Cannell, Fenella. 2005. The Christianity of Anthropology. *Journal of the Royal Anthropological Institute* 11 (2): 335–56.

———, ed. 2006. *The Anthropology of Christianity.* Durham, NC: Duke University Press.

Carrier, James G. 1995. *Gifts and Commodities: Exchange and Western Capitalism since 1700.* London: Routledge.

Casanova, José. 1994. *Public Religions in the Modern World.* Chicago: University of Chicago Press.

Cascardi, Anthony J. 1992. *The Subject of Modernity.* Cambridge: Cambridge University Press.

Chakrabarty, Dipesh. 2000. *Provincializing Europe: Postcolonial Thought and Historical Difference.* Princeton: Princeton University Press.

Clifford, James. 1982. *Person and Myth: Maurice Leenhardt in the Melanesian World.* Berkeley: University of California Press.

———. 1988. Identity in Mashpee. In *The Predicament of Culture: Twentieth-Century Ethnography, Literature, and Art,* 277–346. Cambridge: University of California Press.

Coleman, Simon. 2000. *The Globalisation of Charismatic Christianity: Spreading the Gospel of Prosperity.* Cambridge: Cambridge University Press.

Colenbrander, J. F. 1987a (1932). Eten van Offervleesch. In *Gereformeerde Zending op Sumba: Een Bronnenpublicatie,* ed. Th. van den End, 356–57. Alphen aan den Rijn, Netherlands: Raad voor de Zending der Ned. Herv. Kerk, de Zending der Gereformeerde Kerken in Nederland en de Gereformeerde Zendingsbond in de Ned. Herv Kerk.

———. 1987b (1922). Letter to the Sumba Mission Deputation, October 7, 1922. In *Gereformeerde Zending op Sumba: Een Bronnenpublicatie,* ed. Th. van den End, 219–20. Alphen aan den Rijn, Netherlands: Raad voor de Zending der Ned. Herv. Kerk, de Zending der Gereformeerde Kerken in Nederland en de Gereformeerde Zendingsbond in de Ned. Herv Kerk.

Colijn, H. 1927. Het Vierde Eener Eeuw. In *Tot Dankbaarheid Genoopt: Gedenkboek ter Gelegenheid van de 25-Jarigen Zendingsarbeid op Soemba vanwege de Gereformeerde Kerken in Groningen, Drente en Overijsel,* ed. M. Meijering et al., 10–13. Kampen, Netherlands: J. H. Kok.

Comaroff, Jean. 1985. *Body of Power Spirit of Resistance: The Culture and History of a South African People*. Chicago: University of Chicago Press.

Comaroff, Jean, and John Comaroff. 1991. *Of Revelation and Revolution*. Vol. 1, *Christianity, Colonialism, and Consciousness in South Africa*. Chicago: University of Chicago Press.

Comaroff, John, and Jean Comaroff. 1990. Goodly Beasts, Beastly Goods: Cattle and Commodities in a South African Context. *American Ethnologist* 17: 195–216.

———. 1997. *Of Revelation and Revolution*. Vol. 2, *The Dialectics of Modernity on a South African Frontier*. Chicago: University of Chicago Press.

Constable, Giles. 1996. *The Reformation of the Twelfth Century*. Cambridge: Cambridge University Press.

Cooper, Frederick, and Ann Laura Stoler, eds. 1997. *Tensions of Empire: Colonial Cultures in a Bourgeois World*. Berkeley: University of California Press.

Corner, Lorraine. 1989. East and West Nusa Tenggara: Isolation and Poverty. In *Unity and Diversity: Regional Economic Development in Indonesia since 1970*, ed. Hal Hill, 178–206. Singapore: Oxford University Press.

Coulmas, Florian. 1992. *Language and Economy*. Oxford: Blackwell.

Couvreur, A. J. L. 1914. Jaarverslag Afdeeling Soemba 1914 tevens Memorie van Overgave. Typescript. Algemeen Rijksarchief, The Hague.

Crapanzano, Vincent. 2000. *Serving the Word: Literalism in America from the Pulpit to the Bench*. New York: New Press.

Crump, Thomas. 1981. *The Phenomenon of Money*. London: Routledge and Kegan Paul.

Csordas, Thomas J. 1997. *Language, Charisma, and Creativity: The Ritual Life of a Religious Movement*. Berkeley: University of California Press.

Cunningham, Clark E. 1964. Order in the Atoni House. *Bijdragen tot de Taal-, Land- en Volkenkunde* 120: 34–68.

Daniel, E. Valentine. 1996. *Charred Lullabies: Chapters in an Anthropography of Violence*. Princeton: Princeton University Press.

Davidson, Donald. 1980. *Essays in Actions and Events*. Oxford: Oxford University Press.

Dennett, Daniel. 1976. Conditions of Personhood. In *The Identities of Persons*, ed. Amelie Oksenberg Rorty, 175–96. Berkeley: University of California Press.

Deputaten. 1965. *Rapport inzake de Zending op Soemba aan de Zendingssynode van de Gereformeerde Kerken in de Provincies Groningen, Drenthe, and Overijssel en de Altreformierte Kirche in Niedersachsen*. Groningen: J. Niemmeijer.

Derrida, Jacques. 1973 (1967). Speech and Phenomena: Introduction to the Problem of Signs in Husserl's Phenomenology. In *Speech and Phenomena and Other Essays on Husserl's Theory of Signs*, trans. David B. Allison, 3–104. Evanston, IL: Northwestern University Press.

———. 1982. Signature Event Context. In *Margins of Philosophy*, trans. Alan Bass, 307–30. Chicago: University of Chicago Press.

Derrida, Jacques, and Gianni Vattimo, eds. 1998. *Religion*. Stanford: Stanford University Press.

Dijkstra, H. 1987 (1902). De Duivelen offeren. *Het Mosterdzaad*, vol. 21. In *Gereformeerde Zending op Sumba: Een Bronnenpublicatie*, ed. Th. van den End, 122–23. Alphen aan den Rijn, Netherlands: Raad voor de Zending der Ned. Herv. Kerk, de Zending der Gereformeerde Kerken in Nederland en de Gereformeerde Zendingsbond in de Ned. Herv Kerk.

Dirks, Nicholas, ed. 1992. *Colonialism and Culture*. Ann Arbor: University of Michigan Press.

Douglas, Bronwen. 2001. From Invisible Christians to Gothic Theatre: The Romance of the Millennial in Melanesian Anthropology. *Current Anthropology* 42 (1): 615–50.

DuBois, John W. 1986. Self-Evidence and Ritual Speech. In *Evidentiality: The Linguistic Coding of Epistemology*, ed. Wallace Chafe and Johann Nichols, 313–336. Norwood: Ablex.

———. 1993. Meaning without Intention: Lessons from Divination. In *Responsibility and Evidence in Oral Discourse*, ed. Jane H. Hill and Judith T. Irvine, 48–71. Cambridge: Cambridge University Press.

Dumont, Louis. 1986. *Essays on Individualism: Modern Ideology in Anthropological Perspective*. Chicago: University of Chicago Press.

Duranti, Alessandro. 1993. Intentionality and Truth: An Ethnographic Critique. *Cultural Anthropology* 8: 214–45.

———. 2004. Agency in Language. In *A Companion to Linguistic Anthropology*, ed. Duranti, 451–73. Malden, MA: Blackwell.

Eickelman, Dale F. 2000. Islam and the Languages of Modernity. *Daedalus* 129 (1): 119–35.

Eire, Carlos M. N. 1986. *War against the Idols: The Reformation of Worship from Erasmus to Calvin*. New York: Cambridge University Press.

Ellen, Roy. 1986. Microcosm, Macrocosm, and the Nuaulu House: Concerning the Reductionist Fallacy as Applied to Metaphorical Levels. *Bijdragen tot de Taal-, Land- en Volkenkunde* 142: 1–30.

———. 1988. Fetishism. *Man* (ns) 23: 213–35.

Engelke, Matthew. 2004a. Discontinuity and the Discourse of Conversion. *Journal of Religion in Africa* 34 (102): 82–109.

———. 2004b. Text and Performance in an African Church: The Book, "Live and Direct." *American Ethnologist* 31 (1): 76–91.

Errington, Frederick K., and Deborah B. Gewertz. 1995. *Articulating Change in the "Last Unknown."* Boulder, CO: Westview.

Fabian, Johannes. 1983. *Time and the Other: How Anthropology Makes Its Object*. New York: Columbia University Press.

———. 1986. *Language and Colonial Power: The Appropriation of Swahili in the Former Belgian Congo, 1880–1938*. Berkeley: University of California Press.

Faubion, James D. 2001. *The Shadows and Lights of Waco: Millenialism Today*. Princeton: Princeton University Press.

Feeley-Harnik, Gillian. 2001. The Mystery of Life in All Its Forms: Religious Dimensions of Culture in Early American Anthropology. In *Religion in an Era of Cultural Studies*, ed. Susan Mizruchi, 140–91. Princeton: Princeton University Press.

Ferguson, James. 1999. *Expectations of Modernity: Myths and Meanings of Urban Life on the Zambian Copperbelt*. Berkeley: University of California Press.

Fliegelman, Jay. 1993. *Declaring Independence: Jefferson, Natural Language, and the Culture of Performance*. Stanford: Stanford University Press.

Forshee, Jill. 2001. *Between the Folds: Stories of Cloth, Lives, and Travels from Sumba*. Honolulu: University of Hawai'i Press.

Forth, Gregory. 1981. *Rindi: An Ethnographic Study of a Traditional Domain in Eastern Sumba*. The Hague: Martinus Nijhoff.

Foster, Robert. 1998. Your Money, Our Money, the Government's Money: Finance and Fetishism in Melanesia. In *Border Fetishisms: Material Objects in Unstable Places*, ed. Patricia Spyer, 60–90. New York: Routledge.

Foucault, Michel. 1972 (1969). *The Archaeology of Knowledge and the Discourse on Language*. Trans. A. M. Sheridan. New York: Pantheon.

———. 1979 (1975). *Discipline and Punish: The Birth of the Prison*. Trans. Alan Sheridan. New York: Vintage Books.

———. 1980 (1975). Prison Talk. In *Power/Knowledge: Selected Interviews and Other Writings, 1972–1977*, ed. Colin Gordon, 37–54. New York: Pantheon.

———. 1983. Afterword: The Subject and Power. In *Michel Foucault: Beyond Structuralism and Hermeneutics*, ed. Hubert L. Dreyfus and Paul Rabinow, 208–26. 2nd ed. Chicago: University of Chicago Press.

———. 1992. What Is Enlightenment? In *Ethics: Subjectivity and Truth; the Essential Works of Michel Foucault, 1954–1984*. Vol. 1. Ed. Paul Rabinow, trans. Catherine Porter, 303–19. New York: The New Press.

Fox, James J., ed. 1988. *To Speak in Pairs: Essays in the Ritual Languages of Eastern Indonesia*. Cambridge: Cambridge University Press.

Frei, Hans W. 1974. *The Eclipse of Biblical Narrative: A Study in Eighteenth and Nineteenth Century Hermeneutics*. New Haven, CT: Yale University Press.

Gal, Susan, and Katherine A. Woolard. 2001. *Languages and Publics: The Making of Authority*. Manchester: St. Jerome.

Gaonkar, Dilip Parameshwar, ed. 1999. Alter/Native Modernities. Special issue of *Public Culture* 11 (1).

Geertz, Clifford. 1973. "Internal Conversion" in Contemporary Bali. In *Interpretation of Cultures*, 170–89. New York: Basic Books.

Geirnaert-Martin, Danielle. 1992. *The Woven Land of Laboya: Socio-Centric Ideas and Values in West Sumba, Eastern Indonesia*. Leiden, Netherlands: Centre of Non-Western Studies.

George, Kenneth M. 1996. *Showing Signs of Violence: The Cultural Politics of a Twentieth-Century Headhunting Ritual*. Berkeley: University of California Press.

Goffman, Erving. 1981. Footing. In *Forms of Talk*, 124–59. Philadelphia: University of Pennsylvania Press.

Gombrich, Richard Francis, and Gananath Obeyesekere, 1988. *Buddhism Transformed: Religious Change in Sri Lanka*. Princeton: Princeton University Press.

Goossens, S. J. P. 1987 (1938). Verslag over het Ressort Oost-Soemba in 1936. In *Gereformeerde Zending op Sumba: Een Bronnenpublicatie*, ed. Th. van den End, 404–7. Alphen aan den Rijn, Netherlands: Raad voor de Zending der Ned. Herv. Kerk, de Zending der Gereformeerde Kerken in Nederland en de Gereformeerde Zendingsbond in de Ned. Herv Kerk.

Graeber, David. 2001. *Toward an Anthropological Theory of Value: The Fake Coin of Our Own Dreams*. New York: Palgrave.

Grice, H. P[aul]. 1957. Meaning. *Philosophical Review* 64: 377–88.

———. 1975. Logic and Conversation. In *Syntax and Semantics*. Vol. 3, *Speech Acts*, eds. Peter Cole and Jerry L. Morgan, 41–58. New York: Academic Press.

Guyer, Jane I. 1995. Introduction: The Currency Interface and Its Dynamics. In *Money Matters: Instability, Values, and Social Payments in the Modern History of West Africa*, ed. Jane I. Guyer, 1–33. Portsmouth, NH: Heinemann.

Habermas, Jürgen. 1987. *The Philosophical Discourse of Modernity*. Trans. Frederick Lawrence. Cambridge: MIT Press.

Hacking, Ian. 1995. *Rewriting the Soul: Multiple Personality and the Sciences of Memory*. Princeton: Princeton University Press.

Hampshire, Stuart. 1971. *Freedom of Mind, and Other Essays*. Princeton: Princeton University Press.

———. 1975. *Freedom of the Individual*. Princeton: Princeton University Press.

Hanks, William F. 1992. The Indexical Ground of Deictic Reference. In *Rethinking Context: Language as an Interactive Phenomenon*, ed. Alessandro Duranti and Charles Goodwin, 43–76. Cambridge: Cambridge University Press.

———. 1996. *Language and Communicative Practices*. Boulder, CO: Westview.

———. 2000. Dialogic Conversations and the Field of Missionary Discourse in Colonial Yucatan. In *Les Rituels du Dialogue: Promenades Ethnolinguistiques en Terres Amérindiennes*, ed. Aurore Monod Becquelin and Philippe Erikson, 235–54. Nanterre, France: Société d'Ethnologie.

Hannerz, Ulf. 1996. *Transnational Connections: Culture, People, Places*. London: Routledge.

Harding, Susan Friend. 1991. Representing Fundamentalism: The Problem of the Repugnant Cultural Other. *Social Research* 58 (2): 373–93.

———. 2000. *The Book of Jerry Falwell: Fundamentalist Language and Politics*. Princeton: Princeton University Press.

Haripranata, H. 1984. *Ceritera Sejarah Gereja Katolik Sumba dan Sumbawa*. Ende, Indonesia: Arnoldus.

Harris, Harriet A. 1998. *Fundamentalism and Evangelicals*. Oxford: Clarendon Press.

Hart, K. 1986. Heads or Tails: Two Sides of the Coin. *Man*, n.s., 21: 637–56.

Hefner, Robert W. 1985. *Hindu Javanese: Tengger Tradition and Islam*. Princeton: Princeton University Press.

———, ed. 1993. *Conversion to Christianity: Historical and Anthropological Perspectives on a Great Transformation*. Berkeley: University of California Press.

Heidegger, Martin. 1962 (1927). *Being and Time*. Trans. J. Macquarrie and E. Robinson. New York: Harper and Row.

———. 1977 (1938). The Age of the World Picture. In *The Question Concerning Technology and Other Essays*. Trans. William Lovitt, 115–54. New York: Harper and Row.

Herbert, Christopher. 1991. *Culture and Anomie: Ethnographic Imagination in the Nineteenth Century*. Chicago: University of Chicago Press.

Hill, Jane H. 1985. The Grammar of Consciousness and the Consciousness of Grammar. *American Ethnologist* 12 (4): 725–37.

Hirschkind, Charles. 2001. The Ethics of Listening: Cassette-Sermon Audition in Contemporary Egypt. *American Ethnologist* 28 (3): 623–49.

Hirschman, Albert O. 1977. *The Passions and the Interests: Political Arguments for Capitalism before Its Triumph*. Princeton: Princeton University Press.

Hobsbawm, Eric, and Terence Ranger, eds. 1983. *The Invention of Tradition*. Cambridge: Cambridge University Press.

Holtrop, Pieter N., and Jacqueline A. C. Vel. 1995. Evangelie en Paraingu. In *De Zending Voorbij: Terugblik op de Relatie Tussen de Gerformeerde Kerken in Nederland en de Christelijke Kerk van Sumba, 1942–1992*, ed. W. B. van Halsema et al., 227–46. Kampen, Netherlands: J. H. Kok.

Horton, Robin, and Ruth Finnegan. 1973. *Modes of Thought: Essays on Thinking in Western and Non-Western Societies*. London: Faber.

Hoskins, Janet. 1988. The Drum Is the Shaman, the Spear Guides His Voice. *Social Science and Medicine* 27 (2): 819–29.

———. 1993. *The Play of Time: Kodi Perspectives on Calendars, History, and Exchange*. Berkeley: University of California Press.

———. 1998. *Biographical Objects: How Things Tell the Stories of People's Lives*. New York: Routledge.

Huber, Mary Taylor, and Nancy C. Lutkehaus. 1999. Introduction: Gendered Missions at Home and Abroad. In *Gendered Missions: Women and Men in Missionary Discourse and Practice*, ed. Mary Taylor Huber and Nancy C. Lutkehaus, 1–38. Ann Arbor: University of Michigan Press.

Hutchinson, Sharon E. 1996. *Nuer Dilemmas: Coping with Money, War, and the State*. Berkeley: University of California Press.

Irvine, Judith T. 1982. The Creation of Identity in Spirit Mediumship and Possession. In *Semantic Anthropology*, ed. David Parkin. London: Academic Press.

―――. 1989. When Talk Isn't Cheap: Language and Political Economy. *American Ethnologist* 16: 248–67.

―――. 2001. "Style" as Distinctiveness: The Culture and Ideology of Linguistic Differentiation. In *Style and Sociolinguistic Variation*, ed. P. Eckert and J. R. Rickford, 21–43. Cambridge: Cambridge University Press.

Irvine, Judith T., and Susan Gal. 2000. Language Ideology and Linguistic Differentiation. In *Regimes of Language: Ideologies, Politics, and Identities*, ed. Paul V. Kroskrity, 35–83. Santa Fe, NM: School of American Research Press.

Iskandar, Margaharta, and Siliwoloe Djoeroemana. 1994. Kemiskinan dan Pembangunan: Kasus Kabupaten Sumba Barat. In *Kemiskinan dan Pembangunan di Propinsi Nusa Tenggara Timur*, 56–77 Jakarta: Yayasan Obor Indonesia.

Jakobson, Roman. 1957. *The Framework of Language*. Ann Arbor: University of Michigan Press.

Kahn, Joel S. 1993. *Constituting the Minangkabau: Peasants, Culture, and Modernity in Colonial Indonesia*. Oxford: Berg.

Kammerer, Cornelia A. 1990. Customs and Christian Conversion among Akha Highlanders of Burma and Thailand. *American Ethnologist* 17 (2): 227–91.

Kant, Immanuel. 1956 (1785). Foundations of the Metaphysics of Morals. In *Foundations of the Metaphysics of Morals and What Is Enlightenment?* trans. Lewis White Beck, 3–83. Indianapolis: Bobbs-Merrill.

Kantor Statistik. 1987. *Sumba Barat Dalam Angka 1986*. Waingapu, Indonesia: Kantor Statistik Kabupaten Sumba Barat.

Kapita, Oemboe Hina. 1965. *Sedjarah Pergumulan Indjil di Sumba*. Pajeti, Indonesia: Lembaga Penerbitan Kristen.

―――. 1976a. *Masyarakat Sumba dan Adat Istiadatnya*. Waingapu, Indonesia: Dewan Penata Layanan Gereja Kristen Sumba.

―――. 1976b. *Sumba di dalam Jangkauan Jaman*. Waingapu, Indonesia: Panitia Penerbit Gereja Kristen Sumba.

―――. 1987. *Lawiti Luluku Humba/Pola Peribahasa Sumba*. N.p.: Lembaga Penyelidikan Kebudayaan Selatana Tenri.

―――. n.d. *Pamangu Ndewa/Perjamuan Dewa*. Ende, Indonesia: Arnoldus.

Keane, Webb. 1997a. Knowing One's Place: National Language and the Idea of the Local in Eastern Indonesia. *Cultural Anthropology* 12 (1): 1–27.

―――. 1997b. Religious Language. *Annual Review of Anthropology* 26: 47–71.

―――. 1997c. *Signs of Recognition: Powers and Hazards of Representation in an Indonesian Society*. Berkeley: University of California Press.

―――. 2001. Voice. In *Key Terms in Language and Culture*, ed. Alessandro Duranti, 268–71. Malden, MA: Blackwell.

―――. 2003a. Public Speaking: On Indonesian as the Language of the Nation, in "Technologies of Public Persuasion," ed. Elizabeth Povinelli and Dilip Gaonkar. Special issue, *Public Culture* 15 (3): 503–30.

―――. 2003b. Self-Interpretation, Agency, and the Objects of Anthropology: Reflections on a Genealogy. *Comparative Studies in Society and History* 45 (2): 222–48.

———. 2003c. Semiotics and the Social Analysis of Material Things. In "Words and Beyond: Linguistic and Semiotic Studies of Sociocultural Order," ed. Paul Manning. Special issue, *Language and Communication* 23 (2–3): 409–25.

———. 2004. Language and Religion. In *A Companion to Linguistic Anthropology,* ed. Alessandro Duranti, 431–48. Malden, MA: Blackwell.

———. 2005. The Hazards of New Clothes: What Signs Make Possible. In *The Art of Clothing: A Pacific Experience,* ed. Susanne Küchler and Graeme Were, 1–16. London: UCL Press.

Keyes, Charles F. 1996. Being Protestant Christians in Southeast Asian Worlds. *Journal of Southeast Asian Studies* 27: 280–92.

Kipp, Rita Smith. 1990. *The Early Years of a Dutch Colonial Mission: The Karo Field.* Ann Arbor: University of Michigan Press.

———. 1993. *Dissociated Identities: Ethnicity, Religion, and Class in an Indonesian Society.* Ann Arbor: University of Michigan Press.

Kipp, Rita Smith, and Susan Rodgers, eds. 1987. *Indonesian Religions in Transition.* Tucson: University of Arizona Press.

Kirsch, Stuart. 2001. Lost Worlds: Environmental Disaster, "Culture Loss," and the Law. *Current Anthropology* 42 (2): 167–98.

Klaniczay, Gábor. 1990. Religious Movements and Christian Culture: A Pattern of Centripetal and Centrifugal Orientations. In *The Uses of Supernatural Power: The Transformation of Popular Religion in Medieval and Early-Modern Europe.* Trans. Susan Singerman, 28–50. Princeton: Princeton University Press.

Knauft, Bruce M. 2002. *Exchanging the Past: A Rainforest World of Before and After.* Chicago: University of Chicago Press.

Koentjaraningrat. 1975. *Anthropology in Indonesia: A Bibliographical Review.* The Hague: Martinus Nijhoff.

Koerner, Joseph Leo. 2004. *The Reformation of the Image.* Chicago: University of Chicago Press.

Krijger, L. P. 1927. De Opleidingsschool te Karoeni voor Inlandsche Helpers bij den Dienst des Woords. In *Tot Dankbaarheid Genoop: Gedenkboek ter Gelegenheid van den 25-Jarigen Zendingsarbeid op Soemba vanwege de Gereformeerde Kerken in Groningen, Drente en Overijsel,* ed. M. Meijering et al., 148–51. Kampen, Netherlands: J. H. Kok.

———. 1932. De Zending en de Godsdienst der Heiden. *De Macedoniër* 36: 54–61, 84–96, 151–59.

Kroskrity, Paul V., ed. 2000. *Regimes of Language: Ideologies, Polities, and Identities.* Santa Fe, NM: School of American Research Press.

———. 2004. Language Ideologies. In *A Companion to Linguistic Anthropology,* ed. Alessandro Duranti, 496–517. Malden, MA: Blackwell.

Kruyt (Kruijt), Albert C. 1906. *Het Animisme in den Indischen Archipel.* 's Gravenhage, Netherlands: Marinus Nijhoff.

———. 1921. Verslag van eene reis over het eiland Soemba. *Tijdschrift van het Koninklijk Nederlandsch Aardrijkskundig Genootschap,* 2nd ser., 37: 513–53.

——. 1924. The Appropriation of Christianity by Primitive Heathen in Central Celebes. *International Review of Missions* 13: 267–75.

——. 1936. *Zending en Volkskracht.* 's-Gravenhage: Boekhandel en Uitgeverij voor Inwendige en Uitwendige Zending.

Kuipers, Joel C. 1988. The Pattern of Prayer in Weyéwa. In *To Speak in Pairs: Essays on the Ritual Languages of Eastern Indonesia,* ed. James J. Fox. Cambridge: Cambridge University Press.

——. 1990. *Power in Performance: The Creation of Textual Authority in Weyewa Ritual Speech.* Philadelphia: University of Pennsylvania Press.

——. 1998. *Language, Identity, and Marginality in Indonesia: The Changing Nature of Ritual Speech on the Island of Sumba.* Cambridge: Cambridge University Press.

Kuyper, Abraham. 1898. *Encyclopedia of Sacred Theology: Its Principles.* Trans. J. Hendrik de Vries. New York: Scribners.

——. 1899. *Calvinism: Six Lectures Delivered in the Theological Seminary at Princeton.* New York: Fleming H. Revell.

Lambooy, P. J. 1927. Midden-Soemba. In *Tot Dankbaarheid Genoopt: Gedenkboek ter Gelegenheid van de 25-Jarigen Zendingsarbeid op Soemba vanwege de Gereformeerde Kerken in Groningen, Drente en Overijsel,* ed. M. Meijering, P. I. Jongbloed, W. W. Smitt, and J. H. Lammertsma, 78–86. Kampen, Netherlands: J. H. Kok.

——. 1930. De Godsnaam op Soemba. *De Macedoniër* 34: 275–84.

——. 1937. Het Begrip "Marapoe" in den Godsdienst van Oost Soemba. *Bijdragen tot de Taal, Land- en Volkenkunde van Nederlandsch-Indië* 95: 425–39.

——. 1987a (1932). Aan Deputaten Sumba-Zending. 's Gravenhage, 25 Juli 1931. In *Gereformeerde Zending op Sumba: Een Bronnenpublicatie,* ed. Th. van den End, 342–46. Alphen aan den Rijn, Netherlands: Raad voor de Zending der Ned. Herv. Kerk, de Zending der Gereformeerde Kerken in Nederland en de Gereformeerde Zendingsbond in de Ned. Herv Kerk.

——. 1987b (1932). Zending en Volksgewoonten op Soemba. In *Gereformeerde Zending op Sumba: Een Bronnenpublicatie,* ed. Th. van den End, 340–42. Alphen aan den Rijn, Netherlands: Raad voor de Zending der Ned. Herv. Kerk, de Zending der Gereformeerde Kerken in Nederland en de Gereformeerde Zendingsbond in de Ned. Herv Kerk.

Lancaster, Roger N. 1988. *Thanks to God and the Revolution: Popular Religion and Class Consciousness in the New Nicaragua.* New York: Columbia University Press.

Lansz, C. E. 1919. Memorie van Overgave van de Afdeling Soemba. Typescript, Algemeen Rijksarchief, The Hague.

Latour, Bruno. 1993 (1991). *We Have Never Been Modern.* Trans. Catherine Porter. Cambridge: Harvard University Press.

Lee, Benjamin. 1997. *Talking Heads: Language, Metalanguage, and the Semiotics of Subjectivity.* Durham, NC: Duke University Press.

Lev, Daniel S. 1972. *Islamic Courts in Indonesia: A Study in the Political Bases of Legal Institutions.* Berkeley: University of California Press.

Locke, John. 1952 (1690). *The Second Treatise of Government,* ed. with introduction by Thomas P. Peardon. Indianapolis: Bobbs-Merrill.

———. 1975 (1690). *An Essay Concerning Human Understanding.* Ed. P. H. Nidditch. Oxford: Clarendon Press.

Löwith, Karl. 1949. *Meaning in History: The Theological Implications of the Philosophy of History.* Chicago: University of Chicago Press.

Lucy, John A., ed. 1993. *Reflexive Language: Reported Speech and Metapragmatics.* Cambridge: Cambridge University Press.

Luhrmann, Tanya. 2004. Metakinesis: How God Becomes Intimate in Contemporary U.S. Christianity. *American Anthropologist* 106 (3): 518–28.

Luijendijk, P. J. 1946. *Zeven Jaar Zendingswerk op Soemba (1939–1946).* Groningen, Netherlands: J. Niemeijer.

Lukács, Georg. 1971 (1922). Reification and the Consciousness of the Proletariat. In *History and Class Consciousness: Studies in Marxist Dialectics.* Trans. Rodney Livingstone, 83–222. Cambridge: MIT Press.

MacCormack, Sabine. 1991. *Religion in the Andes: Vision and Imagination in Early Colonial Peru.* Princeton: Princeton University Press.

Mack [Crew], Phyllis. 1978. *Calvinist Preaching and Iconoclasm in the Netherlands, 1544–1569.* Cambridge: Cambridge University Press.

———. 1992. *Visionary Women: Ecstatic Prophecy in Seventeenth-Century England.* Berkeley: University of California Press.

Mahmood, Saba. 2005. *Politics of Piety: The Islamic Revival and the Feminist Subject.* Princeton: Princeton University Press.

Malley, Brian. 2004. *How the Bible Works: An Anthropological Study of Evangelical Biblicism.* Walnut Creek, CA: AltaMira Press.

Marx, Karl. 1978 (1852). The Eighteenth Brumaire of Louis Bonaparte. In *The Marx-Engels Reader,* ed. Robert C. Tucker, 594–617. 2nd ed. New York: W. W. Norton, 1978.

———. 1967a (1887). *Capital: A Critique of Political Economy.* Vol. 1, *A Critical Analysis of Capitalist Production.* Trans. Samuel Moore and Edward Aveling. New York: International Publishers.

———. 1967b (1894). *Capital: A Critique of Political Economy.* Vol. 3, *The Process of Capitalist Production as a Whole.* New York: International.

———. 1978a (1845–1846). The German Ideology, Part 1. In *The Marx-Engels Reader.* Ed. Robert C. Tucker, 146–200. New York: Norton.

———. 1978b (1845). Theses on Feuerbach. In *The Marx-Engels Reader.* Ed. Robert C. Tucker, 143–45. New York: Norton.

Masuzawa, Tomoko. 1993. *In Search of Dreamtime: The Quest for the Origin of Religion.* Chicago: University of Chicago Press.

———. 2005. *The Invention of World Religions: Or, How European Universalism Was Preserved in the Language of Pluralism.* Chicago: University of Chicago Press.

Mauss, Marcel. 1990 (1925). *The Gift: The Form and Reason for Exchange in Archaic Societies.* Trans. W. D. Halls. New York: Norton.

May, Hermann-Josef, Felicitas Mispagel, and Franz Pfister. 1982. *Marapu und Karitu: Mission und junge Kirche auf der insel Sumba.* Bonn: Hofbauer.

McNeill, John T. 1954. *The History and Character of Calvinism.* New York: Oxford University Press.

Meijering, M., P. I. Jongbloed, W. W. Smitt, and J. H. Lammertsma, eds. 1927. *Tot Dankbaarheid Genoopt: Gedenkboek ter Gelegenheid van de 25-Jarigen Zendingsarbeid op Soemba vanwege de Gereformeerde Kerken in Groningen, Drente en Overijsel.* Kampen, Netherlands: J. H. Kok.

Meyer, Birgit. 1998. "Make a Complete Break with the Past": Memory and Post-colonial Modernity in Ghanaian Pentecostalist Discourse. *Journal of Religion in Africa* 34 (3): 316–49.

———. 1999. *Translating the Devil: Religion and Modernity among the Ewe in Ghana.* London: Edinburgh University Press.

———. 2003. Ghanaian Popular Cinema and the Magic in and of Film. In *Magic and Modernity: Interfaces of Revelation and Concealment,* ed. Birgit Meyer and Peter Pels, 200–22. Stanford: Stanford University Press.

———. 2004. "Praise the Lord": Popular Cinema and Pentecostalite Style in Ghana's New Public Sphere. *American Anthropologist* 31 (1): 92–110.

Miller, Daniel. 1987. *Material Culture and Mass Consumption.* Oxford: Basil Blackwell.

Milton, John. 1962 (1649). *Eikonoklastes.* In *Complete Prose Works of John Milton.* Vol. 3, *1648–1649.* Ed. Merritt Y. Hughes, 335–601. New Haven, CT: Yale University Press.

Mitchell, Timothy. 1988. *Colonising Egypt.* Berkeley: University of California Press.

Mitchell, W. J. T. 1986. *Iconology: Image, Text, Ideology.* Chicago: University of Chicago Press.

Miyazaki, Hirokazu. 2000. Faith and Its Fulfillment: Agency, Exchange, and the Fijian Aesthetics of Completion. *American Ethnologist* 27 (1): 31–51.

Moran, Richard. 2001. *Authority and Estrangement: An Essay on Self-Knowledge.* Princeton: Princeton University Press.

Morgan, Lewis Henry. 1877. *Ancient Society; or, Researches in the Lines of Human Progress from Savagery, through Barbarism, to Civilization.* London: Macmillan.

Myers, Fred R. 2002. *Painting Culture: The Making of an Aboriginal High Art.* Durham, NC: Duke University Press.

Nieman, Susan. 2002. *Evil in Modern Thought: An Alternative History of Philosophy.* Princeton: Princeton University Press.

Niesel, Wilhelm. 1956 (1938). *The Theology of Calvin.* Trans. Harold Knight. Philadelphia: Westminster.

Nussbaum, Martha C. 1995. Objectification. *Philosophy and Public Affairs* 24 (4): 249–91.

Onvlee, L. 1973a (1952). De Betekenis van Vee en Veebezit. In *Cultuur als Antwoord*, 10–26. Verhandelingen van het KILTV, 66. 's Gravenhage, Netherlands: Martinus Nijhoff.

———. 1973b (1958). Lucas 2 in het Sumbaas. In *Cultuur als Antwoord*, 206–10. Verhandelingen van het KILTV, 66. 's Gravenhage, Netherlands: Martinus Nijhoff.

———. 1973c (1933). Na Huri Hàpa. In *Cultuur als Antwoord*, 27–45. Verhandelingen van het KILTV, 66. 's Gravenhage, Netherlands: Martinus Nijhoff.

———. 1973d (1938). Over de Weergave van "Heilig." In *Cultuur als Antwoord*, 222–31. Verhandelingen van het KILTV, 66. 's Gravenhage, Netherlands: Martinus Nijhoff.

———. 1973e. Over de Weergave van Pneuma. In *Cultuur als Antwoord*, 211–19. Verhandelingen van het KILTV, 66. 's Gravenhage, Netherlands: Martinus Nijhoff.

———. 1973f (1957). Taalvernieuwing uit het Evangelie. In *Cultuur als Antwoord*, 197–205. Verhandelingen van het KILTV, 66.'s Gravenhage, Netherlands: Martinus Nijhoff.

———. 1973g. Tana Mema, Tana Dawa. In *Cultuur als Antwoord*, 114–32. Verhandelingen van het KILTV, 66. 's Gravenhage, Netherlands: Martinus Nijhoff.

———. 1973h. Woord en Antwoord, Zending en Adat. In *Cultuur als Antwoord*, 133–57. Verhandelingen van het KILTV, 66. 's Gravenhage, Netherlands: Martinus Nijhoff.

———. 1980 (1952). The Significance of Livestock on Sumba. In *The Flow of Life: Essays on Eastern Indonesia*. Ed. James J. Fox, trans. James J. Fox and Henny Fokker-Bakker. Cambridge: Harvard University Press.

———. 1987 (1936). Aan het Hoofdbestuur van het Nederlands Bijbelgenootschap, Waikabubak, 20 Mei 1936. In *Gereformeerde Zending op Sumba: Een Bronnenpublicatie*, ed. Th. van den End, 401–2. Alphen aan den Rijn, Netherlands: Raad voor de Zending der Ned. Herv. Kerk, de Zending der Gereformeerde Kerken in Nederland en de Gereformeerde Zendingsbond in de Ned. Herv Kerk.

Orta, Andrew. 2002. "Living the Past Another Way": Reinstrumentalized Missionary Selves in Aymara Mission Fields." *Anthropological Quarterly* 65 (4): 707–43.

Ouspensky, Leonid. 1992 (1978). *Theology of the Icon*. Vol. 1. Trans. Anthony Gythiel. Crestwood, NY: St. Vladimir's Seminary Press.

Oxford English Dictionary. 1989. 2nd ed., prepared by J. A. Simpson and E. S. C. Weiner. Oxford: Clarendon Press.

Parmentier, Richard J. 1994. The Semiotic Regimentation of Social Life. In *Signs in Society: Studies in Semiotic Anthropology*, 125–55. Bloomington: Indiana University Press.

Pascal, Blaise. 1958. *Pascal's Pensées*. Trans. W. F. Trotter. New York: E. P. Dutton.

Peacock, James L., and Ruel W. Tyson Jr. 1989. *Pilgrims of Paradox: Calvinism and Experience among the Primitive Baptists of the Blue Ridge.* Washington, DC: Smithsonian Institution Press.

Peel, J. D. Y. 1995. For Who Hath Despised the Day of Small Things? Missionary Narratives and Historical Anthropology. *Comparative Studies in Society and History* 37 (3): 581–607.

Peirce, Charles S. 1934. *Collected Papers of Charles Sanders Peirce.* Vol. 5, ed. Charles Hartshorne and Paul Weiss. Cambridge: Harvard University Press.

Pelikan, Jaroslav. 1989. *Christian Doctrine and Modern Culture (since 1700).* Chicago: University of Chicago Press.

———. 1990. *Imago Dei: The Byzantine Apologia for Icons.* Princeton: Princeton University Press.

———. 2003. *Credo: Historical and Theological Guide to Creeds and Confessions of Faith in the Western Tradition.* New Haven, CT: Yale University Press.

Pelikan, Jaroslav, and Valerie Hotchkiss, eds. 2003a. *Creeds and Confessions of Faith in the Christian Tradition.* Vol. 1, Pt. 1, *Rules of Faith in the Early Church;* Pt. 2, *Eastern Orthodox Affirmations of Faith;* Pt. 3, *Medieval Western Statements of Faith.* New Haven, CT: Yale University Press.

———. 2003b. *Creeds and Confessions of Faith in the Christian Tradition.* Vol. 3, Pt. 5, *Statements of Faith in Modern Christianity.* New Haven, CT: Yale University Press.

Pels, Peter. 1999. *A Politics of Presence: Contacts between Missionaries and Waluguru in Late Colonial Tanganiyaka.* Amsterdam: Harwood.

———. 2003. Spirits of Modernity: Alfred Wallace, Edward Tylor, and the Visual Politics of Fact. In *Magic and Modernity: Interfaces of Revelation and Concealment,* ed. Birgit Meyer and Peter Pels, 241–71. Stanford: Stanford University Press.

Pemberton, John. 1994. *On the Subject of "Java."* Ithaca, NY: Cornell University Press.

Pietz, William. 1985. The Problem of the Fetish, I. *Res* 9: 5–17.

———. 1987. The Problem of the Fetish, II: The Origin of the Fetish. *Res* 13: 23–45.

———. 1997. Death of the Deodand: Accursed Objects and the Money Value of Human Life. *Res* 31: 97–108.

Pinney, Christopher. 2005. Things Happen: Or, From Which Moment Does That Object Come? In *Materiality,* ed. Daniel Miller, 256–72. Durham, NC: Duke University Press.

Pol, D. 1931. De Godsnaam op Soemba. *De Macedoniër* 35: 14–20.

Polanyi, Karl. 1944. *The Great Transformation: The Political and Economic Origins of Our Time.* Boston: Beacon Press.

Poovey, Mary. 1998. *A History of the Modern Fact: Problems of Knowledge in the Sciences of Wealth and Society.* Chicago: University of Chicago Press.

Povinelli, Elizabeth A. 2002. *The Cunning of Recognition: Indigenous Alterities and the Making of Australian Multiculturalism.* Durham, NC: Duke University Press.

Prakash, Gyan. 2003. Between Science and Superstition: Religion and the Modern Subject of the Nation in Colonial India. In *Magic and Modernity: Interfaces of Revelation and Concealment,* ed. Birgit Meyer and Peter Pels, 39–59. Stanford: Stanford University Press.

Priest, Robert J. 2001. Missionary Positions: Christian, Modernist, Postmodernist. *Current Anthropology* 42 (1): 29–68.

Rafael, Vicente L. 1993. *Contracting Colonialism: Translation and Christian Conversion in Tagalog Society under Early Spanish Rule.* Durham, NC: Duke University Press.

Ranger, T. O., and John Weller, eds. 1975. *Themes in the Christian History of Central Africa.* Berkeley: University of California Press.

Rapport inzake de Zending op Soemba. 1965. Groningen, Netherlands: J. Neijmeijer.

Reenders, Hommo. 1995. Zending Voor de Oorlog: De Periode 1881–1942. In *De Zending Voorbij: Terugblik op de Relatie Tussen de Gerformeerde Kerken in Nederland en de Christelijke Kerk van Sumba 1942–1992,* ed. W. B. van Halsema et al., 1–33. Kampen, Netherlands: J. H. Kok.

Ricklefs, M. C. 1981. *A History of Modern Indonesia, c. 1300 to the Present.* Bloomington: Indiana University Press.

Riekerk, G. H. M. 1934. Grensregling Anakalang, Oemboe Ratoe Nggai. Typescript no. H975 (2). Archives of the Koninklijk Instituut voor Taal-, Land- en Volkenkunde, Leiden, Netherlands.

———. 1941. Dagboek. Typescript no. H1975 (2). Archives of the Koninklijk Instituut voor Taal-, Land- en Volkenkunde, Leiden, Netherlands.

Robbins, Joel. 2003. On the Paradoxes of Global Pentecostalism and the Perils of Continuity Thinking. *Religion* 33: 221–31.

———. 2004a. *Becoming Sinners: Christianity and Moral Torment in a Papua New Guinea Society.* Berkeley: University of California Press.

———. 2004b. The Globalization of Pentecostal and Charismatic Christianity. *Annual Review of Anthropology* 33: 117–43.

Rodgers Siregar, Susan. 1981. *Adat, Islam, and Christianity in a Batak Homeland.* Athens: Ohio University Center for International Studies.

Rosaldo, Michelle Z. 1982. The Things We Do with Words: Ilongot Speech Acts and Speech Act Theory in Philosophy. *Language in Society* 11 (2): 203–37.

Rot-van der Gaast, A. T., and W. B. van Halsema. 1984. Kerk-zijn temidden van Veranderingen: Verslag van een Bezoek aan de Kerken van Sumba en Timor. Typescript. Archives of the Hendrik Kraemer Instituut, Oegstgeest, Netherlands.

Rubin, Gayle. 1975. The Traffic in Women: Notes on the "Political Economy" of Sex. In *Toward an Anthropology of Women,* ed. Reyna R. Reiter, 157–210. New York: Monthly Review Press.

Rutherford, Danilyn. 2003. *Raiding the Land of the Foreigners: The Limits of the Nation on an Indonesian Frontier.* Princeton: Princeton University Press.

Sahlins, Marshall. 1996. The Sadness of Sweetness: The Native Anthropology of Western Cosmology. *Current Anthropology* 37 (3): 395–428.

Saler, Benson. 1993. *Conceptualizing Religion: Immanent Anthropologists, Transcendent Natives, and Unbounded Categories.* Leiden, Netherlands: E. J. Brill.

Sanneh, Lamin. 1989. *Translating the Message: The Missionary Impact on Culture.* Maryknoll, NY: Orbis Books.

Sartre, Jean-Paul. 1956 (1943). *Being and Nothingness: A Phenomenological Essay on Ontology.* Trans. Hazel E. Barnes. New York: Philosophical Library.

Saussure, Ferdinand de. 1983 (1915). *Course in General Linguistics.* Trans. Roy Harris. La Salle, IL: Open Court Press.

Schieffelin, Bambi B. 2000. Introducing Kaluli Literacy: A Chronology of Influences. In *Regimes of Language: Ideologies, Polities, and Identities,* ed. Paul V. Kroskrity, 293–327. Santa Fe, NM: School of American Research Press.

———. 2002. Marking Time: The Dichotomizing Discourse of Multiple Temporalities. *Current Anthropology* 43: S5–S16.

Schieffelin, Bambi B., Kathryn Woolard, and Paul V. Kroskrity, eds. 1998. *Language Ideologies: Practice and Theory.* Oxford: Oxford University Press.

Schneewind, J. B. 1998. *The Invention of Autonomy: A History of Modern Moral Philosophy.* Cambridge: Cambridge University Press.

Schneider, Jane, and Shirley Lindenbaum, eds. 1987. "Frontiers of Christian Evangelism." Special issue, *American Ethnologist* 14 (1).

Schrauwers, Albert. 2000. *Colonial "Reformation" in the Highlands of Central Sulawesi, Indonesia, 1892–1995.* Toronto: University of Toronto Press.

Schulte Nordholt, Henk, ed. 1997. *Outward Appearances: Dressing, State, and Society in Indonesia.* Leiden, Netherlands: Koninklijk Instituut voor Taal-, Land- en Volkenkunde Press.

Scott, Joan W. 1991. The Evidence of Experience. *Critical Inquiry* 17: 773–97.

Searle, John R. 1983. *Intentionality: An Essay in the Philosophy of Mind.* Cambridge: Cambridge University Press.

Sebeok, Thomas A. 1991. Fetish. In *A Sign Is Just a Sign,* 116–27. Bloomington: University of Indiana Press.

Shapin, Steven. 1994. *A Social History of Truth: Civility and Science in Seventeenth-Century England.* Chicago: University of Chicago Press.

Sharf, Robert H. 1995. The Zen of Japanese Nationalism. In *Curators of the Buddha: The Study of Buddhism under Colonialism,* ed. Donald S. Lopez Jr., 107–60. Chicago: University of Chicago Press.

———. 2000. The Rhetoric of Experience and the Study of Religion. *Journal of Consciousness Studies* 7 (11–12): 267–87.

Shell, Marc. 1982. *Money, Language, and Thought: Literary and Philosophical Economies from the Medieval to the Modern Era.* Baltimore: Johns Hopkins.

Siegel, James T. 1986. *Solo in the New Order: Language and Hierarchy in an Indonesian City.* Princeton: Princeton University Press.

Silverstein, Michael. 1976. Shifters, Linguistic Categories, and Cultural Description. In *Meaning in Anthropology*, ed. Keith H. Basso and Henry A. Selby, 11–56. Albuquerque: University of New Mexico Press.

———. 1979. Language Structure and Linguistic Ideology. In *The Elements: A Parasession on Linguistic Units and Levels*, ed. Paul R. Clyne, William F. Hanks, and Carol L. Hofbauer, 193–247. Chicago: Chicago Linguistic Society.

———. 1993. Metapragmatic Discourse and Metapragmatic Function. In *Reflexive Language: Reported Speech and Metapragmatics*, ed. John A. Lucy, 33–58. Cambridge: Cambridge University Press.

———. 1998. The Uses and Utility of Ideology. In *Language Ideologies: Practice and Theory*, ed. Bambi B. Schieffelin, Kathryn A. Woolard, and Paul V. Kroskrity, 123–45. New York: Oxford University Press.

———. 2003. Translation, Transduction, Transformation: Skating "Glossando" on Thin Semiotic Ice. In *Translating Cultures: Perspectives on Translation and Anthropology*, ed. Paula G. Rubel and Abraham Rosman, 75–105. Oxford: Berg.

Silverstein, Michael, and Greg Urban, eds. 1996. *Natural Histories of Discourse*. Chicago: University of Chicago Press.

Simmel, Georg. 1990. *The Philosophy of Money*. Trans. Tom Bottomore and David Frisby. London: Routledge.

Sinaga, Martin L., Johana Pabontong-Tangirerung, and Steve Gaspersz, eds. 2004. *Misiologi Kontekstual: Th. Kobong dan Pergulatan Kekristenan Lokal di Indonesia*. Jakarta: Sekolah Tinggi Teologi Jakarta.

Skorupski, John. 1976. *Symbol and Theory: A Philosophical Study of Theories of Religion in Social Anthropology*. Cambridge: Cambridge University Press.

Smith, Jonathan Z. 1982. *Imagining Religion: From Babylon to Jonestown*. Chicago: University of Chicago Press.

Snouck Hurgronje, C. 1906 (1893–1894). *The Achehnese*. Trans. A. W. S. O'Sullivan. Leyden: E. J. Brill.

Soeffner, Hans-Georg. 1997. *The Order of Rituals: The Interpretation of Everyday Life*. Trans. Mara Luckmann. New Brunswick, NJ: Transaction.

Special Assembly of Missionaries. 1987 (1934). De Bijzondere Vergadering van Missionaíre Díenaren des Woords aan Deputaten Sumba-Zending, Mei–Juni 1934. In *Gereformeerde Zending op Sumba: Een Bronnenpublicatie*, ed. Th. van den End, 369–70. Alphen aan den Rijn, Netherlands: Raad voor de Zending der Ned. Herv. Kerk, de Zending der Gereformeerde Kerken in Nederland en de Gereformeerde Zendingsbond in de Ned. Herv Kerk.

Spyer, Patricia. 1996. Serial Conversion/Conversion to Seriality: Religion, State, and Number in Aru, Eastern Indonesia. In *Conversion to Modernities: The Globalization of Christianity*, ed. Peter van der Veer, 171–98. New York: Routledge.

———. 2000. *The Memory of Trade: Modernity's Entanglements on an Eastern Indonesian Island*. Durham, NC: Duke University Press.

Stanley, Brian. 2001. Christian Missions and the Enlightenment: A Reevaluation. In Christian Missions and the Enlightenment, ed. Brian Stanley, 1–21. Grand Rapids, MI: William R. Eerdmans.

Steedly, Mary Margaret. 1993. Hanging without a Rope: Narrative Experience in Colonial and Postcolonial Karoland. Princeton: Princeton University Press.

———. 1996. The Importance of Proper Names: Language and "National" Identity in Colonial Karoland. American Ethnologist 23 (3): 441–75.

Stewart, Charles, and Rosalind Shaw, eds. 1994. Syncretism/Anti-syncretism: The Politics of Religious Synthesis. London: Routledge.

Stocking, George W. 1968. Race, Culture, and Evolution: Essays in the History of Anthropology. New York: Free Press.

Stoler, Ann Laura. 2002. Carnal Knowledge and Imperial Power: Race and the Intimate in Colonial Rule. Berkeley: University of California Press.

Sweetser, Eve. 1987. The Definition of Lie: An Examination of the Folk Models Underlying a Semantic Prototype. In Cultural Models in Language and Thought, ed. Dorothy Holland and Naomi Quinn, 43–66. Cambridge: Cambridge University Press.

Swellengrebel, J. L. 1974. In Leijdeckers Voetspoor: Anderhalve Eeuw Bijbelvertaling en Taalkunde in de Indonesische Talen. Verhandelingen van het Koninklijk Instituut voor Taal-, Land- en Volkenkunde 68. 's Gravenhage, Netherlands: Martinus Nijhoff.

Tanner, Norman. 1990. Decrees of the Ecumenical Councils. Vol. 2. Washington, DC: Georgetown University Press.

Targoff, Ramie. 2001. Common Prayer: The Language of Public Devotion in Early Modern England. Chicago: University of Chicago Press.

Taylor, Charles. 1985. What Is Human Agency? In Human Action and Agency: Philosophical Papers I, 15–44. Cambridge: Cambridge University Press.

———. 1989. Sources of the Self: The Making of Modern Identity. Cambridge: Harvard University Press.

———. 1999. Two Theories of Modernity. Public Culture 11 (1): 153–74.

Thomas, Keith. 1971. Religion and the Decline of Magic. New York: Charles Scribners.

Thomas, Nicholas. 1991. Entangled Objects: Exchange, Material Culture, and Colonialism in the Pacific. Cambridge: Harvard University Press.

———. 1994. Colonialism's Culture: Anthropology, Travel, and Government. Princeton, NJ: Princeton University Press.

Tomlinson, Matt. 2004. Ritual, Risk, and Danger: Chain Prayers in Fiji. American Anthropologist. 106 (1): 6–16.

Trilling, Lionel. 1972. Sincerity and Authenticity. Cambridge: Harvard University Press.

Troeltsch, Ernst. 1931 (1911). The Social Teaching of the Christian Churches. Trans. Olive Wyon. New York: Macmillan.

———. 1958 (1912). Protestantism and Progress: A Historical Study of the Relation of Protestantism to the Modern World. Trans. William Montgomery. Boston: Beacon Press.

Tsing, Anna Lowenhaupt. 1993. *In the Realm of the Diamond Queen: Marginality in an Out-of-the-Way Place*. Princeton: Princeton University Press.

Tylor, Edward Burnett. 1864. *Primitive Culture: Researches into the Development of Mythology, Philosophy, Religion, Language, Art, and Custom*. Boston: Estes and Lauriat.

Urban, Greg. 1996. *Metaphysical Community: The Interplay of the Senses and the Intellect*. Austin: University of Texas Press.

———. 2001. *Metaculture: How Culture Moves through the World*. Minneapolis: University of Minnesota Press.

van den End, Th., ed. 1987. *Gereformeerde Zending op Sumba: Een Bronnenpublicatie*. Alphen aan den Rijn, the Netherlands: Raad voor de Zending der Ned. Herv. Kerk, de Zending der Gereformeerde Kerken in Nederland en de Gereformeerde Zendingsbond in de Ned. Herv Kerk.

van der Kooi, P. 1987 (1931). Soemba-Leid I. In *Gereformeerde Zending op Sumba: Een Bronnenpublicatie*, ed. Th. van den End, 329. Alphen aan den Rijn, Netherlands: Raad voor de Zending der Ned. Herv. Kerk, de Zending der Gereformeerde Kerken in Nederland en de Gereformeerde Zendingsbond in de Ned. Herv. Kerk.

van der Veer, Peter. 1996. *Conversion to Modernities: The Globalization of Christianity*. New York: Routledge.

———. 2001. *Imperial Encounters: Religion and Modernity in India and Britain*. Princeton: Princeton University Press.

van der Veer, Peter, and Hartmut Lehmann, eds. 1999. *Nation and Religion: Perspectives on Europe and Asia*. Princeton: Princeton University Press.

van Halsema, W[im]. B. 1987. Kerk van het Kruis? Verslag van een Bezoek aan de Kerken van Sumba en Timor, 3–24 Oktober 1987. Typescript. Archives of the Hendrik Kraemer Instituut, Oegstgeest, Netherlands.

———. 1995. Van Zending naar Oecumenische Samenwerking, de Periode 1947–1992. In *De Zending Voorbij: Terugblik op de Relatie Tussen de Gerformeerde Kerken in Nederland en de Christelijke Kerk van Sumba 1942–1992*, ed. van Halsema et al., 61–99. Kampen, Netherlands: J. H. Kok.

van Halsema, W. B., P. N. Holtrop, H. Reenders, and J. A. C. Vel. 1995. Inleiding. In *De Zending Voorbij: Terugblik op de Relatie Tussen de Gerformeerde Kerken in Nederland en de Christelijke Kerk van Sumba 1942–1992*, ed. van Halsema et al., vi–x. Kampen, Netherlands: J. H. Kok.

van Klinken, Gerry. 2003. *Minorities, Modernity, and the Emerging Nation: Christians in Indonesia, a Biographical Approach*. Leiden, Netherlands: KITLV Press. Verhandelingen van het Koninklijk Instituut voor Taal-, Land- en Volkenkunde 199.

van Rooden, Peter. 1996. Nineteenth-Century Representations of Missionary Conversion and the Transformation of Western Christianity. In *Conversion to Modernities: The Globalization of Christianity*, ed. Peter van der Veer, 65–87. New York: Routledge.

———. 2002. Long-Term Religious Developments in the Netherlands, 1750–2000. In *The Decline of Christendom in Western Europe, 1750–2000*, ed. Hugh McLeod and W. Ustorf, 113–29. Cambridge: Cambridge University Press.

van Til, Henry R. 2001 (1959). *The Calvinistic Concept of Culture*. Grand Rapids, MI: Baker Academic.

Vel, Jacqueline. 1994. The Uma-Economy: Indigenous Economics and Development Work in Lawonda, Sumba (Eastern-Indonesia). Thesis, Agricultural University, Wageningen, Netherlands.

Versluys, J. I. N. 1941. Aanteekeningen omtrent Geld- en Goederenverkeer in West-Soemba. *Koloniale Studiën* 25: 433–83.

Veyne, Paul. 1988. *Did the Greeks Believe in Their Myths? An Essay on the Constitutive Imagination*. Trans. Paula Wissing. Chicago: University of Chicago Press.

Viswanathan, Gauri. 1998. *Outside the Fold: Conversion, Modernity, and Belief*. Princeton: Princeton University Press.

Volkman, Toby Alice. 1985. *Feasts of Honor: Ritual and Change in the Toraja Highlands*. Urbana, IL: University of Illinois Press.

Volkstelling 1930, Deel V: Inheemsche Bevolking van Borneo, Celebes, de Kleine Sunda Eilanden, en de Molukken. 1934. Batavia: Department van Landbouw, Nijverheid en Handel.

Vološinov, V. N. 1973 (1930). *Marxism and the Philosophy of Language*. Trans. Ladislav Matejka and I. R. Titunik. New York: Seminar Press.

Waingapu, Dewan Paroki. 1978. *Waingapu Anda Waraya La Andaluri/Waingapu Jalan Pasir ke Jalan Kehidupan; 25 Tahun Paroki Waingapu*. Ende, Indonesia: Arnoldus.

Waitz, E. W. F. J. 1933. Bestuurs-Memories van den Gezaghebber van West-Soemba. Typescript, Algemeen Rijksarchief, The Hague.

Walker, A. D. M. 1978. The Ideal of Sincerity. *Mind* 89 (348): 481–97.

Wallace, Ronald S. 1953. *Calvin's Doctrine of the Word and Sacrament*. Edinburgh: Oliver and Boyd.

Walls, Andrew F. 2001. The Eighteenth-Century Protestant Missionary Awakening in Its European Context. In *Christian Missions and the Enlightenment*, ed. Brian Stanley, 22–44. Grand Rapids, MI: William R. Eerdmans.

Walzer, Michael. 1974. *The Revolution of the Saints: A Study in the Origins of Radical Politics*. New York: Athenaeum.

Wandel, Lee Palmer. 1995. *Voracious Idols and Violent Hands: Iconoclasm in Reformation Zurich, Strasbourg, and Basel*. Cambridge: Cambridge University Press.

Warner, Michael. 1990. *The Letters of the Republic: Publication and the Public Sphere in Eighteenth-Century America*. Cambridge: Harvard University Press.

———. 2002. Publics and Counterpublics. *Public Culture* 14: 49–90.

Webb, R. A. F. Paul. 1986a. *Palms and the Cross*. Townsville, Australia: James Cook University of North Queensland.

———. 1986b. The Sickle and the Cross: Christians and Communists in Bali,

Flores, Sumba, and Timor, 1965–1967. *Journal of Southeast Asian Studies* 17 (1): 94–112.

Weber, Max. 1946 (1922–1923). The Protestant Sects and the Spirit of Capitalism. In *From Max Weber: Essays in Sociology.* Ed. H. H. Gerth and C. Wright Mills, 302–22. New York: Oxford University Press.

———. 1958 (1904–1905). *The Protestant Ethic and the Spirit of Capitalism.* Trans. Talcott Parsons. New York: Charles Scribners.

Weiner, Annette B. 1983. From Words to Objects to Magic: Hard Words and the Boundaries of Social Interaction. *Man,* n.s., 18 (4): 690–709.

Wellem, F. D. 2004. *Injil dan Marapu: Suatu Studi Historis-Teologis tentang Perjumpaan Injil dengan Masyarakat Sumba pada periode 1876–1990.* Jakarta: PT BPK Gunung Mulia.

White, Geoffrey M. 1991. *Identity through History: Living Stories in a Solomon Islands Society.* Cambridge: Cambridge University Press.

Whiteman, Darrell L. 1983. *Melanesians and Missionaries: An Ethnohistorical Study of Social and Religious Change in the Southwest Pacific.* Pasadena, CA: William Carey.

Wielenga, D. K. 1908. Soemba: Op Reis (van Pajeti naar Memboro). *De Macedoniër* 12: 167–74, 257–69.

———. 1909a. Animisme en Spiritisme. *De Macedoniër* 13: 332–40.

———. 1909b. Soemba: De Dooden en Levenden, v. De Kip die Gouden Eieren Legt. *De Macedoniër* 13: 41–45.

———. 1910. Soemba: Offersteenen. *De Macedoniër* 14: 72–80.

———. 1912. Reizen op West-Soemba. *De Macedoniër* 16: 144–50, 169–74.

———. 1923. Van de Prediking des Evangelies. *De Macedoniër* 27: 137–50.

———. 1926. *Onze Zendingsvelden.* Vol. 5, *Soemba.* 's Gravenhage, Netherlands: Zendings-Studieraad.

Wilson, Bryan R., ed. 1970. *Rationality.* Oxford: Blackwell.

Wintle, Michael. 1987. *Pillars of Piety: Religion in the Netherlands in the Nineteenth Century.* Hull, UK: Hull University Press.

Witin, Fransiska. 1997. Belis dan Harga Diri Wanita. *Dian* August 1, p. 6.

Witkamp, H. 1912. Een Verkenningstocht over het Eiland Soemba. *Tijdschrift van het Koninklijk Nederlandsch Aardrijkskundig Genootschap* 29: 269–79.

Wittgenstein, Ludwig. 1953. *Philosophical Investigations.* Trans. G. E. M. Anscombe. New York: Macmillan.

Wohangara, D. H. 1963. Kawin Mawin menurut Adat Istiadat Suku Sumba Timur. Manuscript.

———. 1985. Sejarah Singkat Kebaktian dan Kebudayaan Sumba Berdasarkan Keyakinan Marapu (Animisme). Typescript.

Wolf, Eric. 1982. *Europe and the People without History.* Berkeley: University of California Press.

Woolard, Kathryn A. 2002. Bernardo de Aldrete and the Morisco Problem: A Study in Early Modern Spanish Language Ideology. *Comparative Studies in Society and History* 44 (3): 446–80.

Woolard, Kathryn A., and Bambi B. Schieffelin. 1994. Language Ideology. *Annual Review of Anthropology* 23: 55–82.

Yewangoe, Andreas A. 1995. Het Theologisch Onderwijs. In *De Zending Voorbij: Terugblik op de Relatie Tussen de Gerformeerde Kerken in Nederland en de Christelijke Kerk van Sumba 1942–1992*, ed. W. B. van Halsema et al., 101–24. Kampen, Netherlands: J. H. Kok.

Zelizer, Viviana A. 1994. *The Social Meaning of Money.* New York: Basic Books.

Index

Page numbers in italics indicate illustrations.

Sumba, 26, 32–33, 285–88; Anakalang, 32, 150–59, 258–60; gongs in, 134; houses in, 257–60; identity in, 89n5; marriage in, 155, 203–6, 273–74; mission, 4, 8, 107–8, 119–26, 150–56; money in, 272–78; religious difference in, 2, 226, 241; representations of, 258–60; Song, 122. *See also* ancestors; Gereja Kristen Sumba; *marapu;* missionaries; Umbu Hina Kapita; Umbu Remu Samapatty; Umbu Sappy Pateduk

Summer Institute of Linguistics, 44

Tagalog, 138, 144
Taylor, Charles, 53, 55, 73, 78n19, 211n10, 214
Taylor, Edward Burnett, 83, 92–96, 118
temporality, 113–16, 158–61, 223, 275; divine, 120. *See also* history
text, 19, 20, 67–68, 109; audience of, 268; denotation in, 269; and entextualization, 14, 68, 74, 171–74, 181n2, 261; as self-representation, 256; textual form, 255. *See also* scripture
theology, 61–63, 100, 114, 126; Ethical Theology, 102–3; and ethnographic context, 239; and materiality, 232; in representational economy, 20
Theophanes, Saint, 61n3
Thomas, Keith, 193
time. *See* temporality
tombs, 159, 168
tradition, 157, 160–62, 257, 274. *See also* modernity
transcendence, 41, 78–81, 136, 213–16, 220; constraints on, 117; of God, 2n2, 59, 65, 73; and money, 280–82; of place, 52. *See also* freedom; materiality
translation: of the Bible, 44, 190–91; in conversion, 129, 136–39, 141–42, 144–45, 173–75; and missionaries, 108–9, 124, 137n18, 185n5; models of, 142; and prayer, 183–84; radical, 286. *See also* Onvlee; scripture

Trilling, Lionel, 185, 209, 211–13
Troeltsch, Ernst, 49n13

Umbu Hina Kapita, 123n8, 152
Umbu Remu Samapatty, 156
Umbu Sappy Pateduk, 156–57, 159, 163, 167–69
Urban, Greg, 21

value: and economic rationality, 242–45; of money, 271, 278–80. *See also* commodity; exchange; fetishism; human
van der Veer, Peter, 81–82
van Dijk, W., 239, 241
van Klinken, Gerry, 45–46n10
van Rooden, Peter, 45n10, 97n10, 120n5
Viswanathan, Gauri, 51
voice. *See* agency; language; sincerity
Vrij Gemaakte Kerk, 241

Wallace, Alfred Russel, 93n8
Waltzer, Michael, 50, 56, 77
Warner, Michael, 16, 38–39, 217
Weber, Max, 38–39, 46, 56–57, 176, 220, 225n2
Weiner, Annette, 211n10
Wellem, F. D., 108n18, 123n8
Wielenga, Douwe Klaas, 186; career of, 151–52; on fetish, 180, 189, 193–94; on sacrifice, 235–38; on value, 242
Wilken, G. A., 97n11
Williams, F. E., 30
Wittgenstein, Ludwig, 71, 183
Wohangara, D. H., 258n1
Wolf, Eric, 46
Woolard, Kathryn, 133n14

Zwingli, Ulrich, 61, 181n1, 237n13

Text: 10/13 Aldus
Display: Aldus
Compositor, printer, and binder: Sheridan Books, Inc.